Turning Points in Curriculum

A Contemporary American Memoir

Second Edition

J. Dan Marshall
Pennsylvania State University

James T. Sears
Independent Scholar

Louise Anderson Allen
Fayetteville State University

Patrick A. Roberts
National-Louis University

William H. Schubert
University of Illinois at Chicago

PEARSON

Merrill
Prentice Hall

Upper Saddle River, New Jersey
Columbus, Ohio

Library of Congress Cataloging in Publication Data

Turning points in curriculum: a contemporary American memoir/J. Dan Marshall . . . [et al.].—2nd ed.

   p.cm.

Rev. ed. of: Turning points in curriculum/J. Dan Marshall, James T. Sears, William H. Schubert. 2000.

   Includes bibliographical references and index.

   ISBN 0-13-112842-6

   1. Education—United States—Curricula—History—20th century. 2. Curriculum planning—United States. I. Marshall, J. Dan. Turning points in curriculum.

LB1570.M36684 2007

375'.0010973—dc22   2006046237

Vice President and Executive Publisher: Jeffery W. Johnston
Executive Editor: Debra A. Stollenwerk
Senior Editorial Assistant: Mary Morrill
Assistant Development Editor: Daniel J. Richcreek
Production Editor: Kris Roach
Production Coordination: Carlisle Publishing Services
Design Coordinator: Diane C. Lorenzo
Cover Designer: Candace Rowley
Cover image: SuperStock
Production Manager: Susan Hannahs
Director of Marketing: David Gesell
Senior Marketing Manager: Darcy Betts Prybella
Marketing Coordinator: Brian Mounts

This book was set in New Century Schoolbook by Carlisle Publishing Services. It was printed and bound by R.R. Donnelley & Sons Company. The cover was printed by R.R. Donnelley & Sons Company.

Pearson Prentice Hall™ is a trademark of Pearson Education, Inc.
Pearson® is a registered trademark of Pearson plc
Prentice Hall® is a registered trademark of Pearson Education, Inc.
Merrill® is a registered trademark of Pearson Education, Inc.

Pearson Education Ltd.   Pearson Education Australia Pty. Limited
Pearson Education Singapore Pte. Ltd. Pearson Education North Asia Ltd.
Pearson Education Canada, Ltd.   Pearson Educación de Mexico, S.A. de C. V.
Pearson Education—Japan   Pearson Education Malaysia Pte. Ltd.

10 9 8 7 6 5 4 3 2 1
ISBN: 0-13-112842-6

In memory of

Alice Miel
1906–1998

and

Arthur Wellesley Foshay
1912–1998

Preface

We do not believe that contemporary shifts in curriculum studies—and the people who played a part in creating these shifts—should be characterized as a movement within the field. Rather, we believe that the field of curriculum, and curriculum work in general, has undergone important changes within the past 50 years. In short, we see movement (i.e., motion). This distinction between *movement* as a noun or a verb lies at the heart of current discussion among curriculum workers, our own curriculum work, and our efforts as authors of *Turning Points*.

As curriculum teachers, we have invited students who represent different levels of background knowledge in curriculum understanding and experience into this great conversation, urging them to (re)locate themselves and others among the players and participants who help to shape the curriculum field. Yet this very desire only complicates our own curriculum making, for few books exist that focus on contemporary (post–World War II) curriculum history. Whether teaching courses in curriculum development, theory, or history, we are inevitably asked where the historical markers might be that illustrate or represent the twists and shifts along the way: the turning points that have helped to shape contemporary curriculum history. This book represents our effort to answer that and other questions.

Turning Points is a text designed to engage readers in a story of curriculum as a field of intellectual study and invite them to identify with and ultimately participate in this important work. Focusing on the United States, it contains five parts, the first of which offers a backdrop or contextual panorama for parts II through V, which present curriculum's journey through the last half of the twentieth century.

Throughout the book we favor the term curriculum *work* over curriculum *studies, theory,* or *development.* To us, the broader notion of *work* allows for variations that include reflection, study, theorizing, construction, inquiry, and deliberation. At the same time, the possibilities for interpretation inherent in the notion of *curriculum work* allow us to steer clear of the more fixed and differential meanings typically associated with more distinctive phrases such as *curriculum theorizing* or *curriculum development.* Our choice of the phrase *curriculum work* reflects, too, our thinking with respect to our readers. Despite some genuinely valuable and welcome advice and criticism from manuscript reviewers, interested colleagues, and graduate students, we decided not to write for an audience conceptualized in some binary way—that is, as scholars *or* teachers, advanced *or* beginning students in curriculum, serious *or* casual readers. To have done so would have helped to perpetuate a theory–practice dichotomy that we believe is not only detrimental to but has outlived its usefulness for the curriculum field.

An important goal of *Turning Points* is to provide readers with multiple levels of engagement in its complex conversation. Toward this end, we have combined five distinct elements (two of which we characterize as unique; see the introduction) into the book with an eye toward personalizing readers' interpretative processes.

1. We have woven a substantial array of published ***curriculum books*** into each chapter as a way to encourage further study by serious students of the field.

2. Chapters 2 through 9 present **Visitor** interviews (done specifically for this book) with a wide range of curriculum workers who speak personally about their actions and perceptions relative to curriculum work.

3. Each of these chapters include a lengthy **Primary Document Excerpt** in an effort to bring the voices of these authors into this complex conversation.

4. We have placed **Varied Tales** taken from America's larger sociocultural milieu within each of these same chapters. The unexpected variety and nature of these tales serve to illustrate curriculum history within its broader cultural contexts as well as to disturb and disrupt reader complacency and spark disjunctive thought.

5. Each of the book's 10 chapters includes reflective questions located within the chapter content itself in an effort to interrupt the reader with a **reflective challenge.**

Whereas other curriculum books rely on one or two of these elements for their strength and relevance, *Turning Points* combines all of these elements in a layered and interactive kind of conversation among numerous storytellers (including readers) from past and present. In the final chapter, we take this conversation through the new millennium.

The renaissance in contemporary American curriculum (often called the reconceptualization) is well chronicled in both broad and meticulously fine strokes elsewhere. What makes *Turning Points* unique is its invitation for readers to become engaged in this story so as to make it part of their own unique life tale. What makes this invitation powerfully salient is our decision to shape this work as a kind of memoir.

As a literary genre, the memoir is a relative to fiction, history, and autobiography. By accepting that these genres are inseparably interrelated (fiction is always part autobiography, history is always part fiction, and so forth), we can more comfortably position ourselves as mindful authors of and participants in *Turning Points*. Like all authors of fiction, history, or autobiography, we made choices and took certain perspectives while writing this book. We assume that readers of this or any other authoritative text recognize that ours is a selective telling of stories.

However, we believe that in recognizing *Turning Points* as a form of memoir, readers might better appreciate that this genre, according to Jay Parini, lends itself to "a society devoted, at least in principle, to the notion of radical equality" (1998, p. A40). In the shadow of the millennium, people want to situate themselves within their own learning. According to Parini, memoirs have become increasingly popular in recent years because their readers are, in the most literal sense,

> learning, quite explicitly, how to construct a self, how to navigate [and narrate] the world, and—perhaps most usefully—how to gain some purchase on the world through the medium of language. (Parini, 1998, p. A40)

Our intentions, from the outset of this project, have included the hope that *Turning Points* might encourage and invite such individual purchase.

New to This Edition

New editions of texts used for teaching often represent desires that are in part cosmetic (like Toyota or Chrysler annually redesigning their vehicles) and economic (think marketing, sales, and royalties from "new" products), as well as ameliorative (in terms of correcting and revising errors and shortcomings) and substantive in nature. This new edition of *Turning Points* represents this mix, certainly, with our most careful attention given to the revision and addition of substance. Thanks to a number of reviewers and readers, we've fixed what turned out to be countless small mistakes throughout the original text and altered the latter portion of the book (Part V) significantly. In this edition, we provide a reshaped and refocused chapter 8, a new chapter (9) that draws attention to the intersection of teachers, schools and important political and ideological struggles over curriculum taking place at the national level during the 1980s and 1990s, and a significantly revised and updated concluding chapter 10.

Also new to this edition are two authors, Louise Allen and Patrick Roberts, a new Introductory Discussion by William Doll, and a new Afterword by Jennifer Snow-Gerono. Unsure of their ability to produce a second edition, the original authors (Marshall, Sears, and Schubert) looked to a new generation of curriculum workers for support. Louise (a former doctoral student with Sears) and Patrick (who studied with Schubert) had the requisite experience as school-based educators, the "chops" as thinkers and writers, and the willingness to work as team players on the project. Evidence of their thoughtful, strong, and meticulous work appears throughout this second edition, but particularly in the content of the new chapter 9. Most of Jenn Snow-Gerono's work here will likely be missed by readers new to *Turning Points* for it was she who, as a doctoral student, worked tirelessly with the original authors to make literally hundreds of small corrections, revisions, additions, and deletions throughout the original manuscript. In her current job as an assistant professor, Jenn has made frequent use of the original *Turning Points* book, and her new Afterword plays an important part in this edition because of the unique perspective she presents as someone who intimately knows and has often used the first edition of this book with her students. While putting together the first edition, we clung to our hope that the book's complex, unorthodox structures would result in differences in the ways in which it was used with and interpreted by students. Jenn's essay, in conjunction with much positive feedback from others, suggests that those hopes have been met.

Inviting William Doll's new Introductory Discussion is a different story entirely. Most within the scholarly field of curriculum studies know and value Bill's work in curriculum theory and philosophy. In early 2002, Bill took part in a panel sponsored by the Society for the Study of Curriculum History that looked critically at what was then a recently published *Turning Points* (see www3.baylor.edu/~Wesley_Null/ssch.html). His remarks in that session, while generally favorable, were thoughtfully and helpfully critical of several aspects of the book—particularly its "Final Conversation." Believing that readers of this second edition would appreciate such thoughtful critique, welcoming provocative criticism about/within an already (in many respects) provocative book, and knowing the author well enough to feel that he would understand and respect our desire to have him speak directly to our readers, we asked Bill Doll to participate in this new edition by writing a new Introductory Discussion. Fortunately for everyone concerned, he agreed to join us here.

Acknowledgments

The actual idea for this book came from our collective years of encounters with students who have taken our curriculum courses. The motivation to propose it came from Marcus Chapman, a sales representative. Embryonic conceptual help was provided by a good friend, Jim Beane. Early and important support came from ASCD's Curriculum Teachers' Network, which funded the survey used to identify many of the primary text documents excerpted here, as well as an enthusiastic collection of participants to our 1994 AERA session (Marshall, Schubert, & Sears, 1994) on the topic of important publications within the curriculum field.

The questions located throughout the book come, in part, from doctoral students at the University of South Carolina who, with James Sears as their instructor, worked through a late draft of the original book. Along with doctoral students Pyeong-gook Kim and Dana Stuchul at Penn State, who helped to review and refine the original working manuscript at several stages, these former graduate students deserve our deepest thanks.

Our various university-based staff assistants in past years, especially Cindy Fetters and Pat Lindler, also deserve acknowledgment and thanks, as does our colleague Connie Yowell.

It was a long and difficult chore to keep the original project afloat in the face of family challenges, career shifts, and natural disasters. Through them all our editor, Debbie Stollenwerk, remained a solid believer. Ultimately, our most profound source of endurance stemmed from our long-time companions—Tara, Bob, and Ann—whose immeasurable faith and understanding continue.

Further Acknowledgments

With the publication of a second edition we remain obliged to those noted above. Regretfully, we failed to acknowledge Shannon Hart and Dana Welte for their research assistance while putting the original book together. Belated thanks to them for all their help.

Producing this second edition led to its own challenges, and we received important help in meeting these from Patricia Gibson, Bryan Lynip, Angela Packer, and Andre Plaisance.

Jennifer Snow-Gerono played a significant role in organizing and cataloging the countless textual corrections and revisions to the first edition generated by the original authors, in addition to conducting important library reference work in preparation for this edition. Other colleagues, too, have helped us to broaden our thinking about curriculum work. They include: Donna Breault, Mary Lynne Calhoun, Deb Freedman, James Henderson, Kathleen Kesson, James Lyons, Tom Poetter, Glenda Poole, Patrick Slattery, Kris Sloan, and Dana Stuchul.

A number of curriculum scholars served as reviewers for this second edition, offering insightful and helpful comments. Our thanks to the following colleagues for doing so: India Broyles, University of Southern Maine; Leigh Chiarelott, Bowling Green State University; Beverly E. Cross, University of Wisconsin, Milwaukee; Francine Hultgren, University of Maryland; Valerie J. Janesick, University of Southern Florida; and Jane McGraw, California State Polytechnic University, Pomona.

Debbie Stollenwerk, our editor, has never doubted the value of this book. Ever. Her faith—and limitless perseverance in particular—has more to do with the appearance of this second edition than almost any other factor. She is a rare collaborator indeed within today's publishing market.

Our two new authors, Louise and Patrick, give special thanks to Dan, Jim, and Bill for generously giving them the opportunity to contribute to this second edition. While the events of September 11, 2001 prevented our first meeting to begin discussing revisions, we persevered and two months later than planned, we (Louise and Patrick) traveled to Dan's house to begin our work. With uncertainty, we embarked on a collaborative journey that was both educative and exhilarating, while exhausting at times. From the beginning, Dan gently guided our efforts with patience, trust and good humor. Much in the world has changed since 2001, but friendship endures. It's been a privilege.

Finally, the five of us wish to underscore the importance of those who provided our most basic levels of support—our partners and family members: John Allen, Tara Fulton, Maria Lettiere Roberts, Ivy and Eva Roberts, Ann Lopez Schubert, and Bob Williamson.

We are pleased to know that so many people found relevance and meaning in the first edition of *Turning Points*. We appreciate those within the curriculum field who have written to use about and/or published formal reviews of the book, as well as the many faculty members and students who have studied, taught, and otherwise used the book in so many different contexts. Their feedback—positive and negative—has helped us to improve our work. With this second edition of *Turning Points* our hope remain to draw readers into the personal journeys that underlie questions of valuable knowledge and experience. Such questions, and the lives they offer meaning to, still move us deeply.

Foreword

by William F. Pinar

In this Weimar-like time of book inflation, when we are nearly overwhelmed by the sheer number of new titles in our field, *Turning Points* stands apart as noteworthy and important. Why? The book is a stylistic achievement. That achievement is not only an aesthetic accomplishment—which would be enough by itself to merit our special attention—but it is an intellectual and pedagogical accomplishment as well. This book represents nothing less than a new genre of scholarship, a genre—what shall its name be?—that combines other genres and in so doing creates a new one. *Turning Points* has within it, as you will see, scholarly commentary, impressionistic portraiture, parallel tales, interviews, and excerpted scholarly materials. Each of these is juxtaposed to the other, all woven together by scholarly commentary into a complex tapestry in which the social and intellectual history of the field and its present circumstances are strikingly visible. There is a continuum of color and weave—from abstract theoretical formulations to concrete material facts and from broad social forces to specific individual lives—so that the reader appreciates how all are in inextricable relation one to another. To change images, one might say that these various subgenres are in a kind of conversation with each other, a "complicated conversation" (Pinar et al., 1995, p. 848) that, in a profound sense, exemplifies curriculum itself as the scholarly field that this book undertakes to teach, understands that term to mean.

The juxtaposition of genres in this book is, I think, most provocative in a pedagogical sense, because it stimulates multiple modes of cognition, reflection, and remembrance. Marshall, Sears, and Schubert place a narrative of IBM or the Roman Catholic Church or gay liberation or NASA (what they term *parallel tales,* although their relation to the primary stream of commentary is not as simple as that phrase implies) next to the intellectual history of the curriculum field, which is then placed next to an impressionistic portrait of the times, which is then generally followed by the singular voice of an individual who recalls that history within the context of his or her individual life. Such a series of juxtapositions provides a multiplicity of vantage points, as Maxine Greene has so eloquently elaborated over the years (see Pinar, 1998c).

And it does something else, something that is stylistically and pedagogically intriguing. By inserting narratives with different themes from apparently very different fields of interest (business, church, sex, athletics, and space exploration) and different ideologies (right, left, and in between), the authors produce a kind of kaleidoscopic effect. The reader samples different knowledges as well as different modes of knowing, recalling (although not equivalent to) what Schwab (1964) termed substantive and syntactical knowledge (see Pinar et al., 1995, p. 161). Such a complex—some would say "chaotic" (W. E. Doll, 1993)—view of knowledge is quite congruent with the contemporary understanding of curriculum as a conversation, disclosing as it does the relational character of ideas, in relation not only one to the other but pointing as well to their embodiment and personification in individual lives, their origin and expression in social movements and trends, their rootedness in the past, their foreshadowing of the future.

Traditionally when curriculum has been conceived as a conversation it meant conversing with the great minds of Western civilization whose ideas transcended the temporal and cultural locales of their origin. That Eurocentric concept is no longer in fashion, for good reason. European high culture is no longer the center of American civilization—was it ever?—especially as that is codified and theorized in scholarship and inquiry. But the political decentering of European knowledges and knowing hardly means that curriculum is no longer students' and teachers' conversation with ideas, including European ones, as they are recorded in primary source material, textbooks, and other curricular artifacts and technologies. Curriculum is also a conversation among the participants, one that supports and expresses the possibilities of unpredicted, novel events and unplanned destinations, conversation that incorporates life history and politics and popular culture as well as official, institutional knowledge. The concept of curriculum as complicated conversation is performed pedagogically in this book, as one listens to individuals describe their professional lives, reads key scholarly products, and recalls, in broad, impressionistic brush strokes, the headlines of the times in which those lives and scholarly theorizations came to form.

While hardly abandoning the sphere of the everyday and the practical, to understand curriculum today requires acknowledging the limits of technique and procedure, what gets subsumed under the umbrella term of *social engineering*. Curriculum conceived as conversation cannot be framed as another technique that will somehow get our educational engine humming smoothly again. Education is of course not mechanical, and yet, astonishingly, much of the field still seems to proceed on the assumption that if we only make the appropriate adjustments—in curriculum, teaching, learning, administration, counseling, and so on—those test scores will soar.

The truth is that much of our obsession with technique and procedure in the field of education is a doomed effort to make an impossible situation possible. That impossible situation is the official or institutional curriculum. The vulgar truth is—and surely everyone knows this even if they feign ignorance when they speak publicly of the curriculum—that everyone will not (despite teaching technique, parental involvement, or curriculum reform) and need not become terribly interested in everything. That all students must take all the major disciplines beyond, say, a middle school level of acquaintance is not educationally sensible. The secondary school curriculum is a somewhat arbitrary historical and political settlement of what Kliebard (1995) characterized as the struggle for the American curriculum. We educators lost that struggle.

What we have today—still, unbelievably—is nineteenth-century faculty psychology, versions of that presumably discredited idea that the mind is a muscle that must be exercised by all the basic weights (or Nautilus machines) if it is to bulge. Once bulging, clearly visible by high test scores, America will be rich, powerful, and so forth. In addition to this masculinized fantasy that conflates test scores with national supremacy, general curriculum requirements also represent a negotiated settlement among competing (and powerful) academic parties (disciplines). With extensive secondary curricular prerequisites for college admission closely linked with two years of "general education," each of the politically powerful disciplines gets a piece of the student enrollment (which equals budget) pie. Forcing students to study each of the "major" fields thus props up enrollment and employment in these various fields. The curricular arrangement that stabilized after *Sputnik* is not, as we know (and despite the pious rhetoric), about the education of students or the preparation of citizens. At the heart of the present vocationalism—academic and otherwise—is the masculinist, militaristic, and economic fantasy that academic achievement (as measured by standardized tests; excellence in mathematics and science is especially crucial) creates the conditions for national supremacy, understood today primarily as economic prosperity but also cultural and military dominance.

Serious students of the curriculum already know this unhappy story. The progressive dream (Pilder, 1974) has long been over, but then it always *was* a dream. Dewey (1916) must have known his was a losing gamble, even if it was a gamble he was compelled, for his own as well as for the nation's sake, to wage. And even while the public sphere was always dominated by conservative and sometimes reactionary political and economic interests, individual teachers have continued—partly due to our promptings—to try to live out that dream. Those individual teachers have always helped to keep hope alive, our faith—*our* denoting those of us in higher education and teacher preparation specifically—that individual educators can somehow find ways to work with children outside official directives and bureaucratic inertia, outside that patriarchal public sphere dominated by right-wing politics and capitalistic economics. We can hear that hope—and its frustration—in the interviews printed in this book; they are also hinted at in several of the parallel tales. Despite the odds, the gamble must be waged, the progressive dream of democratization and self-realization—inextricably intertwined, as each depends on the other—must be performed.

And although each of us must find ways that make sense for us and for those to whom we are bonded and committed, it is instructive to see others engaged in the same struggle. Struggle: we are a long way from barricades in the street (although such events are always only an economic crash or ecological catastrophe away); our battles, our efforts in support of democratization and self-realization must take, well, more subtle forms. That is why questions of style are so very important. The brilliant postwar Italian filmmaker, poet, novelist, and essayist Pier Paolo Pasolini understood this exactly. Because we live in a period in which consumer capitalism has triumphed, as Pasolini (and many others after him) knew, we must now devise new styles of teaching to have any hope of reaching our students. Pasolini's class was large; his students were the citizens of Italy, and his teaching occurred through his art, especially his films. A former schoolteacher, he was very clear that simple didacticism—straightforward instruction—was finished. The triumph of consumption meant that anything that was easily incorporated into existing structures of self and society would in fact be consumed, could make no political difference, teach no moral lessons. What was required were stylistic innovations—forms of indirect discourse intrigued him—that would unsettle one's students, quietly institute a revolution in the self, and thereby unsettle extant social relations. The story of Pasolini's pedagogical efforts in film is exhilarating if tragic (Greene, 1990).

Pasolini was murdered in 1973; his last film, *Salo,* was and is unassimilable, perhaps unpedagogical as well. In *Turning Points,* within our much smaller sphere of influence that is American curriculum studies, students will be provoked, perhaps unsettled, as they work their way through this new genre. The juxtaposition of commentary, interviews, excerpts, and parallel tales can only underscore the provisionality, the instability, the complex and contradictory character of curriculum, indeed of social reality itself, one anachronistic instance of which is the school. The new genre may itself constitute a turning point for students, as they see through the sham of public rhetoric on curriculum to the intensely political and gendered reality.

Congratulations, then, to Dan Marshall, to James Sears, and to William Schubert for this memorable contribution to our effort to understand curriculum. You have devised a new genre, one which performs our contemporary understanding of curriculum, one which teaches the subject matter other textbooks have tended to only describe, a stylistic invention that is profoundly pedagogical. The book itself may indeed someday be described as a "turning point."

Introductory Discussion
for the Second Edition of Turning Points
Wm. E. Doll, Jr.

In light of the perceptive and still-relevant Foreword penned by William Pinar for the inaugural edition of *Turning Points*, I decided to open this second edition with an introductory discussion, or Prolegomena. This decision represents, for me, the sort of response that *Turning Points* itself seeks to elicit.

It is easy to see why, after a few short years, professors, students, and the publisher have asked Dan Marshall, James Sears, and William Schubert—joined, here, by Louise Allen and Patrick Roberts—to write a second edition of *Turning Points*. This book is a living history of the curriculum field from its conceptualization in 1947 at the University of Chicago curriculum conference to the current year, 2006. As a living history, *Turning Points* gives us the voices of those who have lived through those years—such as Michael Apple and William Pinar—who have shaped curriculum in recent decades, of those who will shape it in the future (including the authors), and of those who have been reflective consumers of curriculum. The voices of this eclectic mix are now already, like Keats's lovers, frozen into the panorama of curriculum history: forever to be period pieces, forever to be heard. Paradoxically, this eclectic mix of frozen voices gives to the book its *joie de vie*—its spirit and aliveness.

This is an alive book. It has none of the dustiness of textbooks (about which I have railed so often—Doll, 2005). The conversations here are by real people, concerned with real curriculum issues. The format of the book with its absolutely fascinating interweaving of the historical, the political, the social, and the cultural adds even more depth to the notion of a conversation that is indeed complicated. The virtual and the "real" get blurred in the book and, as such, mirror our present-day being, which, via cybernetics and electronic media, presents us with a blurred reality. It is too early to tell whether we are at a major, paradigmatic turning about in this early part of the twenty-first century, but it does appear that this will be the century of the "virtual," and for this I'd recommend we all look at N. Katherine Hayles's *How We Became Posthuman* (1999). James Sears, one of the authors of the book, alludes to this forthcoming posthuman world in his comments in the "virtual conversations" with which the book ends. This is a spectre, I believe, with which curricularists of our present century will need to wrestle. As Jacob wrestled with the angel (of death?) in the desert, so will future curricularists need to wrestle first with cybernetic reality and then with disembodied consciousness. The quaintness of this book in the year 2106 may well be the vividness of its slice of (curriculum) life a century earlier. I encourage readers to look at this book in two lights: (1) in terms of the complicated conversations that now are and have been the curriculum field; and (2) as the archaic quality our current issues and problems will show themselves to have in future generations. Obviously, I believe that intellectually we are in a transitional phase; hence my attraction to the title, *Turning Points*.

As Dan Marshall says in his new Preface, I was "complementarily critical" (my awkward phrase, not his) of the first edition of *Turning Points*. I was fascinated by the title and worried that in their book the authors had left largely untouched the *linguistic turn* Richard Rorty writes about in his book of the same name (1967). To me *the* major turn of the twentieth century has been this linguistic one. Looking at this second edition I am somewhat, not completely, assuaged. Certainly in the ensuing years, few though they may be, I have grown. N. Katherine Hayles's book on the virtual has led me to better appreciate and fear the final, "imagining" chapter (10) of *Turning Points*. This chapter is not a "real" conversation (or is it?); it is, as I said in 2002, a series of monologues among talking heads. The conversation is not real in our usual sense of the word; the conversants, against all of Hans-Georg Gadamer's advice, did not open themselves to the other, truly accepting the other's point of view, transposing themselves into the other (to whatever extent possible) so that each understands both the other and what the other says. It can be said, in strong defense of the authors, that this most interesting virtual conversational device they devised is indeed just that, a device. My point, though, is that the issue of conversation in a nonfoundational society takes on an importance beyond what occurs in a foundational society. Whatever foundation is left in a non-metanarrative society rests in our ability to converse with each other. That, as Rorty says, is all we have in the dark of night. The linguistic turn, away from the "solid" methodology of science to the hermeneutic one of conversation is, I believe, a turning point in our intellectual and physical move from the human to the posthuman. This move frightens me, as I am sure it does every parent who has a teenage son or daughter connected to the Internet.

My other reaction to the final chapters is a more personal one. Upon reading chapter 8, especially in the first edition, I glanced over the role Michael Peters's comments played in that chapter. In the past, he and I have looked upon the postmodern perspective with rather different, and I fear, nonadjustable lenses.

Peters's comments are most important, may I say foundational, to chapter 8, and with his emphasis on François Lyotards's notion of language games—that which Ludwig Wittgenstein says is all we have once we give up the "reality" of analysis—gives us a peek into a world yet-to-come. The astute reader, which I was not in reading the first edition, will recognize and I hope profit from the authors' most adroit use of Peters's comments here. We may indeed be making the turn from one paradigm to another.

I realize the intent of this book is not to develop or even peek into a paradigmatic change. The intent rather is to present us with a rich background milieu that encompassed the curricular issues unfolding in the postwar and premillennial years. This interplay of culture and curriculum is magnificently, even marvelously and creatively done, making this book valuable not only for contemporary thought—since we are much governed by the decades we have just passed through—but also as an archival piece for future curriculum scholars to better understand both the "whats" and "whys" of the latter part of the twentieth century.

There is more here, though, than just the *whats* and *whys,* important as these are; there is a certain looking into the future—in terms of virtuality, complexity, and in terms of a world ruled by language games. This book will help us enter that world bravely and knowingly.

Doll, W.E. (2005). The culture of method. In W.E. Doll, M.J. Fleener, D. Trueit, & J. St. Julien (Eds.), *Chaos, complexity, curriculum and culture* (pp. 21–75). New York: Peter Lang.

Hayles, N.K. (1999). *How we became posthuman.* Chicago: University of Chicago Press.

Rorty, R. (Ed.). (1967). Introduction. In R. Rorty (Ed.), *The linguistic turn. Recent essays in philosophical method* (pp. 1–39). Chicago: University of Chicago Press.

Teacher Preparation Classroom

TEACHER PREP

MERRILL
PRENTICE HALL

Your Class. Their Careers. Our Future. Will your students be prepared?

We invite you to explore our new, innovative and engaging website and all that it has to offer you, your course, and tomorrow's educators! Organized around the major courses pre-service teachers take, the Teacher Preparation site provides media, student/teacher artifacts, strategies, research articles, and other resources to equip your students with the quality tools needed to excel in their courses and prepare them for their first classroom.

This ultimate on-line education resource is available at no cost, when packaged with a Merrill text, and will provide you and your students access to:

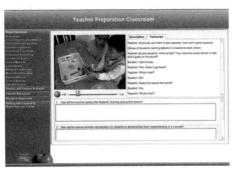

Online Video Library. More than 150 video clips—each tied to a course topic and framed by learning goals and Praxis-type questions—capture real teachers and students working in real classrooms, as well as in-depth interviews with both students and educators.

Student and Teacher Artifacts. More than 200 student and teacher classroom artifacts—each tied to a course topic and framed by learning goals and application questions—provide a wealth of materials and experiences to help make your study to become a professional teacher more concrete and hands-on.

Research Articles. Over 500 articles from ASCD's renowned journal Educational Leadership. The site also includes Research Navigator, a searchable database of additional educational journals.

Teaching Strategies. Over 500 strategies and lesson plans for you to use when you become a practicing professional.

Licensure and Career Tools. Resources devoted to helping you pass your licensure exam; learn standards, law, and public policies; plan a teaching portfolio; and succeed in your first year of teaching.

How to ORDER Teacher Prep for you and your students:
For students to receive a *Teacher Prep* Access Code with this text, instructors **must** provide a special value pack ISBN number on their textbook order form. To receive this special ISBN, please email **Merrill.marketing@pearsoned.com** and provide the following information:
- Name and Affiliation
- Author/Title/Edition of Merrill text

Upon ordering *Teacher Prep* for their students, instructors will be given a lifetime *Teacher Prep* Access Code.

Brief Contents

Contents

Introduction

Visitors and Varied Tales

This is a heady era for curriculum workers: so much to consider, so much to understand, so much to create and re-create, and so many ways to go about it all. Indeed, many curriculum veterans who have been active during the last four or five decades have told us that curriculum work is substantively different today. And while that assertion remains debatable, few would call today's curriculum field moribund, as Joseph Schwab did in 1969 (see chapter 5).

As participating members of the curriculum field and students of curriculum history, we believe that our field and its related forms of work have undergone a renaissance. We base this belief not only on information we read and hear but on our own and others' lived experiences. And like many of our curriculum colleagues, we profit from the ongoing discussions, debates, and questions regarding the separation between theory and practice, the importance of a critical or radical perspective to curriculum work, and, of course, the question of whether the field of curriculum studies remains identifiable and viable.

In *Turning Points* we situate, narrate, and speculate on curriculum history between the end of World War II and the millennium. We do this through a narrative weaving together of curriculum history, personal interviews, and excerpts from relevant and period-specific primary sources within their broader political, cultural, and social contexts.

Choosing Tellers and Tales

Some years ago we conducted a survey of self-identified curriculum people, asking them to identify (among other areas) publications that played a significant role in changing the direction and scope of contemporary curriculum studies (Marshall, Schubert, & Sears, 1994). In terms of curriculum articles, Joseph Schwab's "The Practical: A Language for Curriculum" received the strongest support (see chapter 5), though James Macdonald's "A Transcendental Developmental Ideology of Education" (see chapter 6) also won favor. When asked about noncurriculum books, Jerome Bruner's *Process of Education* was identified more than any other (see chapter 3). As for curriculum books that have helped to change the direction and scope of contemporary curriculum studies, the one most often identified by our respondents was *The Educational Imagination* by Elliot W. Eisner (see chapter 7). To this list we added selections from Herrick and Tyler (see chapter 2), Mager (see chapter 4), those of Ayers, Britzman, Schubert, and Pinar found in *Theory Into Practice* (1992) (see chapter 8) and Cameron McCarthy (see chapter 9) to round out our collection.

When excerpting these materials we fought the ever-present demons of word count and contextual relevance. Through a process of collaborative checking, we determined the most relevant passage for our purposes and then proceeded to edit each to its most fundamental series of points. In the interest of readability we elected not to overwhelmingly employ the use of ellipses but rather to present our edited version of the original text in a more straightforward passage. We urge readers who have not visited these original texts to read them in their entirety; indeed, we hope that our edited presentation of these documents will, in fact, motivate readers to pursue the use of such original documents for a better understanding and appreciation of contemporary curriculum history.

Our choice of interviewees for this book was both personal and purposeful. We selected people, first, whose professional lives in some way coincided with the unfolding stories we present here. Thus, more veteran workers appear early in the book, and certain events or publications connect with certain visitors. When inviting colleagues to participate (and some declined to do so), we tried to represent a range in their reputational status, their "take" on contemporary curriculum work, and their geographic and professional genealogical history while remaining sensitive to gender, racial, and ideological (among other) representational identities.

Each interviewee received a complete transcript of her or his interview along with a draft of the particular chapter in which it was to be featured. Interviewees reviewed the excerpted portions in light of the original transcript and made necessary corrections. However, interviewees were specifically asked *not* to make changes that would formalize the conversational patterns and tenor of their speech since this personalized voice was important to our overall project.

Overall Organization and Chapter Elements

We introduce seven curriculum vectors through which the field's development and struggles since 1947 unfold. These vectors (curriculum people, public interest, outsiders, publications, professional organizations and gatherings, perspectives and paradigms, and marginalized voices) are more than an organizational frame; they constitute forces that have helped to contour and propel the curriculum field. Although all of these vectors are present at all times, we focus on one in each chapter as a way to illuminate that period's important moments.

In addition to curriculum vectors, chapters 2 through 9 contain interviews with people in curriculum who speak directly to their involvement in the field during the period under scrutiny as well as an excerpt from a primary source text document that has direct and important relevance to our historical discussion. These "visits" support our belief in the importance of both portraying history as a personal journey and going to the original source to better understand and appreciate history.

Finally, we include a parallel story or cultural icon designed to correspond to the key point about contemporary curriculum history made in each chapter. These "varied tales" work to situate the development of contemporary curriculum work within a broader sociocultural context and simultaneously illustrate tensions and contradictions.

Part II: The Rise and Fall of Curriculum Specialists (1947–1960). We begin chapter 2 in 1947, the year the Chicago Curriculum Theory Conference took place, and bring it to a close in 1956, the year Benjamin Bloom published his *Taxonomy of Educational Objectives.* This was the true heyday of curriculum development, when most large school districts employed curriculum specialists (who often had graduated from a small but growing number of curriculum doctoral programs) and welcomed the presence of "experts" to help redesign district curricula. While most curriculum people were hard at work making curricula, the 1947 conference originators (Virgil Herrick and Ralph Tyler) hoped to provide for these efforts a more clear and collective theoretical or philosophical framework—or at least some guiding principles. Our excerpt from their impressions of the midcentury curriculum field, "Next Steps in the Development of a More Adequate Curriculum Theory," suggests directions they hoped to see the field take.

Our visitor for this chapter, the late Arthur W. Foshay, was a colleague of Tyler, Herrick, and numerous other curriculum people during this period. As Foshay points out, the essence of curriculum work during this period was guided by a handful of leaders—much like computer technology was originally controlled by IBM, as discussed in our varied tale. However, serious challenges to both lay around the corner.

Chapter 3 highlights national interest in discussing the rapid decline of this heyday of curriculum making that followed the 1957 launching of *Sputnik.* Louis Rubin, our guest for this chapter, offers his experiential insights into the nature and direction of the shifting curriculum field at the time. The key shift is made evident by Jerome Bruner in his introduction to *The Process of Education* (1960), wherein he discusses ties between school curricula and the national interest, the lure of science and technology, and public disappointment with the general state of school curricula (and, by association, curriculum experts in particular). Our tale of the Roman Catholic Church and the "flash of heavenly light" that led to the radical changes of Vatican II underscore this sociocultural shift.

Part III: Reestablishing Agency and Agendas (1961–1969). Those at work today in the field of curriculum have developed their ideas about teaching and learning, teachers and students, and schools and society from various knowledge bases within the social and behavioral sciences as well as the arts and humanities. This was not always the case, however, for certain disciplines and subdisciplines have held privileged positions among educators in general and curriculum workers in particular. As chapter 4 makes clear, chief among these is psychology. Thus many of these "outsiders" have had a major influence on curriculum work.

Five years after publishing *Science and Human Behavior,* B. F. Skinner stepped into the midst of the nation's educational reform craze with his article "Teaching Machines" (Skinner, 1958). The idea of determining end behaviors was not new to this era of curriculum work; however, Skinner's work as a "radical behaviorist" coincided and helped to legitimize various other curriculum efforts. This technological view of curriculum work coincided nicely with moneys made available in the 1950s and 1960s by outside groups (e.g., philanthropic organizations) and the federal government to make schools more efficient through the introduction of what Bruner called "automatizing devices" into the curriculum and instruction process.

Our visitor in chapter 4 is Louise Berman—a woman whose own work during the 1960s sometimes made her feel like a part of some "curriculum underground." Between 1961 and 1964, the federal government strenuously intervened in U.S. schools and their curricula for the first time in history. The virtual disappearance of fundamental curriculum questions is exemplified in our chapter 4 excerpt from Robert Mager's *Preparing Instructional Objectives* (1962), which represents a techno mind-set driving much of the government-funded curriculum projects.

At the same time, a number of progressive ideas related to curriculum work of an earlier period were not only kept alive but nurtured by a small number of curriculum people around the country. While educational psychologists and psychometricians joined academics in producing government-funded "teacher-proof" curricula in almost every discipline (e.g., mathematics and science), some curriculum people remained focused on children and their affective needs as well as the social change possibilities of curriculum—both themes of an earlier progressive era. Like chapter 4's varied tale of the Supreme Court and its shift from judicial activism to judicial restraint, these curriculum outlaws would eventually come to prominence.

On occasion, a single book, chapter, or journal article can generate significant influence among members of a professional group. Though we offer examples of such influential publications within contemporary curriculum studies throughout this volume, we highlight them in chapter 5. Diagnosing the curriculum field as moribund, Joseph Schwab's 1969 article "The Practical: A Language for Curriculum" was arguably the most significant publication for curriculum people since Tyler's *Basic Principles* 20 years earlier. Our excerpt from Schwab in this chapter illustrates the tenor of this wake-up call in which he revisits several ideas found in the Herrick and Tyler excerpt in chapter 2 while proposing new directions.

Publications that enjoy this sort of pervasive appeal do so, in part, because they appear with the right people at the right time under the right circumstances. This describes the feeling we develop in chapter 5, in part through the tale of Stonewall and its resulting effects on the historic homophile movement in this country.

Chapter 5 begins in 1965—a year when, as in 1947, a group of curriculum scholars met in Chicago to consider bases and principles for curriculum theorizing. Despite the overwhelming emphases on science and empiricism evident in most curriculum efforts of the mid-1960s, the group arrived at no consensus regarding a "scientific" basis for curriculum work. Actually, a good deal of curriculum theorizing went on during the 1960s, not only in universities but in classrooms across the country where teachers sought new ideas and practices that made sense for students and schools caught up in the socially, culturally, and politically wrenching changes of the time. Michael Apple, interviewed for chapter 5, understood from experience that the curriculum field needed to shift its attention away from "objective" and empirically based issues to some of the socially oriented, value-based questions posed by many radical thinkers of the past.

Part IV: (Re)Shaping the Contemporary Curriculum Field (1970–1983). The American Educational Research Association (AERA) formed in 1916— the same year John Dewey published *Democracy and Education*. As the association grew and took shape, its members began to organize themselves into specific divisions, the second of which, Division B (formed in 1964), was called "Curriculum and Objectives."

As we indicate in chapter 6, those responsible for overseeing the AERA soon felt the need to formally recognize and encourage the formation of even smaller groups. This need to expand the status quo resulted from a collection of internal and external pressures, much like changes under way then in the game of tennis. Like the amateur tennis players portrayed in our varied tale, AERA members sought to create informal professional gatherings during the annual AERA conference. In 1969, the association sanctioned the creation of these secondary professional organizations, calling them Special Interest Groups, or SIGs. As the curriculum vector in chapter 6, professional organizations and gatherings illustrate the changing face of curriculum studies during the 1970s. These changes are discussed with compelling clarity in James Macdonald's "A Transcendental Developmental Ideology of Education," our primary source excerpt.

The 1970s represent a period during which an enormous energy engulfed the field of curriculum studies as scores of new people and ideas emerged in opposition to traditional practices and procedures. Our newcomers in chapter 6 voice their experiences within AERA and the Association for Supervision and Curriculum Development (ASCD) and as participants in an early series of "alternative" curriculum conferences that became the gathering place for a growing movement to reinvigorate and reconceptualize curriculum work. Our visit with Janet Miller and Alex Molnar provides an insider's view of the dynamic interest in curriculum work as well as the fragile coalition that aimed to see this work legitimized.

In time, however, as this collection of new and refurbished curriculum ideas gained currency, new energies increasingly were spent in disagreement and criticism among the various representatives of this curriculum renaissance. If a new paradigm was not emerging, certainly the old was being challenged as a variety of often competing perspectives vied to replace the Tyler rationale. Chapter 7 brings this vector to bear on the period between 1979 and 1983 when the field had changed unarguably, so it appeared.

The term *paradigm* is popular today thanks to Thomas Kuhn's remarkable book *The Structure of Scientific Revolutions* (1962/1970). We use the term *paradigm* to mean a conceptual framework or way to look at the world composed of knowledge, values, and assumptions that govern activity or inquiry in an academic field such as curriculum. Schubert (1986) offers three analytically distinctive curriculum paradigms that allow one to predict (the perennial paradigm), understand (the practical paradigm), or emancipate (the critical paradigm) through posing and exploring questions about knowledge and experiences in schools, particularly as they relate to curriculum. More recently, Patti Lather (1992), among others, has extended our thinking about paradigms by popularizing a fourth paradigm, variously called poststructural or postmodern. This additional paradigm or framework serves those who wish to deconstruct reality (whether in support of, or in opposition to, the work of understanding or emancipation), moving our notions of reality away from those that are "found" toward those that are "constructed" by participants through their language and actions. In chapter 7, Henry Giroux discusses his participation in the reconceptualization of curriculum work and articulates some of the distinctions among and within these paradigms.

Much of contemporary curriculum work can be said to reflect the practical paradigm, though growing numbers of curricularists have taken what they can from this paradigm (e.g., Schwab's own suggestion to provide an "active intellectualism" for curriculum work) and headed in other directions. In chapter 7, we excerpt Elliot Eisner's *The Educational Imagination,* in which he acknowledges a number of curriculum workers representing multiple perspectives before introducing his own, aesthetic perspective to the work of curriculum evaluation. This book was not only important for its unique take on curriculum work but because it—along with Michael Apple's 1979 publication of *Ideology and Curriculum*—played a major role in popularizing the paradigm shift in contemporary curriculum thinking that took place around this time.

Of course, paradigms lose their conceptual purity in reality, in part because of the multiple perspectives and sophisticated nuances contained within each of them. The idea of developing a tentative coalition for the purpose of breathing new life into an otherwise doomed operation is presented here in the parallel tale about NASA. As chapter 7 suggests, although the curriculum rogues of the time understood themselves as collectively opposed to the perennial paradigm, serious rifts developed over which of the alternative paradigms held the most promise for future curriculum theorizing, leading to what Pinar et al. (1995) call "the paradigm wars"—a phenomenon similar, in some ways, to the earlier split among progressive educators (see chapter 1).

Part V: The Uncertainties of Contemporary Curriculum Work (1984–2002). In a sense, being on the margin of that which is generally accepted, discussed, and done in the name of curriculum is an apt characterization of much contemporary curriculum work. Even when such topics received attention in the early years of the field (e.g., attention paid to social class or spirituality), this attention proved minor compared with the popular discourses of fixing problems and choosing content. More important, even when those representing marginal ideas did manage to make themselves heard (e.g., those promoting "curriculum integration" in the 1930s), their idea was often advanced to serve the business-as-usual mode of making a better curriculum.

In chapter 8, we use the notions of minority and marginal interchangeably to represent several aspects of marginalized voices as a vector for investigating contemporary curriculum work. For example, depending on its place and time in history, anyone representing a certain curriculum agenda (e.g., social behaviorist) might be considered to be in the minority. At a different level, someone like B. F. Skinner was actually considered a minority voice within the world of work done by social behaviorists. To move further away from the familiar, we can also talk about minority voices in relation to the majority surrounding them. Here, P. T. Pritzkau's 1959 text *Dynamics of Curriculum Improvement* serves as an example, for Pritzkau "took a stance that might be labeled existentialist and provided a departure from the usual generalizations found in many of the [other curriculum books of the time]" (Schubert, 1980, p. 143). However, Pritzkau's book title indicates that his overall intentions were much the same as most other curriculum workers of his day: to improve curriculum. And taking another step back, we can recognize how one's ideas might be marginalized both within the broader context of that discourse (i.e., your peers ignore your work) and within a broader context of that discourse (i.e., your peers do not even recognize you as one of them). Contemporary curriculum history represents all of these variations on marginalization.

To be truly marginalized, of course, is to be rendered invisible. In chapter 8 we discuss several discourses that in effect had no visibility (or were ephemeral at best) for much of the curriculum field's existence. During recent decades a variety of voices have surfaced between the cracks in contemporary curriculum discourses. We visit with three curriculum workers—Tom Barone, Susan Edgerton, and Mary-Ellen Jacobs—who work to develop their own voices within and around the imploding narrative called curriculum studies.

Just as we chose to visit multiple people in chapter 8, we also offer multiple excerpts from a special issue of *Theory Into Practice* to show the autobiographical passion underlying contemporary curriculum discourses. Our effort to portray the difficulties inherent in both respecting and rejecting tradition while both requiring and repelling extant labels and identities is aided, in part, by the tale of popular music.

In chapter 9, we link the marginalized voices of the curriculum field to the national school reform agenda of the 1990s. President George H. W. Bush's well-publicized education summit in 1989 marked a shift in the national focus on school reform, as politicians from both political parties took up the cause of accountability and standards. Conflict over national values, priorities, and directions—the so-called "culture wars" of the 1990s—played out in high-profile political debates regarding curriculum. One of the primary source documents in this chapter is an excerpt from the U.S. Senate debate over the National History Standards in January 1995. This debate is striking for the way it frames the classic curriculum question of *what knowledge is of most worth.* We suggest that the stakes surrounding this debate were driven higher by concerns on the part of some politicians and pundits regarding growing racial, ethnic, and cultural differences within the United States.

As the curriculum scholars who had helped diversify the field in the 1980s settled into the 1990s, the fracturing of theoretical unity and disciplinary cohesion we discussed in chapter 8 offered opportunities for new hybrid forms of curriculum theorizing. Our chapter 9 vector, *hybridity,* refers to the condition of heterogeneous assembly—the making of something out of disparate or incongruent parts or elements. The curriculum field's interest in hybridity via work in cultural studies is illustrated in our second primary source document, a piece by Cameron McCarthy titled "The Devil Finds Work: Re-reading Race and Identity in Contemporary Life," which is excerpted from his book *The Uses of Culture* (1998).

Partly in response to the theoretical diversification of the 1980s, and partly in response to changing demographics and cultural values, many in the curriculum field found the idea of hybridity useful to developing new understandings of how curriculum inquiry might approach the always-present institutional concerns of the field. Our visitors in chapter 9, Peter Hlebowitsh, Petra Munro, and Bill Watkins, reflect on these new understandings as they recall their own responses as teachers and curriculum scholars to the national school reform agenda and to the burgeoning theoretical diversity within the curriculum field itself.

In chapter 10, we try to imagine the near future of our field of study and its possibilities through the larger intersections of democracy, globalization, and technology. Toward this end, we introduce and explore the paradox of "consolidated diversity" and its presence in our lives and work. Surfacing within this discussion is a sense that communication and community have become not only more challenging but also more crucial to the work of curriculum. We conclude this chapter by joining all of our visitors to this book in a spirited (albeit artificially constructed) exchange on the past, present, and future of curriculum work. We hope you will imagine yourself as a participant: To whom would you respond and how? How might you connect elements of this exchange with what you've read in the book? With what you know from experience? With what you now understand about contemporary curriculum work?

I

Contextual Panorama for Contemporary Curriculum Work (1897–1946)

▲ **CHAPTER I** *Prelude to Contemporary Curriculum Theory and Development*

1

Prelude to Contemporary Curriculum Theory and Development

The seedbed of contemporary curriculum work is far more complex than an outgrowth of any one decade and extends deeply into the historical and philosophical roots of humanity and society. Far greater than a mere item of curiosity, curriculum lies at the heart of an educator's desire to make a difference in human lives. To ask meaningful questions about what should be taught and learned invokes basic assumptions about what it means to enable the growth of human beings and societies. John Dewey said it well when he defined education as "that reorganization and reconstruction of experience which adds to the meaning of experience, and which increases the ability to direct the course of subsequent experience" (1916, p. 76).

More than any other philosopher, John Dewey influenced the thought of curriculum scholars throughout the twentieth century, and at a new century's beginning, curriculum questions remain easily related to his definition of education. The enduring curriculum question thus becomes "What adds meaning and direction or purpose to experience?" Put another way, the curriculum question is frequently derived from the oft-quoted mid-nineteenth-century work of Herbert Spencer (1861), the social Darwinist:

"What knowledge is of most worth?" We prefer to restate the curriculum question as "What is worth knowing and experiencing?" and would add "Why? When? Where? How? For whom?"

The importance of such questions drew each of us into classroom teaching and, eventually, into higher education in general and the field of curriculum studies in particular. This book represents our collective effort to make some personal sense of this field as it has evolved during our lives. It is also our attempt to show the struggles among people and their viewpoints within the ever-changing social, cultural, economic, and political landscapes of their times. We believe that the essence of curriculum studies lies in the way each educator internalizes fundamental questions of what curriculum is and should be—and the attendant whys, whens, and wheres of its enactment. To personalize such questions and the theoretical and practical discourses that lie behind them is, as Ann Lopez (1993) perceptively contends, an act of embodying perspectives that enrich one's asking of fundamental curriculum questions.

Overview

In a brief chapter such as this, it is impossible to fully set the stage for recent (1947 to the present) contributions in the curriculum field. Here, we highlight some of the basic ideas and debates that fueled contemporary curriculum discourses.

Curriculum history is, in part, a continual recurrence of focus on three elements: subject matter, learners, and society. Dewey (1902) pointed these elements out in his classic essay, *The Child and the Curriculum.* When the nascent field was in danger of disintegrating in the 1920s due to lack of agreement, and Harold Rugg began his quest for common questions (if not common answers), he interpreted these three elements as "fundamentally interdependent factors in curriculum development" (Neil, 1983, pp. 9–10). Rugg's leadership in this process gave some brief stability to a shakily developing curriculum field and resulted in a milestone publication, the *Twenty-Sixth Yearbook of the National Society for the Study of Education* (Rugg, 1927). In the following decade, the curriculum leaders of the renowned Eight Year Study fashioned their model of curriculum development around three similar factors: specialized subject matter, adolescent needs, and social demands (see Giles, McCutchen, & Zechiel, 1942). In the most influential curriculum book of the twentieth century, *Basic Principles of Curriculum and Instruction,* Ralph W. Tyler (1949) summarized several of the key topics that emerged from the first half century while pointing out the need to address balance among these same three sources of curricular knowledge.

Having made the case for the perennial focus on subject matter, students, and society as paradigmatic bases for curriculum considerations throughout the twentieth century, we add two additional elements central to most curriculum debate, dialogue, discussion, and development. First, what is worth knowing and experiencing (to which Schubert [1994, 1995] adds, "and worth sharing")? Different responses to this question obviously shift the balance among subject matter, learners, and society. In fact, as Schubert sought to identify schools of curriculum thought in his earlier scholarship (Schubert, 1980; Schubert & Schubert, 1982), three emerged: intellectual traditionalist, experientialist, and social behaviorist—the underlying assumptions of each reflecting the recurrent emphasis on subject matter, the student or learner, and society, respectively. In our first half-century tour of the curriculum field that follows, you will see how debate shifted among these three curriculum orientations as different spokespersons sought to influence curriculum decisions about knowing, experiencing, and sharing. For those who wish to learn about these pre-World War II orientations, we suggest *History of the School Curriculum* (Tanner & Tanner, 1990), *Curriculum Books: The First Hundred Years* (Schubert, et al., 2002), *The Struggle for the American Curriculum, 1893–1958* (Kliebard, 2004), and *The Transformation of the School* (Cremin, 1961).

Our second additional question or topic of focus has to do with decision *makers:* Who decides (and should decide) what is worth knowing, and who benefits from those decisions? The latter part of this question is more subtle, for it involves the curriculum history equivalent of what Elliot Eisner (1985) calls the "null-curriculum," or that which is not taught. Authors such as Jean Anyon, Catherine Cornbleth, and the late Paulo Freire have steadfastly brought these questions to consciousness during recent decades. Relative to curriculum history, this notion refers to that which has not been part of the debate or that which has been omitted from the field. Here we refer to the many voices that have been suppressed, repressed, oppressed, or ignored. Where, we must ask, are voices at the grassroots, voices of African descent, voices of Latina/Latino origin, voices of Native or first nation people? Where are the voices of women educators, of mothers who are profound educators, of singers and storytellers who create the curriculum of popular culture, of children and youths, of those ignored or cast aside or devalued because of illness, disability, sexual identity, religious views, place of origin, ethnicity, appearance, custom, or belief? The brief history that follows calls for inclusion but is beset with ignorance, a tunnel vision our field has not yet overcome.

The Birth of Curriculum Studies

In the 1890s, one of this country's central and emergent problems was how to provide more universal education. Until then, schooling had been principally for the elite, often taking the form of private tutoring in preparation for higher education that was reserved for the very few. The influence of Horace Mann and Henry Barnard in promoting universal schooling resulted in major debate in the 1890s. Charles W. Eliot led an effort by the National Education Association's (NEA) Committee of Ten in 1893 to broaden the array of subjects for high school students to include contemporary areas of study, not just classical subjects propped up and justified by "faculty psychology" that saw the mind as a muscle to be strengthened. With this broadened array of subjects the committee assumed that the best preparation for college was the same as the best preparation for life.

The question of preparation for elementary students was still open, however, so the NEA established the Committee of Fifteen. Heated debate raged among Herbartians (followers of Johann F. Herbart), with their developmental theories, on the one side, and William T. Harris, a respected Hegelian advocate of the disciplines of knowledge, on the other. In the end, Harris's notion of the disciplines as "five windows of the soul" emerged victorious in the committee's 1895 report. Nevertheless, the Herbartians continued to influence educational practice in America for another decade. They saw child development as the key to curricular decision making and offered detailed plans on how to correlate subject matter around the way child development recapitulates the evolution of the human race. In these efforts we can readily perceive a shift from subject to learner as a basis for curriculum work.

On the social behaviorist front, G. Stanley Hall, who started the first American psychological laboratory, advocated education based on scientific child study. Before Hall's travels to Germany to align himself with the father of experimental psychology, Wilhelm Wundt, his intellectual mentor was William James at Harvard. A pluralistic thinker and Dewey's forerunner in pragmatism, James advocated a curriculum based on conversation and dialogue about fundamental questions, a curriculum focused on the moral and ethical that gives some attention to stream of consciousness and dreamworld elements of life (see Schubert & Zissis, 1988). James—clearly ahead of his time—seemed willing to integrate the subject matter focus of the intellectual traditionalist with the experientialist's focus on individual growth. The grassroots emphasis on the student as legitimate initiator of curriculum was clearly a theme of Dewey's in the years that followed and was anticipated in the debate over the Committee of Fifteen Report. Among the debaters of Herbartian persuasion were Charles DeGarmo, Frank and Charles McMurry, and Francis Parker. Parker, although aligned with the intellectual descendants of Herbart, saw the organizing center for correlation of subject matter as residing precisely in the life world of the child. Frank McMurry (1927) and other fellow Herbartians only later realized the power of Parker's insight into curricular correlation.

Dewey's curricular view (1899, 1902), however, was a balanced integration of emphasis on subject matter, society, and the child. Although much of the debate of the 1890s pitted subject matter advocates against those who favored child-centered approaches, significant emphasis stemmed from the societal front as well. Influencing Dewey directly was the work of Jane Addams (1910; 1981), founder of Hull House in Chicago. A member of her advisory board, Dewey saw firsthand Addams's practical efforts to help the urban poor and immigrant populations to reconstruct their lives and opportunities. Also a minority voice of influence for Dewey was botanist Lester Frank Ward (1883, 1893). Ward, who opposed the social Darwinism of Herbert Spencer (1861), which called for a self-preservationist, survival-of-the-fittest orientation to education, developed what Kliebard (1995) calls a *social meliorist* position built on the argument that human intelligence and a sense of justice make it unnecessary to accept a predator-like interpretation of the laws of nature for human society.

At the turn of the century, Dewey's pragmatic experimentalist educational philosophy, progressive social and educational theory, and experiential and reconstructionist curriculum thinking came to the fore. His central curriculum position, often referred to as the progressive reorganization of subject matter, differed substantially from most educational practice of his day (see Dewey, 1897, 1899, 1902, 1913, 1916) in its argument for the pedagogic necessity of starting with the psychological and moving to the logical. By *psychological,* Dewey meant the concerns and interests of the learner's life world of experience; his *logical* referred to both the disciplines of knowledge and knowledge accumulated by human beings through everyday experiences. Dewey's pedagogical process included identifying individual student interests, encouraging students to share these interests within a community of learners, excavating common human interests symbolized by (but at a deeper level than) the individually identified interests, tapping a broad array of experiential resources (persons who have experienced similar problems) as precedent, and drawing on the fund of written knowledge (the logical or extant disciplines and areas of study) in pursuit of original interests and the discovery of new interests. Thus, for Dewey, the work of educators flows back and forth on a continuum between the logical and the psychological. At the time, many would-be progressive educators were criticized for not being sufficiently rigorous and not acquainting students with the depth of knowledge available in the disciplines. However, having started the Laboratory School of the University of Chicago in 1896, Dewey was able to demonstrate his ideas in practice—a major value for those who advocated experiential learning.

One additional figure from the 1890s should be mentioned. Joseph Mayer Rice, a pediatrician who had studied with Herbartians in Europe and America, sought examples of schools that represented these Deweyan ideals in practice. After surveying U.S. schools he wrote a series of scathing articles in *The Forum*, a popular periodical of the time. Continuing his studies, Rice attempted to determine why some schools were better or worse than others and produced examples of a new form of scientific and comparative study of educational practice in the process. As he learned more, Rice (1913) moved increasingly toward the position that educational progress would only occur if teachers and their leaders were carefully guided, efficiently managed, and systematically controlled.

This story of Rice's saga of survey and investigation does not represent a change in his ultimate ideals but rather in his faith in schools to live up to these ideals. The gross ineptitudes he described remind one of those portrayed by critics of later eras (e.g., Silberman [1970], who coined the term *mindlessness* to characterize mainstream educational practice, or Kozol [1991], who vividly conveyed the "savage inequalities" between urban and suburban schools). The question of the first half century of curriculum debate is symbolized in Rice's story: Can a grassroots, student-centered, democratic community that values the intellectual repertoire available to it (i.e., subject matter, learners, and society rather than one or the other as dominant) be created to support universal education? Or do the hierarchies that govern our world prevent such experience for all but a select few? Dewey's was an inclusive ideal, for if only a few have such educational opportunity, its democratic and communal value is negated and the few become dominant—whether they desire to be or not. Thus, the questions of "Whose knowledge?" and "Who benefits?" must be addressed along with "What knowledge is worthwhile?"

Struggles Surface

Rice's message of efficiency grew loud and strong in the first two decades of the twentieth century. The overwhelming influence of Taylorism (Frederick Taylor, 1911) in business and industry led to a similar emphasis on technical efficiency in education, a tradition that continues today with "high stakes testing." Intelligence testing, popularized during this era, became a means to achieve curriculum efficiency. Believing that one's IQ was a true measure of potential, many curricularists argued for early ability grouping based on such tests. Faith in measurement was further hailed by Edward L. Thorndike (1924), founder of educational psychology, who reasoned that if something exists, it does so in some amount; thus, it can be measured, and we should work to do so. Dewey, however, took a critical and wry look at the emergent popularity of testing, often comparing intelligence testing with hog weighing in his lectures. He observed that in certain rural areas a hog was tied to one end of a board, the board was placed on a fulcrum, and then rocks were placed on the other end of the board until one rock equally balanced with the hog. Then the weight of the rock was guessed. Offered as a joke, this was a deceptively simple but conceptually crushing critique of the construct of intelligence reified as numerical scores.

During the second decade of the new century, the question of how to scientifically make curriculum was addressed directly. Franklin Bobbitt

(1918, 1924), a paragon of the social behaviorist orientation (Schubert, 1986), argued for activity analysis as the basis for curriculum work. Activity analysis was a scientific strategy of surveying the public to see what successful members of society spend time doing and what they must know in order to do those things. Objectives of curriculum would then be derived from gaps between what successful people know and what students know. These activities would then be selected as a means to acquire curricular objectives, which were to be expressed in terms of student behaviors acquired through properly sequenced, organized, taught, and evaluated classroom activities. In a similar vein, W. W. Charters (1923), a former student of Dewey, argued for scientific curriculum making based on survey data representing societal ideals rather than the discreet activities advocated by Bobbitt.

The Deweyan progressive or experientialist tradition was kept alive and promoted in these times through the Progressive Education Association (PEA), founded in 1919. Many progressive educators were influenced by William H. Kilpatrick's small pamphlet, "The Project Method" (1918). Within a few pages and in straightforward language, Kilpatrick illustrated how to integrate curriculum around projects that grow from student interests. Although scholars still debate the authenticity of Kilpatrick's interpretation of Dewey's philosophy, Kilpatrick unquestionably influenced progressive practice.

In the period from 1910 to 1930 the population of students attending high school increased markedly, from about 10% to more than 50% of those eligible. Due in part to the belief that all students could benefit from secondary education, and in part to the passage of the Smith-Hughes Act for Vocational Education in 1917, new subjects (e.g., home economics, business, and industrial arts) emerged in high schools that catered to working-class students. Classic subjects, formerly dominant, gave way to the vernacular in the wake of empirical studies (devised by William James and later by E. L. Thorndike) that "proved" that classic languages (i.e., Greek and Latin) were of minimal value in training the mind.

The decline of faculty psychology, the move away from classic subjects, and the influx of new student populations revived the question "What are the purposes of education?" Again the NEA was at the helm of policy advocacy. Its Commission on the Reorganization of Secondary Education (1918) developed seven cardinal principles, or new curriculum aims: health, worthy home membership, command of fundamental processes, worthy use of leisure time, citizenship, vocational enhancement, and ethical character. Clearly, the purposes of secondary schooling broadened to meet social needs.

Progressive educators, however, argued that addressing existing social needs was insufficient. Both the curricular conciliarists (see Thomas, 1991) and social efficiency advocates had it wrong, because they ignored the need for participatory democracy at all levels of society (even that of students in schools). Curriculum workers guided by the "science" of activity analysis, progressives asserted, merely perpetuated society's seamiest effects. Although the cardinal principles received less criticism, many progressives saw them as favoring a curriculum of personal adjustment rather than social transformation. It is difficult to find a more biting and witty critique of these curriculum orientations than *Modern Educational Theories* by Boyd Bode (1927). However, most accounts of progressive practice during these years were admirable, including the child-centered work described by Harold Rugg and Ann Shumaker (1928); Ellsworth Collings's (1923) portrayal of a project method experiment; and a range of other interpretations of progressive practices penned by female educators, including Margaret Wells's *A Project Curriculum* (1921), Mary H. Lewis's *An Adventure with Children* (1928), *Brief Guide to the Project Method* (1926) by James F. Hosic and Sara E. Chase, *Education on the Dalton Plan* (1922) by Helen Parkhurst, Caroline Pratt's *Experimental Practice in the City and Country School* (1924) and *Before Books* with Jessie Stanton (Pratt & Stanton, 1926), Margaret Naumburg's *The Child and the World* (1928), and Patty Smith Hill's *A Conduct Curriculum* (1923). During our field's early years, female progressive educators played a critical though much neglected role.

Although the 1920s and 1930s became the heyday of progressive practices, progressivism never dominated educational thinking or practice in a popular sense. The intellectual traditionalist position was kept alive (then) by William C. Bagley (1905) and Robert M. Hutchins (1936), followed later by Mortimer Adler (1982) and E. D. Hirsch (1987). This intellectual traditionalist curriculum position has no small kinship with that of the social behaviorist extensions of Bobbitt, Charters, David Snedden, and others in terms of adult-centered authority. For them, curriculum making was a top-down, expert-driven enterprise resulting in selection or creation of products to be systematically delivered to students who were assessed on their retention of knowledge and acquisition of skills.

Sentiments of progressivism would reemerge under numerous guises in subsequent decades. However, by the 1940s the curriculum field was again awash in struggle. But we are getting ahead of our story.

The Progressives Multiply and Divide

By the mid-1920s the curriculum field was in danger of disintegrating because of its many competing positions. With the support of the National Society for the Study of Education (NSSE), Harold Rugg coordinated a virtual all-star team of curriculum advocates from each of the contending schools of thought (among them were Bagley, Bobbitt, Charters,

Counts, Judd, and Kilpatrick). Their challenge: to find commonality in viewpoint about curriculum making. Eventually, they presented a list of 18 questions and subquestions for curriculum developers to consider, along with a 10-page position statement. These were followed by more than 200 pages of rebuttal statements. Nevertheless, this landmark volume (Rugg, 1927) represented the first significant attempt to bring coherence to the expanding field of curriculum.

Despite this search for a common ground, members of the Progressive Education Association felt pressure to demonstrate their successes with the more generalizable, "hard" data of the social behaviorists and traditionalists. Because they found that story, intuition, and experiential insight held little sway in this modern world, progressive educators undertook the most elaborate educational research project in the first half of the twentieth century, the Eight Year Study (circa 1933–1941).

After securing from nearly 300 colleges and universities a willingness to admit high school graduates based on portfolios of their work rather than traditional grades and test scores, 30 school systems agreed to participate in the study. Like their traditional counterparts, these experimental–progressive schools were scattered around the United States and represented public, private, urban, rural, suburban, wealthy, poor, and university constituencies. Ralph Tyler, director of evaluation, and his team arranged curriculum workshops for teachers and developed and employed a host of innovative evaluation instruments. Students from these 30 schools were compared throughout high school and college with students from traditional high schools.

An overview volume, written by Wilford Aikin and published in 1942, tells the story and summarizes the findings. Harper & Brothers published four additional volumes in the same year (*Exploring the Curriculum* by Giles et al.; *Appraising and Recording Student Progress* by E. R. Smith, Tyler, & the Evaluation Staff; *Did They Succeed in College?* by Chamberlin, Chamberlin, Drought, & Scott; and *Thirty Schools Tell Their Story* by educators from the schools commissioned by Progressive Education Association Publications). Collectively, these reports show that on all measures (academic, social, attitudinal, and more), the performance of students from the experimental–progressive schools equaled or exceeded that of students from traditional schools—success in foreign language being the lone exception. Students in many of the experimental–progressive schools engaged in self- or group-designed projects and completed minicourses on a wide range of topics. The progressive explanation for this comparative success was that students learned to love learning, to take charge of the pursuit of meaningful projects, and to sustain and augment their curiosity. They learned skills and amassed knowledge as it became useful for them to do so, and thus they became adept at self-directed learning, group process, democratic interaction, and relating learning to living. Fate, though, was less reliable than modern research methods. Eclipsed by the invasion of North Africa, a spring German offensive, and the Japanese siege of Corregidor, the report received scant public notice when compared with the nation's attention to the events of World War II.

While these progressive liberals were busy planning their massive study, everyday people simply struggled to survive and progressive radicals were arguing for a more extreme approach. In 1932, the year famine in the Soviet Union claimed four million lives, FDR was elected president, squatter camps of World War I veterans were trampled by U.S. tanks, and George S. Counts asked "Dare the School Build a New Social Order?" Stemming from Dewey's efforts to provide curriculum that fostered democratic participation, Counts held—with the world on the brink of destruction—that curricula must be designed to rapidly overcome injustice and oppression and create a more democratic, equitable, fulfilling way of life. Many outside the progressive movement accused these reconstructionists of indoctrination, as did some progressives.

Among prominent reconstructionist progressives, Counts, Harold Rugg, and later Theodore Brameld (1956) disputed the accusation, claiming to foster critical thinking and social action around issues of ethics and justice. Moving beyond social theory and into curricular practice, Rugg went on to develop an influential series of high school social studies textbooks. Though they sold well for a few years, Rugg's texts, like the questions of Socrates and the fables of Aesop, led students to question too many of their elders' values and the books were eventually dashed on the rocks of "un-Americanism."

Despite the fact that these reconstructionists were concerned about individuals and small groups and guided by a social ideology, they were seen as misguided by fellow progressives who favored the tamer, more individualized "child study" ideology. And although these child study advocates were concerned with democratic participation, they were often criticized by reconstructionists as apolitical. Some sought to bridge this rift. Boyd Bode (1938), for example, argued that progressive education must build on the strengths of its common values. Dewey (1938), too, called for a deeper look into these superficial differences, pointing to the need to find reciprocal relationships between individual and political growth. These efforts largely failed, though, and in time this rift among progressives widened, weakening their collective voice and muddying the curriculum waters of the 1940s and early 1950s.

Question

In your community schools, which curriculum approaches are used? What approach do you think is the most appropriate for today's students?

Conclusion

A great deal of terrain has been covered here (from the early 1890s to the late 1940s) as we viewed curriculum history from diverse vantage points. Major figures such as John Dewey, Franklin Bobbitt, Harold Rugg, and Ralph Tyler are examples of established curricularists who were both influenced by and attempted to influence matters of public interest. Intellectual traditionalists cared about preserving sociocultural values and insights from great works and disciplines of knowledge; social behaviorists viewed education as a science and worked for the efficient acquisition of socially admired traits; experientialists promoted their faith in the judgment of grassroots decision making (even among students) to solve problems, enhance meaning, and imagine purpose and possibility; and reconstructionists worked to create a more just and equitable society. That curriculum reflects the social context or milieu of the times is patent. Further, in every era we see those outside the field of curriculum enter to make considerable waves. An example is the work of Lester Frank Ward, an agronomist and outsider who wrote insightfully about the need for social meliorism to overcome the detrimental effects of social Darwinism.

Actually, social Darwinism and the efficiency movement in general were more pervasive socially and economically than educationally. The same can be said about the federal government, which plays a small but important part in the shaping of our early curriculum story. The impact of the Smith-Hughes Act on U.S. curriculum is an illustration of the influence of government agendas.

Publications themselves sometimes serve as benchmarking moments in the history of curriculum. For example, John Dewey, through his publications, helped those doing curriculum work to turn away from the adult-centered curriculum that dominated educational theory and practice in the nineteenth century. Rugg's 1927 *NSSE Yearbook* and Counts's 1932 *Dare the School* are further examples. Emphases on expert science, social behaviorism, and efficient management of curriculum in the Bobbitt and Charters generation (1915–1930) changed as a new generation of curriculum workers, among them Counts and Rugg, turned the field toward a social reconstructionist orientation.

The National Education Association, through several major committees and commissions, proved to be a much greater intellectual forum for curriculum policy making throughout the first half of the twentieth century than any single professional group active today. As professional organizations go, the Progressive Education Association pushed hard on the issue of grassroots authority and influenced curriculum research through progressive and reconstructionist thought published in its two significant journals, *Social Frontier* (1934–1943) and *Progressive Education* (1924–1959). In 1943, a broad range of curricular perspectives combined when the NEA's Department of Supervisors and Directors of Instruction merged with the Society for Curriculum Study to create the huge and influential Association for Supervision and Curriculum Development (ASCD). We will talk about some of ASCD's gatherings later in this book.

Positions such as the intellectual traditionalist, social behaviorist, experientialist, reconstructionist, and even conciliarist represent substantive paradigms, by which we mean conceptual frameworks or ways to look at the world comprised of knowledge, values, and assumptions that govern activity or inquiry in an academic field such as curriculum. These paradigms include various perspectives, all of which shifted and vied for recognition and influence in curriculum debates during the early years of optimism and mission in the field. In more recent years these curriculum debates have moved from their preoccupation with questions about what should be taught and learned and how to develop and package it to problems regarding how best to inquire about such questions. Nevertheless, implicit in the writings of the first half century (especially those of Dewey) is a great deal that speaks to both questions.

Reflecting on the first 50 years of curriculum work finds racial, intellectual, gendered, and other voices largely invisible—a term used perceptively by the African-American scholar W. E. B. DuBois (1903). DuBois wrote on a host of curricular topics throughout the period just discussed, yet his work is rarely cited in curriculum literature. Other African-American voices (Carter G. Woodson [1933], Benjamin Mays, Horace Mann Bond [see Urban, 1992], and Allison Davis [1929]) are missing, too, from the early years of the curriculum field, as is the voice of Cuban liberationist Jose Marti (see, for example, *Deep South* [1940] by Davis, Burleigh, & Gardner, and *On Education* by Jose Marti [1979]). Voices of women and children (*especially* children) remain thin in this history as well. Such marginalized voices are only beginning to be excavated, studied, and integrated fully into our discourse about curriculum (Blount, 2004; Woyshner, 2003/2004). They remain invisible throughout much of this book not because they are unimportant to the story we tell but because ours is an attempt to portray the intellectual and social history of what *has been* rather than what *might or should have been* a part of the background of contemporary curriculum studies. Yet it is our hope to mention them enough that other students and scholars of curriculum will make visible these neglected educators and authors.

Question

What accounts for the marginalization of these various voices? Can you identify voices or individuals who are rendered silent today?

Regardless of collisions among holders of differing perspectives, purposes, questions, or beliefs, the men and women who helped develop and define curriculum work through their engaging struggles were people with a vision of the centrality of curriculum to questions of what schooling and education ought to be. Living through difficult yet remarkable economic, social, political, and cultural times, each had a mission, be it to situate the learner at the center of education, to maintain the integrity of disciplined knowledge, to serve (or subvert) society's apparent needs, or to try to somehow balance all of these. What kept this group of curricularists going was, in part, a deep optimism in the value of their work: The country was changing, its educational mission was changing, and the need for attention to curriculum matters was obvious. By the late 1940s the field of curriculum had arrived.

P A R T

The Rise and Fall of Curriculum Specialists (1947–1960)

2

Curriculum Development at Its Zenith: Curriculum People

Following what oral historian Studs Terkel has called "the good war," men and women anxiously returned to the normalcy of pre—World War II life: marriage and families; movies, dances, and malt shops; steady work; and vacations in the family automobile. Although from hindsight such a view may appear hopelessly romantic, in postwar America it was the zeitgeist of the times.

Living in a country unchallenged as a military and industrial superpower and awash in the benevolence of Uncle Sam's benefits to millions of soldiers, Americans—at least the vast Euro-American middle class—saw a future of social promise and economic prosperity in a land seemingly insulated from the factionalism that had nearly destroyed Europe: Norman Rockwell covers for the *Saturday Evening Post,* Benjamin Spock's *Baby and Child Care,* and comforting Big Band music accompanied by crooning singers such as Rosemary Clooney. It was an era of hope and optimism: the United Nations held its first session in London, the Nuremberg Tribunal reached a summative judgment for crimes against humanity, and the Marshall Plan infused $18 billion into European reconstruction. Top-grossing movies included David Lean's *Great Expectations* and William Wyler's *The Best Years of Our Lives;* inventions including xerography, the transistor, and the long-playing record appeared; and the Jewish state of

Israel entered world politics no less profoundly than Jackie Robinson entered "white" professional baseball.

In the late 1940s most Americans lived in small communities or rural surroundings. In towns with bucolic and patriotic street names, mom-and-pop businesses lined Main Street: the barbershop and beauty salon, the bank and bakery, the grocery and granary. Though social and geographic divisions existed (e.g., the "wrong side of the tracks" variously populated by the working poor and ethnic or racial minorities), they were largely invisible in everyday social life as each person understood his or her role defined against the taken-for-granted symbols and rituals of American life: church steeples, Fourth of July parades, and county fairs.

Yet this good war had already sowed the seeds of social transformation in America. Millions of men and women had stepped onto foreign shores such as those of Normandy and Wake Island or into foreign environments such as General Electric munitions and Bethlehem Steel plants. Now, women were dutifully returned to the kitchen and their role as caregivers, as men reoccupied factories and their role as breadwinners. Neither the economic independence experienced by women on-line nor the cultural diversity experienced by men in uniform would be easily forgotten. In fact, some women and men never returned to their past: homosexual soldiers were discharged into the ports of San Francisco and New York City, working-class women relieved from one job turned around and secured another, and African-Americans and Native Americans refused to accept the indignities of second-class status after proving indispensable in the war effort. Many who did return home soon discovered that both they and their communities were already undergoing change. The world was becoming complicated. So, too, were the communities of school and the small bands of educators known as "curriculum workers."

▨ Curriculum Work as Curriculum Making

These postwar years brought focused attention to American public schooling in general and curriculum work in particular. The curriculum field had established an identity during the 1930s as an informed yet practical endeavor. Expanding cities, immigration (both from abroad and from the American South), and compulsory school laws enmeshed schooling with the American dream, and with more students of all sorts spending more time in schools, it fell to curriculum workers to help schools and school districts answer questions about worthwhile knowledge and experiences.

The work of constructing curricula for schools and districts was done by a small but growing number of curriculum people, most prominent among them Hollis Caswell. Caswell exemplified the scholar-practitioner in that he both theorized about and practiced curriculum making.

Caswell and his colleague Doak Campbell first recognized the need to further professionalize curriculum work by bringing the disparate thinking in curriculum together in a synoptic text. Called *Curriculum Development* (1935), the book was their attempt to provide some uniformity for a field moving in many different directions (i.e., to place much of the literature that had emerged within the curriculum rubric under one cover). Theirs turned out to be an exemplary kind of organizational scheme that provided a pattern for many postwar synoptic texts. Caswell and Campbell also pioneered the combining of varied curriculum publications from journals and book chapters with their 1937 book, *Readings in Curriculum Development*. Such texts became important, in part, because they canonized knowledge for graduate students preparing to be curriculum workers.

Curriculum Meccas and Mentors

In these early years of the curriculum field, curricularists were a small and rather insular group of university-situated academics, many of whom spent considerable time consulting and, as such, influencing school curricula. During the 1930s, 1940s, and 1950s many would probably have identified themselves as generalists. There were subject matter specialists, of course—those in mathematics education or social studies education—but they had less interaction with the general curriculum field than did their colleagues in the social and philosophical or psychological foundations of education. Indeed, to a large extent, there seems to have been a competition between people whose origins were in the philosophical and social foundational areas (who, by the 1940s, seemed to intellectually dominate curriculum work) and those primarily influenced by educational psychologists. Although the curriculum field was being nurtured by faculty at the University of Illinois, Ohio State University, and the University of Wisconsin, most important curriculum mentors worked at Teachers College—Columbia University and the University of Chicago.

Few people actually sought doctorates in curriculum during this era because few universities offered such a degree. Teachers College—a flagship institution for progressivism—was the IBM of curriculum studies. Indeed, the first academic department to employ the term *curriculum* (the Department of Curriculum and Teaching) was inaugurated in 1935 at Teachers College under the leadership of Hollis Caswell. Caswell was influential in helping to legitimize curriculum studies there and move the field toward greater status. Though influenced markedly by progressive theory, Caswell's curriculum work is best characterized as eclectic. Largely because of Caswell's presence, the main place that people from all over the world went to study curriculum was Teachers College.

At Teachers College in the 1940s and early 1950s one could also find L. Thomas Hopkins, who was the research director of the Horace Mann-Lincoln Laboratory School. Other great curriculum or foundations faculty members at Teachers College included Florence Stratemeyer, Harold Rugg, George S. Counts, John Childs, Gordon McKenzie, George Axtell, Alice Miel, and William H. Kilpatrick. Though some had retired by the early 1950s, the institutional legacy continued.

Probably the only serious rival for graduate curriculum studies during the 1940s and 1950s was the University of Chicago. Ralph Tyler, midway in the Eight Year Study (1936), brought his work in evaluating this great, progressive curriculum experiment from Ohio State University to the University of Chicago. Not yet 40 years old, Tyler became head of the Department of Education, dean of social sciences, and educational examiner at Chicago. Just as he would influence his new department by recruiting influential faculty members (including Virgil Herrick, Carl Rogers, Robert Havighurst, and Joseph Schwab), he would contribute to the curriculum field's continued sophistication through his impact on students (including Benjamin Bloom, Lee J. Cronbach, John Goodlad, and Elliot Eisner). Tyler was—for years—responsible for teaching the major curriculum course for graduate students at the University of Chicago. And in 1949 he published a version of his syllabus under the title *Basic Principles of Curriculum and Instruction.*

▼ ARIED TALE

IBM: THE RISE OF BIG BLUE

The emergence and dominance of IBM in the new field of business technology and computing reflects both the optimism of this postwar generation and the underbelly of nascent multinational corporatism. This story is a harbinger to how a young field such as curriculum studies (with its own niche at Teachers College producing curriculum workers to serve a monopoly of educational clients) was first challenged from within and later from without.

Once a National Cash Register (NCR) salesperson from upstate New York, Thomas Watson was the quintessential "NCR man" (intelligent, aggressive, and tenacious) at the turn of the century. Within three years he rose to the top in sales, and by 1910 he was a member of company president John Patterson's inner circle and his heir apparent. However, following a nationally publicized antitrust trial and disagreements on marketing strategies, Watson found himself holding his last paycheck.

Watson quickly assumed management responsibility for the fledgling Computing-Tabulating-Recording (CTR) Company. There he created an experimental laboratory

(continued)

for a new generation of advanced and superior business machines, expanded the well-trained and richly rewarded sales force, and developed new markets by ruthlessly undercutting his competitors. Emphasizing hard work, Watson valued cooperation and loyalty as much as he discouraged independence and individualism. In 1924, Watson was named chief executive officer, and CTR was renamed International Business Machines.

During the next two decades Watson oversaw the quadrupling of revenues as IBM weathered the Depression, took advantage of the electrification and urbanization of America, and emphasized research and development (R&D). Leasing its machines to large corporations and the government (whose demand exploded with its New Deal agencies), providing low capitalization requirements for leased equipment, selling operating supplies at inflated prices, and providing free training to the predominantly female IBM operators created a "harmonious whole … [that] provided IBM with a stability that the other companies in the industry lacked" (Sobel, 1981, p. 81). It was also the formula for IBM's success a generation later when its reputation for customer service, its monopoly on critical components, and its sales emphasis on leasing and upgrading would enable it to dominate the computer market.

The Depression found Watson developing relationships with institutions of higher education and academics. Serving on the boards of trustees for universities such as Columbia not only gave Watson and IBM a small market advantage but, more important, provided them with a source for cutting-edge technology and ideas. For example, IBM came to dominate the educational testing market by developing the 805 test scorer in the 1930s. IBM subsidies provided to Columbia University's Statistics Bureau contributed to the development of the calculator, which in turn led to the alliance of leading Harvard academics and researchers (e.g., James B. Conant, Harlowe Shapley, and Howard Aiken) with IBM to develop the automatic controlled sequence calculator that was unveiled in February 1943 as the Mark I.

Schools of education, like public schools, enjoyed their own monopolies. In the field of curriculum, these included Teachers College—Columbia University, synonymous with progressivism and experientialism, and the upstart University of Chicago, built on the pillars of perennialism and empiricism under the leadership of Robert Hutchins. Like IBM and its youthful rival Rand, these two curriculum meccas would redefine the curriculum field.

Arthur Wellesley-Foshay

VISITOR Arthur Wellesley (Wells) Foshay, a 1949 doctoral graduate of Teachers College, studied with many of curriculum's early progressives. Entering the curriculum field around midcentury, he recognized the change in traditions under way, though he has steadfastly maintained his support for the progressive ideals he embraced at Teachers College. However, as Foshay explains,[1] it was Caswell's stature within the curriculum field more than Teachers College's progressive reputation that drew him to New York City:

> My father was an old fashioned family doctor who made house calls. Well, during the depression his practice collapsed and here I was in college at the University of California in Berkeley, so I thought I'd better get off his back. In 1936, I got a job as a high school teacher in Oakland. After that year enrollments were dropping and I was transferred to a junior high school in East Oakland where I taught science, mainly, along with French, English, music, and social studies. I was there for three years before becoming an elementary school principal in 1939—a job I kept through the war.

Following the war, Wells and his wife agreed that he should go on to pursue a doctorate in curriculum. As for where to attend, Foshay's choice seemed obvious. As he put it:

> The best place to go at that time was Teachers College. I had heard about Hollis Caswell at Cal in several courses. He was the leading curriculum man in the country at that time. Where was he? He was at Teachers College. So I followed him there. In the medieval university, you go to the man.
>
> My first meeting with him was formal. I went there in the summer of 1945 to let them look me over and to look them over. When I sought Caswell out, he said, "Well, here are some courses you probably ought to take, and there's a test you need to take"—it was a graduate intelligence kind of thing. He told me to come back when I'd done that.
>
> The following summer I returned with a high score on that test—and his whole manner changed! He rolled out a red carpet, offered me a job as Assistant Principal at the Horace Mann-Lincoln School at Teachers College, later invited me onto the faculty [1949], and invited me to do a book with him (*Education in the Elementary School*, 1950). In general he treated me as a protégé. It's a funny thing, because I never knew him awfully well in a personal sense.
>
> Mind you, there were plenty of well-known people at Teachers College at the time, including Harold Rugg, Florence Stratemeyer, and Arthur Jersild. Jersild even became my doctoral sponsor when Caswell became dean of the college and couldn't take on any more sponsorships. But Caswell remained my mentor, and while at Teachers College I developed a strong sense of membership in the curriculum field.
>
> Upon graduation, Caswell invited me to join the faculty as a Research Associate in the Horace Mann-Lincoln Institute of School Experimentation. The institute was to carry on experimentation in public schools, not in laboratories, and the income from the endowment was used to support a research staff. Much of my time as a researcher [1949–1952] was spent in Springfield, Missouri, working with school staff doing action research.

---

[1]Personal communication, A.W. Foshay, August 17, 1994.

I left Teachers College in 1952 to become Director of the Bureau of Education Research at Ohio State University. Caswell invited me to come back to Teachers College in 1957 as Head of the Horace Mann-Lincoln Institute. So I went back.

Seeking Guidance and Direction

As we have illustrated thus far, an increasing amount of curriculum work was being done by a small but growing number of established curriculum workers and their students, largely educated at *two philosophically different* institutions. Caswell the eclectic, who provided Wells Foshay with numerous opportunities on the one hand and yet no specific direction for curriculum work on the other, represented one sort of curriculum mentor. Ralph Tyler the assessor, who was establishing evaluation as a fundamental aspect of curriculum work on the one hand, and teaching his curriculum students at Chicago to begin with a small and manageable set of "basic principles" for curriculum work on the other, represented a different form of curriculum leadership. Too, most curriculum leaders of this era spent a good deal of time in school environments working with their clients—teachers and administrators—to make curricula. And most new curriculum workers typically began their careers after taking only a few curriculum development courses and consuming one or another of the popular synoptic texts.

Our beginning point for contemporary curriculum history is 1947 because it coincides with a curriculum conference held at the University of Chicago on October 16 and 17 of that year. Convened under the leadership of Virgil Herrick and Ralph Tyler, participants were gathered to develop theoretical principles that might extend curriculum development and research. In the conveners' eyes, the time had come to try and move beyond the competing paradigms of neopositivist, analytic, and normative-prescriptive curriculum theory.

Although no grand theory emerged, Herrick and Tyler identified several ideas in their conclusion to the published conference proceedings, including the state of curriculum theorizing at that time and a foreshadowing of changes in the field. These ideas include their belief that an adequate curriculum theory could only be produced by the combined efforts of people at all "levels of curriculum work." Additionally, they foresaw the need to address curriculum questions on a "broad front" via multidisciplinary teams or "committees" that employed "creative scholarship" in their efforts. Herrick and Tyler further understood that curriculum questions were inherently questions about values and should be acknowledged and critically discussed as such. And recognizing that "a theory of curriculum becomes very close to a theory of education" (Herrick & Tyler, 1950, p. 124), they invited a diverse group of curriculum workers to begin the more comprehensive and compli-

PRIMARY DOCUMENT EXCERPT

Next Steps in the Development of a More Adequate Curriculum Theory

by Virgil E. Herrick and Ralph W. Tyler

One useful outcome of a conference . . . is to provide its audience with a sense of the present status of the thinking in the field and of the future directions to be taken. It is likely too that professional workers in the curriculum were disappointed to realize that, in spite of this conference's being the first of its kind, the past fifteen to twenty years had produced few, if any, new or significant contributions to the topic of the conference. This sense of disappointment should not, however, lead to cessation of work in the field. It should merely point out the great opportunity for work and contribution in curriculum development. . . .

Additional Concerns about Curriculum Theory

Curriculum development by its very nature is a co-operative problem. The teacher working with a group of young people is engaging in a co-operative learning project whether he recognizes it or not. . . . In the same way, the development of curriculum theory is a co-operative enterprise. No one person is going to be able to encompass all the knowledges or to perceive all the problems that would be essential in the formulation of an adequate conception of curriculum. On the other hand, there must be, on the various levels of curriculum work, people who are consciously trying to see the ideas which are important in clarifying and relating the various curriculum activities in their sphere of interest. At present, there is not even any clear-cut conception of what these levels of curriculum work are, but it is quite likely that they must have both a horizontal and a vertical orientation to curriculum activities. . . . The belief of the editors of this monograph is that the task of curriculum theory is not the question of either the grass-roots approach or the mountain-top attack but that any program must have both, proceeding through proper communication and interaction to evolve and creatively project a more adequate curriculum theory.

The implications of this point of view are many and pose some interesting problems for the profession itself. It is time that these problems be posed frankly and honestly.

For example, is it possible for workers in education and in fields of study such as sociology, psychology, political science, human development, and the other content fields to communicate and work together so that their individual contributions can be utilized in the solution of common problems of curriculum? . . . Curriculum problems demand a range of competencies and a co-operative attack. There is need for communication and synthesis of results. . . . Improvement in curriculum theory will probably come as rapidly or as slowly as we make progress in securing such co-operation.

As a part of the above, if we are to have more comprehensive theory, we have to have more people thinking and struggling with its problems. The simplest solution would be to say, "Give this task to the philosophers." And while the philosopher might welcome the task, he would have to become acquainted with the subject matter of his theory, just as the worker in education would have to become acquainted with the disciplines of the philosopher and with the points of his preoccupations. Actually, this task will not be given to any group unless they are willing to assume it. The persons naturally concerned with curriculum theory on the different levels are the teacher who tries to encompass the total program of his group; the curriculum co-ordinators and supervisors in the public schools; the workers on the horizontal levels of education, such as elementary education, secondary education, higher education, or adult education; the specialist in curriculum organization and development, both in general and in special fields; and the educational philosophers....

The Problem of Basic Orientations

The problem of basic orientations is not different from the problem of more adequate curriculum theory because one of the most important decisions in formulating a good curriculum theory is the one regarding the basic orientation of that theory. This problem of the orientations of the curriculum is mentioned specifically because it serves to point up an aspect of theory which runs through all the specific problems of curriculum development.

In the derivation of objectives, there is general agreement that the society, man's accumulated knowledge, and the individual must be considered. Approaches to this problem differ, however, not in the fact that these three backgrounds are not considered at some point, but in the fact that they differ primarily at the base which is given prior importance. The problem simmers down not to whether you are or are not going to consider the individual, man's knowledge, or the society but to whether you believe the society, man's knowledge, or the individual should be the initial and basic orientation of the curriculum in general and of the derivation of objectives in particular.

Question

In the derivation of objectives, the authors note "general agreement" (although not on their importance or priority) on three backgrounds for curriculum development: society, knowledge, and the individual. In everyday school life, how do you see these three backgrounds variously defined and operationalized?

Similarly in the problems of selection, organization, and sequence, the approaches to these problems do not differ in the sense that different elements are considered in the decisions involved in determining the selection of learning experiences and their organization into a learning program with adequate breadth and continuity. The differences in the approaches to these problems grow out of the differences in the order in which certain bases are used as initial considerations in the selection process. . . .

How does one decide the basic orientation of a curriculum for determining objectives, for selecting and organizing the learning experiences, and for determining the role and function of the learner and teacher in the educational process? It has been suggested that this decision is one of the major value judgments of curriculum. But what does one look at as a value when making these judgments? At this point, much of our curriculum thinking starts to sound like a phonograph record stuck at a certain spot; society is the basic orientation to the curriculum because the society is the basic orientation of the curriculum because the society is the. . . . Perhaps . . . we need a theory of value to help us make a theory of curriculum.

In relation to this question, many have suggested that the solution consists in applying the methods of scientific education or the products of present knowledge about how individuals learn and develop. With this suggestion, the discussion usually gets hazy, for no one seems to know what to apply the methods of scientific education to or how, after having applied them, that would eliminate the ultimate need for making some kind of judgment on a base still outside the data being considered. The knowledge of how individuals learn and develop is confronted with its own dilemma in this connection. The different points of view regarding learning and development rest their case ultimately upon some conception regarding the basic orientation of the learning and developmental process. Differences in this conception account for, in the main, the differences in findings and point of view. And we are back again where we started.

The editors of this monograph have only two suggestions to make at this point. First, the problem would be clarified and the issues would be kept clear if the writers on the various topics of curriculum development would make sure that the reader is always told what decisions are being made and exactly how these decisions are being reached. It would be especially helpful if the points where value judgments operate were honestly recognized and critically discussed in the writings on curriculum theory. The second suggestion is that some critical study be made of the role of values in curriculum investigation and that the implications of this study be shown for the development of curriculum theory and practice.

Research on Broad Fronts

Most fields of study are constantly being enriched by discoveries and advances in related fields. This fact is especially true in the field of curriculum. . . . Many times, however, similar advances do not take place in curriculum theory either because everyone assumes that the implications of such advances in other fields are obvious for the field of curriculum or because no one really faces up to the task of determining the actual import of such advances for the improvement of educational programs. Frequently, too, when the implications of a new knowledge or new understanding of what educational programs might be are honestly put into practice, that practice is so different from the traditional practice of the school that it seems impossible of achievement and is consequently discarded or ignored as being too radical or too impractical....

Two ideas which may have some significance seem to grow out of this discussion. First, many research studies in education and its related fields are, very properly, being made by committees which represent an array of backgrounds and interests. Could it be that a person interested in the problem of the curriculum might profitably be a part of such research groups?

Second, the kind of creative scholarship which would deal with the synthesis of these related fields of knowledge and with the seeing of the import of this synthesis for curriculum theory and improved curriculum practices, deserves as much recognition and status in the professional field of education as that now given to the so-called "pure research" specialists. It is very likely that the contribution to humanity on the one hand and the demand on creative scholarship on the other is not very different in either case.

Leadership in Curriculum Development

The emphasis on curriculum theory in this monograph does not mean that the problem of curriculum improvement in schools is not regarded as important. In fact, the value of curriculum theory is not realized until it serves to aid the teacher in making curriculum decisions in his classroom. Curriculum theory in its broadest aspects is not a problem apart from the development of curriculum programs in schools. Rather, the two merely illustrate the important ingredients of the same problem. It is difficult to visualize a program of in-service education of any value in which the program of activities is not directed by some kind of "working hypotheses" of education and curriculum. The power and capacity of a school staff to improve its own program grows correspondingly when these working hypotheses are part of the thought and action pattern of each teacher. When this is true, future experience can supply data for the evaluation and improvement of such hypotheses. When this is a conscious part of the in-service training, there is real hope for the continued improvement of the school's program.

The most important part of this point of view is the fact that the above process is the very foundation of an educational program through which we hope each learner will become increasingly competent to deal with his own problems. In this sense, a theory of curriculum becomes very close to becoming a theory of education. If this is true, then there is no more worthwhile project demanding the attention of workers in education.

Source: Herrick, V., & Tyler, R. (Eds). (1950). Next steps in the development of a more adequate curriculum theory. In *Toward improved curriculum theory* (pp. 118–124). Chicago: University of Chicago Press. Copyright 1950 by The University of Chicago. All rights reserved. Published 1950. Composed and printed by The University of Chicago Press, Chicago, Illinois, U.S.A.

V ARIED TALE

IBM: LEADERSHIP IN COMPUTER DEVELOPMENT

Like the place of curriculum people in the development of school programs, IBM's place in business machines at the end of World War II was unchallenged. Yet despite the unparalleled resources held by IBM in terms of its network of scientists and institutional affiliations, extensive patents and profits, and market range, its 73-year-old patriarch showed more enthusiasm for the known market than the potential market: computers. Further, the death of vice president Charles Kirk silenced the only executive championing the potential of computer technology—which lacked commercial applications and carried an undetermined R&D price tag. Smaller companies such as NCR, Bell of AT & T, and RCA were unable to enter the computer technology field because of legal, financial, or marketing considerations. Thus, IBM failed to take advantage of its resources and networks due to lack of competition and insularity.

Content with developing electronic variations of IBM's card-sorting machines, the elder Watson sat as board chairman and his son, Tom Watson Jr., assumed the vice presidential seat occupied by Kirk. While research continued elsewhere on computers, IBM's emphasis on commercial viability and its reliance on the customer to direct its efforts resulted in the loss of John von Neumann, the most prominent theoretician in the field of computers, to RCA; two additional IBM scientists quit to form the first computer-focused firm, Electronic Control Corporation (ECC). By 1950, RCA had completed the EDVAC computer for the Army, and in 1951, ECC—bought out by Remington Rand—delivered its UNIVAC computer to the Census Bureau for a hefty $1.1 million. In 1954, General Electric became the first nongovernmental firm to own a computer—another UNIVAC.

Admitting in 1952 that IBM was probably two years behind its competitors, the elder Watson handed corporate control to his son, who quickly initiated the largest capital borrowing campaign in the company's history. Faced with competition on the home turf and fueled by the military needs of the Korean War, IBM quickly developed the 701, a computer that, although inferior to the UNIVAC, found military applications. IBM also began taking orders for its first commercial computer, the 702, two years later and, in 1955, unveiled the 705, which competed favorably against the UNIVAC with a price tag well below the Remington Rand model.

In the space of three years, Watson junior had doubled IBM's long-term debt, tripled its income, and, most important, overtaken Rand in the production and marketing of commercial computers. By 1956, 85% of the retail value of computer sales was generated by IBM; UNIVAC had less than 10%.

(continued)

What accounted for the dramatic turnaround of a company that had been two years behind? Certainly one can cite IBM's effective and well-rewarded sales force, its reputation for service and customer satisfaction, and the integration of academic, technological, and business acumen—long characteristics of IBM—coupled with heavy capitalization and youthful vision. But the single most powerful reason was market advantage.

The move of government agencies and large corporations toward computer technology increased the demand for peripheral office equipment and supplies ranging from printers to punch cards. IBM not only reaped enormous profits from this increased demand but its monopoly over card readers dictated that all other computer manufacturers had to rely on these units (which were leased from IBM). In other words, every computer customer leased at least one piece of IBM equipment. The result was guaranteed profits and a direct sales link to IBM service personnel. These service contacts eventually translated into lease contracts for entire computer systems at less than one-half their actual cost and well below that of the competition. Thus, market advantage—not technological lead—proved key to IBM's dramatic reemergence as the computer leader.

IBM's governing structure also changed during this transition of leadership. In the spring of 1956, shortly before Watson senior's death, 100 executives attended a reorganization conference. "We went in a monolith," Sobel (1981, p. 161) quotes Watson junior; "we emerged three days later as a modern, reasonably decentralized organization."

Whereas Watson senior supervised and exercised decision-making authority in almost every area, this now multinational conglomerate delegated authority and dispersed power. The new corporate climate emphasized innovation, hard work, and open communication. Executives were given greater authority, and the entire corporation was separated into different divisions; the greatest resources were placed in R&D, where the first computer generation of vacuum-tube technology would soon give rise to a second generation of transistorized, solid-state computers. In comparison, the curriculum field's early R&D work was still under way at the University of Chicago and Teachers College.

cated challenges awaiting them as the century passed its midpoint. The preceding excerpt is from their concluding essay to the conference proceedings, published in 1950 as *Toward Improved Curriculum Theory*.

Serving and Shaping School Personnel

Clearly, the 1947 Chicago Conference was a call from Herrick and Tyler for more attention to curriculum theory and research. Meanwhile, much of curriculum work remained focused on developing and revising actual school curricula to meet the needs of "customers." One of the major figures at Teachers College at the time was Alice Miel, whose 1946 book, *Changing the Curriculum: A Social Process,* could be considered a precursor of today's contemporary ideas of group process, cooperative learning, and action research. Her colleague Steven Max Corey published *Action Research to Improve School Practices* in 1953. Today's "action research" was essentially born at Teachers College from the earlier work of Dewey as developed in his *The Sources of a Science of Education* (1929). And Wells Foshay pursued this:

> In 1954, I published a book with K.D. Wann called *Children's Social Values.* It grew out of our discussions with teachers in Springfield, Missouri. Springfield was a member of the Network of Schools associated with the Horace Mann-Lincoln Institute at Teachers College. As a researcher with the Institute I was sent to Springfield as the curriculum person who was going to work with them on whatever they wanted to work on. Well, what they wanted to work on was social values, not subject matter—which I would have preferred. Everybody was very much influenced in those days by Daniel Prescott's work in child study and child development (Prescott, 1957). They'd had courses in child study, so that's what they wanted to do: study children.
>
> Actually, the work I'm most proud of is also tied to action research. In 1956, while serving as a member of the Association for Supervision and Curriculum Development's National Executive Committee, the association's director of publications, Bob Leeper, invited me to edit the 1957 ASCD yearbook with James Hall. As editors, we wanted to put together a curriculum book that provided an eclectic feeling for the field, but the book turned out to be loaded with action research. At the time, that seemed to be the solution to everything. The people I had asked to come together on the project—Hilda Taba, Virgil Herrick, Margaret McKim and others of that sort—all had this action research perspective in common.

For the curriculum field, then, action research represented a kind of compromise between the field's need for theoretical and research legitimacy (to better define itself) and its largely service orientation. This action research focus during the 1950s also grew from an increasing interest in teachers as important players in curriculum development efforts—attention rekindled from an earlier Progressive Era emphasis on the importance of the teacher.

Question

How do teachers know what classroom actions merit inquiry? Imagine what, if any, difference there might have been in mid-twentieth-century and early twenty-first-century inquiries.

Curriculum development remained, however, either "expert work" done by hired curriculum developers and presented to teachers in the form of curriculum guides and wholesale plans of study or, as in Foshay's experience, the work of curriculum expert as facilitator of whatever teachers wanted to do.

On the national scene, "life adjustment education" was a kind of hybrid curriculum effort occurring during this same period, with Charles Prosser as its major proponent. Prosser (1939) believed that the traditional high school curriculum of the day was best suited for the 20% of college-bound students, while another 20% of high schoolers were well served by vocational and technical curricula in place in most schools. That left 60% of students who, Prosser argued, would be best served by a "life adjustment" curriculum designed to prepare them to go into various roles and lines of work that did not require college or vocational training.

Some high schools did move in the direction of life adjustment curriculum; however, as memories of World War II became increasingly replaced with more immediate cold war concerns, many educators agreed with a growing public sentiment that we should move away from any curriculum that would smack of being frivolous or catering to the interests of students when such interests veered too far from rigorous study of skills, basics, and disciplines of knowledge. As a result, life adjustment curricula were rather quickly overwhelmed by a kind of back-to-basics movement. Such movements often follow wars and other kinds of national emergencies when the public is understandably more concerned with preservation than experimentation. The growing cold war chill had much to do with this turn.

Civil strife, multinational corporations and the resulting "organization man," the cultural discovery of adolescence, and the grudging acknowledgment of a seamy side of American social life would all combine with cold war effects to influence an entire generation of young people. The A-bomb detonation tests of the Soviet Union and the elevation of Joseph McCarthy as the nation's chief communist catcher, the publication of Orwell's *1984*— a not-so-optimistic rendition of our totalitarian future—and Camus's *The Plague*—a not-so-pleasing portrait of the human condition; the death of Babe Ruth and the retirement of Joe Lewis; the communists' triumph in the newly declared People's Republic of China around the time that rail and road traffic ceased between east and west Berlin and North Korea invaded South Korea; the passage of the antilabor Taft-Hartley Act as threats of rail and coal strikes marked the legitimacy of big unions; and the establishment of both the Vietnamese state in Saigon and apartheid policy in South Africa: In 1950, these and other events signaled the emergence of American society into a new world that would be defined by fear, uncertainty, ennui, and misanthropy while simultaneously associated with certainty of progress, trust in social institutions, and pride in oneself and one's country. It was an era when "the people" turned their attention to public schools like never before.

Most curriculum workers at the time were politically liberal and socially progressive. Almost by definition, their work required a vision of what could be rather than what had been. For example, Hollis Caswell and others identified exemplary curriculum projects across the country in a book called *Curriculum Improvement in Public School Systems* (1950). A decade later, Harold J. McNally, A. Harry Passow, and their associates at Teachers College published a similar book titled *Improving the Quality of Public School Programs* (1960). Neither of these books contained examples of school curriculum projects that were especially radical, leftist, or truly alternative, though some could rightfully be labeled as progressive.

By the 1950s, what was left of the Progressive movement was largely its student-centered focus: With the exception of a small handful of writers such as Theodore Brameld, few curriculum leaders were calling for social reconstruction of the sort proposed in the 1930s and 1940s by George Counts and Harold Rugg. Whatever "social" attention remained within curriculum work was geared more toward serving than steering society. Professor Foshay, who has been around long enough to recollect the active span of the Progressive movement, offers these comments:

I had a course with George Counts and, frankly, I didn't think much of it. Although I saw Harold Rugg around, I never had a course with him at Teachers College. Nonetheless, he came out to Ohio once, after he retired and had been in Egypt working, and we had a long talk about the way things were back in the 1930s. This was in the early '50s and the right wing Macarthyesque kind of thing was in full bloom, so we talked about that. Of course, Rugg had been a target of its earlier efforts.

You see, during the 1930s and '40s, progressive education was kind of an elite matter. I read "The New Yorker" during that period, when it was a kind of elite magazine, and it presented progressive education over, and over, and over again. Well, that discussion and those issues got into the popular media and became a matter of general discussion during the 1950s. Why that happened, I don't think I understand particularly. I'm glad it did, though. I think that the Cold War and competition with Russia had something to do with it. The drama of the Sputnik business has never been fully appreciated as much as it deserves. It really turned things around. Anyway, the blame for some things fell on the schools which is, in a way, silly though not ironic, for in a way, it belonged there. The schools represented the evolution of popular culture and had become largely vocational and ideological. I think the progressive movement—which had a life period from approximately 1920 to 1960—was a period when curriculum was seen as an ideological tool. And that's what it was.

Actually, during the 1950s, the teaching machine was even bigger news—a way of making the teachers' work easier, technified. It was a clever idea, though not Skinner's idea, originally. The teaching machine acquired its popularity with the press and public because, again, it offered a promise for a way to directly address self-teaching and subject matter—things that the schools apparently were ignoring. They weren't, really, but the public perception was overwhelming.

Discovering the Public's Perceptions

Of all the era's curriculum-related research, Benjamin Bloom's would lead to one of the most influential books of the 1950s: *Taxonomy of Educational Objectives, Handbook 1: Cognitive Domain*. Though published in 1956, the book had its origins in Giles et al.'s (1942) volume of the Eight Year Study, *Exploring the Curriculum;* that is, Bloom developed and refined his ideas for the taxonomy during his own involvement in that great progressive experiment. In his *Taxonomy,* Bloom identified "social behavior" as a kind of demarcation between the cognitive and affective lives of school students—a demarcation that significantly influenced schooling, educational discourse, and curriculum thought for decades. Bloom described six hierarchical levels of cognitive functioning and provided explorations of each level—from memorization (the least sophisticated) to evaluation (the most sophisticated). Although not perceived as a curriculum person in the traditional sense, Benjamin Bloom typifies the shift in emphasis from social and philosophical to psychological foundations in curriculum work. His taxonomic scale of cognitive abilities further lent itself to the coming attention to subject matter content, a focus on which the curriculum field had not paid serious attention.

But subject matter content had become central to the public's interests. Albert Lynd published *Quackery in the Public Schools*—a major criticism of the schools—in 1950 (reprinted in 1953); Rudolph Flesch followed in 1955 with *Why Johnny Can't Read,* which criticized the state of reading instruction in the public schools. Throughout the 1950s Arthur Bestor disparaged the schools in articles such as "Life-Adjustment Education: A Critique" (1952), in which he addressed anti-intellectualism in the schools, and books such as *Educational Wastelands* (1953), which he subtitled *The Retreat from Learning in Our Public Schools.* By the mid-1950s, steelworkers and seamstresses, priests and politicians, homemakers and heiresses all seemed concerned about what was *not* happening in schools. While curriculum workers attended to what Herrick and Tyler called orientations toward "the society" and "the individual," society at large grew increasingly concerned with an orientation toward "man's accumulated knowledge." The unarticulated question became "What are these curriculum experts doing?"

A number of "invisible" curriculum projects were going on at the time. Max Beberman, for instance, was at work at the University of Illinois at Urbana-Champaign in the area of mathematics education developing the "new" or "modern" math. Similar projects had begun at Harvard and MIT with Zacharias and others developing new, inquiry-oriented approaches to science education. Joined by smaller movements in foreign language education, none of these received wide-scale attention. But all of this would soon change when the field lost its market advantage. A curriculum coup lay just around the corner.

▼ isitor Bibliography   Arthur W. Foshay

Foshay, A.W. (Ed.). (1980). *Considered action for curriculum improvement.* Alexandria, VA: Association for Supervision and Curriculum Development.

Foshay, A.W. (1984). The peak/spiritual experience as an object of curriculum analysis. ERIC Document Reproduction Service No. ED247169.

Foshay, A.W. (1994, Summer). Action research: An early history in the United States. *Journal of Curriculum and Supervision, 9*(4), 317–325.

Foshay, A.W. (1998, Summer). Problem solving and the arts. *Journal of Curriculum and Supervision, 13*(4), 328–338.

Foshay, A.W. (2000). *The curriculum: Purpose, substance, practice.* New York: Teachers College Press.

Foshay, A.W. (2001). You and me and I and thou. In J. T. Sears & J.D. Marshall (Eds.), *Teaching and thinking about curriculum* (pp. 273–279). Troy, NY: Educator's International Press.

3

Transfer by Eminent Domain: National Interest

During the second half of the twentieth century, American society and Americans' self-image was forever altered amidst revolutionary upheavals in politics, business, popular culture, religion, and technology. The underlying stresses and hidden anomalies of everyday life in the apparently transparent 1950s were often portrayed by America's artists. Literary writers such as J. D. Salinger (*Catcher in the Rye,* 1951) and Jack Kerouac (*On the Road,* 1957); playwrights such as Samuel Beckett (*Waiting for Godot,* 1952), Tennessee Williams (*Cat on a Hot Tin Roof,* 1955), and Lorraine Hansberry (*Raisin in the Sun,* 1958); poets such as Dylan Thomas (*Under Milk Wood,* 1954) and Allen Ginsberg (*Howl,* 1956); and film directors such as Nicholas Ray (*Rebel Without a Cause,* 1955), Billy Wilder (*Twelve Angry Men,* 1957), and Alain Resnais (*Hiroshima Mon Amour,* 1959) captured the decade's fears, uncertainties, and anxieties.

These novels, plays, poems, and films strike at odd juxtapositions to the more mainstream popular culture found in the black-and-white television world of *Father Knows Best* and *I Love Lucy,* where hosts like Milton Berle (*Texaco Star Theater*) and Ronald Reagan (*General Electric Theater*) transported the American viewer elsewhere. Game shows such as *Twenty-One* and *The $64,000 Question* promised that anyone could be transfigured into *someone* by separating right from wrong responses. In the law-and-order TV world of the Wild West, heroes wearing white hats drove the *Wagon*

Train, rode in posses with *Wyatt Earp,* or joined in shoot-outs on *Gunsmoke* (during the 1958–1959 season the three television networks broadcast 31 westerns series). Television, which could boast only 15 stations nationwide in 1948, was received in more than 37 million homes within 10 years—connecting the American consciousness and transforming U.S. social and political culture in ways unfathomable to prior generations.

The emphasis on the sublime and the ephemeral in popular culture can also be found in innocuous pop music (*Davy Crockett* and *The Chipmunk Song*), the nostalgic plays of Rodgers and Hammerstein (*King & I,* 1951) or Lerner and Loewe (*My Fair Lady,* 1956), and escapist fiction such as *Lord of the Rings* (1954), *Peyton Place* (1956), and *Hawaii* (1959). Within another decade, popular culture would replace them with rock and roll, the Broadway production of *Hair,* and science fiction novels.

Artifacts and icons such as these suggest a desire within America's postwar generation to retreat from the inevitable march of humankind's progress, inhumanity, and indifference: polio, tuberculosis, and influenza proved more immediately fearsome than the federal government's refusal to intervene in the Rosenbergs' executions or its military interventions in Korea, Guatemala, and Lebanon; kitchen gadgets, long-playing stereo records, and color television helped to diminish the desegregating sting of events resulting from *Brown v. Board of Education* (1954).

Beginning quietly enough with Rosa Parks on December 1, 1955, the Montgomery, Alabama bus boycott lasted almost a year, ended not by the acquiescence of the city's white politicians, lawyers, or police but by a U.S. Supreme Court decision judging Montgomery's bus-segregation law to be unconstitutional. As David Halberstam (1993, p. 652) notes, "the battle was won. But the war was hardly over. It was a beginning rather than an end; the boycott became the Movement, with a capital M. The blacks . . . had gained the sympathy of the white majority outside the South." Within a year (September 3, 1957), Governor Orval Faubus sent Arkansas National Guard troops to block 15-year-old Elizabeth Eckford, a black student, from entering Little Rock Central High School amidst shouts of "Lynch her! Lynch her!" "Go home, you bastard of a black bitch!" and "No nigger bitch is going to get in our school!" (Halberstam, 1993, p. 675). Eventually, President Eisenhower deployed U.S. military troops to see that nine young black students found their way into Central High and that a segregationist southern governor upheld the constitutional law of the land.

By 1957, television correspondents were presenting these and numerous other troubling incidents to millions of viewers. Yet while African-American representations of the culture of nonviolence proved important, for American youth, black influence on popular culture—particularly through music and sports—proved truly revolutionary. Elvis Presley's success opened the door for other white recording artists to borrow as freely as he had from the music of black artists; by the late 1950s, black artists including Fats Domino, the Platters, and Sam Cooke were recognized on America's white hit charts. And while most major sports had been integrated by 1960, television pushed them (and their players) to nationwide prominence. "Clearly, a social revolution . . . was in many ways outstripping the revolution engineered by the Supreme Court of the United States and by Martin Luther King, Jr., in the streets of the nation's Southern cities. If the face of America . . . was still almost exclusively white, then the soul of America, as manifested in its music and sports, was changing quickly" (Halberstam, 1993, p. 693).

▰ Louis J. Rubin: Curriculum Consultant

V ISITOR Changing far less quickly was the face of curriculum work. Tightly tied to the expressed needs of public school educators, curriculum workers continued on a national path cut some years earlier by the NEA's Educational Policies Commission (EPC) and contained in two of that commission's major publications, *Education for ALL American Children* (1948) and *Education for ALL American Youth: A Further Look* (1952). The commissioners—who included James B. Conant, a former government diplomat and Harvard University president, and Dwight D. Eisenhower during his presidency of Columbia University—spelled out the need to address students' diverse educational needs through a core curriculum of common learnings coupled with various "differential studies" (e.g., vocational, advanced academic, and elective courses) within an untracked system from grades 7 through 12. As the 1950s marched on, the first wave of war babies had made their way through elementary schools and were entering the very high schools where educators grew increasingly concerned about working in "blackboard jungles" with growing numbers of diverse youth becoming disinterested in school itself.

Professor Lou Rubin, a decade earlier, was himself a somewhat disinterested high school student. Born in Oakland, California, in 1926, his Depression era childhood resulted in ambivalent feelings toward schooling. His high school experience, in fact, heralded the precise EPC argument supporting massive curriculum renovations. In Rubin's words:[1]

> I enjoyed school because it was much better than anything I could find elsewhere. Much school work was not very challenging or interesting, but the culture was appealing. I wasn't much of a student simply because I diverted my attention elsewhere.
>
> Going to college was not part of a tradition that I grew up with. When I saw my high school counselor during my senior year and asked about going to college, he said, "Well, based upon your grades I don't think you have the ability to get through college. Why not consider some sort of job instead?" My father agreed, suggesting "If you're a good carpenter they'll

---

[1]Louis J. Rubin, personal communication, November 23, 1994.

always want you." I was annoyed with that. In fact, I think I was driven to survive college and get a teaching credential primarily in anticipation of going back and student teaching in the same school to pique the counselor. My intent was to teach a couple of years to earn money for law school. Well, I taught the first year and was captivated—absolutely consumed by the joys of helping kids learn. Law school became a lost cause and fifty-one years later I still prefer teaching to retirement.

Indeed, Rubin spent eight more years as a high school teacher, during which time he completed a master's degree (in musicology) and a doctorate (in curriculum) at Berkeley. As a teacher interested in higher education, however, his choice of doctoral studies within education proved limited at the time:

In those days you followed the prescriptive sequence out of consensual faith, in curriculum, finance, administration, or whatever. I found a pliable professor at Berkeley named Cecil Parker, liked him, and simply affiliated. He taught me that people are more important than ritual. I found the curriculum field a little more interesting than the others simply because it had a greater capacity to circulate ideas. I took the normal sequence of courses at Berkeley—a matter of two curriculum courses.

Leaving the high school classroom in 1956, Rubin began his work as a curriculum consultant. Typical of most others then in his field, the work proved to be explicitly teacher oriented and educationally "progressive." At the time, the progressive ideals of many curriculum people, particularly those linked to Teachers College, remained largely prominent. In 1957, for example, a second edition of *Developing a Curriculum for Modern Living* by Florence Stratemeyer, H. L. Forkner, M. G. McKim, and A. H. Passow appeared in the curriculum literature. The book offered an expanded and revised conceptualization of building school curricula around what the authors called "persistent life situations," reasoning that "transfer" is best accomplished when problems studied in school mirror those encountered later in life. Harkening back to W. H. Kilpatrick's "project method," the popular student-centered Stratemeyer text remained proudly progressive.

Despite the public storm approaching, most curriculum texts of the late 1950s, especially those addressed to secondary schooling, continued to pay attention to curricula for a "general education" or the "core curriculum" idea while addressing democratic ideals and their related aspects such as interpersonal relations. Writers who spoke to particular content areas or disciplines (e.g., mathematics) tended to emphasize their subject matter and ways to present it. Generally, they ignored normative questions: How can content knowledge be selected and situated relative to knowledge about students and society? How might it best be understood within the entire curriculum endeavor? The two published exceptions to this were the "subjects" of citizenship and social living (Schubert & Lopez-Schubert, 1980).

Thus, impetus from the EPC, residue from the once-prominent life adjustment education movement, progressive education ideals, and alienated young people continued to drive the felt needs of educators and the related work of curriculum. By this time, belief that too few students were appropriately served by the traditional, "scholarly oriented" high school curriculum had, as Kliebard notes, "become conventional wisdom in the educational world" (1986, p. 257). He continues, however:

> Life adjustment education turned out to be the prod that awoke the slumbering giant. . . . After a period of neglect almost amounting to disdain, an intense interest began to develop among leading scholars in a variety of disciplines as to the state of the curriculum in the lower schools. . . . Almost without warning, the decade of the 1950s became a period of criticism of American education unequaled in modern times. (pp. 258, 260)

Educational critics offered an effective conservative critique of the progressive ideas promoted by John Dewey and his fellow travelers. This age-old tension between "conserve" and "progress" was apparent in most aspects of American life, including the religious. As the decade mixed the sacred with the profane and long-standing proselytizing tent shows were reborn as nationwide pulpits through the new medium of television. Just as Hollywood served the Allied war effort, so now its services were turned to promote Christian themes, myths, and value. Marquees announcing blockbuster movies such as *The Robe, Exodus, The Ten Commandments, The Greatest Story Ever Told,* and *Ben Hur* shared their space with films such as *Roman Holiday, The Seven Year Itch, Gigi,* and *Around the World in 80 Days.* Like the curriculum field, religious life was in serious flux. The transfiguration of the Roman Catholic Church in America illustrates this period of change.

VARIED TALE

TWENTIETH-CENTURY ROMAN CATHOLIC CHURCH: IN A POSTWAR WORLD

The postwar world marked the emergence of ecumenicalism and challenges to religious teachings and practices. The World Council of Churches and the National Council of Churches formed in 1948 and 1950, respectively, heralding a "new theology," developed through the writings of Jews such as Martin Buber (*Eclipse of God,* 1952), Protestants such as Richard Niebuhr (*The Purpose of the Church and Its Ministry,* 1956), and Roman Catholics such as Pierre Teilhard de Chardin (*The Phenomenon of Man,* 1959). Also published was the New Revised Standard Version of the Bible.

Throughout this era, nevertheless, religious conservatism remained the distinguishing characteristic of American society: reflective talks by Archbishop Fulton J. Sheen and the inspiring sermons of Reverend Billy Graham; the Catholics' Legion of Decency and strictly followed Code for Television and Motion Pictures; and the emergence of a new generation of secular and religious conservative thinkers such as William Buckley, Russel Kirk, and Thomas Molnar (a vociferous critic of Deweyan-styled public education), building on an earlier generation of Catholic conservatives led by Ross Hoffman and Francis Graham Wilson (another vehement Deweyan critic).

Since the founding of Maryland by Roman Catholics who sought religious freedom from the intolerance of fellow colonists, the Catholic community in America has viewed itself as an embattled minority. Postwar anti-Catholic nativism was evident in religious bigotry ranging from the influential publication of *American Freedom and Catholic Power* (Blanshard, 1949), which questioned Catholic Americans' patriotism and ability to think freely, to John F. Kennedy's difficulties seeking national office in 1956 and 1960.

To be Roman Catholic in postwar America was to be at once different and similar. It meant enduring anti-Catholic jokes and sentiments expressed by the very Protestant neighbors with whom you shared a common social class and immigrant background. It meant reading from Catholic newspapers such as *Our Weekly Visitor* and newsmagazines such as *Catholic World*. It meant abiding by catechistic teachings, respecting priestly authority, and eating fish on meatless Fridays. And it meant worshipping in Latin through a sixteenth-century Eucharistic ritual of genuflections, sacred songs, and scriptural readings while being accused of statue worshipping and "brainwashing." The latter allegation grew from the fact that postwar Catholics tied their pro-American, anticommunist ideology to a separate, integrated school system that included thousands of elementary schools, single-sex secondary schools, colleges, and seminaries as well as a handful of illustrious universities such as Notre Dame, Georgetown, and the Catholic University of America.

Then, like now, Catholic schools were seen as places where strict, no-nonsense learning occurred: educational critics during this period wanted no less for public school students. As we noted in chapter 2, prominent intellectuals and pundits lambasted long-standing progressive ideas and practices like serving all students' needs or offering numerous elective courses. Rather than providing a common curriculum within a high school designed to educate everyone, they argued strenuously for the opposite: an efficient, dual, European-like system of secondary schools—one academic and the other vocational. They feared that so much attention to dropouts and the general education of all students had taken time, attention, and resources away from the schools' ability to mine the intellectual potential of their best students. Schools that wished to support the country's best students should go back to a curriculum of mathematics, science, English, history, and foreign language—the academic basics, the true liberal arts. After all, the Russians were surpassing us.

Upside Down in a Satellite's Glow

Though educational critics might have paid little attention to the 1957 election of Jimmy Hoffa as president of the Teamsters Union, and while most adults probably gave little thought to the 1957 premier of a new television show called *American Bandstand,* none could ignore the following news report taken from the Soviet News Agency, Tass (Gordon & Gordon, 1990, p. 352): "The first artificial earth satellite in the world . . . was successfully launched in the USSR. . . . The new socialist society turns even the most daring of man's dreams into reality." The small (184-lb.) Soviet satellite, launched early on October 4, 1957, was called *Sputnik.* As Halberstam notes, its success

> seemed to herald a kind of technological Pearl Harbor. . . . Suddenly, it
> seemed as if America was undergoing a national crisis of confidence. . . .
> Soon there was *Sputnik II.* Launched on November 3, 1957, it weighed
> 1,120.29 pounds . . . and it carried a small dog, Laika. Clearly, the
> Soviets intended to put a man in space soon. It was another
> psychological triumph. (1993, pp. 625–627)

Shockwaves rolled across America's heartland. Shortly after the *Sputnik* launchings, Americans learned that the Soviets' nuclear program was advancing as ours slipped. "The Russians seemed to be ahead of us in all aspects of defense and weapons technology, and even worse, their GNP was said to be growing at a faster rate than ours. . . . Clearly, the barbarians were not merely at the gate, they were able to fly over it with missiles and nuclear warheads" (Halberstam, 1993, p. 700). Almost overnight, the federal government rolled into action in defense of our national security. Previously published books of critics such as Bestor and Flesch sold out of stores while popular magazines published countless articles and series about America's educational problems.

"With Sputnik, curriculum in particular and education in general became much more of a political issue," Lou Rubin recalls, "because it was at that point that we began comparing the achievement of American youths, along with the status of our culture and our scientific progress, with the communist block. The argument was that if we took a page out of their book we could create better scientists." In 1958, as *Life* magazine identified poor curricula as a significant problem in its "Crisis in Education" series, the U.S. government created the National Aeronautics and Space Administration (NASA) to unify and develop the country's nonmilitary space efforts.

At the same time, large-scale curriculum work proceeded along its tenuously constructed theoretical track. Professor Rubin, like most other curriculum consultants, relied on the thinking found in the enormously popular second edition of the Smith, Stanley, and Shores synoptic text, *Fundamentals of Curriculum Development* (1957). Rubin recalls it being "a careful and well done treatment of prevailing curriculum theory," and that it was. Its authors were among the first to set the work of curriculum development within its sociocultural context and the first to carefully explore criteria for various curriculum tasks (going well beyond the earlier "basic principles" suggested by Ralph Tyler). They situated all of this within a discussion of three differing curriculum orientations (subject, activity, and core) and carefully explored theoretical assumptions and issues related to curricular problems.

Encyclopedic in nature, *Fundamentals of Curriculum Development* was a book well suited for the curriculum experts at work in the schools. Here's how Professor Rubin described such work:

> When I began my work in California [1957], staff development was in its infancy and yet to be recognized as a fact of professional life. It had become clear that you couldn't really accomplish curriculum change without teacher change, so I got involved in both. At that time, people called curriculum scholars were widely used as consultants: it was just assumed that some lettered sage from afar could come inform teachers on what and how the young should be taught. Back then, when I met with the Professors of Curriculum group at ASCD, for example, it was a day of glory to sit with people like Alice Miel, Gordon McKenzie, Florence Stratemeyer, and "Bunny" (B. Othanel) Smith—the curricular greats of the moment—and debate substance and method.
>
> Curriculum was viewed as a local process of decision-making: Denver, San Francisco, Toledo and Macon would each ponder weighty instructional questions. The eminencies of the day—like Hilda Taba and William Stanley—would guide school districts in thinking through what was important to teach. Curriculum has always been something of a political football, but in that period two particular issues began to emerge. One was the general concern over what I referred to as the thinking aspects of curriculum: curriculum as particular content and intellectual processes. You could teach kids history, math, and science and, at the same time, increase their imaginal capacities, reasoning skills, and creativity—all worthy by-products. The other notable shift was to conceive of curriculum, both positively and negatively, as a key factor in the society's well-being. As a consequence of Sputnik it suddenly became commonplace to use schools as whipping posts—to argue that the nation was in difficulty because schools taught the wrong stuff, and in the wrong ways. Hence, as an add-on to the fledgling interests in process as content, the politicization of the curriculum, among a variety of vested interest groups, became fashionable.

Question

Do you agree with Rubin's implication that staff development has become "a fact of professional life" for teachers? In your experience, how much staff development is connected to curriculum work?

What Rubin recalls was an ever-so-slow shift in the interests of curriculum work. Many of the "curriculum gurus" of the time were still emphasizing practical, client-centered curriculum construction and repair based on still-evolving theory and research bases. Those bases reflected heavy doses of progressive, experientialist thinking and practice. Meanwhile, educators of all sorts—including curricularists—had begun to take note of Bloom's *Taxonomy* and its obvious relationships to curriculum work (see Anderson & Sosniak, 1994), particularly Bloom's connecting of "objectives" to "cognition." Just as the stereophonic records introduced in 1958 would rapidly make obsolete monophonic recording, the strong theoretical foundations of educational psychology were poised to overwhelm the more progressive philosophical and sociological roots of curriculum work. Still needed were a vision, funding, and a spokesperson.

The U.S. Senate was in high gear in 1958. Its Committee on Labor and Public Welfare conducted hearings to determine the causes of our intellectual lag behind the Russians. Testimony, not surprisingly, indicated serious problems with public schools, particularly their seeming inability to produce intellectually superior graduates. Swiftly, Congress moved to pass the National Defense Education Act (NDEA) on September 2—an unprecedented governmental intrusion into community schooling and curriculum work. As Kliebard (1986, p. 266) notes, federal intentions were made clear in the act's opening paragraph:

> The Congress hereby finds and declares that the security of the Nation
> requires the fullest development of the mental resources and technical
> skills of its young men and women. The present emergency demands
> that additional and more adequate educational opportunities be made
> available. The defense of this Nation depends upon the mastery of
> modern techniques developed from complex scientific principles.

Kliebard continues: "Their credibility impaired, . . . professional educators were no longer to be given free reign in curriculum matters. Congress had clearly accepted the verdict of the academic critics that educators had foisted a soft and intellectually puerile curriculum on American schools" (p. 267).

Like IBM, public schools and curriculum workers confronted the harsh realities of the marketplace; unlike IBM, few responded with independent R&D initiative. So, the federal government, accompanied by corporate foundations, entered the vacuum and redefined curriculum work: the field was taken over by eminent domain. This single law (NDEA), designed to fund curriculum improvement in science, mathematics, and foreign languages, was quickly followed by significant funding efforts from the likes of the Ford and Carnegie Foundations and subsequent legislation to address additional subject areas. These events and efforts radically changed the focus of curriculum work, the role of the curriculum worker, and the influence of progressive thought.

VARIED TALE

TWENTIETH-CENTURY ROMAN CATHOLIC CHURCH: A NEW DAY DAWNS FOR CHURCH AND STATE

As public education and the curriculum field were turning away from progressivism, Roman Catholicism was about to embrace it. This postwar generation was to become a bookend for traditional Catholicism, and America's Roman Catholics would mark 1958 as a year of unforgettable change. Catholic life in America was essentially unchanged for generations, and the Church had shown great antipathy toward modernism (variously disguised as ecumenicalism, the new theology, institutional democracy, and positivism)—a prejudice developed and refined throughout the reigns of five popes.

During the 1870s, two crucial events served as the other bookend: the loss of the papal states (and the papacy's accompanied sovereignty, financial resources, and political power) to the nation-state building of modern Italy and the ecumenical council of bishops (Vatican I), which condemned modernism and declared the doctrine of papal infallibility.

Following these events, Leo XIII—elected in 1878 as the 256th pope—found himself within a reduced dominion (from 16,000 square miles to 108 acres) and an ideologically defensive position. As a "prisoner of the Vatican," his 25-year reign suffered modernistic assaults: Freud and Darwin, Einstein and Heisenberg, Marx and Engels, Nietzche and Kierkegaard, Chaplin and Edison. Leo's successor, Pius X, lambasted modernism as a "synthesis of all heresies" and directed his bishops to eradicate it. Toward this end he issued a decree that required all clergy to take an annual pledge against modernism (revoked by Pope Paul VI in 1967). Later, under the shepherdship of Pope Pius XII (1939–1958), the "new theology" would be linked to modernism: his 1950 encyclical, *Humani Generis,* declared that Catholics were to subordinate their "will and intellect" to papal judgment and Church teaching. In these modern times, Pius XII declared, the theologian's task was to justify orthodoxy through Scripture and tradition.

During the postwar era, however, some U.S. bishops, most notably James Cardinal Gibbons of Baltimore and Archbishop Ireland of St. Paul, challenged this position. Arguing for an Americanization of Catholicism, they acknowledged the separation of church and state, religious pluralism, and the importance of institutional democracy. For most of the church hierarchy and thousands of Roman Catholic parishes throughout the United States, however, the position was more traditional: religion would change man; it was not man's role to change religion.

Leading Catholic intellectuals began to exert a profound influence on secular society. Heavily influenced by antimodernist ideology, large numbers of Catholic editors and writers produced conservative journals including *National*

(continued)

Review and *Modern Age*. Embracing natural law, they rejected relativism and pragmatism and championed democratic capitalism and rationalism. Defending
Church authority, they rejected not only calls for institutional democratization
but also claims of undue papal influence on American politics; praising God and
Western culture, they opposed communism, internationalism, and liberalism and
dismissed pleas for isolationism and laissez-faire capitalism espoused a generation earlier by conservatives.

At the cusp of a new decade, the Catholic role in American public life was
more prominent than ever before, as evidenced by these public intellectuals
on the emerging right (and on the left, for example, with John Cogley, soon to
be religious editor for the *New York Times*), as well as the rise of a brash, young
Massachusetts senator named Kennedy. The health of the Church, too, seemed
unquestioned: its seminaries and convents were at capacity, its churches were
prosperous and full, its clergy were respected, and its papal authority was
unquestioned.

The death of Pius XII in 1958, like the demise of America's technological and
educational supremacy a year earlier, altered this hegemony. His successor was
a compromise candidate among the College of Cardinals—a pope whose role
was to be marginal, status quo, and brief. It was brief. Selected on the 12th bal-
lot by an assemblage of his peers was Cardinal Roncalli, known forever after as
Pope John XXIII. Within a year, in a "flash of heavenly light" as he would later describe it, this new father of the Roman Catholic Church informed a small group
of cardinals of his intention to call a great council. Following his January 1959
declaration, the goals of Vatican II became visible: modernization of the Church
and unification of all Christians.

In one swift decision, John XXIII ushered in a new era that would sweep
away 100 years of antimodernism and place the Church at the vanguard of ecumenicalism. Vatican II witnessed bishops in the Council relying on the very the-
ologians dishonored, marginalized, silenced, or excommunicated by the Church
since the last ecumenical council in 1870. Similarly, local school governance,
school-based curriculum development, and education professors as curriculum
experts would quickly disappear as comprehensive high schools, consolidation,
and behavioral instructional objectives quickly gained ascendancy by congressional and foundational demand.

A Curriculum Spokesperson Emerges

As the decade drew to a close, curriculum workers became more reflective,
publishing empirical studies, bibliographies, and historical reviews of
their work as curriculum consultants and coordinators (see Schubert &
Lopez-Schubert, 1980, pp. 154–159). Progressive ideals and the democratic aims of American education were disappearing as fast as had the
results from progressives' grand experiment, the Eight Year Study, in the

face of greater attention to the nation's more "advanced" students. In an effort designed, in part, to blunt the idea of a European-like two-tiered system of secondary schools, the Carnegie Corporation had financed a major study by James Conant (formerly of the Education Policies Commission) that was published in 1959 as *The American High School Today* and distributed, with Carnegie financing, to school superintendents throughout the country. Conant's study found that students who graduated from large, comprehensive high schools (those with the faculty expertise and material resources to offer everything from vocational to advanced academically specialized" schools. Thus, went the argument, smaller high schools would need to be phased out and more comprehensive high schools built— schools large enough to offer a strong yet diverse curriculum. Conant also offered recommendations concerning the nature and number of specific courses needed for graduation. The book proved especially important because it suggested that popular concerns regarding educational excellence could indeed be met within the subject-centered high schools of the day without altering their basic curriculum structures.

In 1959, "above-average" elementary school students, as a benefit of post-NDEA federal experimentation programs, were permitted to take foreign language instruction while their high school counterparts received early college admissions. At the same time, efforts were under way by representatives from the National Academy of Sciences, the U.S. Office of Education, the Air Force, the National Science Foundation, and the Rand Corporation to organize and finance a conference at a place called Woods Hole, on Cape Cod, which was run by the U.S. Navy. It is doubtful that many educators even knew that the conference would take place: amidst the collection of eminent psychologists, mathematicians, scientists, and others (e.g., historians and cinematographers) invited to participate, only three were identified as educators and none represented the field of curriculum.

In retrospect, Professor Rubin can identify the motivations of the conference chairperson, Jerome Bruner, though like his curriculum peers, he learned about the conference from Bruner's report published in 1960 and titled *The Process of Education.*

> The late 50s brought an effort to instill rigor into the curriculum, and a renewed concern about whether it was time to shift attention to the cognitive direction. The landmark event was when Jerry Bruner collected that group at Woods Hole. What he wanted was to poll the judgment of disciplinary specialists on how to convey the essential structure of a subject to learners in ways that maximized functional understanding. The result [*The Process of Education*] really wasn't to be a curriculum book, but as a great psychologist and adroit conceptualizer he was able to view the curriculum through a very different kind of lens: synthesizing complex knowledge into transferable chunks.

Jerry came in with a cognitive background and a keen interest in how knowledge could be made applicable. He wanted to focus on the essence of a discipline's key ideas and present this in provocative ways which permitted integration and facilitated thought. He did not want a student who could successfully answer a couple hundred recall questions; he wanted the student to be able to tell you what was significant and what the deeper implications meant. In Bruner's rhetoric, the best way to perfect educational theory is to assess its practicality.

"The contribution of university scholars in the creation of the most advanced weapons systems had led the nation's political leadership to look to the university scholars for devising curricula in science and mathematics for the elementary and secondary schools" (D. Tanner & Tanner, 1980, p. 434). And the university scholars came through. Bruner's publication of the Woods Hole results became, as Tanner and Tanner note, a curriculum manifesto for the 1960s. As such, it marks a turning point. Most who excerpt this influential text highlight the "structure of the disciplines" and "spiral curriculum" (a curriculum wherein subjects were revisited in subsequent years with increased sophistication) aspects of its theoretical discussion, for with the publication of *The Process of Education,* curriculum work finally found a theory (at least for the moment). We, in contrast, find the book's original introduction more pertinent. Our excerpt illustrates the polite and highly professional dismissal of curriculum workers as people in need of support from disciplinary scholars. Too, it announces a rekindled interest in curriculum problems by educational psychologists and expresses concern for schools' ability to produce sufficient numbers of scholars, scientists, poets, and lawmakers. Finally, Bruner suggests two extremes related to "how best to aid teachers" in the forthcoming curriculum revolution.

PRIMARY DOCUMENT EXCERPT

The Process of Education

by Jerome Bruner

Each generation gives new form to the aspirations that shape education in its time. What may be emerging as a mark of our own generation is a widespread renewal of concern for the quality and intellectual aims of education—but without abandonment of the ideal that education should serve as a means of training well-balanced citizens for a democracy. Rather, we have reached a level of public education in America where a considerable portion of our population has become interested in a question that until recently was the concern of specialists: "What shall we teach and to what end?" The new spirit perhaps reflects the profound scientific revolution of our times as well. . . .

One of the places in which this renewal of concern has expressed itself is in curriculum planning for the elementary and secondary schools. Several striking developments have taken place. There has been an unprecedented participation in curriculum development by university scholars and scientists, men distinguished for their work at the frontiers of their respective disciplines. They have been preparing courses of study for elementary and secondary schools not only reflecting recent advances in science and scholarship but also embodying bold ideas about the nature of school experience....

The main objective of this work has been to present subject matter effectively—that is, with due regard not only for coverage but also for structure. The daring and imagination that have gone into this work and the remarkable early successes it has achieved have stimulated psychologists who are concerned with the nature of learning and the transmission of knowledge. The Woods Hole Conference ... was one response to this stimulation of interest....

An additional word of background is needed to appreciate the significance of present curricular efforts in the changing educational scene. The past half century has witnessed the rise of the American university graduate school with its strong emphasis upon advanced study and research. One consequence of this development has been the growing separation of first-rank scholars and scientists from the task of presenting their own subjects in primary and secondary schools—indeed even in elementary courses for undergraduates. The chief contact between those on the frontiers of scholarship and students in schools was through the occasional textbooks for high schools.... For the most part, however, the scholars at the forefront of their disciplines ... were not involved in the development of curricula for the elementary and secondary schools. In consequence, school programs have often dealt inadequately or incorrectly with contemporary knowledge, and we have not reaped the benefits that might have come from a joining of the efforts of eminent scholars, wise and skillful teachers, and those trained in the fields related to teaching and learning. Now there appears to be a reversal of this trend. It consists in the renewed involvement of many of America's most distinguished scientists in the planning of school study programs in their field, in the preparation of textbooks and laboratory demonstrations, in the construction of films and television programs.

This same half century saw American psychology move away from its earlier concern with the nature of learning as it occurs in school.... For their part, educational psychologists turned their attention with great effect to the study of aptitude and achievement and to social and motivational aspects of education, but did not concern themselves directly with the intellectual structure of class activities.

Other considerations led to a neglect of curriculum problems by psychologists. The ever-changing pattern of American educational philosophy played a part in the matter as well. There has always been a dualism in our educational ideal, a striving for a balance between what Benjamin Franklin referred to as the "useful" and the "ornamental." As he put it, in the mid-eighteenth century: "It would be well if they could be taught everything that is useful and everything that is ornamental: but art is long and their time is short. It is therefore proposed that they learn those things that are likely to be most useful and most ornamental." The concept of the useful in Franklin and in the American educational ideal afterwards was twofold: it involved, on the one hand, skills of a specific kind and, on the other, general understanding, to enable one better to deal with the affairs of life....

The American secondary school has tried to strike a balance between the two concepts of usefulness—and most often with some regard for the ornamental as well. But as the proportion of the population registered in secondary schools increased, and as the proportion of new Americans in the school population went up, the balance between instruction in the useful skills and in disciplined understanding was harder to maintain. Dr. Conant's recent plea for the comprehensive high school is addressed to the problem of that balance.

It is interesting that around the turn of the last century the conception of the learning process as depicted by psychology gradually shifted away from an emphasis upon the production of general understanding to an emphasis on the acquisition of specific skills. The study of "transfer" provides the type case—the problem of the gain in mastery of other activities that one achieves from having mastered a particular learning task. Whereas the earlier emphasis had led to research studies on the transfer of formal discipline—the value obtained from the training of such "faculties" as analysis, judgment, memory, and so forth—later work tended to explore the transfer of identical elements or specific skills.... Virtually all of the evidence of the last two decades on the nature of learning and transfer has indicated that, while the original theory of formal discipline was poorly stated in terms of the training of faculties, it is indeed a fact that massive general transfer can be achieved by appropriate learning, even to the degree that learning properly under optimum conditions leads one to "learn how to learn." These studies have stimulated a renewed interest in complex learning of a kind that one finds in schools, learning designed to produce general understanding of the structure of a subject matter. Interest in curricular problems at large has, in consequence, been rekindled among psychologists concerned with the learning process....

Clearly there are general questions to be faced before one can look at specific problems of courses, sequences, and the like. The moment one begins to ask questions about the value of specific courses, one is asking about the objectives of education. The construction of curricula proceeds in a world where changing social, cultural, and political conditions continually alter the surroundings and the goals of schools and their students. We are concerned with curricula designed for Americans, for their ways and their needs in a complex world. Americans are a changing people; their geographical mobility makes imperative some degree of uniformity among high schools and primary schools. Yet the diversity of American communities and of American life in general makes equally imperative some degree of variety in curricula. And whatever the limits placed on education by the demands of diversity and uniformity, there are also requirements for productivity to be met: are we producing enough scholars, scientists, poets, lawmakers, to meet the demands of our times? Moreover, schools must also contribute to the social and emotional development of the child if they are to fulfill their function of education for life in a democratic community and for fruitful family life. If the emphasis in what follows is principally on the intellectual side of education, it is not that the other objectives of education are less important.

We may take as perhaps the most general objective of education that it cultivate excellence; but it should be clear in what sense this phrase is used. It here refers not only to schooling the better student but also to helping each student achieve his optimum intellectual development. Good teaching that emphasizes the structure of a subject is probably even more valuable for the less able student than for the gifted one, for it is the former rather than the latter who is most easily thrown off the track by poor teaching. . . . One thing seems clear: if all students are helped to the full utilization of their intellectual powers, we will have a better chance of surviving as a democracy in an age of enormous technological and social complexity. . . .

Four themes are developed in the chapters that follow. The first of these has already been introduced: the role of structure in learning and how it may be made central in teaching. . . .

The second theme has to do with readiness for learning. Experience over the past decade points to the fact that our schools may be wasting precious years by postponing the teaching of many important subjects on the ground that they are too difficult. The reader will find the chapter devoted to this theme introduced by the proposition that the foundations of any subject may be taught to anybody at any age in some form. . . .

The third theme involves the nature of intuition—the intellectual technique of arriving at plausible but tentative formulations without going through the analytic steps by which such formulations would be found to be valid or invalid conclusions. Intuitive thinking, the training of hunches, is a much-neglected and essential feature of productive thinking not only in formal academic disciplines but also in everyday life. . . .

Question

Individuals with a preference for intuition constitute about one-quarter of the general population (based on research on the long-standing Myers-Briggs Type Indicator [MBTI]. Can educators be effective in "the training of hunches" when three-fourths of our student body prefers "sensing"?[2]

---

[2]We thank Kathy S. Quinn for this particularly insightful question.

The three themes mentioned so far are all premised on a central conviction: that intellectual activity anywhere is the same, whether at the frontier of knowledge or in a third-grade classroom. . . . The difference is in degree, not in kind. The schoolboy learning physics is a physicist, and it is easier for him to learn physics behaving like a physicist than doing something else. The "something else" usually involves the task of mastering what came to be called at Woods Hole a "middle language"—classroom discussions and textbooks that talk about the conclusions in a field of intellectual inquiry rather than centering upon the inquiry itself. . . .

The fourth theme relates to the desire to learn and how it may be stimulated. Ideally, interest in the material to be learned is the best stimulus to learning, rather than such external goals as grades or later competitive advantage. While it is surely unrealistic to assume that the pressures of competition can be effectively eliminated or that it is wise to seek their elimination, it is nonetheless worth considering how interest in learning per se can be stimulated. There was much discussion at Woods Hole of how the climate in which school learning occurs can be improved, discussion that ranged over such diverse topics as teacher training, the nature of school examinations, the quality of curriculum. . . .

While there was considerable discussion at Woods Hole of the apparatus of teaching—films, television, and audio-visual aids, teaching machines, and other devices that a teacher may use in instruction—there was anything but consensus on the subject. Virtually all of the participants agreed that not teaching devices but teachers were the principal agents of instruction, but there was a division of opinion on how the teacher was to be aided. The disagreement, perhaps, can be summarized (though oversimplified in the process) in terms of the relative emphasis placed upon the teacher as such and upon the aids that the teacher might employ. The two extreme positions—stated in exaggerated form—were, first, that the teacher must be the sole and final arbiter of how to present a given subject and what devices to use, and, second, that the teacher should be explicator and commentator for prepared materials made available through films, television, teaching machines, and the like. The implication of the first extreme position is that every effort should be made to educate the teacher to a deep knowledge of his or her subject so that he or she may do as good a job as possible with it, and at the same time the best materials should be made available for the teacher to choose from in constructing a course that meets the requirements of the syllabus. The other extreme implies a massive effort to prepare films, television programs, instructional programs for teaching machines, and so on, and to teach the teacher how to use these with wisdom and understanding of the subject. . . .

No Turning Back

Bruner's new "theory of instruction," like John XXIII's "new theology," radically transformed the educator's role in the classroom, the student's role in learning, and the curriculum worker's role in development. Teachers became either subject matter specialists or human conduits for the transmission of subject matter knowledge, students became child-scientists and the curriculum worker took a backseat to psychologists and other discipline scholars of the "first rank." Within a few years neither traditional curriculum developers nor devout American Catholics recognized their long-time sanctuaries.

However, in an ironic reversal of roles, while the Church opened the doors for participation at the local level, the schoolhouse became the dominion of the federal government funders and the foundations, with primary curricular control exercised by noneducators. Whereas church governance grew to include parishoners, the control of public education shifted dramatically from teachers, school boards, and the states to Ivy League scientists, foundation boards, and the federal bureaucracy. Just as the central role of the parish priest as confessor, father figure, and shepherd was changing to accommodate greater participation by the laity, so, too, was the central role of the teacher as instructor and curriculum developer supplanted by prepackaged curricula authored by subject specialists. The new curriculum evidenced in Biological Sciences Curriculum Study (BSCS) and Man: A Course of Study (MACOS), like the new liturgy, revealed a radical transformation of curriculum and curriculum development. Inquiry into the discipline supplanted inquiry into the self, comprehending the structure of knowledge was more important than understanding the structure of society, and theories of learning were prized above theories of knowledge. There was no turning back.

In the very same month that the Harvard University Press published Bruner's book, U.S. pilot Gary Powers was shot down over the Soviet Union while on a spying mission, and the most popular hobbies in 1960 America were playing with science kits and building model rockets. Meanwhile, the civil rights movement produced more than 100 sit-ins at lunch counters across the country as Kennedy and Richard Nixon "were magnified to the status of heroic gladiators" during "the most exciting democratic election of the twentieth century" (Aitken, 1993, p. 274). The largest television audience to date, some 74 million, watched the candidates debate in what became a boon for the nation's soon-to-be first Catholic president, and "After a century of American Presidents who refused to deal with the issue of overpopulation, Kennedy expressed cautious approval of federal support for contraceptive research" (Halberstam, 1993, p. 606). What a different place America had become.

As president, John Kennedy also supported the growth and acceleration of government-supported curriculum projects, which had come to represent

> the end of an era in several respects. First, almost without exception, the directors of these major projects were drawn from academic departments in major universities. Control of curriculum change in other words had reverted from its traditional locus in the professional education community to specialists in the academic disciplines. Secondly, as would be expected, the effort to replace the academic subjects as the basic building blocks of the curriculum, going back about half a century, was brought to an abrupt end. . . . Third, the long-standing emphasis on local efforts at curriculum change was replaced by a pattern of centrally controlled curriculum revision. (Kliebard, 1986, p. 268)

We proceed into the next chapter with Professor Rubin's story of first meeting Ralph Tyler. It was during the height of externally controlled curriculum work:

> In 1964, I went to the University of California to work on a major grant. Those were the halcyon days when the feds welcomed new ideas, made money available, and believed that research and development could advance education. These were the early days of Title III and Title IV [of the Elementary and Secondary Education Act], R & D Centers, and all kinds of local projects. High optimism prevailed, and foundations gave large sums to various experiments.
>
> In my case, the Ford Foundation funded the Center for Coordinated Education on the premise that we needed greater connective tissue between high schools and universities. I came on as Assistant Director, and when Ernie Boyer, the first director, went east to the stewardship of the New York Higher Education System, I succeeded him. Ralph Tyler was on the Board. He became a superb mentor. A legendary giant, Tyler was a living portrayal of Bruner's educational ideal: broad knowledge, social consciousness, and a finely-honed repertory of intellectual skills.

▼ isitor **Bibliography**   Louis J. Rubin

Rubin, L. (1987). The thinking teacher: Cultivating pedagogical intelligence. *Journal of Teacher Education*, 40(6), 31–35.

Rubin, L. (1991). The arts and artistic curriculum. In W. H. Schubert & G. Willis (Eds.), *Achieving better curriculum*. Albany, NY: SUNY Press.

Rubin, L. (1994). Muddy curriculum waters. *Peabody Journal of Education*, 69(4), 21–37.

Rubin, L. (1994). Ralph W. Tyler: A remembrance. *Phi Delta Kappan*, 75(10), 784–785.

Rubin, L. (1994). The Ralph Tyler legacy. *Educational Researcher*, 23(5), 32–33.

Rubin, L. (1997). The essence: Process as content. In A. L. Costa & R. M. Liebmann (Eds.), *The process-centered school: Sustaining a renaissance community* (pp. 207–211). Thousand Oaks, CA: Corwin Press.

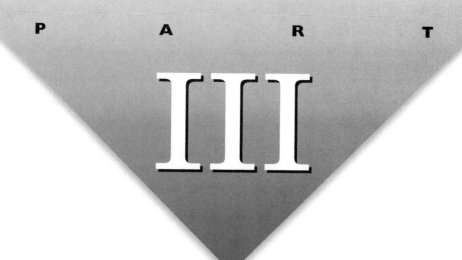

Reestablishing Agency and Agendas (1961–1969)

4

Muted Heretics Endure (1961–1964): "Outsiders"

The painstaking work of developing a curriculum alongside teachers and school administrators quickly diminished when the curriculum field was repossessed by psychologists and discipline specialists funded by foundation moneys and empowered by federal decrees. Bruner's *Process of Education* was the new curriculum bible, with its "military and nationalistic objectives ... buried in erudite discussions of the structures of the disciplines" (Pinar, Reynolds, Slattery, & Taubman, 1995, pp. 159–161).

This erudite curriculum discourse of the early 1960s was dominated by the psychological language of cognition, development, and behavior. As Tanner and Tanner (1990, pp. 300-301) note, psychology had

> become the basic educational science. Most educational controversies rage around theories of learning rather than the content of the curriculum. . . . As a result of this domination, the educational problem has been recast in terms of method. The underlying assumption of this point of view is that there is an agreed-upon body of knowledge called the curriculum.

In time, curriculum people such as Dwayne Huebner and James Macdonald would develop potent critiques and alternative possibilities to such discourse.

To be fair, Bruner's ideas were far more complex than the manner in which they were eventually employed. Bruner brought attention to the structure of knowledge, the importance of the disciplines, and the kind of inquiry that produces discipline-specific knowledge, yet he also emphasized intuition and different ways of knowing through inquiry. Overall, however, many of the post-*Sputnik* curriculum reform projects, their teacher-proof character, and their evaluation-heavy aspects modeled on Bruner's ideas reflected an unmistakable social behaviorist flavor. Indeed, they seemed to promote a belief in human similarity that could be addressed through an information-processing model of curriculum—much like the widespread influence of faculty psychology during the late nineteenth century (Willis, Schubert, Bullough, Kridel, & Holton, 1993, p. 355).

Moreover, though inquiry and structure were touted as fundamental in this new take on curriculum work, inquiry was usually divorced from action (D. Tanner & Tanner, 1990, pp. 282–283) as structure was transformed into "a means-ends rationality with predetermined objectives that governed, or at least rationalized, systematically designed learning activities. Such a turnabout was promoted in many synoptic texts . . . [and] embodied the technology of behaviorism and simplistic systems applications . . . a new version of social behaviorism" (Schubert, 1980, pp. 175–176). Ironically, as the curriculum field moved away from action toward rational, removed, planned experiences, its larger sociocultural context moved in opposition.

Through the midpoint of the decade, curriculum books suggested a confused and uncertain field. Many 1960s curriculum books were new or revised editions of earlier synoptic texts. Additionally, this decade welcomed the full-fledged production and popularity of collected readings in the field.

The true swan song for the disappearing field of curriculum development, however, would emerge in 1962 with the publication of Hilda Taba's *Curriculum Development: Theory and Practice.* Taba, one of the few women in the curriculum field whose work had achieved broad notoriety, had long been associated with Ralph Tyler. In addition to her work on the Eight Year Study evaluation, she had produced an oft-cited chapter in the 1945 National Society for the Study of Education (NSSE) yearbook, which Tyler edited (NSSE, 1945).

Curriculum Development: Theory and Practice was, like many preceding synoptic texts, a work in general curriculum that built on the Tylerian formula for curriculum making. This book was distinguished by Taba's ability to draw from multiple disciplines in describing the forces that influence curriculum and her special emphases on diagnosis and unit construction (Schubert, 1980). Taba was especially interested in developing a strong theoretical base for curriculum development and in moving from the perceived linearity of Tyler's "steps" to a more Deweyan or "circular" process wherein new goals or purposes could emerge through the utilization of ongoing (formative) evaluation at the school level (Pinar et al., 1995, p. 175).

Louise M. Berman

VISITOR Dewey's progressive and experiential influence managed to remain recognizable during the technical and behavioristic curriculum work of the early 1960s, thanks in no small part to a growing number of women entering the curriculum field. Though we may take for granted the presence of women in academia or curriculum work today, few such role models existed for earlier generations. This situation changed, in part, because women such as Florence Stratemeyer, Margaret Lindsey, and Alice Miel were quietly at work in places like Teachers College recruiting and mentoring increasing numbers of young women teachers. One of these recruits was Louise Berman,[1] professor emerita of education at the University of Maryland, who has spent more than 35 years as a curriculum worker involved with issues of curriculum development as a rational and organized process undertaken by meaning-making human beings.

> I grew up in West Hartford, Connecticut, which at the time was a rural area. My father was a lawyer and my mother stayed home with their four children. Being the oldest I often had responsibility for my siblings care. I enjoyed being with them, but I didn't have the kind of freedom to spend with peers that many youngsters have today. Because we had lots of open space around, we could play in the fields, pick fruit in nearby orchards, and watch the horses of one of my classmates. We built tree houses and all kinds of things outdoors.
>
> I can recall all my teachers. I usually liked them, yet I can also recall spending an awful lot of time sitting and watching the clock. Education was quite formal and classical, and considered very good. Communication skills and writing skills were emphasized in my elementary and high schools. I seldom thought much about possibilities beyond high school because career options for women in the late 1940s were scarce.

Louise was deeply affected by World War II. Not only was her father an air raid warden, but her parents helped many European refugees immigrate to the United States, offering them temporary lodging until they could find a place to settle. Professor Berman continues:

> I recall one very poignant story. Among the people who stayed with us were two young girls, one of whom had sent this huge wooden box ahead—it was her hope chest. She settled in Hartford and worked in a little store. The next thing she knew her fiancé had been killed. I felt such compassion for her; the war seemed to be so close.

---

[1]Louise M. Berman, personal communication, September 27, 1994.

Nearing high school graduation, the president of Wheaton College in Illinois, a long-time friend of Louise's mother, encouraged the family to send Louise to college in the Midwest. Despite encouragement from her high school principal to consider other options, Louise felt that she had little choice but to attend Wheaton. She continues:

> When I graduated from college I didn't know I was going to be a teacher. I had taken a fairly traditional liberal arts program at Wheaton, majoring in English literature, because the field invited a love of language. I did take a few education courses and became interested in certain of John Dewey's ideas. As the father of progressivism, Dewey was no favorite at Wheaton, but I stored some of his ideas in the back of my head.
>
> While at college I took a course in personnel and guidance with the Dean of Students. During that course we learned how to administer, score, and interpret many tests. In that process we took the tests. The professor came to know us both through how we took the tests and how we interpreted what we were learning from them. I think he probably was interested not only in how I was coming out on these tests but also the kinds of questions I was raising when looking at results, because the day I graduated from Wheaton College, he called me into his office and pointed out some things that I didn't see in myself, such as my potential to do graduate work. Further study didn't even occur to me because of my family situation: There were other children to educate. Besides, to my knowledge, most women didn't have graduate degrees.

Leaving Illinois, Louise returned home, soon finding herself invited to work as a part-time kindergarten teacher in Hackensack, New Jersey. She took the job, in part, because it would enable her to consider graduate study in English. As a novice teacher feeling a need for some advanced help, she enrolled in the Department of Curriculum and Teaching at Teachers College-Columbia University.

> I taught half a day and attended Teachers College afternoons and evenings, completing half of my master's work that year (1950–51). Roma Gans was my major professor during that period. And even though she worked with hundreds and hundreds of students, she got to know many of us. She seemed interested in what was happening in my classroom. Gans was very much concerned about injustice.
>
> For example, she was furious about women not getting the same salaries as men. That was in the '50s! Roma also published some down-to-earth writings. Her course on the role of the teacher was a hands-on kind of class in which she asked teachers to know their neighborhood and their world. She once took us on an all-night trip to New York City to observe the markets being set up, to eat an early morning meal in Chinatown, and to witness life on the docks. Gans was tuned in to the relationships between life in the city and classroom teaching.

I was working very hard that first year of teaching and became quite ill, so I moved back to Connecticut that spring to find a job. I taught in the East Hartford public schools (1951–54) and later at the Laboratory Schools associated with Central Connecticut State College in New Britain (1954–58).

Professor Berman's early interest in social justice and progressive ideals grew during her professional maturation as a teacher and graduate student in the 1950s. As we noted earlier, that was a decade of seemingly unending economic bounty leavened by communist fear for many Americans. "Only later—in some cases much later—would the nation confront in anything like a comprehensive fashion the era's racism, gender exploitation, nuclear and environmental hazards, and vast class disparities" (Boyer, 1993, p. 217).

VARIED TALE

U.S. SUPREME COURT: SOCIAL ACTIVISM AND JUSTICE

The seeds of this eventual confrontation were sown early in the civil rights movement, and the U.S. Supreme Court played a major role. Yet the Court, too, was undergoing a change of its own. Since its inception, jurists, legal scholars, politicians, and the public at large have argued about the Court's primary role as a branch of government: Is it to practice judicial restraint or judicial activism? The Warren Court would tack hard toward the latter. Beginning in 1954, judicial conservatives, like curriculum progressives, were left with no alternative but to batten down the hatches and endure.

When mediocre Stanford Law School graduate, state attorney general, three-term California governor, vice presidential nominee, and one-time presidential hopeful Earl Warren joined the Supreme Court as its 14th chief justice in the summer of 1953, *Brown v. Board of Education* had already been argued before the justices. In reconsidering the separate-but-equal principle articulated in *Plessy v. Ferguson,* Justice Felix Frankfurter—a Roosevelt appointee with a cautious jurisprudential temperament—had successfully avoided a mixed decision to overturn the 60-year precedent.

Rising from his German-Jewish émigré parents' Lower East Side home, Frankfurter had transformed his stellar Harvard Law School performance into a career as a Wall Street insider whose network of relationships, fostered by his interpersonal and legal skills, extended from the business community and academe into governmental agencies and the judiciary. He advised presidents, developed close friendships with prominent jurists and political architects, and mentored talented young men who later assumed prominent positions throughout the legal, business, political, and academic establishments. A student of the Progressive Era who echoed the importance of the professional and intellectual elite in expanding democracy, Frankfurter was an ardent advocate of judicial reason and the hopeful heir apparent of Supreme Court Chief Justice Holmes—about whom he wrote a book a year before his nomination to the Court in 1939.

Frankfurter's fascination with Chief Justice Holmes reflects their similarity in judicial philosophy, best characterized as "judicial restraint." In his biography of Holmes, Frankfurter extols the chief justice's ability to "transcend personal predilections and private notions of social policy" (Frankfurter, 1939, p. 45) and rely, instead, on rationality, due process, and judicial tradition.

However, although Felix Frankfurter and Earl Warren shared progressive views of a "good society," were born of immigrant parents, and encountered controversy in their outspoken views, their judicial philosophies diverged. For Frankfurter, who had denounced the ruling of the Sacco and Vanzetti case in the 1920s, political preferences were to be sidelined in deference to judicial restraint and legal precedent. For Warren, an "old progressive," the law was a political instrument to right social ills through sweeping decisions that the other branches of government lacked the political will or ideological conviction to make.

In short, Frankfurter and Warren were a study in contrasts. Frankfurter was a long-time judicial insider with a razor-sharp mind for case law and a traditionalist's fervor for interpreting law; Warren was a judicial outsider who had little knowledge of the Court's activities or personal contacts, who lacked recent or sustained legal experience, and who believed that the Court should create the law when necessary. An appointee of an activist president (Franklin Delano Roosevelt), the flamboyant Frankfurter was the consummate inside New Deal lawyer and legal scholar, whereas Warren, selected by a Republican conservative (Eisenhower) whose first two choices (John Foster Dulles and Thomas Dewey) had both declined, was pragmatic, affable, and communicative. Both Warren and Frankfurter would cast long shadows on the Supreme Court well through the remainder of the century.

Brown v. Board of Education, the first in a series of hallmark constitutional cases of the Warren Court, illustrates the role of both men as political activists and strategists while marking a shift from the judicial conservatism of the often embattled Vinson Court. Although the Vinson Court had signaled the eventual end of segregation with unanimous rulings against property covenants that restricted resale on the basis of race (*Shelley v. Kraemer,* 1948) and segregated universities (*Sweatt v. Painter,* 1950), the Court limited its role by adopting a progovernment, anti-individual rights view and refusing to overrule Congress's restriction of free speech or to bound the search and seizure procedures—positions that Frankfurter found unjustified by legal precedent.

The untimely death of Chief Justice Vinson, a former minor league baseball player and political appointee of the Truman administration, created an opportunity for a unified Court ruling in *Brown* based on precedent, evidence, and reason—

(continued)

a political necessity given the certainty of southern hostility. The request for a second hearing before the newly constituted Warren Court allowed Frankfurter the opportunity to encourage a former law clerk and now a Justice Department official, Philip Elman, to draft a compelling argument and for Warren to assume a statesman-like role in forging the 9-0, tightly worded decision that called for school integration "with all deliberate speed" (a phrase suggested by Frankfurter).

The Court's *Brown* decision (May 17, 1954) "laid the foundation for a civil rights struggle that eventually confronted the whole vast reality of a racially stratified society (Boyer, 1993, p. 215). Rosa Parks's civil disobedience (1955), the desegregation of Little Rock Central High School, and the first Civil Rights Act since Reconstruction (1957) all led the way for the 1960 lunch counter sit-ins, out of which grew the Student Non-Violent Coordinating Committee (SNCC). In 1961, efforts to desegregate public buses were begun by the civilly disobedient Freedom Riders led by the Congress of Racial Equality (CORE) and SNCC. The search for racial justice continued with James Meredith, a black Air Force veteran, whose effort to attend the all-white University of Mississippi was blocked by Governor Ross Barnett in 1962. Violent civil rights demonstrations rocked Birmingham, Alabama, in 1963—the same year that Dr. Martin Luther King Jr. delivered his "I Have a Dream" speech to tens of thousands who had marched on Washington. SNCC's Mississippi voter registration efforts during the "Freedom Summer" of 1964 resulted in dozens of resident blacks and visiting young people being beaten and jailed—and James Chaney (black), and Andrew Goodman and Michael Schwerner (white Jews) being murdered.

Modeling Compassionate and Democratic Ideals in Curriculum

To be sure, curriculum dissent was also in the air. Efforts to keep alive the more experientialist, progressive ideals of earlier decades prevailed in the early 1960s, though their advocates were few, their voices muffled, and their writings marginalized. Those who would persist in working to bring such ideas back into the curriculum discourse of the 1960s were mentored during the 1950s at institutions such as Teachers College and Ohio State. In the case of Teachers College, many of the women faculty were busy modeling their ideas. Louise Berman was there.

> While teaching kindergarten and primary grades in Connecticut, I continued at Teachers College during the summers, completing my master's and accumulating 30 credits toward a professional diploma. It was during my years with the three Lab Schools, which were closely affiliated with Central

Connecticut State College, that I first became involved in general curriculum development. I chaired the Curriculum Committee—a group of some 60 college professors and lab school teachers. At that point I saw curriculum as composed of the separate subjects. The Committee realized that we couldn't possibly explore the curricula of all the grades as they related to teacher education. So we decided to focus on social studies. This experience awakened my desire to gain more insight into curriculum development.

At some point, one of the Central Connecticut professors who had studied with Alice Miel suggested that I make contact with her, so I wrote and requested a conference. We met Dr. Miel one Saturday morning and talked about what I was doing and what I wanted to know. Of course, she was very skilled at curriculum development, and that's what I was doing at New Britain.

Beginning full-time doctoral study in 1958, Louise knew that most Teachers College faculty "seemed to have some kind of ongoing curriculum development project." She continues:

For example, Marcella Lawler and Gordon McKenzie were working in suburban New Jersey . . . [and] Alice Miel was involved in suburban New York—a project which ultimately led her to publish a little booklet with Edwin Kiester, Jr., called *The Shortchanged Children of Suburbia*. The book focused upon what schools do not teach about human differences. Creativity, social learning, knowing how to know, and issues of justice were central to Miel's teaching as well as to the teaching of several other faculty at Teachers College.

Professor Berman worked closely with Miel, creating an annotated bibliography for Miel's book *Creativity in Teaching,* assisting in creativity workshops, and coteaching a course called "Social Learning in the Elementary School." Louise also benefited from the presence of faculty members Margaret Lindsey and Florence Stratemeyer.

During my time at TC, a dichotomy was evident among the faculty between those concerned with curriculum in a "pure" or theoretical sense and those interested in life in schools as their starting point. From my perspective as a student, both viewpoints were instructive. Stratemeyer used to say that you couldn't just talk big curriculum ideas; you had to operationalize them. Her book, *Developing a Curriculum for Modern Living* (Stratemeyer, Forkner, & McKim, 1947; 1957), was quite influential in helping me to see the importance of considering the philosophical and psychological bases of curriculum development while at the same time giving examples of the activities and knowledge congruent with these bases.

The women with whom I studied at TC were vitally concerned with social issues, values, and real life situations. Women faculty had extraordinarily large numbers of students because they had reputations for offering wise counsel and being completely committed to the profession.

In time, Louise selected Miel as her major professor and Lindsey as one of her doctoral committee members: "With such strong role models, I began feeling as if I wanted to enter the curriculum field and an academic career in a more whole-hearted way." Herself an independent thinker, Berman had made a good choice:

> In the 50s, psychologists like Arthur Combs and Donald Snygg were popularizing notions of non-directive counseling, and supervision, and so on. Similarly, doctoral advisors encouraged the telling of your story, clarified what they heard, pointed out places where your perceiving might be accurate or faulty, noted creative ideas worthy of exploration, and energized you with the sharing of appropriate knowledge. Advisors like Alice Miel were generators of independent thinkers, though a certain continuity of curricular thought often resulted from these advisor/advisee relationships. I still pursue interests I can relate to my days of being a new advisee of Alice Miel's. And like many other former advisees, my personal relationship with her lingered.

The concerns for social issues, values, personal responsibility, and real-life situations that so greatly impressed Berman remained quietly alive within the early 1960s curriculum field. In 1961, for example, an important conference took place at Teachers College where, for three days, "two hundred educators interested in curriculum and representative of the various academic disciplines" (Passow, 1962, p. iii) explored the frontiers of the curriculum field. The edited proceedings published as *Curriculum Crossroads* (Passow, 1962) include an essay by Dwayne Huebner entitled "Politics and Curriculum" that explores curriculum from the vantage point of political theory, arguing "that the curriculum field permits the use of all major disciplinary systems, not only behaviorist psychology" (Pinar et al., 1995, pp. 171–172).

The small but committed group of curriculum dissidents who agreed with Huebner's plea was soon gifted with the publication of the Association for Supervision and Curriculum Development's (ASCD's) 1962 yearbook, *Perceiving, Behaving, Becoming*. One of the organization's best-selling curriculum books of all time, it influenced curriculum thought in the 1960s and beyond. Edited by Arthur W. Combs, a protégé of Carl Rogers, the text brought humanistic or "third-force" psychology as discussed by Rogers, Abraham Maslow, R. D. Laing, Eric Fromm, Gordon Allport, and Erik Erickson into the curriculum field. The chapters by Maslow and Rogers, especially, were the benchmark "alternative to mainstream educational psychology, and more narrowly, behaviorism, which had dominated the school curriculum so thoroughly at the time. Their pioneering work would be acknowledged and extended in the humanistic movement in the field later in the 1960s and during the 1970s" (Pinar et al., 1995, p. 172).

Rather suddenly, a movement appeared that provided "internal challenges to the Tylerian paradigm" (Pinar et al., 1995, p. 178) and seemed to
be more enthusiastically received by educators than the earlier social
reconstructionist ideas offered by Counts, Rugg, L. Thomas Hopkins, and
Brameld, though some of their more politically charged ideas and practices would soon reemerge from the likes of Dwayne Huebner, James
Macdonald, and their students.

At the time, however, the rapidly increasing popularity of humanistic
psychology and its accompanying emphases on the importance of providing students with choices, a sense of belonging, and opportunities for creative expression did little to slow the advancing juggernaut of big-budget,
discipline-centered, top-down curriculum projects. The early 1960s produced numerous reports of these national endeavors in mathematics, science, English, and various other school subject areas (see, for example,
Fraser, 1962; Gilchrist, 1963; Heath, 1964). Most were so thoroughly
planned and carefully packaged that they would later be called "teacher
proof." To the extent that teachers had any flexibility in their decisions,
this flexibility was wrapped within the need to adhere to developmen-
talist tenets and be accountable to behaviorist principles. How narrow
were these parameters? With the publication of Robert Mager's *Preparing
Instructional Objectives* (1962), error proofing the teaching-learning
process reached a peak.

Benjamin Bloom had published his *Taxonomy of Educational Objectives, Handbook 1: Cognitive Domain* in 1956 (dedicating it to Ralph
Tyler)—a time when the importance of educational objectives among
classroom teachers, at least, was rather underwhelming. The arrival of
Robert Mager's "little book" helped to move the perennial Tylerian concern for educational objectives toward inevitably more instruction-
oriented, measurably explicit notions of instructional (and later behavioral
or performance) objectives. This shift, with its focus on specificity of language and lack of attention to questions of content or intentions (among
other missing elements), created serious constraints for curriculum workers. Interestingly, Ralph Tyler both supported and opposed this shift (see
Airasian, 1994; Sosniak, 1994).

Mager's book—itself a programmed learning text—represents the
popular state of affairs of the time with respect to the direct, one-way relationships between goals, objectives, and assessment as well as the apparent unimportance of the teacher (curriculum worker) in matters of
what should be taught and why. The language of this excerpt exhibits
these attempts rather explicitly and stands out as a curriculum turning
point.

PRIMARY DOCUMENT EXCERPT

Preparing Instructional Objectives

by Robert F. Mager

Before you prepare instruction, before you choose material, machine, or method, it is important to be able to state clearly what your goals are. This book is about instructional objectives.... The book is NOT about the philosophy of education, nor is it about *who* should select objectives, nor about *which* objectives should be selected.

It is assumed that you are interested in preparing effective instruction.... It is further assumed that you are interested in communicating certain skills and knowledge to your students, and in communicating them in such a way that your students will be able to *demonstrate* their achievement of *your* instructional objectives. (If you are *not* interested in demonstrating achievement of your objectives, you have just finished this book.)

Why We Care about Objectives

An objective is an *intent* communicated by a statement describing a proposed change in a learner—a statement of what the learner is to be like when he has successfully completed a learning experience. It is a description of a pattern of behavior (performance) we want the learner to be able to demonstrate....

When clearly defined goals are lacking, it is impossible to evaluate a course or program efficiently, and there is no sound basis for selecting appropriate materials, content, or instructional methods.... Too often ... one hears teachers arguing the relative merits of textbooks or other aids of the classroom versus the laboratory, without ever specifying just what goal the aid or method is to assist in achieving. I cannot emphasize too strongly the point that an instructor will function in a fog of his own making until he knows just what he wants his students to be able to do at the end of the instruction.

Another important reason for stating objectives sharply relates to the evaluation of the degree to which the learner is able to perform in the manner desired. Tests or examinations are the mileposts along the road of learning and are supposed to tell the teacher and the student the degree to which both have been successful in the achievement of the course objectives. But unless goals are clearly and firmly fixed in the minds of both parties, tests are at best misleading; at worst, they are irrelevant, unfair, or useless. To be useful they must measure *performance in terms of the goals*. Unless the programmer himself has a clear picture of his instructional intent, he will be unable to select test items that clearly reflect the student's ability to perform the desired skills, or that will reflect how well the student can demonstrate his acquisition of desired information.

An additional advantage of clearly defined objectives is that the student is provided the means to evaluate *his own* progress at any place along the route of instruction and is able to organize his efforts into relevant activities. With clear objectives in view, the student knows which activities on his part are relevant to his success, and it is no longer necessary for him to "psych out" the instructor.

The Qualities of Meaningful Objectives

Basically, a meaningfully stated objective is one that succeeds in communicating to the reader the writer's instructional intent. It is meaningful to the extent it conveys to others a picture (of what a successful learner will be like) identical to the picture the writer has in mind.... What you are searching for is that group of words and symbols that will communicate your intent exactly as YOU understand it....

A meaningfully stated objective, then, is one that succeeds in communicating your intent; the best statement is the one that excludes the greatest number of possible alternatives to your goal. Unfortunately, there are many "loaded" words, words open to a wide range of interpretation. To the extent that you use ONLY such words, you leave yourself open to *mis*interpretation.

Question

From your experience, is correct textual interpretation always desirable or even possible?

Consider the following examples of words in this light:

Words Open to Many Interpretations	**Words Open to Fewer Interpretations**
to know	to write
to understand	to recite
to *really* understand	to identify
to appreciate	to differentiate
to *fully* appreciate	to solve
to grasp the significance of	to construct
to enjoy	to list
to believe	to compare
to have faith in	to contrast

...Though it is all right to include such words as "understand" and "appreciate" in a statement of an objective, the statement is not explicit enough to be useful until it indicates how you intend to sample the "understanding" and "appreciating." Until you describe what the learner will be DOING when demonstrating that he "understands" or "appreciates," you have described very little at all. Thus, the statement that communicates best will be one that describes the terminal behavior of the learner well enough to preclude misinterpretation. . . .

Identifying the Terminal Behavior

A statement of an objective is useful to the extent that it specifies what the learner must be able to DO or PERFORM when he is demonstrating his mastery of the objective. Since no one can see into another's mind to determine what he knows, you can only determine the state of the learner's intellect or skill by observing some aspects of his behavior or performance (the term "behavior," as used here, means overt action). . . .

Further Defining the Terminal Behavior

But simply specifying the terminal act may not be enough to prevent your being misunderstood. . . .

To state an objective that will successfully communicate your educational intent, you will sometimes have to define terminal behavior further by stating the conditions you will impose upon the learner when he is demonstrating his mastery of the objective. Here are some examples:

Given a problem of the following class . . .
Given a list of . . .
Given any reference of the learner's choice . . .
Given a matrix of intercorrelations . . .
Given a standard set of tools . . .
Given a properly functioning . . .
Without the aid of references . . .
Without the aid of a slide rule . . .
Without the aid of tools . . .

Stating the Criterion

Now that you have described what it is you want the learner to be able to do, you can increase the ability of an objective to communicate by telling the learner HOW WELL you want him to be able to do it. You will accomplish this by describing the criterion of acceptable performance. . . .

Probably the most obvious way to indicate a lower limit of acceptable performance is to specify a *time limit* where one is appropriate. . . .

Another way to indicate a criterion of successful performance is to specify the *minimum* number of correct responses you will accept, the *number* of principles that must be applied in a given situation, the *number* of principles that must be identified, or the *number* of words that must be spelled correctly. . . .

An alternative to indicating *number* is to indicate *percentage* or *proportion*. . . .

Another way of describing criterion behavior is that of defining the important characteristics of performance accuracy. . . .

As you try to write objectives that meet the requirements discussed in this book, you will undoubtedly find other ways of specifying the excellence of performance you intend to accept as evidence of the learner's success. One good way to get started is to look over the examinations you use; they will tell you what you ARE using as standards of performance, and you can improve your objectives by putting these standards into words. Once this is done, you can ask these questions of your statements to test their clarity and completeness:

1. Does the statement describe what the learner will be doing when he is demonstrating that he has reached the objective?
2. Does the statement describe the important conditions (givens or restrictions, or both) under which the learner will be expected to demonstrate his competence?
3. Does the statement indicate how the learner will be evaluated? Does it describe at least the lower limit of acceptable performance?

...To familiarize you with a strategy for preparing objectives, only examples of content objectives have been used. But, of course, you frequently intend to reach objectives other than those relating merely to the content or subject matter. Where, for example, it is intended that the learner develop a certain amount of "confidence" in his handling of the subject matter, or if he is expected to acquire certain "critical attitudes," it is appropriate to decide what you will accept as evidence of "confidence" or of "critical attitudes" and describe these behaviors in separate objectives. Statements of objectives should include *all intended* outcomes, whether related to content or not; only when this is accomplished will you have a sound basis for selecting the learning experiences to include in an instructional program.

This excerpt from Mager's text illustrates the epitome of the social behaviorist takeover of curriculum work in the early 1960s. Soon to follow were "mastery learning" (Carroll, 1963), Krathwohl, Bloom, & Masia's (1964) publication of objectives for the affective domain (in which humanism meets behaviorism), and Gagne's connecting of objectives to accountability in *The Conditions of Learning* (1965). All of this transpired as the curriculum community continued to function within Bruner's structure of the disciplines mode (see, for example, Elam, 1964; G. W. Ford & Pugno, 1964).

▓▓ Dissidence Comes Alive

Strengthened by the popularity and intellectual respectability of *Perceiving, Behaving, Becoming,* dissident curriculum voices multiplied. In 1964 alone, John Goodlad critiqued the national curriculum reform projects, A. Harry Passow revisited the focus on individual development, and Dwayne Huebner reassessed the dominant state of curriculum affairs.

Reassessment and critique were also a part of the larger sociocultural landscape. Unlike the chilling atmosphere of the 1950s, the early 1960s seemed to welcome a culture of dissent emanating from the previous decade's outlaw literature (e.g., *On the Road* and *Catcher in the Rye*), comedy (e.g., Mort Sahl and Lenny Bruce), films (e.g., *To Kill a Mockingbird* and *On the Waterfront*), and music (the Weavers and Elvis). The difference was that this 1960s dissent would eventually take center stage.

The civil rights struggle had opened many eyes to the problems of the marginalized and those taken for granted. For a significant proportion of young, white, middle-class Americans (forever after to be dubbed baby boomers), morality and justice would motivate their actions. As Gottlieb (1987, pp. 32–33) recalls:

> Only action could cleanse you. . . . In the early Sixties, we felt that the nation had awakened from its Fifties sleep. There was much to set right, but there was reason for pride as well. The ideals of the Founding Fathers were still alive, and the transition from the old to the new America might just be accomplished by moral force alone.

Or by the political force of the New Left. From the beginnings of the Students for a Democratic Society (SDS) in 1960, to the Port Huron statement in 1962, to Mario Savio and the free speech movement at Berkeley in 1964, early university protests over discipline, drinking, visitation rules, and course content led to occupied buildings, strikes, and protests. By 1964, much of this self-serving energy would shift to antiwar efforts. This largely campus-centered dissent stood both in contrast to and in concert with the ongoing civil rights struggle, creating a wholesale cultural unraveling from America's coasts to the heartland. Common for a time, among protesters, were

> things like ethics, equality, and justice—everything they'd been taught in eighth-grade civics class and seen in Frank Capra movies. They expected, especially in America, everybody to get a fair deal. And they could see that nobody was getting a fair deal. . . . If the system was a fraud, it was up to them to fix it. And by action more direct and more effective than mere voting and letter writing, immediately. Undistracted, innocent, and responsible, children of the sixties brashly attacked injustice, irritation, and idiocy head on. The undertaking was, though quixotic and naive, supremely heroic. And it was massive. (Pichaske, 1989, p. 52)

▓ Acting on Ideals, Seeking New Priorities ▓▓▓▓▓▓▓▓

This sense of being driven by issues and ideals missing in the world around you existed among some within the curriculum field as well during the early 1960s. In the following passage, Louise Berman talks about this feeling as she arrived at her first university job at the University of Wisconsin in Milwaukee.

> There is usually some kind of a voice in curriculum work with which you resonate. It's sometimes a small voice, but fortunately I happened to participate. When I was at Columbia, people like Alice Miel and Dwayne Huebner continued to sing different songs. Doing an annotated bibliography for Miel's book on creativity propelled me to join the chorus, to venture elsewhere. That project put me in touch with people like Paul Torrance, Calvin Taylor, Marie Hughes, Wells Foshay, Ross Mooney—many imaginative people. Faculty at the University of Wisconsin at Milwaukee (UWM) knew of my connections and interest. In a sense, we were all part of an underground, singing on a subway platform as opposed to on the stage at Lincoln Center.

Louise found exciting colleagues at UWM, including Jim Raths and Bernard Spodek, Jim Macdonald and George Denemark, Martin Haberman and Earl Johnson. She quickly became involved in a project called Creativity in Teaching, which enabled her to combine teaching with professional development and present everything through a series of videotapes (produced by public television) and study guides for teachers. All the while, she labored in an initial teacher preparation program "in which the professors spent all morning in the schools supervising student teachers and all afternoon teaching courses. In other words, you worked with the same students all day, five days a week." But it was her evening class that caused her serious concern:

> I was also teaching at night—a basic graduate-level curriculum course that I think most institutions offered. I had taken many hours in curriculum at TC and had done work in curriculum development, yet I wondered what to do with these students. I started out teaching a little from this person and a little from that one until I realized this way of teaching wasn't where I wanted to go, so I began spelling out what I believed students needed to know. I would spend nights in class talking with them about creating, about perceiving, about caring and other process skills. Over time I developed an outline for what eventually became my own curriculum priorities, resulting in the book *New Priorities in the Curriculum* (1968).
>
> I was given an advance so that I could take a few months off to write the book. I saw no educators during that period unless it was necessary: I didn't visit the campus or talk to my former mentors. I just had to think through: Who am I as a person? What am I interested in? What's important for students to know and be? How can curriculum be developed in a logical manner when I believe that knowledge is fluid and person-oriented? Where

am I in relation to all of this? What's my role going to be? I was reading in many areas: psychology, sociology, history, literature, religion, and the philosophy of science. My curriculum work is eclectic, which is both a strength and a weakness. And I was aware at that point in time that my curriculum orientation was a minority perspective.

The Sixties were a strange period of time. On the one hand efforts in discipline-oriented curriculum development were taking place; on the other hand, many in society were dealing with confounding issues pertaining to freedom, morality, and ethics. I was constantly trying to balance all of this within myself by hunting for different ways of knowing, thinking, valuing and being. It was a very lonely time because I was extraordinarily aware of mainstream curriculum thought and realized I was out of step.

I guess I was young enough and brash enough at the time to think that that work might have changed the course of education more. On the other hand, I never wanted to see a school that was built on *New Priorities* because I am a strong believer that people have to develop their own curriculum. I hoped persons would have looked at the book for insight, but I wanted people to go through the thinking and feeling processes I did. Although writing the book was a very painful process, the learnings have endured.

We Shall Overcome (and Endure) . . . Someday

Of course, some progressive and seemingly unusual ideas relating to curriculum organization did find the light of day in this otherwise constrictive curriculum environment, including modular scheduling (Trump & Baynham, 1961), core curriculum (Wright, 1963), and the call to look differently at the needs of junior high school students—the precursor of the middle school movement (van Til, Vars, & Lounsbury, 1961). ASCD continued its habit of exploring new terrain with its 1963 publication of *The Unstudied Curriculum* under the leadership of Norman Overly, and 1964 would bring the most careful, thorough, and creative statement on the structure of knowledge in curriculum in the Philip Phenix's book *Realms of Meaning: A Philosophy of the Curriculum for General Education*. Nonetheless, these voices like those of Louise Berman and others, were muted by sounds of curriculum construction and development projects.

The moral imperatives that drove curriculum heretics such as Berman, Huebner, and Miel were no different from those at work in the larger sociocultural milieu. Millions of Americans were losing faith in, working to change, simply ignoring, or planning to subvert "the system." All, it seemed, was open to question and doubt. New subcultures of difference born with the civil rights "ban the bomb" generation, the emerging market of rock-and-rock adolescents—easily dismissed by America in the 1950s—stood four square on center stage by the mid-1960s. As David Pichaske (1989, p. 24) explains, using the beat writers of the 1950s as an example, this was in part a result of a growing tribalism.

> This sense of close community, built on the principles of male
> friendship, more than anything else, differentiated the beats from
> other forms of fifties counterculture and anticipated an important
> element in the sixties mix: the impulse toward tribalism. The voices
> of Salinger, Mailer, and . . . Hemingway were individual voices. The
> central concern of social critics like Goodman and Whyte was the
> liberation of the individual from society's annihilating homogenization.
> The beat shared [this concern] . . . and he, too, glorified the individual. . . .
> But the beat sought in a mystical fashion to communicate those
> experiences beyond words, to share them, to feel them with outsiders,
> to transcend experiences into Experience. So the outsiders with whom
> he shared became insiders, an in-group, a subclass, an elite. And you
> "made the scene" communally. The ethics of the beat subculture were
> the ethics of the tribe.

We would see this ethic across subcultures in the 1960s: from lunch
counter sit-ins to city park love-ins, from the growth of the underground
press to the popularity of alternative schools, and from the Velvet Underground to the Weather Underground.

By the time the Limited Nuclear Test Ban Treaty was signed in 1963,
widespread American dissent had situated itself much closer to home
around issues of race and class, power and authority. The sense of community among these subcultures and between them and a good deal of
mainstream America grew real on November 22 of that year with the assassination of President Kennedy. As Annie Gottlieb (1987, p. 34) writes
of the baby boom generation:

> That day, and in the days that followed, television became our tribal
> bard, weaving an unforgettable visual ballad out of live coverage, news
> photos, the frames of Abraham Zapruder's home movie. . . . These were
> images that finally fused us into one, even as they shattered our
> childhood innocence. . . . now, for the first time we became conscious of
> our unity—and our vulnerability.

SNCC's "Freedom Summer" in Mississippi, the arrival of the Beatles
in the United States, and the beginnings of unrest at Berkeley characterized 1964. "It was the first year after the presidential assassination, the
first year of the new era in which the fifties images were already becoming tinged with nostalgia" (Jones, 1980, p. 106). It was also the year President Johnson signed the Civil Rights Act of 1964, which "outlawed racial
discrimination in all public accommodations and authorized the Justice
Department to move with greater authority on school and voting issues.
It also prohibited discrimination in hiring. . . . The act was one of the greatest achievements of the 1960s and destroyed the legal sanctions for the
segregation system" (Winkler, 1993, p. 224). On August 4 of that same year
Congress approved the Tonkin Gulf Resolution and the Vietnam era began in earnest. "Over the next decade, the entire generation was clapped

between the hands of war" (Jones, 1980, p. 106). And "as the world came apart, we began to come together, reaching out for physical comfort and power of our numbers. In November 1963, we watched history together. By August 1968, we were making it together in the streets, while the whole world watched us" (Gottlieb, 1987, p. 34).

As this chapter illustrates, the world of curriculum workers had come apart as well during these four years. Gone were the precedent and form of curriculum gurus as grassroots curriculum makers, replaced by psychologists, subject matter specialists, and national efforts to supply America's schools—regardless of their location or participants—with the best curricula that money could buy. Yet in time, as later chapters will show, curriculum workers bent on keeping alive the centrality of the student as a whole person, the unmistakable role of society and culture in shaping curriculum, the primacy of philosophical and historical questioning in curriculum deliberation, and the growing imperative to understand the forms and functions of curriculum in new ways and from new perspectives would coalesce to form a kind of dissident tribe of curriculum people. For the time being, however, they would continue as muted heretics in the eyes of the curriculum mainstream. But they would, like the conservative Supreme Court jurists suffering through the activist years of the Warren Court, endure.

VARIED TALE

U.S. SUPREME COURT: PERSEVERANCE AS THE MOTHER OF SATISFACTION

The most activist phase of the Warren Court began with the 1962 departure of Justices Frankfurter and Whittaker and the appointments of Arthur Goldberg and former football star and nonideologue Byron White to the Court. These two newest members often joined the four most activist jurists (Black, Douglas, Brennan, and Warren) to form a shifting majority characterized by its innovative approaches to constitutional analysis—a majority that would expand with the eventual appointments of Abe Fortas (replacing Goldberg) and Thurgood Marshall.

Even before the departure of Whittaker and Frankfurter, however, the loss of influence of the judicial conservatives was signaled in the 1962 reapportionment decision by six justices in the landmark case of *Baker v. Carr*. While some state legislatures had not been reapportioned for generations and thus reflected disproportionately the minority interests of rural areas over the increasingly more densely populated cities and suburbs, the Court had steadfastly refused to enter this "political thicket" (*Colegrove v. Green,* 1946).

Abandoning the Holmes-Frankfurter philosophy of judicial restraint, the newly emerging majority of the Warren Court adopted the principle of "one man, one vote." In their dissent, the disappearing conservative jurists defended judicial restraint to the end. Two weeks later, Justice Whittaker, who had already withdrawn from the *Carr* case, announced his retirement. Although Byron White would eventually fill Whittaker's seat, former Howard Law School dean and court of appeals judge William Hastie, an African-American, was President Kennedy's first choice (but was eventually passed over for political reasons). Several months later, Frankfurter resigned. Replacing the "Jewish seat," Kennedy appointed his secretary of labor, Arthur Goldberg; three years later, Lyndon Johnson pressed Goldberg to accept the ambassadorship to the United Nations and replaced him with Abe Fortas, who served through the end of the Warren Court before resigning for alleged financial improprieties.

The *Baker v. Carr* decision was soon followed by a series of landmark decisions handed down by what Chief Justice Warren himself called "the people's court." These decisions dramatically altered criminal procedures (*Gideon v. Wainwright,* 1963; *Miranda v. Arizona,* 1966), the rights of privacy (*Griswold v. Connecticut,* 1965), and the separation of church and state (*Engle v. Vitale,* 1962; *Abington School District v. Schempp,* 1963). These and other such cases reflected a vision of the Court justices as social engineers who, in the national interest, sought to redefine the Constitution by discovering new areas of rights (most notably the right to privacy) previously absent from its most liberal reading.

Justice John Marshall Harlan was the leading (and eventual lone) muted voice arguing against the chaos of the later Warren years when precedent, historical analysis, and legal form were abandoned with ever-increasing zeal in favor of swift and substantive "active justice." Appointed two years after the Warren nomination, Harlan pummeled the Warren Court for its misuse of judicial power in forging "poor constitutional law" on the anvil of social justice. Agreeing in the case of criminal reform (where the poor were often left without counsel or protection against self-incrimination), he nonetheless dissented from *Miranda*—echoing Frankfurter's admonishment that the Court stay out of the "political thicket" that rightfully belonged to legislators. Similarly, in his stinging dissent in the Warren Court's unilateral decision to apportion state legislatures, Harlan challenged the majority's niew "that every major social ill in this country can find its cure in some constitutional 'principle,' and that this Court should 'take the lead' in promoting reform when other branches of government fail to act." Harlan—following in the tradition of Holmes and Frankfurter—concluded: "The Constitution is not a panacea for every blot upon the public welfare" (Steamer, 1986, p. 84). For integrity of the Constitution was the watchword; in the tradition of Frank sought to judge on the merits of a case without regard to social contexts or needs. But these conservative jurists were a persevering lot.

The demise of the activist court began with Richard Nixon's presidential election in 1968 and his subsequent appointment of Warren Burger as chief justice. Like the Supreme Court, the balance within the curriculum field during the 1960s was itself about to change.

Question

How have recent issues before the Supreme Court influenced educational practices and policies?

Visitor Bibliography   Louise Berman

Berman, L. (1968). *New priorities in the curriculum.* Columbus, OH: Merrill.

Berman, L. (1977). *Curriculum: Teaching the what, how, and why of living.* Columbus, OH: Merrill.

Berman, L., & Aoki, T. T. (1991). *Toward curriculum for being: Voices in education.* Albany, NY: State University of New York Press.

Berman, L., & Roderick, J. A. (Eds.). (1977). *Feeling, valuing, and the art of growing: Insights into the affective.* Washington, DC: Association for Supervision and Curriculum Development.

Lashley M. E., Neal M. T., Slunt E.T., Berman L. M., & Hultgren, F. H. (1994). *Being called to care.* Albany, NY: State University of New York Press.

5

Transcending a Muddled Juncture (1965–1969): Publications

From the Singing Nun to the Age of Aquarius, Camelot to Chappaquiddick, the Valachi testimony to *The Godfather,* from *The Making of the President* to *The Selling of the President,* the SNCC to the Black Panthers, Hootenannies to Woodstock, and *Blue Moon* to *Bad Moon Rising,* the beginning and end of the 1960s enclosed a decade of transformation. Forty-six million Americans entered adolescence during a decade that began with the banning of the rock song *Teen Angel* and ended with the arrest of Jim Morrison, singer for the rock group The Doors, an era that segued from black-and-white TV sitcoms such as *Car 54 Where Are You?* and *Mr. Ed* to shows with more social immediacy including *60 Minutes, Rowan & Martin's Laugh-In,* and *All in the Family.*

It was a span of 10 years that seemed more like a century as values and beliefs, fashions and music, language and politics changed utterly. A decade of political turmoil and social change, the 1960s are remembered for assassinations and resignations, urban unrest and generational conflict, scientific breakthroughs and technological growth. As the 1970s arrived, the *Saturday Evening Post* had suspended publication, Jack Kerouac was dead, and the New York Mets had won the World Series.

To the watchful futurist, however, there were already harbingers of America's transformation from an era of New Frontier innocence and idealism to the realpolitik of the Nixon-Kissinger legacy. The publication of Rachel Carson's *Silent Spring,* Betty Friedan's *Feminine Mystique,* Vine Deloria's *Custer Died for Your Sins,* James Baldwin's *Another Country,* and Toni Morrison's *The Bluest Eye* prefigured soon-to-be environmentalist, women's, Red and Black Power, and sexual liberation movements; the generational shift from Woody Guthrie to his son, Arlo, symbolized the important role music would play in this generation's coming of age event: the antiwar movement.

(Re)Emerging Differences and Traditions

As we suggested in chapter 4, similar signs of change were apparent within the ebb and flow of curriculum traditions. Throughout the 1960s, the massive quantity of curriculum books continued to amalgamate these traditions—a practice begun with the earliest synoptic texts. The large curriculum projects had created new foci (e.g., objectives, measurement and evaluation, and the importance of administrators in supervising curriculum and instruction)

> that took on the character and rhetoric of business, industry, and technology. This, too, was an amalgam, but the tendencies toward the social behaviorist [tradition] were obvious. Still . . . the intellectual traditionalists dominated practice . . . [while] a new experientialist movement began to emerge under several, often different guises. (Schubert, 1980, pp. 193–194)

The array of mid-decade curriculum books published included still more synoptic texts and collections of readings joined by discussions of curriculum change (often discussions of the need to monitor and manage change). ASCD published two books focused on administering and supervising curriculum work. Other writers continued the mining of various organizational schemes as an alternative to the structures of the disciplines model, which, by the mid-1960s, "had become commonplace, a taken-for-granted fact" (Pinar et al., 1995, p. 161). Noteworthy in this regard was the appearance of *Strategies in Curriculum Development* (Anderson, Macdonald, & May, 1965), an edited collection of the works of Virgil Herrick that emphasized his attention to "organizing centers" for curriculum.

Two notable events took place this year as well, both sponsored by ASCD. The association's Commission on Curriculum Development explored the role of the humanities in curriculum work—an effort that featured Louise Berman, who later edited this commission's deliberations, published in 1967 as *The Humanities and the Curriculum.* Meanwhile, ASCD's Commission on Curriculum Theory met in Chicago to try and produce a clearly articulated framework for curriculum theorizing (a purpose similar to the 1947 Chicago conference discussed in chapter 2). Given the problematic state of affairs within the mid-1960s curriculum field as well as the rapidly changing intellectual, social, cultural, and political environments within the United States, this group of theorists was "unwilling to adopt an exclusively 'empirical' or 'scientific' framework for theory development in curriculum" (Pinar et al., 1995, p. 173). Despite continuous refinements to the Tyler rationale, the popularity of humanistic psychology and its loosely related experientialist tradition had created real possibilities for curriculum workers themselves to refashion their field and its work. The time to reembrace multiple curriculum traditions had arrived.

Much as the post-World War I and Great Depression era in this country created an opening for liberal, progressive, and radical thought and action earlier in this century, the post-Korean War and Great Society era created a reopening. Long-quiet humanist and radical traditions reemerged during the 1960s to counter, in part, the country's overwhelming conservative hubris:

> During those years, the bases of U.S. nationality had taken a beating. Doubts had replaced certainties. Youthful historical innocence, a belief in our exceptional historical status, faith in quick solutions, and conceptions of politics as sets of universalistic principles that can be applied anywhere and anytime became debatable in a world that had previously been inhabited by certainties. (McQuaid, 1989, p. 6)

By the mid-1960s, the civil rights movement had permanently altered American life. In 1965, the U.S. government situated itself in unprecedented ways into the business of public schools through the Elementary and Secondary Education Act (ESEA), which poured more than a billion dollars into schools, libraries, and universities, with most of this money targeted for "educationally disadvantaged youth." The ESEA signaled President Johnson's declaration of war on the culture of poverty as the white economic and political power structures of the old South eroded and the civil rights movement migrated north and west. Dr. King's march in Cicero, Illinois, was greeted with armed police, angered protesters, and sporadic violence. The Los Angeles neighborhood of Watts exploded in racial turmoil during the summer of 1965: five August days of rioting left 34 dead, 1,000 injured, and more than 4,000 under arrest in a preview of subsequent summers of racial turmoil.

This was a period of transitions. Founded on principles of nonviolence, coalitions, and optimism, the civil rights movement began to evidence principles of confrontation, racial separatism, and pessimism. At the same time, young, white, middle-class university students were becoming politicized by the military buildup. In April 1965 the United States had some 25,000 troops deployed in Vietnam—about the same number of demonstrators who participated in an antiwar rally in Washington. Meanwhile, many young people began to recognize themselves as part of a growing counterculture.

The 1960s were a decade of enormous identity shifting. Broad, global desires for social justice evolved into more personal struggles as young people began to seek

> a sense of themselves as members of an identifiable group, be they
> blacks, gays, feminists or radical youth. . . . As individuals, but
> especially as members of these defined groups, . . . their attitude
> throughout the sixties became one of questioning, rather than
> accepting, society's definition and treatment of them as second-class
> citizens. (Kessler, 1990, p. 16)

By 1966, the curriculum field was undergoing its own identity adjustment in quiet and mostly imperceptible ways. By and large, the field was presented with more synoptic texts, continued discussion about curriculum organization—both discipline centered and otherwise (especially "core curriculum")—new national imperatives, and additional works pertaining to evaluation.

Jerome Bruner was clearly moving away from his structure-of-the-disciplines emphasis and, as he titled his new book, *Toward a Theory of Instruction* (Bruner, 1966) which recognized the importance of students as players in the curriculum mix. John Goodlad published four books in 1966, including *School, Curriculum, and the Individual,* in which he "wrote of the interwoven nature of [society, institutions, and individuals within the] curriculum fabric. . . . These three areas carried considerable influence in subsequent study of curriculum problems" (Schubert, 1980, p. 188). Macdonald and Leeper's 1966 *Language and Meaning* represented the results of an ASCD Curriculum Research Institute and included a thoughtful critique of the disciplines focus from James Macdonald. And Mary Louise Seguel's *The Curriculum Field: Its Formative Years* took a look back at the early formation of the field's varied traditions.

The National Organization for Women (NOW) formed in 1966, with Betty Friedan as its first president. The second wave of the women's movement was born with a strong sense of its own history—a factor ignored by many of the decade's "revolutionaries." Too many activists of the time, as Angela Davis notes of herself, "expected the revolution to happen tomorrow. . . . [W]hat we didn't have that we should have had in the sixties was a clear relationship to the generations that had been involved before us" (in Kessler, 1990, p. 13). The same critique might be made of the transforming curriculum field.

Michael W. Apple

VISITOR Michael W. Apple was a young teacher when NOW formed. Apple, who holds the John Bascom Professorship in Education at the University of Wisconsin at Madison, entered teaching and later the curriculum field with a strong sense of its history and traditions. Today he is one of the curriculum field's best-known workers within what people variously refer to as the critical, political, or social reconstructionist tradition. In the following segment he describes the source of his political consciousness and its relationship to his commitment to schooling.[1]

> All of us carry biographies. Much of my political consciousness is related to a particular kind of immigrant tradition that's articulated in various ways in different ethnic communities. In my own community in Paterson, New Jersey, my grandfather literally taught himself how to read by buying "nickel books." He was working in a textile mill at the time and saving up his money to buy books by O'Henry and Mark Twain. I grew up sitting on his lap while he read Twain to me. The stuff that came through was remarkable: the slight anger, the questioning of authority in some ways, and the idea that there are literate traditions which can raise issues about the nature of politics and culture.

Professor Apple's extended family reflected the politically active context of Paterson, "home to the first anarchist and Communist strikes in the United States. Most of my family worked in textile mills, airplane manufacturing plants, or as printers." From his parents he learned the value and importance of spirited conversation and debate through dinner table arguments over "politics, race, gender, sexuality. The expectation was that children would, in fact, have things to say, and while you were respectfully listened to and argued with, you had to defend yourself." Given the importance his parents placed on formal schooling and the sacrifices they made to enable their children to go to college, Michael Apple understood his parents' questioning of "teachers who didn't treat you seriously and respectfully or who clung to the normal, boring textbook materials. All of those kinds of things were challenged."

Graduating from high school several years early, Apple began work as a printer and enrolled in evening college classes. He became deeply involved in reading, consuming "Romaine Roland, Turgenyev, Dostoyesvesky. Or I'd be reading all of Samuel Clemens at the same time I'd be reading W. E. B. DuBois—very strange kinds of reading material for a fifteen or sixteen year old. But it had to be long and it had to be serious." His college classes, in contrast, seemed far from serious. Exhausted part-time faculty hosted "huge, boring classes held in dirty, old rooms on the top two floors of an elementary school in Paterson." The combination of youth, "awful schooling," and a full-time job became too much, and

---

[1]Michael W. Apple, personal communication, October 11, 1994.

Michael Apple was "dropped" from the roles within a year. He continues his story:

At the time (1960), if you were dropped you had a variety of choices, one of which was the army. That's what I did. The army gave me the dual careers of truck driver and teacher: I drove kitchen equipment and taught first aid, compass reading, etc.

With my one year of college credits and army training as a teacher, and because I was a warm body at a time of teacher shortage in inner city schools, I was able to get a job as a teacher. Actually, my mother happened to be friendly with the assistant school superintendent in Paterson. I got out of the army one week before school started, and they couldn't find anyone to go into classrooms. He asked my mother whether her son had any interest in teaching? Well, it was something I had dreamed about doing since I was about five or six, in part because of the great respect that was instilled in me—by especially my grandmother and grandfather—for a critical schooling process. The idea of being involved in that was very important to me. Secondly, it was the natural path to working class mobility. For kids growing up in poor communities you really were limited in some respects with your choices.

Between 1962 and 1966, I taught with what was called an "emergency certificate," first in Paterson, later in Pitman, New Jersey, while attending Glassboro State at night and during the summers to get my bachelor's degree and permanent teaching certificate. While teaching in Paterson I was working in CORE (the Congress On Racial Equality), when it was still possible for coalitions across race within CORE, and deeply involved in the issue of segregated schools. So there's always a connection in my mind between those kinds of struggles and education itself. In the tradition that I come from—not only Marxist, but a strong element of working class socialist tradition in my family among the women and the men—there has always been this emphasis on the utter centrality of education: that through education, working class and other groups could, in fact, learn what reality was. It's a little naive in some ways, but the faith that education itself was one of the paths toward social, personal, and group emancipation through understanding power was always very clear. So going into education was, again, a path that was almost chosen for me in some ways.

But my career as an academic was quite accidental. I had moved from Paterson to Pitman—a small, rural prayer meeting community in southern New Jersey—where I taught sixth grade for two years. I became very angry, politically, about what I was forced to do there. For example, I was teaching about the history of racism in the United States and I brought in the normal kinds of reading material that all teachers have used. One story told of hundreds of African-Americans who had been lynched during and after the Reconstruction period. So we got into a long conversation in class about the history of African-Americans and the struggle that was going on then, in the mid-1960s. Well, one of the parents, who happened to be a pastor at a very conservative church, came in and wanted me fired because there had been no such lynching; he claimed that my lesson was simply fiction! Those kinds of things drove me to go to graduate school to try and find a way to make better curriculum, a way of getting better stuff in school, and a way to deal with teachers more respectfully. I applied to Columbia University's graduate program at Teachers College while still working toward teacher certification at Glassboro State.

Undercurrents to the Mainstream

The curriculum field was, in 1967, beginning to recognize its own traditionally optional paths. The experientialist tradition was unmistakably evident in books by Leeper and Berman that year. At the same time, both Gagne and Glaser made attempts to tie the experientialist-humanist respect for individual difference to more behaviorist desires for systemic curricular cohesion. Most prominent among the book-length efforts of that year, however, is the dominance of evaluation as a crucial step in the Tylerian curricular process: ASCD devoted its annual yearbook to this topic (Wilhelms, 1967), and the American Educational Research Association (AERA) published the first in its series of monographs on curriculum evaluation (R. W. Tyler, Gagne, & Scriven, 1967). The dominant path of rational curriculum making remained in place.

A major curriculum theory conference took place in 1967 at Ohio State University, the proceedings of which were edited by Paul Klohr and published in the journal *Theory Into Practice* (Vol. 6, No. 4). The conference, significant in its collection of fringe members of the curriculum field, highlighted Dwayne Huebner's recent work on temporality and James Macdonald's call for the incorporation of "aesthetic" (in contrast to technical) rationality. Along with Louise Berman, Ross Mooney, Maxine Greene, and Elliot Eisner, a growing number of younger curriculum scholars began pushing the field to revisit and rethink mainstream curriculum work.

Surrounding the curriculum field were various (and sometimes overlapping) social, political, and cultural streams of thought channeling away from the mainstream. Thus, at the October 1967 March against the Pentagon, one could find among the more than 100,000 participants a loose alliance of people ranging from members of the Old and New Left, to women's and civil rights activists, to those using drugs, enjoying sex, and listening to rock and roll (McQuaid, 1989). Represented in the 1960s by organizations such as the Students for a Democratic Society, the New Left framed the state of social and cultural affairs in revolutionary political and economic language. Though it would eventually dissolve into numerous factions (including the Weather Underground), political activism was a strong undercurrent in 1967.

A larger though often different passage being forged was social activism. From civil rights marches and antiwar rallies to acts of civil disobedience, huge numbers of people often submerged personal issues of race, sexuality, and gender in favor of more global concerns for disarmament, peace, and social justice. In time, this generic social activism would evolve from amalgamated antiwar gatherings into collections of smaller, more distinct groups seeking "power" (often racialized) and "liberation" (often gendered).

The social current that most rivaled the status quo in ease of travel, however, was that taken by the counterculture. The counterculture generally welcomed any and all, regardless of race, class, gender, age, or sexual identity. Unlike paths of activism, it had no apparent political or ideological agenda: its adherents were busy altering their personal mindscape and, in the process, the cultural landscape. Its 1967 "coming out" gala in San Francisco—known as the Summer of Love—"burned the values of the counterculture permanently into the body social and at the same time slowed its forward momentum" (Unger & Unger, 1988, p. 415). In time, even the counterculture would redistribute itself into selective subgroups ranging from those in pursuit of deeper spirituality and harmony with the earth to those seeking the ultimate high or the world's greatest rock and roll band.

The largely ahistorical nature of the times grew not only from the zeitgeist of immediacy and self-importance but from a shared disgust for "the Establishment" and its defenders (especially white men over the age of 30). Consequently, change was often sought from outside of existing institutions and structures through renegade institutions (e.g., underground presses and FM radio stations) and alternative settings. Among the most dynamic of these settings were the hundreds of "free schools" and "freedom schools" of the 1960s and the later "alternative schools" of the 1970s. These efforts were spawned in part by the "romantic critics" of public schooling—including Paul Goodman (*Compulsory Mis-Education,* 1966), Jonathan Kozol (*Death at an Early Age,* 1967), Ivan Illich (*De-Schooling Society,* 1971), and Carl Rogers (*Freedom to Learn,* 1969)—who, in book after damning book, denounced mainstream educational institutions.

▓ Apple and Curriculum Traditions ▓▓▓▓▓▓▓▓▓▓▓

VISITOR

As a teacher, Michael Apple had been influenced by some of these very writers, though he continued to search for a more politicized understanding of school problems.

When I began doctoral studies in 1966, it was the first time I had been in school full-time at an intellectually and politically exciting campus. Going to Columbia was a very lively kind of thing which transformed me from someone who certainly didn't belong in a place like Teachers College— because after all, I'd flunked out of college earlier—to someone who found it all quite interesting. You could be politically active, you could learn an immense amount of stuff, and at the same time you could hopefully transform other folks who are going to be teachers, curriculum workers, etc. So slowly but surely, your vision of yourself changes and your vision of your career changes as well.

At the time, TC was Mecca if you were involved in this political stuff. Though it's odd: My major reason for going to TC was not because of the intellectual and political ferment. It was because Leland Jacobs, a professor at TC in language arts, literacy studies, and reading, had given an in-service workshop in my school district and I was just thrilled. He was so engaging and as practical as you can get at the same time. Throughout my time at Teachers College I was constantly working in classrooms, quite often making films with kids or helping with integrating curriculum materials or working on black studies programs. So there was a sense of gritty reality to my time there. While TC was disconnected in some ways, those connections were pretty visible for people who wanted to make them.

A lot of people at TC influenced me, turning me from particular kinds of things I was interested in toward curriculum. I came in, first of all, not in curriculum, but in philosophy. You couldn't go through that period of the middle '60s without reading Herb Kohl, Jonathan Kozol, Jules Henry, Paul Goodman—people now known as the romantic critics. Well, I'd read enough of the romantic critics and other kinds of folks to believe that maybe the problems with education stemmed from simply thinking about kids and teachers and curriculum and schools in the wrong ways.

There were three traditions and philosophies available at TC at that time. One was the analytical philosophical tradition, which focused on how language works. Another was a sort of discipline centered theory, arguing that the disciplines of knowledge are the fundamental forms under which curriculum should be organized. We all got a dose of that. Then there was Maxine Greene, who was largely marginalized at the time because most people did not understand what critical phenomenology was about. Maxine was not a jazzy type of analyst, though if I were to point to people who influenced me, my major influences in philosophy would be Maxine and Jonas Soltis.

In time I became less enthusiastic about the analytic philosophical tradition, though it provided me with some very helpful tools. I was missing the connections between analytical philosophical work and daily school life; the analytic stuff was powerful but more arid than I wanted, and it was not political. Then I took a course from Alice Miel. I recall walking into her office and telling her what I was interested in, and she said, "Well, I know one person here you should speak to—Dwayne Huebner."

I owe more than I can ever say to Dwayne. When I first went into his office I found him loving and off-putting at the same time. I showed him my master's paper, which was an analytic philosophical treatment of the difference between indoctrination and training, and he said, "Well, this is smart. But it's not very useful, is it?" He listened very respectfully to me, then said, "You know, I think you really need to change traditions here, because what you're trying to do can't be found in where you're going now." He gave me a list of specific titles and authors, including work exploring the linkage between the analytic and phenomenological philosophic traditions, along with some initial political material. He said, "Read these. And then if you've got some serious questions, let's get together." With Dwayne, the invitation was always there. And that started conversations which lasted for three and a half years between us. It was clear that the person I wanted to work with was Dwayne. He was a taskmaster—a very disciplined, sometimes difficult, but always caring and loving person.

Dwayne taught courses in curriculum theory, but he also had a joint appointment at Union Theological Seminary. He and Arno Bellack were the two people in curriculum theory, per se. TC, at the time, had a mandatory sequence of curriculum courses which was quite demanding: courses in curriculum development, curriculum reform, and curriculum theory. I was part of a group of 10–15 folks who entered at the same time and took the same curriculum classes with Huebner, Bellack, Miel, etc. In effect, that experience created a small group of urban terrorists, because we were all in classes together. It created friendships within a tradition that was quite massive. You became a curriculum person because you took courses in curriculum. Period.

Struggles Suggest the Beginnings of Change

The collection of curriculum books published in 1968 was quite mixed in perspectives and purposes. While largely routine in terms of topics such as curriculum orientations and curriculum evaluation, authors had begun employing phrases like "social realities" and "survival of self" in the titles of books dedicated to technology, cognition, and curriculum design in an attempt to acknowledge the larger sociocultural milieu that they still wished to manage and control.

However, three 1968 curriculum books signaled a burgeoning legitimacy to topics outside the realm of behavior and control. *The Emergent Middle School* (Alexander, Williams, Compton, Hines, & Prescott) exemplified a text that argued that curriculum structures for adolescent students needed to be differently understood and constructed. Another was Louise Berman's *New Priorities in Curriculum,* in which she combined humanistic or third-force psychology and existentialism in critiquing the prevailing structures-of-the-disciplines orientation—a "courageous call" for new priorities at the time (Pinar et al., 1995, p. 174). A third text that appeared in 1968 was Philip Jackson's *Life in Classrooms,* a book that illustrated how both the planned and unplanned or "hidden" curriculums are perceived and enacted within classrooms. This book helped to reintroduce the classroom as a central site of curriculum work and renew "political" discussions of curriculum work (Pinar et al., 1995, p. 174). These three texts represented a renewal of vibrant intellectual discussion and debate among curriculum workers anxious to resuscitate their field.

Apple and Curriculum Transformation

VISITOR In preparation for his preliminary or qualifying examinations at Teachers College, Michael Apple read these and numerous other curriculum books and documents, "from the *Cardinal Principles*, to Rice's original studies on school spelling, to contemporary ASCD documents in curriculum." He came away with two lasting realizations. First, that curriculum work contained *multiple* traditions under "an umbrella tradition of trying to answer the question, 'What knowledge is of most worth?' " Second, that the field, itself, was in struggle. Apple continues:

> During those years, it was very clear to us how the movements within the curriculum field were being transformed. It was clear, for instance, that behavioristic traditions were becoming increasingly prominent, as people began to argue that we ought to have this thing called behavioral objectives. We would go to ASCD meetings or Professors of Curriculum meetings—when they were still vital and their struggles were very, very real—or to AERA meetings and watch Dwayne Huebner or Jim Macdonald and behavioral objectives folks like Popham go at it in public. Jim, who was Dwayne Huebner's best friend, actually had quite a strong influence on me as well. . . .
>
> But as for the more political curriculum ideas, we were aware that we were a minority. Yet in an odd way that gave us strength, because these were the days of the Vietnam War and an immense anti-racist struggle. And for those of us who had been formed by the combination of politics and education activism before coming to TC, it was like swimming uphill saying, "Look. There is a dominant culture with dominant political and economic powers. Why should we assume that the curriculum field won't have those representations as powerful at the same time?"

Swimming Uphill with History at Your Back

The struggle to see that the curriculum field adequately continued to reflect the political links between schools and larger political and economic powers would turn in Apple's favor eventually, though this was not a new fight. The political tradition in curriculum work can be cautiously traced from Huebner and Macdonald back to Theodore Brameld, L. Thomas Hopkins, and Ross Mooney, to Virgil Herrick and Harold Rugg, to George Counts and John Dewey. Michael Apple was at a juncture in time when this rich tradition could, with the addition of new and deeper insight, reemerge with pertinence.

The year 1968 was a turning point for those in the larger society who were attempting to change the dominant beliefs and practices of its overseers. The nonviolent civil rights movement died with the assassination of Reverend Martin Luther King Jr. that April, tens of thousands of students in Germany and France protested the Vietnam War in April and May, and presidential hopeful Bobby Kennedy was murdered in June. During 1968, the United States passed the 50,000 mark in war casualties, exceeded a troop strength of 500,000, and amassed a war debt of $100,000,000. Respected physician Benjamin Spock, Yale chaplain William Sloan Coffin, and Catholic priest Daniel Berrigan were all convicted of antiwar activities. The growing antiwar sentiment produced a presidential candidate (Eugene McCarthy) as well as public condemnation from established religious organizations such as the Methodists and Unitarians.

It was 1968 when "the Great Society petered out, when the civil rights movement stopped dead, when the liberal consensus of the Sixties came apart, when the Vietnam War leveled off, and when the cultural outsiders found their voice" (Unger & Unger, 1988, p. 532). What had begun as the women's movement with Friedan's *Feminine Mystique,* for example, turned the corner toward women's liberation with Kate Millett's *Sexual Politics.* Women freed themselves from the currents of the New Left and antiwar movements. In Washington, more than 5,000 women expressed their disillusionment with their place in the antiwar movement by burying "traditional womanhood" at Arlington National Cemetery and later picketing the Miss America pageant in Atlantic City.

Other cultural outsiders were soon to follow the example set by women in 1968.

> One rebel group still in the wings . . . was the homophile community, the nation's gay and lesbian outsiders. It had already begun to stir . . . [b]ut it was still a part of a social underground, a half-world, its members anxious to avoid identification or detection. No sector of the nation's outsiders had more to gain from making the personal political. (Unger & Unger, 1988, p. 447)

V ARIED TALE

FROM THE HOMOPHILE MOVEMENT TO GAY LIBERATION

On three sultry June nights in 1969, near a seedy Greenwich Village bar, drag queens, beats, and various other youthful and malcontent deviants rebelled against police harassment that had for decades been tolerated. Known simply as Stonewall, this event turned from riot, to battle cry, to gay icon in the span of a generation, and with it the homosexual was transformed from meek and mild. *Homosexual* was replaced by *gay,* which in turn was replaced by *queer,* as lesbians, gay men, bisexuals, and transgendered persons gained voice, influence, and momentum. The number of campus homophile organizations, including several dozen in the south (Sears, 2001), increased 10-fold during the year following the Stonewall "disturbance" (transformed into gay liberation fronts). Stonewall was the most visible result of a new movement enlivened by a new generation of activists who, often unknowingly and sometimes begrudgingly, built on the efforts of past generations of sexual malcontents. In short, Stonewall was both cause and effect.

As sexual outsiders, many homosexuals in postwar America reflected the social conformity, self-hatred, or sexual inferiority epitomized in novels such as *The City and the Pillar,* films such as *Rope,* and plays such as *The Children's Hour.* Through the cold war and Camelot eras, the nuclear family was reaffirmed with strict enforcement of compulsory heterosexuality: blacklists and blackmail, entrapment and interrogation, purges and witch-hunts, surveillance and harassment. "Sexual deviates" were committed to state hospitals, remanded to prisons, dismissed from jobs, denied professional licenses, and abandoned by family and friends.

While homosexuals such as Bayard Rustin, Lorraine Hansberry, James Baldwin, Tennessee Williams, Audre Lorde, Lilian Smith, and Paul Goodman contributed their considerable talents to the emerging civil rights movement or other protests in the arts and education, their sexual identities generally remained private. In a society increasingly fractured by conflicts of race, gender, social class, and age, only a few determined persons sought a place at the banquet table of capitalism.

A fledgling homophile movement began in earnest during the early 1950s with the founding of the male-led Mattachine Society and the women's group Daughter of Bilitis. Relying heavily on the professional expertise of psychologists, ministers, and researchers, these homophile groups sought social acceptance and eschewed political activism. With chapters in more than a dozen cities, these groups published professional looking magazines, *Mattachine Review* and *The Ladder,* that included news stories, book reviews, prose and poetry, and scholarly essays (D'Emilio, 1983). The traditionalists' goals were assimilation and toleration—quite radical aims for the intolerant times of McCarthyism and the sleepy silence of the Eisenhower years (Sears, 2006).

In 1961, Illinois became the first state to decriminalize homosexual behavior between consenting adults. This Model Penal Code became the pattern for other states and, more important, the first organizing wedge among homosexual activists. During that same year, a government astronomer, Frank Kameny, and his friend Jack Nichols established a Washington, DC chapter of the Mattachine Society. Fired because of homosexuality, Kameny declared war on the federal government, advocating militant (for the times) tactics among the loosely confederated homophile organizations: direct action through respectable demonstrations at the White House and Pentagon (gentlemen wore suits, ladies dresses), less reliance on outside experts, and a repudiation of the "sickness" conception of homosexuality (Loughery, 1998). Although many long-time activists rejected this militant new agenda, others embraced it; some were called by it. One of these was 37-year-old Florida entrepreneur turned taxi driver Richard Inman.

Inman launched a state-chartered corporation in 1964—the Atheneum Society of America—that sought "to secure the civil rights and equal protection under the law of all persons regardless of libidinous orientation." Refusing to

(continued)

release membership lists to Florida's state attorney, Inman quickly gained statewide attention from the media, the Miami police, and the infamous Johns Committee (which clandestinely spied on civil rights groups, communists, and homosexuals). A political pragmatist, Inman sought to abolish Miami's antihomosexual ordinances and to rescind the state's sodomy statute. As the first openly gay man in the United States to legally challenge homosexual discrimination and criminalization (the case, funded by the American Civil Liberties Union, was lost in the Florida Supreme Court and denied a hearing by the U.S. Supreme Court), Inman used a wide network of homosexual political insiders to influence state legislation. Eventually, Florida, too, adopted the Model Penal Code, though Inman's biggest obstacle would remain the apathy and sometimes open hostility of the local homosexual community, which rejected or ridiculed his aims as "outlandish," "radical," and "unrealistic" (Sears, 1997, chap. 7).

During this era of the Green Giant and Charlie Brown, slim-line pantsuits and miniskirts, there was zero tolerance for the homosexual or homosexuality in the school, the classroom, or the curriculum. However, in a mid-1960s society increasingly fractured by conflicts of race, gender, social class, and age set against the panorama of the civil rights movement and the Vietnam War, a new generation of gay activists emerged whose only memories of the McCarthy era were Bette Davis and Howdy Doody. Social integration or polite demonstration was replaced by social separation and confrontation. Gay militants enveloped in the antiwar, women's, and civil rights movements pushed beyond the boundaries of the old order. Much like Michael Apple and his fellow students in curriculum studies at Teachers College, Stephen Donaldson and his fellow Columbia University students organized the nation's first university chartered gay organization. In the year following Stonewall, scores of gay liberation fronts spouted on college campuses from the Carolinas to California (Sears, 2001; Teal, 1971).

This new generation of homosexual leadership also included Carl Wittman, who in 1971, heavily borrowing from Marxist analysis, penned the now seminal document "The Gay Manifesto," which concluded:

> Revolution differs from reform in that it means that the oppressed, with the full consciousness of their oppression, create social change through their own power. Historically, revolution is the method by which one class overthrows another. Gay revolution will see the overthrow of the straight male caste and the destruction of all systems of caste and class that are based in sexism. (Jay & Young, 1972, pp. 343–344)

A year earlier, along similarly revolutionary lines, the New York-based lesbian-feminist group known as Radicalesbians, employing early feminist analysis, had written:

> Lesbian is a label invented by men to throw at any woman who dares to be his equal. . . . [F]or a woman to be independent means she can't be a

woman—she must be a dyke.... Only women can give each other a new sense of self.... This consciousness is the revolutionary form which all else will follow, for ours is an organic revolution ... facing the basic heterosexual structure that binds us in one-to-one relationships with our own oppressors. (Jay & Young, 1972, pp. 173, 176)

During the 1970s, however, these youthful calls for revolution were not realized. Gay liberation would be contoured by capitalism, not Marxism, as the stonewall generation danced to disco music and engaged in conventional political organizing (Loughery, 1998; Sears, 2001). Similarly, feminism splintered across ideological and political lines while experiencing the crushing defeats of the Equal Rights Amendment. Nevertheless, although changes articulated by the radicals never materialized, once-radical concepts and strategies articulated by Kameny and Inman became the norm. Within a decade nearly half of the states had repealed their sodomy statutes and several dozen municipalities had enacted nondiscrimination ordinances.

The youthful Stonewall protesters' scribbles, "They Invade Our Rights; Support Gay Power," on the riot-torn bar's front window was as much an effect of the homophile generation's resistance to the mainstream as it was a cause for the burgeoning gay politics and culture before AIDS. Stonewall—the Boston Tea Party of the gay movement—had, like the curriculum revolution of 1969, been long in the making.

1969: A Year of Declarations

By 1969, the traditional curriculum field had become as seemingly irrelevant and illegitimate to growing numbers of educators and curriculum people as had "the Establishment," the military-industrial complex, patriarchal hierarchies, heterosexual orthodoxies, and conventional wisdom to social and political activists and members of the counterculture. Issues of relevancy and legitimacy stood at the center of antiwar activism and countercultural growth as college and university students across the country spent their spring semester in protest. At Columbia University, for example, 3,500 students and 100 faculty refused to attend classes in mid March; in April, "after several weeks of relatively polite protest concerning the on-campus presence of a cold war think-tank and the university's expansion into the surrounding black community, SDS and local black activists led close to 1,000 Columbia students in a week-long occupation of five campus buildings" (Kessler, 1990, p. 75).

Yet even the legitimacy of the activist and counterculture movements would suffer in 1969: Charles Manson and several of his followers would be arrested and charged with multiple gruesome murders, injuries and death would visit the Altamont rock concert, and some antiwar radical activists would accidentally die while building bombs. As the 1960s came to a close the decade's cultural and political dark sides were showing as the war that had given it so much meaning raged on.

Like other institutions, it seemed the traditional curriculum field had by 1969 "lost its legitimacy" (Pinar et al., 1995, p. 179) as well. Too many large-scale curriculum projects had failed due to their global orientation, teacher proofing, discipline specificity, and more. Curriculum people themselves had so technicized the Tyler rationale that even the act of curriculum making had become a quasi-empirical empirical science, ushering in an entire new field of study (evaluation) while placing teachers in a vulnerable new state of accountability (for student learning) without adaptability (in terms of what and how to teach).

This identity crisis within the curriculum field is apparent in the curriculum books published in 1969. Although a few authors remained on the reemerging experientialist-humanist path (including those who were busy expanding the area of middle school curriculum), others remained on the well-trodden path toward measurement, behavioral objectives, and instructional technology. The two notable exceptions were Joseph Schwab's publication of *College Curriculum and Student Protest* (1969a) and S. F. Walton's *The Black Curriculum* (published by Black Liberation Publishers, 1969). According to Schubert (1980, p. 193), "Schwab and Walton each responded to a major societal problem of the Sixties by providing curriculum perspectives relative to it; Schwab to student protests and Walton to the civil rights movement."

For the most part, however, the 1969 array of curriculum books suggested a field caught in a holding pattern. As Schubert notes: "A barrage of books that offered advice and caution for the future, reviewed past developments, and reemphasized prior thrusts appeared in 1969" (1980, p. 192). Yet from the perspective of published scholarly work, a key appearance in the curriculum field was Joseph Schwab's essay "The Practical: A Language for Curriculum," in which he argued for paradigmatic change in curriculum work. His essay, first delivered at an invited symposium for AERA members, was the Stonewall of the new curriculum movement. As much an effect as a cause, his paper was a clarion call for renewal.

Joseph Schwab: Coroner for Conventional Curriculum Making

Schwab was a theoretical geneticist who first taught in the field of biology and genetics. He is said to have been an excellent teacher—which may have inspired him, in part, to embrace the field of education. By 1969, Schwab had been teaching in the curriculum and philosophy department at the University of Chicago for quite a while. Brought to the university by Robert

Maynard Hutchins, Schwab was a contemporary of Ralph Tyler whose scholarship was largely dedicated to the nature of scientific inquiry, though he was a well-read scholar in numerous fields (see Westbury & Wilcoff, 1978).

Joseph Schwab was an interesting amalgam of different influences. One of his mentors, Sewell Wright, had invented "path analysis" in statistics as a way to solve certain kinds of unique problems. The work of John Dewey also influenced Schwab, as did that of his colleague, Richard McKean, an Aristotelian scholar in the philosophy department at the University of Chicago.

The combined attention to the structures of the disciplines, measurement and evaluation, curriculum knowledge and principles being generated from large, wholesale curriculum projects, and the seeming omniscience of behavioral objectives had all but killed the curriculum field, Schwab believed. In "The Practical: A Language for Curriculum," he carefully outlines this sad state of affairs before explaining the need to see curriculum problems differently. Moving away from the theoretic toward a more practical form of curriculum work might, he argued, revive the field.

Within this article Schwab also questions the curriculum field's reliance on Jerome Bruner's disciplinary structures, behavioral objectives, psychological emphases, and a narrow focus on any one of the generally accepted sources for curriculum (students, subject matter, or society). Additionally, he criticizes the growing "accountability movement" in curriculum work that relied on findings from large-scale research studies to produce highly generalized knowledge and principles. What schools need, says Schwab, are curriculum workers who wish to know and understand what goes on in classrooms, who wish to make the teaching–learning process (and curriculum) function better, who are sophisticated enough to anticipate new problems, and who see their work as fundamentally practical or "deliberative" (context specific and decision oriented). Our excerpt from this significant essay follows (all emphases in original).

PRIMARY DOCUMENT EXCERPT

The Practical: A Language for Curriculum

by Joseph Schwab

I shall have three points. The first is this: that the field of curriculum is moribund, unable by its present methods and principles to continue its work and desperately in search of new and more effective principles and methods.

The second point: the curriculum field has reached this unhappy state by inveterate and unexamined reliance on theory in an area where theory is partly inappropriate in the first place and where the theories extant, even where appropriate, are inadequate to the tasks which the curriculum field sets them....

The third point, which constitutes my thesis: there will be a renaissance of the field of curriculum ... only if the bulk of curriculum energies are diverted from the theoretic to the practical, to the quasi-practical and to the eclectic. By "eclectic" I mean the arts by which unsystematic, uneasy, but usable focus on a body of problems is effected among diverse theories, each relevant to the problems in a different way. By the "practical"... I refer ... to a complex discipline ... concerned with choice and action, in contrast with the theoretic, which is concerned with knowledge. Its methods lead to defensible decisions where the methods of the theoretic lead to warranted conclusions and differ radically from the methods and competencies entailed in the theoretic. ...

A Crisis of Principle

The frustrated state of the field of curriculum is not an idiopathology and not a condition which warrants guilt or shame on the part of its practitioners. All fields of systematic intellectual activity are liable to such crises ... because any intellectual discipline must begin its endeavors with untested principles. ...

A crisis of principle arises ... [in the case of theoretical enquiries] when principles are exhausted—when the questions they permit have all been asked and answered—or when the efforts at enquiry instigated by the principles have at last exhibited their inadequacy to the subject matter and the problems which they were designed to attack. ... [T]he latter holds in the case of curriculum: the curriculum movement has been inveterately theoretic, and its theoretic bent has let it down. ...

Characteristics of Theory

Consider first the early, allegedly Herbartian efforts (recently revived by Bruner) [which] took the view that ideas were formed by children out of received notions and experiences of things, and that these ideas functioned thereafter as discriminators and organizers of what was later learned. Given this view, the aim of curriculum was to discriminate the right ideas (by way of analysis of extant bodies of knowledge), determine the order in which they could be learned by children as they developed, and thereafter present these ideas at the right times with clarity, associations, organization, and application. A theory of mind and knowledge thus solves by one mighty coup the problem of what to teach, when, and how; and what is fatally theoretic here is not the presence of a theory of mind and a theory of knowledge ... but the ... vast simplicity which grounds this purported solution to the problem of curriculum.

Consider, now, some of the numerous efforts to ground curriculum in derived objectives. One effort seeks the ground of its objectives in social need and finds its social needs in just those facts about its culture which are sought and found under the aegis of a single conception of culture. Another grounds its objectives in the social needs identified by a single theory of history and of political evolution.

A third group of searches for objectives are grounded in theories of personality. . . . Freudianism persuaded its followers to aim to supply children with adequate channels of sublimation of surplus libido, appropriate objects and occasions for aggressions, a properly undemanding ego ideal, and an intelligent minimum of taboos. Interpersonal theories direct their adherents to aim for development of abilities to relate to peers. . . . Theories of actualization instruct their adherents to determine the salient potentialities of each child and to see individually to the development of each.

Still other searches for objectives seek their aims in the knowledge needed to "live in the modern world," in the attitudes and habits which minimize dissonance with the prevailing mores of one's community or social class, in the skills required for success in a trade or vocation, in the ability to participate effectively as member of a group. Still others are grounded in some quasi-ethics, some view of the array of goods which are good for man.

Three features of these typical efforts at curriculum making are significant here, each of which has its own lesson to teach us. First, each is grounded in a theory as such. . . . Second, each is grounded in a theory from the social or behavioral sciences: psychology, psychiatry, politics, sociology, history. . . . Third, they are theories concerning *different* subject matters. . . .

Need for an Eclectic

The significance of this third feature is patent to the point of embarrassment: no curriculum grounded in but one of these subjects can possibly be adequate, defensible.

It is clear, I submit, that a defensible curriculum or plan of curriculum must be one which somehow takes account of all these subsubjects which pertain to man. . . .

It is equally clear, however, that there is not, and will not be in the foreseeable future, one theory of this complex whole which is other than a collection of unusable generalities. Nor is it true that the lack of a theory of the whole is due to the narrowness, stubbornness, or merely habitual specialism of social and behavioral scientists. Rather, their specialism and the restricted purview of their theories are functions of their subject, its enormous complexity, its vast capacity for difference and change. . . . As far, then, as theoretical knowledge is concerned, we must wrestle as best we can with numerous, largely unconnected, separate theories of these many, artificially discriminated subsubjects of man.

I remarked in the beginning that renewal of the field of curriculum would require diversion of the bulk of its energies from theory to the practical, the quasi-practical, and the eclectic. The state of affairs just described . . . constitutes the case for one of these modes, the necessity of an eclectic, of arts by which a usable focus on a common body of problems is effected among theories which lack theoretical connection. . . . There is no foreseeable hope of a unified theory in the immediate or middle future, not of a metatheory which will tell us how to put those subsubjects together or order them in a fixed hierarchy of importance to the problems of curriculum. What remains as a viable alternative is the unsystematic, uneasy, pragmatic, and uncertain unions and connections which can be effected in an eclectic. And I must add . . . that changing connections and differing orderings at different times of these separate theories, will characterize a sound eclectic.

The Place of the Practical

. . . The significance of the existence of theory as such at the base of curricular planning consists of what it is that theory does not and cannot encompass. All theories . . . necessarily neglect some aspects and facets of the facts of the case. A theory covers and formulates the regularities among the things and events it subsumes. It abstracts a general or ideal case. It leaves behind the nonuniformities, the particularities. . . . Moreover, in the process of idealization, theoretical enquiry may often leave out of consideration conspicuous facets of all cases because its substantive principles of enquiry or its methods cannot handle them. . . .

Yet curriculum is brought to bear not on ideal or abstract representatives but on the real thing, on the concrete case in all its completeness and with all its differences from all other concrete cases on which the theoretic abstraction is silent. The materials of a concrete curriculum will not consist merely of portions of "science," of "literature," of "process." On the contrary, their constituents will be particular assertions about selected matters couched in a particular vocabulary, syntax, and rhetoric. They will be particular novels, short stories, or lyric poems, each, for better or for worse, with its own flavor. They will be particular acts upon particular matters in a given sequence. The curriculum will be brought to bear not in some archetypal classroom but in a particular locus in time and space with smells, shadows, seats, and conditions outside its walls which may have much to do with what is achieved inside. Above all, the supposed beneficiary is not the generic child, not even a class or kind of child out of the psychological or sociological literature pertaining to the child. The beneficiaries will consist of very local kinds of children and, within the local kinds, individual children. The same diversity holds with respect to teachers and what they do. The generalities about science, about literature, about children in general, about children or teachers of some specified class or kind, may be true. But they attain this status in virtue of what they leave out, and the omissions affect what remains. . . .

. . . If, then, theory is to be used well in the determination of curricular practice, it requires a supplement. It requires arts which bring a theory to its application: first, arts which identify the disparities between real thing and theoretic representation; second, arts which modify the theory in the course of its application, in the light of the discrepancies; and, third, arts which devise ways of taking account of the many aspects of the real thing which the theory does not take into account. These are some of the arts of the practical.

Question

How have the arts of the practical since influenced theory underlying curriculum practice?

Theories from Social Sciences

. . . Nearly all theories in all the behavioral sciences are marked by the coexistence of competing theories. . . . All the social and behavioral sciences are marked by "schools," each distinguished by a different choice of principle of enquiry, each of which selects from the intimidating complexities of the subject matter the small fraction of the whole with which it can deal.

The theories which arise from enquiries so directed are, then, radically incomplete. . . . Further, there is perennial invention of new principles which bring to light new facets of the subject matter, new relations among the facets and new ways of treating them. In short, there is every reason to suppose that any one of the extant theories of behavior is a pale and incomplete representation of actual behavior. . . .

It follows, then, that such theories are not, and will not be, adequate by themselves to tell us what to do with human beings or how to do it. What they variously suggest and the contrary guidances they afford to choice and action must be mediated and combined by eclectic arts and must be massively supplemented, as well as mediated, by knowledge of some other kind derived from another source.

Some areas of choice and action with respect to human behavior have long since learned this lesson. Government is made possible by a lore of politics. . . . Institution of economic guidances and controls owes as much to unmediated experience of the market place as it does to formulas and theories. Even psychotherapy . . . relies as much or more on the accumulated, explicitly nontheoretic lore accumulated by practitioners, as it does on theory or eclectic combinations of theory. The law has systematized the accumulation of direct experience of actual cases in its machinery for the recording of cases and opinions as precedents which continuously monitor, supplement, and modify the meaning and application of its formal "knowledge," its statutes. It is this recourse to accumulated lore, to experience of actions and their consequences, to action and reaction at the level of the concrete case, which constitutes the heart of the practical. It is high time that curriculum do likewise.

The Practical Arts

The arts of the practical are onerous and complex; hence only a sampling must suffice to indicate the character of this discipline and the changes in educational investigation which would ensue on adoption of the discipline. . . .

The practical arts begin with the requirement that existing institutions and existing practices be preserved and altered piecemeal, not dismantled and replaced. It is further necessary that changes be so planned and so articulated with what remains unchanged that the functioning of the whole remain coherent and unimpaired. These necessities stem from the very nature of the practical—that it is concerned with the maintenance and improvement of patterns of purposed action, and especially concerned that the effects of the pattern through time shall retain coherence and relevance to one another....

The same requirements would hold for a practical program of improvement of education. It, too, would effect its changes in small progressions, in coherence with what remains unchanged, and this would require that we know *what is and has been going on in American schools.*

At present, we do not know....

What is wanted is a totally new and extensive pattern of empirical study of classroom action and reaction; a study, not as basis for theoretical concerns about the nature of the teaching or learning process, but as a basis for beginning to know what we are doing, what we are not doing, and to what effect....

This is an effort which will require new mechanisms of empirical investigation, new methods of reportage, a new class of educational researchers, and much money. It is an effort without which we will continue largely incapable of making defensible decisions about curricular changes, largely unable to put them into effect and ignorant of what real consequences, if any, our efforts have had....

A second facet of the practical: its actions are undertaken with respect to identified frictions and failures in the machine and inadequacies evidenced in felt shortcomings of its products. This origin of its actions leads to two marked differences in operation from that of theory. Under the control of theory, curricular changes have their origin in new notions of person, group or society, mind or knowledge, which give rise to suggestions of new things curriculum might be or do [with] ... little or no account of the existing effectiveness of the machine or the consequences to this effectiveness of the institution of novelty.... The practical, on the other hand, because it institutes changes to repair frictions and deficiencies, is commanded to determine the whole array of possible effects of proposed change, to determine what new frictions and deficiencies the proposed change may unintentionally produce.

The other effective difference between theoretical and practical origins of deliberate change is patent. Theory, by being concerned with new things to do, is unconcerned with the successes and failures of present doings.... The practical, on the other hand, is directly and deliberately concerned with the diagnosis of ills of the curriculum....

A third facet of the practical I shall call the anticipatory generation of alternatives. Intimate knowledge of the existing state of affairs, early identification of problem situations, and effective formulation of problems are necessary to effective practical decision but not sufficient. It requires also that there be available to practical deliberation the greatest possible number and fresh diversity of alternative solutions to the problem. . . . The problems which arise in an institutional structure which has enjoyed good practical management will be novel problems, arising from changes in the times and circumstances and from the consequences of previous solutions to previous problems. . . . They cannot be well solved by apparently new solutions arising from old habits of mind and old ways of doing things.

[Further], . . . practical problems do not present themselves wearing their labels around their necks. Problem situations, to use Dewey's old term, present themselves to consciousness, but the character of the problem, its formulation, does not. This depends on the eye of the beholder. And this eye, unilluminated by possible fresh solutions to problems, new modes of attack, new recognitions of degrees of freedom for change among matters formerly taken to be unalterable, is very likely to miss the novel features of new problems or dismiss them as "impractical." Hence the requirement that the generation of problems be anticipatory and not await the emergence of the problem itself. . . .

As the last sampling of the practical, consider its method. . . . It is deliberative. It cannot be inductive because the target of the method is not a generalization or explanation but a decision about action in a concrete situation. It cannot be deductive because it deals with the concrete case, not abstractions from cases, and the concrete case cannot be settled by mere application of a principle. . . .

Commitment to Deliberation

Deliberation is complex and arduous. It treats both ends and means and must treat them as mutually determining one another. It must try to identify, with respect to both, what facts may be relevant. It must try to ascertain the relevant facts in the concrete case. It must try to identify the desiderata in the case. It must generate alternative solutions. It must make every effort to trace the branching pathways of consequences which may flow from each alternative and affect desiderata. It must then weigh alternatives and their costs and consequences against one another and choose, not the right alternative, for there is no such thing, but the best one.

I shall mention only one of the new kinds of activity which would ensue on commitment to deliberation. It will require the formation of a new public and new means of communication among its constituent members. . . .

This will require penetration of the curtains which now separate educational psychologist from philosopher, sociologist from test constructor, historian from administrator; it will require new channels connecting the series from teacher, supervisor, and school administrator at one end to research specialists at the other. Above all, it will require renunciation of the specious privileges and hegemonies by which we maintain the fiction that problems of science curriculum, for example, have no bearing on problems of English literature or the social studies. The aim here is not a dissolving of specialization and special responsibilities. Quite the contrary: if the variety of lights we need are to be obtained, the variety of specialized interests, competencies, and habits of mind which characterize education must be cherished and nurtured. The aim, rather, is to bring the members of this variety to bear on curriculum problems by communication with one another.

Concretely, this means the establishment of new journals, and education of educators so that they can write for them and read them. The journals will be forums where possible problems of curriculum will be broached from many sources and their possible importance debated from many points of view. . . .

. . . Similar forums, operating viva voce and in the midst of curriculum operation and curriculum change, are required: of the teachers, supervisors, and administrators of a school; of the supervisors and administrators of a school system; of representatives of teachers, supervisors, and curriculum makers in subject areas and across subject areas; of the same representatives and specialists in curriculum, psychology, sociology, administration, and the subject-matter fields.

. . . By [such] means . . . , the educational research establishment might at last find a means for channeling its discoveries into sustained improvement of the schools instead of into a procession of ephemeral bandwagons.

▓ The Time Has Come for Change ▬▬▬▬▬

Ready or not, the curriculum field was poised for the very renaissance Schwab awaited. A small but sufficient number of its own people had quietly spent the 1960s working to push the boundaries of the Tylerian tradition. They patiently waited and eventually critiqued the myriad of national curriculum reform projects that, by the decade's end, had predictably failed in most respects. Across the country, those who called themselves curricularists had begun to look to their field's own history and traditions, to look toward other fields within and outside of education, and to look within themselves for new insights and meaning. While so much about curriculum work in the 1960s seemed headed toward even greater precision, control, and efficiency, this small and scattered tribe of renegades understood all too well that the decade's social, political, personal, and cultural metamorphoses could not be separated from their own lives and educational work. Most important, they shared their expanding inquiries, their deep desire to inquire and understand, and their persistent faith in the importance of curriculum work with the many classroom teachers and graduate students they encountered through their teaching and writing. Those whom they influenced over the next three decades would change the countenance of curriculum studies.

Joseph Schwab's critique was among "the first of a decade of attacks on the traditional curriculum field." Internally, the field had reduced its own conventional framework (the Tyler rationale) to a mere technique; externally, the field had been thoroughly co-opted by educational psychologists and subject-matter specialists. A sort of "cardiac arrest" had taken place (Pinar et al., 1995, pp. 176–177). Fortunately, a critical mass had formed within the curriculum underground. Joined by a handful of curriculum deviants, a disparate collection of younger upstarts was about to surface. With little more in common than a disdain for the present state of affairs, they set out to resuscitate the work of curriculum. Michael Apple, who earned his doctorate in 1970, was among them.

Michael Apple

VISITOR The people who profoundly affected me during my career at TC were the somewhat politicized phenomenologists. It wasn't a situation where first we did political criticism, then we did phenomenology, etc. None of that was going on. We felt no revolutionary overtones, but we were aware of multiple traditions within the field—some of which had been drawn from the others, all of which were in tension with each other.

There was no doubt in our minds that this was a time of generational shifts. Huebner, Macdonald and others exerted a great deal of effort in making sure that their doctoral students knew each other. There was this sense of being children of the children of a number of vibrant voices which were dissident and striking—and caring at the same time: the humanist tradition with some teeth in it. There was a sense of our trying to find something that was humanist, because Huebner was a phenomenologist and very much a disciplined humanist. Yet I can't imagine Dwayne not allowing that he was deeply affiliated with Joseph Schwab or Virgil Herrick, and that that tradition worked through Ralph Tyler in the same way. But ours was a search for an economic and cultural and political form that could enable humanist values to actually take place in schools: we were both humanist and wanting to go beyond it at the same time, disciplining ourselves and distancing ourselves from the humanist tradition which, we felt, had the right intuitions but insufficient power.

Yet I don't like to talk about it in terms of generational shifts. It's one of the reasons why I totally reject any language that talks about curriculum reconceptualists: I have never been one; I don't think there ever have been any in the field; and I think it's a total misreading of history. Certainly, Herb Kliebard, myself, and many others who were included in that tradition never saw ourselves as reconceptualizing anything. We are simply standing on the shoulders of a very, very long and valuable tradition that has its roots in the very beginning of the curriculum field.

Question

What similarities, if any, do you see in Apple's reading of curriculum history and the cause and effect of Stonewall?

I have always thought that I am standing on the shoulders of Counts and Rugg and Dewey and numbers of other folks from the 1920s, like DuBois, who were socialist educators and anti-racist educators. If there was any reconceptualizing going on, it was because we were trying to figure out how to make their claims more political—and make them work. That's why we turned to Marcuse, Polanyi, and a number of other radical, neo-Marxist, and humanist-Marxists who were critics; that's why I was so strongly influenced by the combination of phenomenology and Marxism I found in Sartre and Merleau-Ponty.

And all the while we knew that we were standing on people's shoulders, yet Huebner and others insisted that we weren't to be clones. And that's something that I try and do with my own doctoral students. My task is not to create the new generation of "Apples." I want my students to be political, but there are multiple politics. And I want them to care about a particular tradition represented by a very important curriculum question that I've tried to transform, which is not *what* knowledge is most important, but *whose* knowledge. That's my task—that kind of generational shift. For me, recognizing one's traditions has always been very important.

▼ isitor Bibliography   Michael Apple

Apple, M. (1979, 1990). *Ideology and curriculum.* New York: Routledge.

Apple, M. (1982, 1995). *Education and power.* New York: Routledge.

Apple, M. (1988). *Teachers and texts.* New York: Routledge.

Apple, M. *Official knowledge.* (1993, 2000). New York: Routledge.

Apple, M. (with James Beane). (1995). *Democratic schools.* Alexandria, VA: ASCD.

Apple, M. (1996). *Cultural politics and education.* New York: Teachers College Press.

Apple, M. (1999). *Power, meaning, and identity.* New York: Peter Lang.

Apple, M. (2001). *Educating the "right" way.* New York: Routledge.

Apple, M. *The state and the politics of knowledge.* (In Press). New York: Routledge.

(Re)Shaping the Contemporary Curriculum Field (1970–1983)

6

The Renaissance Blossoms: Professional Organizations and Gatherings

■ Janet L. Miller

VISITOR Many of us who enter the curriculum field have not spent our prior years planning carefully for such work. This is true of Janet Miller, professor of education at Teachers College, Columbia University.[1] Janet happened into teaching and eventually pursued graduate school and curriculum studies in serendipitous turns. Her timing—relative to the changing nature of curriculum work at least—could not have been more fortuitous for us.

I was born in Ottumwa, Iowa, in 1945. My dad was a pharmacist and we moved around quite a bit when I was very young. I went to first and second grade at the St. Paul [Minnesota] Cathedral School—part of a big, imposing parish on a hill. My search for whatever community I might need really originates there, because as a non-Catholic I felt very outcast. I went on to spend third and part of fourth grade living in Kansas City before we finally settled in Pittsburgh, Pennsylvania, when I was in the middle of fourth grade. Moving around was very traumatic for me. I was very shy as a child.

---

[1]Personal communication, 16 October, 1994.

Janet met her future husband, Phil, in fourth grade. They began dating in high school. After graduation, Janet headed off to Grove City College—two hours north of Pittsburgh.

> I think I became an English major because I had always loved to read. I received a really wonderful background in English literature at Grove City College. But I knew I would teach, because at that time my career options were teacher, nurse, secretary. . . . I had no other idea of what I could possibly do. So I took Grove City's one course in secondary education, one in English methods, one in audio-visual aids, and then did student teaching. But frankly . . . I really, truly thought I would teach three years and then have kids and stay home for a while.
>
> I graduated with an A.B. in English in 1966, married Phil, and moved to Massena, New York where he had a job with Alcoa as an industrial engineer. Massena's a little town on the St. Lawrence River, about an hour and a half south of Montreal. I was in eight other weddings that summer. Everyone got married, taught three years, and then had kids. I think the only reason that didn't happen with me was because I got rheumatic fever, which really put a halt to our family plans for a while. By the time I was healthy enough and strong enough to consider it again, Phil and I were separated.
>
> When I interviewed for a job at the high school in Massena, they said, "Well, we've got four positions here. What would you like to teach?" So I constructed my own job: I taught three sections of senior-level Modern Literature, one class of juniors preparing for the New York Regents exam, and one class of English 12D for kids who tested low. I also sponsored the cheerleaders, which meant I went to every basketball, football, hockey, soccer and wrestling match the school ever had. And I loved it.
>
> Massena's also where I met two of my best friends in life, Arlene and Kay. Kay taught English with me and Arlene taught French. We did all kinds of creative, wild, and crazy things in school. I taught for six years in Massena. It was great.

The 1970s Unravel

It may have been fate that took Janet Miller from the expected to the unexpected, from the joys of teaching to the sadness and pain of a separation from her childhood sweetheart. Yet on a grander scale, life in the United States itself had turned inside out and upside down.

The 1970s were years of chaos, crisis, and change bracketed by the social ferment of the 1960s and the "greed is good" Reagan era. It was, in President Jimmy Carter's words, "a crisis of confidence . . . that strikes at the very heart and soul and spirit of the nation." Symptoms included cultural malaise and personal melancholy, institutional distrust and political disillusionment, international aimlessness and global impotence.

From the perspective of the Reaganesque New Millennium, the 1970s were, in some ways, a disaster waiting to happen: our overconsumption of technology and natural resources, our overindulgence with sexual freedom and freedom of expression, and our overreliance on federalism and individualism. It was a decade-long series of national ruptures: the ecological Armageddons of Three Mile Island and Love Canal; an economy of stagflation, with production declining by 10%, official unemployment reaching 9%, inflation touching 18%, interest rates rocketing to 20%, the Dow Jones Industrial Average falling below 600, and our first trade deficit since 1888; a meltdown of political credibility with the publication of the Pentagon Papers, the later Watergate revelations, and the hearings of the House Select Committee on Assassinations. It was a decade when the Organization of Petroleum Exporting Countries (OPEC) and the Pacific Rim nations first challenged America's economic superiority, Iranians and Vietnamese challenged America's military superiority, activists at Wounded Knee, Attica, and Kent State challenged America's moral superiority, and the tragedies of *Apollo 13* and Yom Kippur challenged our technological prowess. This decade marked the collapse of the steel industry, creating the rust belt of riot-torn Midwestern and Northeastern cities, as well as the collapse of New Deal liberalism marked by the emergence of populist conservatism evidenced in Howard Jarvis's Proposition 13, Jerry Falwell's Moral Majority, and Anita Bryant's Save Our Children.

This crisis of spirit found ample expression in popular culture: disaster movies such as *The Towering Inferno* and *The Poseidon Adventure,* escapist fantasies of *Star Wars* and *Saturday Night Fever,* horror films such as *The Exorcist* and *The Shining,* ethnic exploits in *The Godfather* and *Shaft,* post-Vietnam revisionist films such as *Apocalypse Now* and *The Deer Hunter,* cynical political post-Watergate thrillers *Three Days of the Condor* and *The Parallax View,* and the futility of individual actions and the false reality of surface appearance represented in the films *Network* and *Shampoo.* This chaotic ferment was also mirrored in best-selling books, including *The End of Affluence, Passages, Diet for a Small Planet,* and *Andromeda Strain,* reflected in architecture such as Richard Meier's Bronx Development Center, apparent in the sculpture of Wendy Taylor, and clear in the birth of punk and glitter rock during the heyday of disco.

As crisis, chaos, and change marked most aspects of intellectual, political, social, and cultural life during the 1970s, the "curriculum field would be no exception" (Pinar et al., 1995, p. 187). Curriculum books continued to pour forth. The master's-level synoptic text designed to prepare "budding curricularists to become able to influence practice" (Schubert, 1980, p. 247) remained popular. Like most synoptic texts of the 1970s— the amalgamistic sort presented as free of ideology—curriculum development remained central while curriculum evaluation grew in prominence.

At the same time, however, a new trend in synoptic curriculum efforts appeared in a more considered approach to delineating curriculum studies while attempting to historically situate the field (e.g., Zais, 1976). The still-popular exemplar is Tanner and Tanner's 1975 publication *Curriculum Development: Theory into Practice* (now in its third edition [1995]). Taken together, such books signaled an effort to elaborate on the parameters of curriculum work as articulated in earlier "standard works" by Taba or Smith, Stanley, and Shores while staying focused on the *development* of curriculum.

Textbooks aside, most mainstream curriculum writing throughout the decade remained intent on influencing practice (e.g., English, 1978; Frymier & Hawn, 1970; Rubin, 1977a, 1977b, 1977c) by joining curriculum thought and classroom practice. Adopting the epistemological stance of social behaviorism, mainstream curriculum workers sought to continue the legacy of the expert curriculum consultant, often through setting curriculum policy. Goodlad's *The Dynamics of Educational Change: Toward Responsive Schools* (1975) exemplifies this effort.

In part, a consequence of the previous decade's national curriculum projects and their requisite funding accountability, developing localized curriculum policy became entangled with measuring success through curriculum evaluation (e.g., Hamilton, 1976; Lewy, 1977; P. A. Taylor & Cowley, 1972). Attention to evaluation grew in weedlike fashion. Eventually a thoughtfully skeptical response to such measurement fervor appeared (Hamilton, Macdonald, King, Jenkins, & Parlett, 1977). Others would soon follow (most notably, *Qualitative Evaluation* [Willis, 1978] and *The Educational Imagination* [Eisner, 1979; 1994]), reminding the field that how we come to know is as important as what we think we know.

This large-scale policy and measurement direction was precisely where Joseph Schwab did *not* want the field to head. Schwab, who directed "the turn taken by curriculum writers in the Seventies" (Schubert 1980, p. 242) and has been called "one of the most brilliant and influential minds the curriculum field has known" (Pinar et al., 1995, p. 197), saw a huge influx of interest in attempts to solve curriculum problems at large. Much concerned about the values of the social and behavior sciences turning completely in the neopositivist direction (empirical design and measurement seeking broad generalization), his antidote was a move to the practical and quasi-practical (see chapter 5).

Interestingly, Schwab also had a major hand in bringing teachers (back) into focus with respect to curriculum work. Clearly, the earlier work of curriculum progressives paid serious attention to teachers' place in the work of curriculum, but the importance of the classroom teacher as an active agent had largely disappeared in the mainstream of curriculum work during the 1950s and 1960s.

The centrality of the teacher as a living force in understanding the nature of curriculum work took on great importance in other ways as well.

As Schubert (1980, p. 271) note, another "significant variation" in curriculum books emerged in the 1970s: books highlighting "contrast and commentary," which both "sharpened problematic areas" (e.g., Eisner & Vallance, 1974) and, in the case of a new generation of collected readings, helped to shape the field's major concerns (e.g., Bellack & Kliebard, 1977; Gress & Purpel, 1978; 1988; Purpel & Belanger, 1972).

What began as a humanistic psychological look at curriculum and schooling evolved into "a new variation, perhaps a profound one, in the experientialist line of curriculum thought" during the 1970s (Schubert, 1980, p. 243). This influence, represented early in the decade by Weinstein and Fantini's *Toward Humanistic Education: A Curriculum of Affect* (1970), came alive through such practices as affective education, confluent education, open education, personalized education, and values education. ASCD, still the organizational "home" to most curriculum workers as the decade began, remained prominent in its promotion of these and related ideas. Like the so-called romantic writings of the 1960s and early 1970s, this sort of "personal humanism" greatly appealed to teachers. Ironically, the humanistic psychology promoted by ASCD was intellectually, politically, and often ideologically unrecognizable from the early works of people such as John Holt, Jonathan Kozol, James Hearndon, and Herb Kohl (who were steeped in the humanities and philosophy in particular and, to a lesser extent, race and class politics), all of whom wrote from a teacher's autobiographical vantage point without any initial understanding of their progressive heritage (Marshall & Sears, 1985; Sears & Marshall, 1984).

Personalizing the curriculum had already been complicated by ideas borrowed from existential philosophy, phenomenology, and autobiography as well as insights from the humanities, theology, and depth psychology. What humanistic and third-force psychology provided the field of curriculum more than anything else was an opportunity to recognize that schooling had become absurd, that we had left *people* out of curriculum work. Yet as this personal humanism was being popularized, a more unnerving "sociopolitical humanism" was being shaped and discussed through mainstream outlets, as exemplified in ASCD's *Schools in Search of Meaning* (1975), coedited by James Macdonald and Esther Zaret (a former Macdonald student) and featuring chapters by Dwayne Huebner, William Burton, John Steven Mann, and Michael Apple.

Alex Molnar

VISITOR Alex Molnar, professor of curriculum and instruction at Arizona State University, came to the curriculum field with a highly developed sense of sociopolitical humanism. Today, in addition to his teaching and continued social activism, Alex is a practicing psychologist. During the 1970s he worked closely with James Macdonald and joined the struggle to reinvigorate the work of curriculum.[2]

> I was born on Wednesday, February 6, 1946, in Chicago. I had one sister who was almost 14 years older than me. She married at 17 and moved out of the house. My dad died when I was nine, so for most of my childhood I was raised by my mom. So I had a very small family, you might say, and I frequently spent time alone.
>
> I recall thinking that school was fun. I can't say that school was terribly important to me, though; I was more or less impervious to school. I had a great time in elementary school and throughout high school, too. I did quite well in English and history because I was interested in them, yet during my senior year I signed up for the lowest track math/science classes and spent probably three and a half hours a day in physical education hanging around lifting weights, swinging on ropes, shooting hoops. I was largely regarded as a child who had terrific potential but was unlikely to ever realize it. While I was a good kid, I just didn't apply myself and wasn't properly deferential to adult authority.

After graduating from high school in 1963, Alex immediately began college and married at the age of 18. He became "pretty much a straight 'A' student" and chose teaching as a career not only because it interested him but because he had a family to support, and teaching was a degree he could complete relatively quickly. He continues:

> I graduated from college in 1966 with a history major and both political science and education minors. I was certified to teach grades six through twelve but couldn't find a job teaching high school, so I was planning to enroll at Northwestern University and get a degree in African history, which interested me. But that was during the war in Vietnam, and that October a job opened up at the high school I had graduated from when a teacher was drafted. So, in 1966, I started teaching high school at the age of 20. I was draft exempt because I was married and also the father of a child.
>
> I taught junior-level World Civilizations in my first year, and during my second and third years I taught senior-level courses that I wrote. For example, my second year course involved four themes: poverty, intolerance, the environment, and war. In my third year I taught a course on African-American history that I developed. I chuckle, now, because it was an all-white school and the course was considered quite extraordinary at the time.
>
> I had heard about behavioral objectives and all of that, but this school was built around the teacher. Ridgewood Community High School was among the first high schools in the country to employ flexible modular scheduling and faculty teams. We had no required textbooks and we never spent more than 50% of our scheduled time in class, the rest being available to plan, work on curriculum, and meet with students. So it was a terrific school for somebody with a lot of ideas and interests in doing different things.

---

[2]Personal communication, 30 October, 1994.

Once teaching, Alex soon began a master's degree in history. Upon completing his master's, he applied and was accepted into an unusual residential program for experienced teachers run by Merrill Harmin, one of the coauthors of the book *Values and Teaching* (Raths, Harmin, & Simon, 1966). During that year (1969–1970), he also earned a certificate in educational administration. As Alex explains:

> Through this program I became very immersed in what was then called third force psychology, along with humanistic education, values clarification, and so on. I can't say that I was ever terribly interested in any of this beforehand. I mean, the whole idea of sensitivity training, expressing your true feelings, having authentic relationships and so on was certainly in the air in the late '60s and it was something that the faculty at Ridgewood had talked about and debated and tried to figure out. But I didn't really know much about it until I arrived at Southern Illinois University and found myself in it up to my eyeballs.
>
> This was a live-in program, with all night or weekend sensitivity groups. It was very, very intense, designed to educate just 18 people to educate their fellow teachers. It was run from a little farmhouse out in the field there in southern Illinois, very much like a community.
>
> Well, myself and three other guys decided to see if we couldn't go on to get our doctorates together at the same place and set up an experimental teacher education program as kind of an extension of the work we'd been doing at Southern Illinois and also as a way of earning our doctorate. We were a multi-racial team, three white guys and a black guy, with quite diverse backgrounds.
>
> We applied to graduate schools all over the country together, and though a couple of schools were indeed interested, the only school that put up the money was the University of Wisconsin-Milwaukee. UWM was kind of a wide open place at that point because they had just begun a new doctoral program in urban education and were looking for a way to attract some high quality doctoral students. So, in the fall of 1970, UWM brought us there to work on our doctorates together and set up this experimental teacher education program. And that's where I met Jim Macdonald.

The Slow Dismantling of Convention

For some, the idea that four friends would expect to be accepted to a doctoral program in all-or-none fashion and that their purpose would be to design an unconventional initial teacher preparation program may seem hugely presumptuous. But for those involved in education and curriculum at the time, dismantling conventions seemed natural. Ironically, Alex would find himself at the University of Wisconsin-Milwaukee working closely with James Macdonald who was himself in the midst of theoretically dismantling the conventional field of curriculum.

The need for this intellectual and practical deconstruction and reconstruction was evident in two works published in 1970. In the first, Kuhn's significantly revised *The Structure of Scientific Revolutions,* intellectuals seemed finally to begin to appreciate "that the conventional paradigm of scholarship in any given era is not the only possibility" (Schubert, 1980, p. 240). Silberman's *Crisis in the Classroom,* a thorough, deeply invasive critical report on public schools, constituted a second warning offered in language that everyone could readily understand: our schools had lost their meaning.

Curricularists could now begin to take a critical look at the causes of this crisis, which included the failed curriculum reforms of the previous decade. More numerous, however, were those who argued for a need to sharpen the procedures and principles used in developing curricula for schools. Work begun by individuals such as Mager (whose *Preparing Instructional Objectives* enjoyed a second edition in 1975) and others (e.g., Baker & Popham, 1973; Drumheller, 1972; Hannah & Michaelis, 1977) continued through the decade, gaining momentum within the emerging field of school-based curriculum evaluation while simultaneously losing space within the curriculum literature as more "complex" ideas found life in print.

Generally speaking, mainstream curriculum workers entered the 1970s with a mission to fix what was wrong with schools through the building of better curricula using more sophisticated tools and measures. It was still too early for the overall field to embrace the symbiotic relationship among school, society, and culture, though a handful of books that appeared during this period pointed in that direction through titles such as *Black Studies: Threat-or-Challenge* (N. A. Ford, 1973), *Curriculum and the Cultural Revolution* (Purpel & Belanger, 1972), *Feminist Resources for Schools and Colleges* (Ahlum & Fralley, 1973), *Heightened Consciousness, Cultural Revolution, and Curriculum Theory* (Pinar, 1974), and *Curriculum for Better Schools: The Great Ideological Debate* (Schiro, 1978). As Pinar, the author of one of these seminal books, later wrote with others: "It was becoming clear that the conceptual and instrumental 'tools' provided by the traditional paradigm of curriculum development no longer adequately addressed rapidly changing social and cultural realities. Somehow, the traditional paradigm attempted to insulate itself from these indications of 'cultural revolution' " (Pinar et al., 1995, p. 209).

This sort of resistance to unpredictable influences by the "keepers of the curriculum field" is certainly understandable, in part, following a decade when large-scale curriculum work had been taken over by outsiders. But the deeper struggle during this era would be over the very nature of curriculum work itself. Here, struggles within the curriculum field differed in function if not in form from their progressive antecedents. In general, the multiple directions taken during the curriculum theorizing efforts of the 1970s (e.g., politics, autobiography, phenomenology) reflect some of the themes developed by the early curriculum progressives, though "their function during the 1970s was to reconceptualize the character of the American curriculum field, both conceptually and methodologically. The field would shift from a primary and practical interest in the *development* of curriculum to a theoretical and practical interest in *understanding* curriculum" (Pinar et al., 1995, pp. 186–187).

Historically, these internal curriculum struggles were not unlike those found elsewhere. Whenever we find something that was created, developed, and popularized by a self-identifiable group of people, sanctioned by its own leaders and organizations, and managed so as to control not only the rules of the game but also who plays it, we are eventually likely to see slippage, compromise, and outright internal struggles. Tennis is a good example of this phenomenon.

▼ ARIED TALE

TENNIS: A CIVILIZED SPORT, INDEED

Tennis has a long and distinguished, if not truncated, history. Its roots have been traced back to the early Romans and Greeks. During the early part of the fourteenth century, *jeu de parre* was played in France with the ball hit by the player's hand. The modern game of lawn tennis is attributed to Major Walter Wingfield, who developed it as an outdoor sport for the ladies of his British castle. Freely borrowing from the rules, scoring, and equipment of related games, Wingfield added these to an hourglass-shaped playing court. Patenting the game as *Sphairistike,* the Greek command for "play ball," Wingfield's lawn tennis rules were published in pamphlet form during the early 1870s. But variations and rule changes quickly appeared.

The most significant revisions to Wingfield's game were made and published by the Marylebone Cricket Club in 1875 and recodified by the All England Croquet Club, whose dwindling membership and empty croquet lawns necessitated accommodation with this new lawn sport. The court's hourglass shape was abandoned in favor of a rectangle, the length of the court extended and its width shortened, scoring methods changed to 15s, and the serving location moved. The first British lawn tennis championships, held in 1877 at the Wimbledon Club, employed the revised Marylebone rules.

In the winter of 1874 while vacationing in Bermuda, an American visitor, Mary Ewing Outerbridge, had the "grand fortune" to experience Sphairistike at the British garrison. Heralded as an exciting new game for America's gentry, lawn courts soon appeared in Nahant, Massachusetts; Newport, Rhode Island; and Tuxedo, New York.

The first national championship was held on Staten Island in 1880, but the tournament was moved to the exclusive enclave of Newport a year later (where it remained until 1914). During these early tournaments most of the players came from major eastern cities, competing literally within a boundary of wooden chairs—called "socialities"—placed around the court's edges to accommodate the audience of well-heeled women, dressed in elaborate summer gowns, shaded by silk and lace parasols, and escorted by men in formal attire topped with stiff derbies. There was neither a grandstand nor a press box and neither prize money nor "guarantees."

Tennis was an amateur's game that required "money to play it, money that one earned or one's father earned.... [While] a handful of teaching professionals at a few clubs ... derived direct financial benefit from the game ... nothing accrued, either directly or indirectly, to the amateur player himself" (Cummings, 1957, p. 61). During the era of robber barons and no income tax, the Newport of the 1890s was the summer watering hole of the Belmonts, the Vanderbilts, and the Astors, who built million-dollar "cottages" of opulence. Here, residents enjoyed Tennis Week, with its annual men's singles champions of the United States Lawn Tennis Association (USLTA). College athletes turned tennis players, such as four-time champion Bob Wreen, enjoyed lavish parties and bathed at Newport's fashionable Bailey's Beach. The game was increasing in speed, expanding in the number and styles of players, and attracting public interest. In 1892 a portable grandstand replaced chairs around the court's edge at Newport.

After World War I, the emergence of Maurice "Mac" McLoughlin, a Californian whose father worked at the government mint, marked the movement of tennis toward a more popular and fast-paced game. He introduced his cannonball serve and overhead return to the Newport leisure class, which was equally shocked by his proletarian parentage. As the game evolved, the championship site moved to Long Island's Forest Hills, with a grandstand built around clubhouse courts to accommodate 15,000 people. During this time, the American Tennis Association was formed, as were separate singles championships for black players. Much like those in the Negro Baseball League, African-American tennis champions such as Reginald Weir and Althea Gibson were never able to test their talents and skills against white stars.

Clearly, tennis was a game of style and convention. The 1928 book *Tennis* (Wills, 1928) devoted two chapters to dress and etiquette. The book admonished that "[t]o play in any other color [than white] is a great mistake in the eyes of one who knows tennis.... In tennis it isn't to be done" (p. 137). Etiquette, too, remained traditional. Player etiquette included allowing the foreign player to enter the court first and ignoring bad calls; audience etiquette included no applause except at the end of rallies, no questioning the umpire, and "no remarks about players since their family or relatives may be in the audience" (p. 154). Such were the shared understandings of a sport played almost exclusively by and for the well-to-do—understandings shaped by those who created and controlled its conventions. But serious conflict loomed, fueled by struggles over power and control much like those so evident during the 1970s in the United States.

Transition and Transformation

The 1970s were a time of modernist conflict. The war in Vietnam continued as Nixon's "incursion" into Cambodia sparked campus violence. International tensions continued in the Middle East as Arab countries invaded Israel on Yom Kippur and quadrupled oil prices in a 12-month period. The century of Pax Americana continued with coup d'etats backed by the Central Intelligence Agency (CIA) as the ancestral remnants of Pax Britannica imposed direct rule on Northern Ireland. It was a world divided: the cold war certainties of communism and capitalism, the economic disparities of North and South, and the philosophical differences of East and West. It was a geopolitical chess game of détente, Strategic Arms Limitation Talks (SALT) and mutually assured destruction (MAD), the fall of the Shah and Somoza, the "China card," and Olympic tragedy, protest, and boycott.

Nationally, the Supreme Court adjudicated but did not resolve the abortion conflict while violence erupted over forced busing. Such troubles appeared in TV sitcoms including the top-ranked *All in the Family,* in which an embattled Archie lived with his intellectual "meathead" son-in-law near the upwardly mobile Jeffersons, as well as in real life when motorists fought at neighborhood gas stations over a few gallons of fuel.

The decade witnessed the building of infrastructures on both the Left and the Right. In response to the energy crisis came groups such as New Hampshire's Clamshell Alliance and David Rockefeller's Trilateral Commission. In response to the feminist movement Congress passed the Equal Rights Amendment, activating groups such as the Concerned Women for America and the Eagle Forum. In response to the crisis of faith in politics came liberation theology and the Moral Majority. In response to voter apathy and alienation arose the Citizens Party, the American Party, and the Committee for the Survival of a Free Congress. It was the time of Earth Day and May Day, of DDT and SST, of public interest research groups and voter referenda, of MIRVs and MXs.

Often characterized as the "me decade," the previous, existential 1960s turned into the pragmatic (some say narcissistic) 1970s. This was a transitional era wherein many activists turned inward and liberationists turned outward, an era of self-obsession and self-reliance marked by the collapse of idealism and the resurgence of cynicism: Club 54 and The Farm, Zen centers and food co-ops, *How to Be Your Own Best Friend* and *Greening of America,* Altamont and Farm Aid, pet rocks and preppy alligators.

It was a time, too, of transformation: from Karl W. to John Paul II, from *Good Housekeeping* to *Ms.* magazine, from activists Tom Hayden and Angela Davis to Representative Hayden and Professor Davis, from Big

Blue to *Small Is Beautiful,* from the Beatles to Queen, from the Gulf of Tonkin Resolution to the War Powers Act, from the death of John Wayne to the $16 million inauguration ceremony of Ronald Reagan.

The transformation Janet Miller underwent in 1972 also involved crisis, chaos, and change as she set out to reformulate her life.

> When I separated from Phil in 1972 I moved to Rochester, New York. I substitute taught for a year but it was probably the worst year of my life. I was just devastated not to have my own classes, my own students—not to mention my own home.
>
> My friend Kay and I had gone to Columbia University for six weeks in the summer of 1967 and taken two literature courses, plus I had another graduate course from SUNY Potsdam. I knew that I'd have to finish my master's if I wanted to be on my own as a teacher, because in New York you have to get a master's within five years to acquire permanent credentials.

Driven by the economic need to complete her master's degree in order to continue teaching, Janet enrolled in the English education program at the University of Rochester. William Pinar was assigned as her academic adviser. She recalls:

> In January, 1973, I began taking classes. In my first class, everyone was an English teacher of one sort or another. That's where I met Madeline Grumet, who was just starting her master's also, and we became friends. The class was taught by this very mysterious 24-year-old (I was 27 at the time) who had us reading things by Louise Rosenblatt and others in English education as well as works by R. D. Lang and Maxine Greene. His name was Bill Pinar, and his was a totally new world to me. I had no idea about any educational components of my studies in English, no real background in education per se. I was an English major, but this was a master's in English *education.* Bill was having us read things by people I had never heard of before and a lot of the teachers in that class kept saying, "What's he talking about?" I was sort of amazed and intrigued.
>
> I remember one novel I read in one of my master's English classes, Kate Chopin's *The Awakening.* It's set in the 1800s and really considered one of the first feminist novels around because it's about a woman's awakening to her own sense of being and really is a fairly stringent critique of patriarchy. I read that novel and thought gosh, this feels like me. During my master's work at Rochester I was also exposed to ideas about curriculum and teaching that I had never thought about before, such as structures of power relations, or the sort of psychoanalytic tack that Bill was heavily into in terms of how we construct our realities of classrooms. Well, shoot, you know, I hadn't had any idea about *any* of this.

After she earned her master's degree, Janet took a full-time job teaching English at Honeoye High School in southern Rochester. However, within a month she realized that she was too interested in these new ideas to continue teaching high school. With the help of Pinar, Janet decided to head to Ohio State University for doctoral study with Don Bateman in English and Paul Klohr in curriculum theory—Pinar's own doctoral mentors. As Janet recalls:

> Once I got to Ohio State, it started to become a little clearer to me what I was embarking on. Don Bateman and Paul Klohr were wonderful people to have as mentors. In 1974, Don was at the height of his radical period, so we were reading people like Paulo Freire. I actually taught a class with him as part of my teaching assistantship. And Paul's brilliant mentoring in curriculum studies changed my life.
>
> At the time, you were pretty free to construct your own doctoral program, so I was lucky enough to be able to sit down with Don and Paul and work out a program that let me take courses in both areas as well as meet the university requirements. We were reading all over the place in a very interdisciplinary kind of way. It opened me up to the understanding that curriculum is not just about this traditional conceptualization but also about interdisciplinary understanding of how knowledge gets constructed in the world. It was just an unbelievable sort of immersion. . . . And I was free to create my own direction.

A Field in Search of Meaning

Like Alex Molnar, Janet Miller began doctoral studies during a period of uncertainty within the curriculum world and accompanied by an outstanding thinker (in Janet's case, Paul Klohr, and in Alex's case, Jim Macdonald). Curriculum theorizing came to prominence in the 1970s in a way that had not been seen for many decades. We are referring here to theorizing that leaned heavily on such schools of thought as European critical and neo-Marxist thinking, depth psychology, phenomenology, literature, and existential philosophy rather than the standard areas of developmental (and, more recently, humanistic and cognitive) psychology from which the curriculum field had previously borrowed.

Question

These terms are umbrella characterizations of profound ideas about the human condition. What books or individuals would you associate with these ideas? How can they affect our understanding of curriculum?

For example, Paulo Freire's *Pedagogy of the Oppressed* (1970; 1972) became a major impetus for resuscitating "critical" reconstructionist developments in the field, as did further development of Jackson's (1968) notion of the hidden curriculum (e.g., Overly's *The Unstudied Curriculum* and Snyder's *The Hidden Curriculum,* both published in 1970).

The flurry of social reconstructionist curriculum work popularized in the 1930s and 1940s by Counts, Rugg, and others had been almost singularly kept alive into the early 1960s by Theodore Brameld. Overall, however, mainstream curriculum work had developed an "apolitical blindspot" (Pinar & Bowers, 1992, p. 187) that would be corrected through political curriculum scholarship of the 1970s. One early proponent (though he eventually abandoned this perspective) was James B. Macdonald.

Macdonald is credited with, among other contributions, foreshadowing "the move to reconceptualize the field" in his 1971 article titled "Curriculum Theory." Moreover, his own career "spans what we might tentatively call the four theoretical movements of the field: scientific thinking, personal humanism, sociopolitical humanism, and transcendental thought" (Pinar et al., 1995, pp. 217, 218). After working with Virgil Herrick at the University of Wisconsin-Madison (as did Huebner), Macdonald held four positions before his University of Wisconsin-Milwaukee professorship. At the time of Macdonald's death in 1983, he held a distinguished professorship in education at the University of North Carolina-Greensboro. As a preface to Macdonald's work titled "A Transcendental Developmental Ideology of Education," an excerpt of which appears in this chapter, Alex Molnar talks about his doctoral advisor.

> Although he was not one of the principal people involved in bringing us to Milwaukee, I got to know Jim because he was then director of doctoral studies. I had no consciousness of something called a curriculum field when I arrived at UWM and I'd never heard of Jim Macdonald.
>
> I took a curriculum theory course from him the first semester. Because I came there with a ton of credits as well as a master's and a specialist's degree, the bulk of my doctorate ended up being independent work. And I did a lot of that with Jim. One day I said, "I just assumed you were going to be my major professor." And he said, "Yeah, I assumed I would be, too." I said, "Yeah, okay." And that was pretty much it.
>
> Descriptions of Jim Macdonald will differ depending on who you ask. As a doctoral advisor he once told me that you should only work with people you love, and that your job was to get things out of their way so that they can do what they want to do, because you have faith in them and believe that if you got stuff out of their way they would never let you down. So I would not call him a directive kind of a guy. He had high standards. He wrote a lot. He expected a lot. But he just allowed me to produce a lot; he didn't demand anything. Jim didn't produce disciples. He did what he said he'd do: he ran interference.

> One of the other doctoral students who Jim advised, Bob Ubbelohde, had been in the doctoral program at Madison and moved to Milwaukee expressly for the purpose of working with Jim Macdonald. And Bob was in the curriculum field because he had *chosen* the curriculum field! Jim and I and Bob spent a lot of time together discussing issues and lots and lots of things we were reading. But I can't really say that any of it had any particular attachment to something that in a technical sense might be called curriculum. In that regard I don't think Jim provided me with a very solid foundation in curriculum history or any other field.

During his doctoral program (1970–1972), Alex recognized Macdonald as an intellectual, not a curriculum theorist per se, and learned about Macdonald's various curriculum journeys "retrospectively, in dribs and drabs." As Alex puts it:

> I never felt as though I was some new generation of curriculum scholar, and I didn't care one way or another. I had little consciousness, for example, of the ideas being promoted by Joseph Schwab in '69 and '70 regarding the moribund curriculum field. I mean, I read some things and people quoted Schwab a lot. But I wasn't terribly interested in it.
>
> Jim never really discussed *himself* within that situation either: and he *participated* in it! In our curriculum theory classes we didn't get any kind of didactic exposition of the field and what he was trying to do within it. Instead, he just had us attempting to theorize. And while we read some of the papers he was writing at the time, there was no historical context in terms of what he had written, where he had come from and so on. They were just what Jim Macdonald was thinking, and to the extent we talked about those things, that's what we talked about.
>
> I've always been what I wanted to be; Jim encouraged that. And I don't think it was necessary for Jim Macdonald to be a professor in something called curriculum because for Jim, curriculum—or any intellectual discipline—was really only a device for extending your intellect. I don't really think that Jim would have ever called himself a curriculum person in the sense most people define a curriculum person. Jim Macdonald was a curriculum person because he made curriculum be what he was interested in studying; or perhaps he made what he was interested in studying be curriculum.

James Macdonald was on a life journey during the 1970s, continuing to explore his interests. In the following excerpt from his 1973 Rochester curriculum conference presentation (Macdonald, 1974), he explores his thinking regarding the importance of moving beyond the sociopolitical humanism (political ideology) of his earlier times toward a place that is best described as transcendental.

PRIMARY DOCUMENT EXCERPT

A Transcendental Developmental Ideology of Education

by James B. Macdonald

The title of this chapter was prompted by the Kohlberg and Mayer article entitled "Development as the Aim of Education."[3] They talk about three ideologies: romantic, developmental, and cultural transmission. It is clear to me that there are at least two other potential ideologies that I am calling radical and transcendental developmental.... It is my contention that the radical and transcendental ideologies are the most potentially useful in the modern world....

The romantic ideology ... is fundamentally concerned with human nature and the unfolding or maturation of the individual. Knowledge in this ideology is said to be existential or phenomenological, and it refers directly to the inner experience of the self. Truth is self-knowledge and extends to others by sympathetic understanding of other selves. The ethical theory of the romantic is based upon the freedom of the individual to be himself, assuming that individuals, when free, are essentially good unless society makes them otherwise.

The cultural transmission ideology is grounded in behaviorist psychology. Essentially the individual is shaped by his environmental experiences in terms of the associations and stimulus-response sets he encounters and acquires. Knowledge is the outer reality, the "objective" world, that can be found in sense experience and culturally shared. Value theory is either an ethically neutral stance or a social relativism that accepts the present cultural values for which there would appear to be consensus.

Between these two, in the sense that it is neither a model of inner experience or outer experience but a dialectic between inner and outer, lies developmental ideology. The transaction itself creates reality which is neither an inner nor an outer phenomenon, but something else. Dewey's method of intelligence and the cognitive-developmental work of Piaget with its concern for inner structures and outer structures encountered in interaction are the psychological models for this ideology. Knowledge is equated with a resolved relationship between inner experience and outer reality. Truth is pragmatic in that it depends upon its relationship to the situation in which we find ourselves. Values are based upon ethical universals derived philosophically, and they serve as developmental means and ends. Thus rational ethical principles, not the actual values of the child or the culture, serve as arbiters for defining aims.

---

[3]Lawrence Kohlberg and Rochelle Mayer, "Development as the Aim of Education," *Harvard Educational Review* 42, No. 4 (November 1972), 449–96.

Analysis of these ideologies suggests … the inner and outer aspects of ideology and the dominant directions of the critical flow of the human encounter. Thus, the romantic conception is mainly from inner to outer, the cultural transmission from outer to inner, and the developmental is dialectical.

Kohlberg and Mayer assume that the radical position is equivalent to the romantic, or at least they use these terms interchangeably at times. This I believe to be in error.…The political radical is committed to a dialectical model, as is the developmental. However, as the work of Paulo Freire[4] shows, it had a fundamentally different interpretation of the dialectic.

The developmental and radical models look identical only on the surface, for the radical model is weighted on the side of social realities.…The progressive position assumed that democracy was the ideal social reality and continued its analysis of the interaction process with that assumption in mind. The radical model, on the other hand, is essentially based upon an analysis of why democratic ideas are not realized, thus emphasizing environmental structures.…

The radical point of view takes off from the essential proposition that the critical element in human life is the way people live together. It further posits that the way people live together is determined essentially by the structure of our economic arrangements, the ownership of means of production, and the distribution of goods and services through the possession of power.…

At this level of analysis, radical ideology claims that liberal developmental ideology and romantic ideology are embedded in the present system. That is, the emphasis upon the individual and his unfolding or developing necessitates an acceptance of the social structures as status quo in order to identify in any empirical manner the development of the individual. Thus, developmental theory is culture and society bound, and it is bound to the kind of a system that structures human relationships in hierarchical dominance and submission patterns and alienates the person from his own activity in work and from other people. Given the level of analysis of the radical, the individual cannot fully develop out of the very conditions that are central to the improvement of human life. Only when new social conditions arise will we be able to begin to empirically identify and talk about human development in the new social context.…

My problem with the radical or political view of curriculum is not its level of analysis or the questions it asks, per se; instead, it is the feeling I have that it is also one step behind the world. Thus, I feel that, as McLuhan once said, we are traveling down a superhighway at faster and faster speeds looking out the rearview mirror. Kohlberg and Mayer's three ideologies are "over the hill," so to speak, but the political view is in the mirror. It does provide us with some idea of how straight the road is ahead.…What we need is some way to look beyond, if only a few feet.

---

[4]Paulo Freire, *Pedagogy of the Oppressed* (New York: Herder and Herder, 1970), p. 186.

The radical view of education in its political manifestations does provide us with a historical analysis—as well as with concepts for analyzing contemporary phenomena. Yet I find this historical view limiting in its materialistic focus, and I suspect that it is grounded fundamentally in the Industrial Revolution and reflects the same linear rationality and conceptualizing that characterizes the rise of science and technology. It is a "social science" of human relations and a "science" of history. Like all history, this is a special reading of the past that helped make sense out of the nineteenth-century present. The world today is not the same, and a different reading of history is needed to help make sense of our contemporary world.

The radical-political perspective as a base for curriculum thinking does not adequately allow for the tacit dimension of culture: it is a hierarchical view that has outlived its usefulness both in terms of the emerging structure of the environment and of the psyches of people today. *I propose that the structure of the world environment today must be approached through the existence of a nuclear, electronic-computerized, multimedia technology rather than the more linear, single-media machine world.* [emphasis added] . . .

I believe we have entered a new hierarchical level with our electronic world. This passage may have seemed gradual, but its impact has essentially been to produce a difference in kind (instead of in degree) in the condition of human existence. The institutionalization of nuclear and electronic technology . . . is an operating pattern, a cultural milieu that has never existed before.

The sense of powerlessness and impotence we feel is not a sign of alienation in the traditional Marxian sense. It is a true reflection of the state of human beings. . . . No longer are we dominated by the owners of the tools of work; they are also dominated by the need for survival and power sources.

We have in effect created our first man-made gods in material form. . . . Now all people must serve the technical "gods" in some nonthreatening way in order to insure social and perhaps personal survival. Political action and political analysis of the human condition is now too limited a perspective with which to view our conditions of existence. . . . Precisely because radicals have been so busy pushing and tugging at the means of production and distribution, they do not see that they share the same technological world view—what liberals love, radicals hate, and both are equally possessed by technology. . . .

Curriculum thinking should be grounded in cultural realities. . . . In my own developmental speculation I see the present and future technological domination of man as a step in the road toward human evolution. . . . Technology, in other words, is a necessary development for human beings in that it is the means of externalizing the potential that lies within. Humanity will eventually transcend technology by turning inward, the only viable alternative that allows a human being to continue to experience oneself in the world as a creative and vital element. Out of this will come the rediscovery of human potential. . . .

A Transcendental Developmental Ideology

A transcendental ideology seems to be necessary because I find the source of value positions to be inadequate in the other four. . . . In other words, I find all four ideologies unclear in their ontological and phenomenological grounding. . . .

My position is best approached through the concept of a dual dialectical process. A dialectic exists not only between the individual and his environment but also within the individual himself. . . . [The outer dialectic deals with] the explicit knowledge systems of the individual and the situational context within which he acts. This represents a position similar to that held by radical ideologists, as far as it goes. Thus, I would agree that human activity is in part created by the reflective transaction of human consciousness in situational contexts. . . .

It is clear, however, that within the limits of [this dialectic] there can be no access to values or ethical principles that do not arise out of a utilitarian reflection upon the objective historical or personal consequences of human activity. Without positing a method of reflective intelligence based upon an analysis of the consequences of human activity, there could be no assessment of "good" other than a bare survival adjustment to reality, much in the manner of most other animals.

Utilitarianism as a source of values is, however, a relatively unsatisfactory position. It does not allow or account for phenomena in human experience that have been readily apparent to persons throughout history and in contemporary society. Central to this discontent is the cognitive orientation of reflection as the method of intelligence and the only source of analysis for human activity. Thus, an a priori valuing of rationality is necessary in utilitarianism. Where does it come from?

That this gives only a partial account of human beings is indicated by the second [inner] dialectic, between the explicit awareness of the individual and the nonexplicit nature of the individual. The self, in other words, is composed of both conscious awareness and unconscious data at any given time.

Values, I believe, are articulated in the lives of people by the dual dialectic of reflecting upon the consequence of an action and sounding the depths of our inner selves. Only a process something like this can explain why "what works is not always good." Some dual dialectic is also needed to explain the existence of reason, or aesthetic rationality, to counterbalance purely technological rationality. . . .

The inner dialectic of the self is a critical element if we are to advance the position that culture is in any way created by human beings. The possibility of value may well be limited in alternatives by the individual-biological-social dialectic, but the validation of values would seem to demand some source other than explicit and rational knowledge. . . .

Components of Epistemology

The epistemological components of a transcendental ideology are grounded in the concept of personal knowledge. Thus, knowledge is not simply things and relationships that are real in the outer world and waiting to be discovered, but it is a process of personalizing the outer world through the inner potential of the human being as it interacts with outer reality.

At this level I am ... referring to the idea that the created culture of human life is a common set of personal constructs. Personal in the sense that all cognitive constructs are grounded in individual personal meaning and that our shared culture, as well as language usages, serves as a pragmatic survival device. This outer necessity does not change the fundamental nature of knowledge....

An epistemology must further come to grips with the so-called hard knowledge of our culture. It seems doubtful if any knowledge is "harder" than modern physics, and it is instructive to note epistemological implications found in the knowledge of modern physical science....

As Sir James Jeans[5] said, "Today there is a wide measure of agreement ... that the stream of knowledge is heading toward a non-mechanical reality; the universe begins to look more like a great thought than like a great machine." ...

An epistemology that does not recognize tacit knowledge components, or the fantastic possibilities and implications of our most advanced fields of inquiry, is simply weighted down with the baggage of philosophical and materialistic biases. How, what, and why are far more open questions than we are often led to believe, and the possibilities of accessibility to knowledge from "hidden" inner sources operating on acausal, or integrative, or serial and synchronistic bases point directly toward the awareness of another ground of knowledge in human being.

Centering as the Aim of Education

The aim of education should be a centering of the person in the world....

Centering does not mean mental health.... Further, centering does not mean self-actualization, for that process ... is filled with assumptions about personality development that seem arbitrary and somewhat closed to me....

The idea of centering may be found in a wide variety of sources throughout history and the contemporary world. It is essentially what William James called a religious experience.... It is a human experience facilitated in many ways by a religious attitude when this attitude encompasses the search to find our inner being or to complete one's awareness of wholeness and meaning as a person....

---

[5]Sir James Jeans, *The Mysterious Universe* (Cambridge, England: Cambridge University Press, 1937), p. 172.

Spiritual energy does not shape the explicit knowledge of the person in absolute or noncultural ways. Centering takes place within the culture of the individual, and the process of centering utilizes the data of an individual's culture, what he explicitly knows through social praxis. . . .

Centering as the aim of education calls for the completion of the person or the creation of meaning that utilizes all the potential given to each person. It in no way conflicts with the accumulated knowledge of a culture; it merely places this knowledge in the base or ground from which it grows. As such, centering is the fundamental process of human being that makes sense out of our perceptions and cognitions of reality. . . .

The Processes in Curriculum

Centering is the aim of a transcendental ideology. As such, it is a process one enters into. Thus, the question of the objectives of a transcendental curriculum must be seen in process terms also. But processes . . . refer to the engagement of the individual in human activity, which facilitates the process of centering.

. . . There are a number of possible processes that would facilitate centering.

Pattern making. This critical process reflects itself in the need to transform reality symbolically, to create order in search of meaning, and it is fundamental for locating oneself in time and space and for providing cognitive awareness that may facilitate centering. . . . Thus, pattern making would emphasize the creative and personal ordering of cultural data as the individual engaged in activity.

Playing. The attitude and activity of play is a critical aspect of the pattern-making process. Play in this sense refers to playing with ideas, things, and other people. . . . Thus, the process of "playing" would seem to be necessary to facilitate pattern making and to provide for self-regulation of activity.

Meditative thinking. "Why" is the fundamental thought question for a transcendental ideology, why in the sense of examining the fundamental meaning of things. . . . Rather than fostering the activity of thought in a functional, utilitarian way, a problem-solving process, we must foster what Martin Heidegger[6] called a "releasement toward things" and an "openness to the mystery." Thus, nothing can be accepted simply on its own terms in its social utility. Rather, we must encourage the young to say both yes and no to culture and probe the ground from which our culture arises, through meditative thinking.

Imagining. Another way of approaching pattern making, play, and meditative thinking comes through the activity of . . . imagining as a process in contrast to verbalizing. Our verbal culture and language culture and language forms, as useful and necessary as they are, have also become the dominant form of thinking and expressing ourselves. . . . Imagining, on the contrary, provides an internal

---

[6]Martin Heidegger, *Discourse on Thinking,* Harper Torchbook (New York: Harper and Row, 1966), p. 93.

referent for the external world. ... Thus, imagination as the ability to picture in the mind what is not present to the senses is a perceptual power that involves the whole person, that puts him in contact with the ground of his being.

The aesthetic principle. It is clear that the guidance of much of the arrangement of physical facilities, interpersonal relations, and individual expression must come from what Herbert Read[7] called the aesthetic principle. Read called the guidance of human education by the aesthetic principle the natural form of education ... [which] should move from feeling to drama, sensation to visual and plastic design, intuition to dance and music, and thought to craft. Then, from the play of children emerging from their feelings, sensations, intuitions, and thinking, the individual could gradually grow toward cultural art forms guided by the aesthetic principle. Thus, the activities of dramatization, designing, dancing, playing music, and making or crafting are important in a transcendent ideology.

The body and our biology. Physical education, Alan Watts[8] has said, is "the fundamental discipline of life" ... [i.e.,] coming to grips with our own biological being and all that it means. ... Although we rarely admit to a mind-body separation on a philosophical level, it is clear by the way we educate the young that we do not consider the biological aspects of the person to be relevant to the real business of education. Thus, the emphasis upon cognitive-verbal learning not only separates us from our inner resources but it divorces us from our biological organism. To be at home in our bodies is critical for human centering, and it would seem to me that far more attention should be paid to this phenomenon.

The education of perception. ... I refer to perception in the sense of William James's many other worlds of consciousness that exist aside from our present one, rather than in the sense of a functional psychological mechanism. ... I am sure that the creation of altered states of consciousness is a human potential that is important to the process of centering.

Question

How might these processes look different when intended to facilitate centering as compared to when intended to enhance learning?

The Teacher in the Process

The developmental ideology of Dewey, Piaget, and others ... perceives the teacher to be a person who comes to know the students but who also makes judgments about the long-range implications of experiences on the development of the children. ...

---

[7]Herbert Read, *Education through Art* (London: Faber and Faber, 1958), p. 308.
[8]Alan Watts, *In My Own Way* (New York: Pantheon Books, 1972).

The teacher from a transcendental point of view is also in process. That is, the developmental aim of centering is as valid and important to the person of the teacher as it is to the child. . . . Thus, the relationships between students and teachers are mutually responsive to the aim of centering.

The key distinction between these two developmental ideologies is the fundamental difference between knowing and understanding. In a secular or psychological developmental ideology . . . the predominant rationality of the teacher is still a technical process of planning, manipulating, and calculating, even though the intentions and relationships are, for example, more humane, perhaps, than those found in cultural transmission ideology. A transcendental ideology would shift the predominant rationality toward the aesthetic, intuitive, and spontaneous in the mutual process of centering.

. . . Teachers cannot be said to understand children simply because they possess a considerable amount of explicit knowledge about them. Understanding is a deeper concept. It demands a sort of indwelling in the other, a touching of the sources of the other. . . . Understanding provides the ground for relating, for being fully there in the presence and as a presence to the other, for what Huebner called a continuance of the joint pilgrimage. . . .

This is the process of locating one's center in relation to the other: to "see" one's self and the other in relation to our centers of being; to touch and be touched by another in terms of something fundamental to our shared existence. . . .

Implicit understanding is to poetry as explicit knowledge is to science. The explicitness of science is in contrast to the unity and expressiveness of poetry. Science "adds up"; poetry integrates. . . . When we make a poem of the other in ourselves, we do not trap either in categories and classes. When we understand each other, we create a shared poem of our existence. Understanding is the crystallization of our aesthetic knowing; explicit knowledge is its rational handmaiden. To know a child is to describe his characteristics; to understand him is to be able to write a poem that captures his essence.

The teacher in such a process is, therefore, engaged in the art of living. The task of both student and teacher is the development of their own centering through contact with culture and society, bringing as much of their whole selves as they can to bear upon the process. . . . It is primarily a willingness to "let go" and to immerse oneself in the process of living with others in a creative and spontaneous manner, having faith in ourselves, others, and the culture we exist in as a medium for developing our own centering.

From William Pinar: *Heightened Consciousness, Cultural Revolution, and Curriculum Theory.* Copyright 1974 by McCutchan Publishing Corporation, Berkeley, California 94702. Permission granted by the publisher.

▬ Letting Go of the Past

In so many respects, Janet Miller's life seemed in synch with Macdonald's ideas regarding "the art of living" through a process of "centering." It was, for Janet, a time to let go.

> I remember in 1974 listening and reading and thinking about things that had happened to me personally; finding myself totally and abruptly removed from any life I had ever known heretofore and being really scared yet totally excited about it. Having no idea what any of it meant and no idea of what anything would mean in the future, yet unable to turn back. I remember thinking well, I don't know what the hell I'm doing, but I can't go back. It was just like it erupted in me—the intertwining ideas of what I was reading about, what was happening to me and what I was feeling really coincided. Feminism by then had moved into the arena of literature studies, and I got a lot of strength and energy from my academic work realizing that others were out there exploring these ideas and perceptions around women, women in society, women in education. But I never had one course that focused on women in any way. Instead, I was taking courses like philosophy, literature, and film theory plus talking with Bill, Madeline and Maxine Greene. These were the very beginnings of my exorcism.
>
> I was at Ohio State during an absolutely golden time, with fellow students like Craig Kridel, Bob Bullough, Jack Holton, Leigh Charliotte, and George Dixon. While there, I developed a better sense of curriculum studies because of all the courses I had with Paul Klohr. Because we studied with Klohr we had a background in history of curriculum. And of course, the curriculum conferences were happening then, too.

Women's lives and work have remained fundamental to Janet's curriculum efforts since her days as a doctoral student. The early 1970s were an important time, as well, for the larger ongoing struggle to understand, articulate, and change the gendered status quo—a struggle known then as the women's movement. Yet despite exuberant 1960s activism among women, minorities, and the poor, the 1970s warranted few reasons for celebration. In 1940 only one-quarter of adult women held jobs; 30 years later that figure had doubled. During that same period the ratio of the female-to-male pay range actually declined from 63 to 57% with white women earning 54 cents on the Euro-male dollar. As youngsters returned to school following their summer recess in 1970, two of every three African-American children went to a school with a student population that was 95% black. Although fewer than one in seven black children attended segregated schools in the South, more than three-fourths attended such schools in northern cities. By 1980, the proportion of whites in these northern urban schools had declined significantly.

The 1970s were a decade of economic recessions, though this burden was not shared by all. When Carter assumed the presidency fewer than

1 in 10 whites lived below the poverty line compared with nearly one-quarter of Hispanics and one-third of blacks. But the burden of poverty was mostly shouldered by women and children. Two-thirds of poor black families were absent a father, and the proportion of all nonwhite families headed by women increased in the 1970s from one in five to one in three (a proportion that would rise to two in five by 1980). Even among the rising middle and upper-middle class, black economic gains paled in comparison with those of whites. Combining 100 of the top-grossing black-owned businesses would form only a midrange corporation on the Fortune 500; by 1975, year-end corporate profits for white-owned businesses had increased 25-fold over profits generated by black-owned enterprises.

Voter apathy was also deepening and widening. The percentage of nonvoters rose from 18% in 1964 to 42% in 1972. By 1974, with a disgraced American president, voter turnout for the congressional elections was the lowest since World War II—38%. Nationwide, trust and respect for physicians, lawyers, and educators slipped to record lows as money got tight, nothing seemed right, and the "good old days" slipped away.

VARIED TALE

TENNIS: AT THE CROSSROADS

Back in those "good old days," however, issues of race, class, gender, money, and control lay at the heart of the controversy that engulfed the sport of tennis. The roaring 1920s produced the first tennis superstar, "Big Bill" Tilden. As the number-one-ranked player throughout the decade, he not only appeared in plays and films but also wrote tennis books and newspaper articles—all for a fee. Tilden—the first "bad boy" of tennis—pushed the issue of his amateur status like he did the game's own etiquette.

Traveling the circuit of a half dozen or so championships as an amateur tennis player brought fame and social prominence but not money. This mostly wealthy group of tennis players made the latter as unseemly as it was unnecessary. But as the game transformed from a leisure activity into a full-time sport, money increased in importance.

In 1926, sports entrepreneur C. C. Pyle irrevocably changed tennis by forming the first professional tour. Players who "turned pro," like Tilden, easily enticed amateur greats such as Suzanne Lenglen and Vincent Edwards into their ranks. Originally viewed as a leisurely activity pursued by persons of status and wealth, the tennis professional had arrived while the use of club facilities for professional matches or mixed professional-amateur exhibitions (known as opens) remained forbidden by the USLTA. In 1937, the Greenbrier Golf and Tennis Club violated this position by holding the first U.S. Open tennis championships. All amateur participants were subsequently suspended. By the late 1950s, the loss of outstanding amateur talent had nearly devastated the ability of the USLTA to build, attract, and retain top players and large audiences. It also handicapped American efforts to regain the Davis Cup and resulted in the rise of the "shamateur" (amateurs who received complimentary rackets, clothing, and often inflated travel expenses).

The 30-year debate between amateur and professional status reached a peak in the late 1960s when major tennis countries such as the United States, Britain, and France supported open tournaments only to find their will blocked through a United Nations-like structure composed of the smaller federation countries (led by tennis giant Australia), which feared the impact of such competition. At an impasse, England challenged the International Lawn Tennis Federation (ILTF) by declaring the 1968 Wimbledon Tournament an "open championship." Blocking the tournament, the ILTF committee suspended the British Lawn Tennis Association, seriously jeopardizing the Davis Cup, the federation, and the entire sport.

Tennis was at a crossroads. When it became clear in 1968 that leading amateur players planned to participate at Wimbledon, other countries—most noticeably Australia—joined in support. Accepting the inevitable, the ILTF voted unanimously to hold open tournaments, saving face only in its refusal to end the amateur-professional distinction.

Revisioning Curriculum History

Knowing the history of tennis allows us to appreciate the numerous struggles and forces that have helped to shape the game as we know it today. The same can be said, of course, of the curriculum field, whose own history would come to a crossroads a few years later.

Pursuit of history proved to be another distinguishing characteristic of the curriculum field during this period. Tyack's *The One Best System* (1974) appeared as historians Herb Kliebard (1970) and Larry Cuban were busy exploring curriculum history for the National Institute of Education's Curriculum Development Task Force, commissioned in 1975 (see Pinar et al., 1995, pp. 207–208). And Dwayne Huebner continued his call for "a need to examine curriculum historically, with the present situation very much linked to both the past and the future, . . . a view the majority of curricularists found eccentric at best" (Pinar et al., 1995, p. 213).

What seems to have awakened most interested curriculum workers, however, was the sharp, "revisionist" turn in educational history, as exemplified in *Class, Bureaucracy, and Schools* (M. B. Katz, 1971), *The Great School Legend* (Greer, 1972), *Education and the Rise of the Corporate State* (Spring, 1972), *Roots of Crisis* (Karier, Violas, & Spring, 1973), *Education and Social Control* (Sharp & Green, 1975), and *Schooling in Capitalist America* (Bowles & Gintis, 1976). In essence, these "new histories" of American schooling raised troubling questions about the complicity of curriculum workers in helping to create and sustain problematic situations.

During this decade we also begin to see collections of individuals' work (e.g., L. W. Anderson & Macdonald, 1975; Foshay, 1975); ASCD's yearbook celebrating America's bicentennial, *Perspectives on Curriculum Development, 1776–1976* (O. L. Davis, 1976); Louise Tyler's *A Selected Guide to Curriculum Literature: An Annotated Bibliography* (1970); and the reprinting of a 1948 book titled *Bibliographical Essays on Curriculum and Instruction* (Brickman, 1974/1976). The American curriculum field had discovered a growing interest in its history.

In 1977, Laurel Tanner gathered a group of people (including Wells Foshay, Arno Bellack, Lawrence Cremin, Ralph Tyler, Gordon Mackenzie, and O. L. Davis Jr.) at Teachers College to discuss the importance of historical study within the curriculum field. This small group eventually formed the Society for the Study of Curriculum History (SSCH), which had its first official meeting in Toronto in 1978.

Another small cadre welcoming this new emphasis on historical understanding was a newly formed special interest group (SIG) within the AERA called "The Creation and Utilization of Curriculum Knowledge." Begun in 1973 with 45 members, the SIG welcomed and promoted the exploration of new ways of thinking about curriculum. Indeed, this group welcomed a young doctoral graduate named Schubert, whose early historical and bibliographic research later became the basis of *Curriculum Books: The First Eighty Years* (Schubert, 1980). In time, the SIG grew to more than 300 members and changed its name to "Critical Issues in Curriculum" (see Short, Willis, & Schubert, 1985). Yet in its earlier and smaller days, this SIG, along with the SSCH, provided welcome spaces of encouragement for the historical study of curriculum work—despite Schwab's criticism that a sure sign of a dying field was its retreat to the past.

▣ The Hassles of History Making

The early 1970s converged an interest in U.S. curriculum history with the intensification of seemingly offbeat ideas and constructs within the field as well as an influx of international scholarly work[9] in a way that seriously

---

[9]We remind the reader that ours is a story focused on American curriculum work. This is a difficult and arbitrary focus that, as our tale continues, becomes unnatural and difficult to maintain. During the 1970s, for example, European political and cultural perspectives significantly impacted U.S. curriculum theorizing. One of the most influential publications in this respect was Michael F. D. Young's *Knowledge and Control: New Directions for the Sociology of Education* (1971). Numerous European

disrupted the status quo of mainstream American curriculum work. At the same time, the radical caucus within ASCD and the AERA SIG worked to collectively personalize the lives and work of like-minded curriculum workers like never before.

ASCD's major upheavals during its 1969 and 1970 conferences (see Pinar et al., 1995, pp. 209–210) had politicized a significant number of curriculum workers, including James Macdonald. For several years, many of these members (among them Steve Mann and Alex Molnar) functioned within what was called the radical caucus. Yet despite the organization's long-standing "efforts to bring together professors of curriculum, school district curriculum supervisors, school administrators, and teachers" (Pinar et al., 1995, p. 208), ASCD would shrink in importance to curriculum scholars by the decade's end.

Most important, 1973 marked the year when Bill Pinar (at the University of Rochester) hosted the first in a contentious series of non-mainstream curriculum theory conferences. Similar to the 1968 Wimbledon tournament in relation to tennis, the 1973 Rochester gathering would become the first sanctioned event in the rebirth of curriculum studies.

---

authors found their educational ideas available within the United States via England's Open University Press and the eminent publishing house of Routledge & Kegan Paul. As a whole, our international curriculum colleagues pushed U.S. curriculum workers in the direction of theoretical inquiry at an important moment in our history.

At the same time, U.S. curriculum workers reciprocated. Alice Miel, for example, sought an international focus as she and Louise Berman published *In the Minds of Men: Educating the Young People of the World* (1970; see also Razik, 1972). Later, both would promote the World Council for Curriculum and Instruction. This internationalization of curriculum studies can be seen throughout our field, too, in the teacher-as-researcher work explored by Foshay, Miel, Corey, and others at Teachers College, popularized by Britain's Lawrence Stenhouse (1975), and since refined and advanced by the work of Canadians D. Jean Clandinin and F. Michael Connelly (1992).

Joseph Schwab's work was pivotal in internationalizing curriculum study. For example, in 1975 Decker Walker (who studied with Eisner) published a book with Britain's William Reid called *Case Studies in Curriculum Change* that connected curriculum deliberation with policy decision making. Reid later published *Thinking about the Curriculum: The Nature and Treatment of Curriculum Problems* (1978), which expanded Schwab's notion of deliberation. And Ian Westbury and Neil Wilkof produced a collection of Schwab's work in 1978 called *Science, Curriculum, and Liberal Education.*

And although curriculum-specific journals had their beginnings in the 1960s, they truly came of age in the 1970s thanks to international efforts. For example, the largely informal publication known as "Curriculum Theory Network" became *Curriculum Inquiry*—an international journal under the leadership of F. Michael Connelly, who had studied with Schwab at the University of Chicago. And the *Journal of Curriculum Studies,* edited by Philip H. Taylor, who was later joined by William Reid and Ian Westbury (who was also influenced by Schwab while at the University of Chicago), came to prominence in England.

VARIED TALE

TENNIS: FULL-CIRCLE TRANSFORMATIONS

For the game of tennis, 1968 at Wimbledon marked the first sanctioned meeting between amateur and professional players. Tournament play surprised many, as top-ranked amateurs such as Arthur Ashe often beat professional foes. By 1969, even recalcitrant Australia found attendance booming and public interest soaring. Inevitably, big money followed.

With tennis reborn as an open sport, prize money skyrocketed. By 1978, American Jimmy Connors collected $175,000 for his Wimbledon victory—in sharp contrast to the Wimbledon umpires, who received a princely sum of $50 per match. The size of the purse was often dwarfed in comparison with income from commercial endorsements, business franchises, and tournament "guarantees" for big-name players even before they stepped onto the court. One-half of Billie Jean King's 1972 income of $200,000, for example, came from endorsements.

But the revitalized sport of tennis only grudgingly included a larger role for women (for whom the game was ostensibly invented), coinciding with greater involvement of girls in high school sports (the number of girls involved more than doubled between 1971 and 1973). Here, Billie Jean King's leadership was pivotal:

> Tennis was one of the few major spectator sports where men and women had traditionally competed together, although . . . in different events. . . . As tennis staggered toward professionalism, however, it became pretty clear that it was a sport controlled by men who were unwilling to even think about giving women a fair shake. . . . The disparity with prize money started right with that first open. . . . In the United States the ratio was 4 to 1, sometimes 5 to 1. . . . At some tournaments . . . [women] didn't get a cent unless we reached the quarter finals. . . . And since promoters were now putting all the money they used to give us under the table into the prize-money pot . . . we were worse off than we'd been in the good old shamateur days. (King, 1974, pp. 100–101)

King ultimately formed the Women's Tennis Association, organized the Virginia Slims circuit in 1971, battled and beat Bobby Riggs, began a women's sports magazine, and garnered headlines equal to those of Australian Rod Laver and American Arthur Ashe.

Ashe's 1970s activism also helped to change the game. When open tennis arrived, Ashe observed the loss of "cooperation and camaraderie" among players who scrambled for the pots of money now available and who viewed the "concept of values and standards . . . [as] quaint and obsolete, like wooden racquets" (Ashe & Rampersad, 1993, p. 66). As a leader and eventually president of the newly formed Association of Tennis Professionals, Ashe (like King) found the ILTF and the Big Four (the tennis governing bodies of America, France, Australia, and Britain) pursuing a "reactionary strategy ... impeding us at almost every turn ..., [resisting] change in defense of privilege and a stuffy conception of the tradition" (Ashe & Rampersad, 1993, p. 66).

By the end of the decade, the game had changed in other ways. There were more than 2,500 clubs in the United States, and the number of tennis tournaments multiplied as well-equipped stadiums holding tens of thousands of paying spectators replaced stodgy country clubs with small, self-centered crowds. Tennis, animated by public interest, television coverage, and megacorporate sponsorships, had been transformed from an amateur sport among the well-heeled aristocracy to a professional career opportunity open to a more diverse collection of players. Notably, tennis has come full circle from a game *for* the rich to a game *of* the rich.

Assisting the Blossoming of Contemporary Curriculum Studies

Like Wimbledon and the U.S. Open for tennis, annual performance gatherings play a key role in the life of every profession. Until the 1970s, ASCD's annual conference was *the* place for curriculum people. And while that venue surrendered its importance by the decade's end to the annual AERA meeting, curriculum's "misfits" had begun their own small gatherings in 1973. These meetings, held at different locations until 1979, had an effect on curriculum work similar to that of the opening up of tennis: turmoil.

Alex Molnar and Janet Miller each played a role in the revitalization of the curriculum field during this time and helped organize these curriculum theory conferences. Each has a different perspective on those particular events, as the following exchange suggests. Alex begins:

> **Alex:**   Jim Macdonald never asked me to go to an AERA meeting, though he was active. However, he did buy me a plane ticket to the ASCD convention in St. Louis in 1971 or 1972. A lot of the people associated with the radical caucus of ASCD felt very close to Jim and that's how I got to know Steve Mann. Afterwards, I really got involved in the radical caucus at a time when it was becoming more of a presence in the organization.
>
> In May, 1973, they had a curriculum theory conference in Rochester. I didn't even know it took place until afterwards: Macdonald never told me. In fact, I never knew about the second one of these off-shoot conferences at Xavier University except for my work with Steve (see Mann & Molnar, 1975).

I didn't regard many of these folks as serious people. I was sort of dismissive of their work, particularly since I was very well informed about humanistic psychology. When I looked at some of this stuff I said, "This is curriculum? Not in my book. This is just an excuse for trotting out your own internal dialogue and calling it curriculum."

At the same time, I was having considerable difficulty respecting the academic community or regarding myself as an academic. I mean, coming from where I had in my life and the way I got through school, I had a sort of arrogant idea about academics. I tended to regard them as sort of privileged poodles yapping around about nothing terribly important and establishing academic careers which were in some existential sense not very important at all, while the world was going to hell in a handbasket. So I was having a great deal of difficulty reconciling my own membership in something called the academic community. I had some serious doubts about whether or not I was, in fact, making myself absurd.

I did attend the 1975 conference at the University of Virginia. I remember I roomed with Jim, though I can't really remember why I was there. Maybe it was just to spend some time with Jim? Ours was really a kind of father/son relationship. I mean, I don't want to make too much of this, but it was more complete than this sort of intellectual fathering or mothering that goes on. I knew that some people saw him as a kind of guru, but I don't think he cared much for that. Anyway, I can remember being on the University of Virginia campus and sharing a room with Jim and all that, but I don't remember very much about the 1975 curriculum conference.

Janet Miller recalls these earliest conferences in rather stark contrast to Alex's perspective.

Janet: I was a master's student at Rochester for the 1973 conference and a doctoral student at Ohio State the next year for the University of Cincinnati conference. During those first two curriculum conferences I had no idea what was going on, other than I heard presentations by people who I had started to read. The most predominant among them for me was Maxine, although I was also drawn to Dwayne Huebner and Jim Macdonald. At Rochester, where I first heard Bateman and Klohr speak, I remember taking notebooks full of notes and then going home and thinking I have no idea what all of this means. But, I was always able to talk to Bill [Pinar] about it and that was incredibly instructive in terms of helping to situate each person's perspective within a larger history, helping to see connections.

When the conference moved to Virginia (1975), I remember giving a paper there and feeling for the first time like a part of something that was happening. There seemed to be a huge number of graduate students there from Rochester, Ohio State, and other places. I remember Chuck Beegle [the conference organizer] had a big party afterwards, and people were excited because they thought something important was really happening—though nobody could name it. I don't think anybody was naming it as such, although the word reconceptualist had by then been used in a 1971 article by Jim Macdonald. That entire Macdonald era was very influential to me.

By the end of the Virginia conference plans had already been made regarding who would organize the next one [it would be Alex Molnar]. So every year I began to feel a little more like I understood the conferences in relation to the curriculum field and then later, JCT's [Journal of Curriculum Theorizing] relationship to the field; how this work differed from the mainstream field; and why it was important to provide a means for the type of work that was emerging. But it took me a while to understand why it was all important.

For Alex, none of what he'd seen at Virginia seemed of much importance. He continues:

Alex: Many of the ways in which curriculum was being talked about at the 1975 Virginia conference seemed silly, so I volunteered to organize a conference for the following year that in my view represented a somewhat more serious approach to the work of trying to think through what curriculum was and what was important about it. And I did just that. I sat down and said, "Well okay, what do I want to talk about here?" Then I just invited people: a different point of view with regards to the humanities represented by Elliot Eisner; a phenomenological perspective in psychology—that's Bernice Wolfson; a kind of hermeneutic analysis represented by Dwayne Huebner; historical artifacts in the form of Ralph Tyler; Jim Macdonald and several others. Those were the key presenters, though we had lots of sectionals. It was a political event within the field—that's why I did it.

Look, I'm a combative kind of guy and I have my values. So while I certainly was aware of Bill Pinar's work and this whole coterie of people associated with what was loosely called reconceptualism, I was dismissive of it on a number of different levels. The 1976 conference would not be ahistorical and would have a solid set of ideas that you could sink your teeth into, along with some experimental elements done within a context. At the conclusion of the (1976) Milwaukee conference I felt that I had accomplished what I set out to accomplish and figured that was it; my job was done.

The following year (1977) I went to the curriculum conference at Kent State, but that was my last one. I quit paying attention after Kent because the subsequent conferences weren't interesting enough to me. They didn't seem important enough. I heard something about the journal, JCT, afterward, but stuff like that was sort of unextraordinary to me at the time because I was doing other things.

Published collections of the papers from these early conferences have become requisite historical readings in contemporary curriculum history. After the initial conference in Rochester, Pinar published *Heightened Consciousness, Cultural Revolution, and Curriculum Theory* (1974), followed by his 1975 collection titled *Curriculum Theorizing: The Reconceptualists* (1975). Some of the major papers from Alex's 1976 Milwaukee conference appeared as *Curriculum Theory* in 1977 (edited by Molnar and Zahorik and published by ASCD).

The 1973 founding conference thematically mapped the various projects of the reconceptualization as political, historical, and autobiographical. However,

> While the Rochester conference conveyed a sense of the intersections of these projects, indeed a sense of the fundamental interconnectedness of these theoretical interests, subsequent conferences revealed antagonisms not evident in May, 1973. . . . The basic division occurred between . . . [those interested in] macro-structural issues and [those] more interested in the individual. (Pinar et al., 1995, p. 223)

This division coincided with places of graduate study (University of Wisconsin-Madison and Teachers College versus Ohio State University and the University of Rochester, respectively) in that the affiliation of each year's conference organizer "reveals this institutional as well as thematic aspects of this division within the movement" (Pinar et al., 1995, p. 223). Thus, we can more readily see Molnar's frustration with the early conferences when we note that following Pinar's (an Ohio State graduate) hosting of the inaugural 1973 conference was Tim Riordan's (another Ohio State alum) 1974 event at Xavier University. The 1975 gathering at the University of Virginia was put together by Charles Beegle, another Ohio State graduate.

Molnar, though a University of Wisconsin-Milwaukee graduate himself, had deep ties to both Jim Macdonald (a Madison alum) and Steve Mann (another Madison graduate and Marxist scholar). The Kent State meeting in 1977 was organized by Richard Hawthorne (UW-Madison) and, like the Milwaukee gathering, seemed heavily populated by the "political" or "structural" contingent of contemporary curriculum thought.

The conference returned to Rochester in 1978 and was held at the Rochester Institute of Technology and organized by Ronald Padgham (an alum of the University of Rochester). By this time, troublesome rifts had developed between numerous curriculum theorists over the nature, control, and direction of this overall theorizing effort. Coincidentally, *JCT* began publication that year with Janet Miller and Bill Pinar as editors. Concerned with the potentially disabling power struggles over conference location and ideological direction, Miller and Pinar—through the auspices of *JCT*—took over the sponsorship and organization of this increasingly popular event, moving it to the Airlie House (in Virginia, near Washington, D.C.) from 1979 through 1982, then to the Bergamo Conference Center outside of Dayton, Ohio, from 1983 through 1993. Janet offers her impressions of why events played out the way they did at the time:

> The tensions were very apparent in 1978. People like Jim Macdonald had been talking about differing viewpoints or differing ideologies and

theoretical frames within which people were working, suggesting that we seek some position of collective agreement. All of us were against the major technical paradigm; what we shared was the interest of knowing that no matter what particular vantage point you spoke from it was still important to get all of these contrary ideas out there and to try and do it in a collective way so that there would be some momentum; so that these ideas just wouldn't get eaten up either by each other or by the larger forces of the dominant paradigm.

Although Jim Macdonald had tremendous influence on everybody, there was never any overt agreement amongst the various players from these differing ideologies. And others refused to even be identified with the reconceptualist effort in curriculum studies: people like Maxine Greene, Mike Apple and Elliot Eisner.

In terms of the journal and the conferences after 1978, the whole idea was let's just keep going and see what happens. And if people want to be there and want to participate, there's room there to do so. A lot of it still became turf and ego wars among some of the main players. I don't think that ever went away.

Little by little, year after year, new turf was identified and old turf re-fashioned by curriculum workers. Individuals and small groups that had grown to sizable collections of irreverent curricularists met yearly on their own and within the AERA SIG they populated and managed to publish collections of their work as they struggled to alter the parameters of what was "appropriate" curriculum scholarship. Whether ready to accept a collective label ("the reconceptualists") or not, they were fashioning the renaissance from within the field. In time, the dominant curriculum paradigm would be defaced from within.

Despite the various egotistical and ideological spats that splintered their collective strength, Pinar was asked to represent them and their "reconceptualist movement" by delivering the very first "state-of-the-art" address to the curriculum division of AERA in 1978. John McNeil was selected to represent the field's mainstream, and Maxine Greene served as respondent. Pinar et al. (1995, pp. 230–238) present a detailed description of what transpired afterward. As they note: "As long as the movement to reconceive the field appeared marginalized in conferences attended mostly by those committed to the movement, the threat to the traditional field seemed to be contained." Following this prestigious major address, however, "the situation for traditionalists became critical and intolerable" (p. 231). We will pick up the story from the perspective of one of the actual participants in this significant, open struggle for control of the field during the late 1970s and into the 1980s—Henry Giroux—in chapter 7. Suffice it to say that the many different inquiries and forms of work we take for granted within the contemporary curriculum field did not come about without some ugly wrangling.

▼ isitor Bibliography   Janet L. Miller

Ayers, W. C., & Miller, J. L. (Eds.) (1998). *A light in dark times: Maxine Greene and the unfinished conversation.* New York: Teachers College Press.

Miller, J. L. (1990). *Creating spaces and finding voices: Teachers collaborating for empowerment.* Albany: State University of New York Press.

Miller, J. L. (1998). Autobiography as a queer curriculum practice. In W. F. Pinar (Ed.), *Queer theory in education* (pp. 365–373). Mahwah, NJ: Lawrence Erlbaum Publishers.

Miller, J. L. (1998a). Biography, education, and questions of the private voice. In C. Kridel (Ed.), *Writing educational biography: Explorations in qualitative research* (pp. 225–234). New York: Garland Publishing, Inc.

Miller, J. L. (1998b). Autobiography and the necessary incompleteness of teachers' stories. In W. C. Ayers and J. L. Miller (Eds.), *A light in dark times: Maxine Greene and the unfinished conversation* (pp. 145–154). New York: Teachers College Press.

Miller, J. L. (1999). Curriculum reconceptualized: A personal and partial history. In W. F. Pinar (Ed.), *Contemporary curriculum discourses: Twenty years of JCT* (pp. 498–508). New York: Peter Lang Publishers.

Miller, J. L. (1999). Putting cultural studies to use: "Translating the curriculum." *Journal of Curriculum Studies, 31* (1), 107–110.

Miller, J. L. (2000). English education in-the-making. *English Education, 33*(1) 34–50.

Miller, J. L. (2000). What's left in the field . . . . A curriculum memoir. *Journal of Curriculum Studies, 32* (2), 253–266.

Miller, J. L. (2005). *Sounds of silence breaking: Women, autobiography, curriculum. (complicated conversations). Collected essays on feminist curriculum theorizing.* New York: Peter Lang.

▼ isitor Bibliography   Alex Molnar

Arizona State University at Tempe, Education Policy Studies Lab. Eric Document Reproduction Service No. ED483415.

Molnar, A. (Ed.). (1985). *Current thought on curriculum.* Alexandria, VA: Association for Supervision and Curriculum Development.

Molnar, A. (1996). *Giving kids the business: The commercialization of America's schools.* Boulder, CO: Westview Press.

Molnar, A. (Ed.). (1997). The construction of children's character. *96th Yearbook of the National Society for the Study of Education (pt. 2).* Chicago: University of Chicago Press.

Molnar, A. (2004). *Virtually everywhere: Marketing to children in America's schools.* The Seventh Annual Report on Schoolhouse Commercialism Trends, 2003–2004.

Molnar, A., & Lindquist, B. (1989). *Changing problem behavior in schools.* San Francisco: Jossey-Bass.

Molnar, A., & Reaves, J. A. (2002, Fall). The growth of schoolhouse commercialism and the assault on educative experience. *Journal of Curriculum and Supervision, 18*(1), 17–55.

CHAPTER 7

From Chorus to Cacophony: Paradigms and Perspectives

William Pinar's 1978 address to the curriculum studies division of AERA debuted a revisionist curriculum juggernaut. American curriculum workers exploring new ideas, perspectives, and paradigms were moving the Tyler rationale off center stage; the renaissance of curriculum studies had come of age. Among the rogues' gallery of curriculum "discontents" who bore credit for this coup was Elliot W. Eisner.

Eisner, who has never felt comfortable being recognized as a contributor to the reconceptualization of contemporary curriculum work, became active in the field during the late 1960s. With a doctorate in curriculum studies from the University of Chicago and a formal background in art, some of his earliest work expressed a critical view of the potential of technology and behavioral objectives to minimize the expressive role of the teacher. He is equally recognized for his work in the area of evaluation and qualitative inquiry.

Eisner's conceptual work revolves around ideas of classroom experience, aesthetic cognition, expressive objectives, enactment, and multiple forms of knowing. In addition to the concept of *null curriculum,* he is perhaps best known for introducing into curriculum discourse his ideas of educational connoisseurship and criticism. First published in 1979, *The Educational Imagination,* now in its third edition (1994), introduced aesthetic theorizing and aspects of functional curriculum making within a historical framework.

We begin this chapter with a substantive excerpt from *The Educational Imagination: On the Design and Evaluation of School Programs*. In his opening chapter, Eisner presents his understanding of the current (late 1970s) field of curriculum in three parts: present, past, and future. What follows is his 1979 image of the future of curriculum studies.

PRIMARY DOCUMENT EXCERPT

Where We Are Going*

by Elliot W. Eisner

The position that Tyler advocated regarding curriculum planning is in many ways a far more liberal and far less mechanistic position than the views espoused by those who made their curriculum mark during the 1960s. From the 1960s to the present [1979], this nation has seen the emergence of individuals, trained not in the curriculum field but rather in psychology, developing both curriculum materials and ideas about curriculum planning that have had considerable impact in the field of education. . . . For each of these individuals, the essential characteristic of curriculum and instruction is that it be a planned, sequential series of steps that leads to ends that are known in advance and that are realized with a minimum of pedagogical efficiency. Mager's monograph on instructional objectives . . . succeeds in reducing educational aspirations into test items, even when they lose what might be educationally significant in the translation.

Popham [1969] follows this [technical] tradition, . . . [focusing] on how one should form objectives—and if one cannot or does not want to create them, one can purchase them from the Instructional Objective Exchange that Popham has established in Los Angeles. For Glaser [1963], one of the central problems of teaching and curriculum planning is that of finding or creating the correct sequence of tasks for a student; again, systematics that yield predictable forms of student behavior is the desired end in view.

Perhaps the ultimate position that this line of thinking has led to is found in Bereiter's [1972] argument that schools are misguided in their attempts to educate students. The role of the schools, according to Bereiter, is to . . . provide training; they should not attempt to influence the values or visions that students hold. That, according to Bereiter, is for the family. . . .

The problems with Bereiter's views in this regard are abundantly clear.

Question

A generation later, however, this is precisely the argument made by secular and religious conservatives. What, then, is the appeal of this view and its benefits for educators who embrace it?

What is perhaps not so clear are the consequences that views such as these have not only for the field of curriculum, but for education and educational research in the United States.

Consider the influence these views have had on educational research. To do research has come to mean to do scientific inquiry, and to do such scientific inquiry in education has meant to do inquiry in which variables are identified, measured, and analyzed statistically. The desired image of the educational researcher is that of a scientist who as far as possible emulates his colleagues in the natural sciences. To engage in other forms of inquiry, to do historical or critical analysis of existing educational or social problems, to engage in philosophic inquiry, is not to do research. To pursue such activities is to write, as they say, "think pieces," a phrase that is curiously pejorative. To count is somehow better, perhaps, because counting or measuring . . . provides the illusion of precision. . . .

The consequences of the scientific view for education as a field and for curriculum as a part of that field emerge not only within the conception and conduct of educational research, but also within the methods that people believe appropriate for educational evaluation. Because evaluation methods are largely the offspring of the educational research community as it is presently defined, this is not surprising. But surprising or not, I believe that these practices have had deleterious consequences for the curricula that are provided to children in American schools. One of these consequences is to reduce the term *evaluation* to *measurement*. . . . When this occurs, the fields that are most amenable to measurement are measured and those that are difficult to measure are neglected. What is measured then is emphasized in school programs because measurement becomes the procedure through which educational quality is determined.

For the curriculum of the school this means that evaluation practices . . . influence to a very large degree the kinds of programs that will be offered to the young. Educational practices based on a scientific model too often become not a tool for improving the quality of teaching and learning but rather an impediment to such ends. . . .

The consequences of scientifically based approaches to educational evaluation extend beyond the issue of what subject matters should be emphasized. In many schools they influence how curricula will be organized and how teaching will occur. If one conceives of the curriculum as a kind of assembly line that produces at predictable intervals a certain complex of behaviors, then it appears reasonable to specify those behaviors and to set up the mechanism through which they can be measured. . . . When combined with a reward structure to care for problems of student motivation and a set of minimum standards to ensure the public of good-quality education, we have a complete system—at least in theory—for the management and control of school programs. What happens is what Lewis Mumford [1934] described in the 1930s: The technology we design to expand our freedom and flexibility becomes our constraint. . . .

What is truly sad is that those of us in the field of education ... have so seldom tried to help the public understand the complexities of education as a process. ...

All in all, when one looks back on the consequences the behavioristic, positivistic, scientific tradition has had on education in general and the curriculum field in particular, the following seem to me to be important.

First, the dominance of a scientific epistemology in education has all but excluded any other view of the way in which inquiry in education can legitimately be pursued. ...

Second, the kind of science that has dominated educational research has ... been preoccupied with control. ... The offshoot of this view has been to regard educational practice, including curriculum development, as a technology that uses knowledge provided by the social sciences as the primary basis for its management and control. ... In the field of curriculum this has found its apotheosis in the aspiration to create teacherproof curriculum materials. In teaching it has manifested itself in the belief in the diagnostic-prescriptive model. In school evaluation it has showed up in an input-output model of productivity. Seldom have the basic assumptions underlying such beliefs been subject to the kind of critical scrutiny they deserve.

Third, a consequence of these assumptions has been the preoccupation with standardized outcomes. The testing movement that has grown out of the field of educational psychology depends on assumptions that required a uniform set of test items and a uniform set of methods of test administration to measure educational achievement. Indeed, until quite recently, the major function of tests was to differentiate student from student on a common scale. ... Such practices, built into the technology of test construction, undermined any educational inclination to cultivate the student's positive idiosyncrasies or to use forms of assessment that were different for different students. ...

Fourth, under such assumptions, little or no role can be given to the pupil for participating in the creation of his or her educational program because the provision of such opportunities would make the system difficult to control, hard for educators to manage, and complex to evaluate. ... The result of such assumptions in educational practice is to regard the pupil as an essentially passive material to be molded by the impact of the treatment. ...

Fifth, the consequences for curriculum of the interest in control measurement have been to break up complex tasks into small, almost microunits of behavior and in the process to render much of the curriculum meaningless to children. If one is primarily interested in control and measured outcome, the best way to do it is to disallow the adventitious, to focus attention on highly discrete and highly defined tasks, and to assess after each task in order to determine whether the objectives of the tasks have been achieved. ... The aspiration is for an errorless program. ... The tacit image is that of an assembly line.

Finally, one is struck by the sober, humorless quality of so much of the writing in the field of curriculum and in educational research. The tendency toward what is believed to be scientific language has resulted in an emotionally eviscerated form of expression; any sense of the poetic or the passionate must be excised. Instead, the aspiration is to be value neutral and technical. . . . Cool, dispassionate objectivity has resulted in sterile, mechanistic language devoid of the playfulness and artistry that are so essential to teaching and learning.

Now the reason for the paucity of scientifically based educational practice is not that teachers are ignorant or recalcitrant or unwilling to use what's new and effective, but that there is little that conventional forms of educational research have to offer educational practitioners. At the very minimum, as Dewey himself said, scientific conclusions have to be artfully interpreted and applied to particular educational situations, even if we grant that there is something to apply. What I think is beginning to occur is that more and more of the really bright, courageous students of education are beginning to look elsewhere to find ways of dealing with the problems of practice. The line of former educational scientists that are engaged in this search is growing longer. Donald Campbell, Lee Cronbach, Gene Glass, Philip Jackson, Lou Smith, and Robert Stake are a few. . . . There are others within the curriculum field itself who have long held this view: Mike Apple, Mike Atkin, Herbert Kliebard, Steve Mann, Jim Macdonald, Joseph Schwab, Decker Walker, and myself. In Europe people like Torstein Harbo in Norway, Ulf Lundgren in Sweden, Lawrence Stenhouse and Barry Moore in England, and Hartmut von Hentig in Germany, represent individuals whose views of curriculum, teaching, and evaluation are considerably more complex than can be encompassed by a simple means-ends model of educational practice.

Now the significance of this discontent is the promise it provides for the development of new ways of conceptualizing educational problems, formulating educational questions, and pursuing educational aims [emphasis added]. What we badly need are models that are heuristic and useful, ways of talking about educational problems that are clear but not stilted. We need to avoid the pitfall that so many progressives fell into, both in the 1930s and in the 1960s: namely, the tendency toward romantic obscurantism, the infatuation with vague rhetoric that has little intellectual rigor. . . . What I believe we need are approaches to the study of educational problems that give full range to the varieties of rationality of which humans are capable, that are not limited to one set of assumptions about how we come to know, that use methods outside of *as well as* inside the social sciences to describe, to interpret, and to evaluate what occurs in schools. Orthodoxy often creates blinders to new possibilities, and I believe the field of education has worn such blinders for too long.

I believe that we need evaluation methods that exploit the variety of expressive forms through which we understand and make public what we know. . . . We need evaluation methods that give students the opportunity to use, for example, artistic forms of expression as intellectually legitimate and that cease penalizing students whose aptitudes and interests motivate them to work in such areas. Evaluation methods should be instrumental to the ends we seek; they should not, as so many of them do now, impede the realization of such ends.

I believe we need theory that unapologetically recognizes the artistry of teaching and that is useful in helping teachers develop those arts. The model of the teacher as a scientist who first hypothesizes before he or she acts may fit some aspects of teaching but certainly does not fit all of teaching. . . .

I believe we need to be willing to recognize the interaction between the character of the curriculum and the kind of teaching that occurs, and the ways in which the school is organized and how the reward structure of the school is employed. For too long we have operated as though decisions about school organization were one thing and decisions about curriculum were something else. All of us who work in schools, whether elementary schools or universities, work and live within a culture. This culture functions as an organic entity that seeks stability yet reacts to changes in one part from changes made in others. We need to try to understand these interactions if we seek intelligently to bring about significant change in schools. . . .

Finally, I believe we need to develop methods that will help us understand the kinds of experience children have in school and not only the kind of behavior they display. The behavioristic-positivistic tradition in American educational research tended to regard experience as unknowable and focused therefore on what children did. . . . As students of the hidden curriculum have told us, students learn more than they are taught and teachers teach more than they know. Attention only to what the school explicitly teaches or to what students do may be misinformative with respect to what they are learning and experiencing.

To deal with the newfound appreciation of experience will require methods that differ markedly from those of behavioristic psychology. . . . The precedent for such inquiry already exists and is found largely in the work of continental philosophers. I believe its potential utility for the study of educational phenomena is quite promising.

Also promising is the tradition of ideographic inquiry and the analysis of the practical in education. The fertile but unplowed field of art criticism is also available to us. Art criticism, in particular, has much to offer to help us understand the arts of teaching and the qualities of the particular situations in which curriculum decisions must ultimately be made and applied. . . .

What I believe we are seeing is the emergence of new models, new paradigms, new sets of assumptions that are finding increasing acceptance in the professional educational community. Whether the salient model will turn out to be a literary form of ethnography, the legal adversary model of evidence, or the model of art criticism is not yet clear. I believe the field has more than ample room for these three models and for scientific models, as well. For what I believe the study of education needs is not a new orthodoxy but rather a variety of new assumptions and methods that will help us appreciate the richness of educational practice, that will be useful for revealing the subtleties of its consequences for all to see....

Among growing numbers of his curriculum peers, Eisner was about the work of creating new bases for a revitalized field of curriculum studies. As Eisner, Pinar, Greene, and others questioned educators' confidence in the old scientific paradigm of curriculum construction, the richness of educational practice and the subtleties of its consequences became more apparent.

Decline in the confidence of conventional curriculum thinking and practice bottomed out in the late 1970s, as did the decline in our national confidence. President Carter's "national malaise" speech of 1979 articulated our collective disquietude. During the second half of his presidency, Carter presided over a nation under siege, from the takeover of the Iranian embassy with its 444-day-by-day countdown on nightly television to an assassination attempt on the chief of Allied Forces in Europe and the successful assassination of the U.S. ambassador to Afghanistan. Despite successes with the Camp David Accords and Salt II, the Carter presidency was also under domestic siege by Ted Kennedy's electoral challenge, a recalcitrant Democratic Congress, and a significant tilt toward the political right.

From the ashes of the 1970s slowly arose the Phoenix of political conservatism to dominate well into the next century, effectively challenging progressive assumptions about the role of the state in social and economic progress as well as individual and collective rights and responsibilities. The conservative onslaught of the 1980s began in earnest in 1979 with the defeat of liberal Canadian Prime Minister Pierre Trudeau and the election in England of Prime Minister Margaret Thatcher. A year later Americans voiced a resounding "no" to his question "Are you better off now than you were four years ago?" and elected Ronald Reagan—whose campaign proclaimed "It's morning in America!"

By 1983, the neoconservative revolution was evident to all: the publication of *A Nation at Risk* decrying poor test scores equated to a declining share of the global market, the scientific designation of acquired immunodeficiency syndrome (AIDS) propelling abstinence-based curricula and diminishing support for gay rights, and the dedication of the Vietnam War Memorial inscribing the names of 58,000 on a black granite wall guarded by infantrymen.

The early 1980s also brought a balkanization of peoples. Boundary disputes and the resurrection of old border controversies characterized the last quarter of the twentieth century much as it did the first quarter: the emigration of 120,000 "undesirable" Cuban refugees or a flood of Mexican refugees over America's 1,000-mile "unprotected" border; disputes between Iran and Iraq or the United Kingdom and Argentina; the crossing of Pope John Paul II over the communist border or the refusal of 50 nations to journey to Moscow for the 22nd Winter Olympic Games; religious wars of intolerance in Lebanon, Northern Ireland, or the United States—where Jerry Falwell, Richard Vigerie, James Dobson, and Pat Robertson declared "cultural war" on American others.

In American popular culture, the 1970s legacy of political cynicism and corporate weariness was no match for the feel-good era of the 1980s American family led by Ronald and Nancy Reagan. The shrillness of leftist critique and liberal angst fell against ears deafened by the conservative sirens of optimism and nostalgia, visible in contrasting movies and plays of this time: *Norma Rae* and *Coal Miner's Daughter, Missing* and *E.T.*

Divisions also became more evident along economic borders. The language of the early 1980s (e.g., *yuppie, beamer, thirty-something, dink*) and variegated consumers in the marketplace (e.g., Sharper Image versus Radio Shack and L.L. Bean versus JC Penney) marked the economic disparities arising within a generation. During a span of 20 years, for example, the proportion of mothers with children five years of age or younger working full- or part-time doubled to 47%, the proportion of heads of households between the ages of 18 and 24 who owned their home dropped by one-third, and the percentage of pretax income needed for mortgage payments on a median-priced home doubled. Meanwhile, the median American family income dropped 10% and unemployment rose to its highest level since 1941. These were trying times for the working and middle classes.

Henry Giroux

VISITOR Historically, most educators come from working- and middle-class families. This was the case with Henry A. Giroux, who currently holds the Waterbury Chair in Secondary Education at Pennsylvania State University. Recognized as one of the current field's earliest spokespeople to develop a contemporary critical or political perspective, he spent a number of years negotiating economic and intellectual borders to arrive at that curricular position. In his words:[1]

> I grew up in a working class neighborhood in Providence, Rhode Island.
> I came from a small family: just myself, my sister and my parents.
> My parents never owned a house. I went to Catholic schools for about seven

---

[1] Personal communication, 22 March, 1995.

years before my neighborhood was taken over under the right of Public Domain and the entire community was dispersed. We ended up living on the third floor of a three family house in a new neighborhood, and I found myself moving to a public school in that neighborhood during the 7th grade. It was a very difficult transition for me, particularly since the neighborhood was a very tough place. That's when I got involved playing basketball as a way to negotiate the neighborhood and to in some way establish my own identity outside of the traditional options of either gang violence or doing dope.

Henry, who attended Hope High School, remembers little about his academic experiences beyond "a sense of being trapped" as a working-class kid at the lower end of a tracking system designed to maintain social distinctions. His basketball playing earned him a college scholarship, and though he was the first in his family to go to college, he dropped out "before the basketball season even started in 1961." After working for two years, he again began college. He continues:

I got a scholarship to a place I didn't know anything about, actually. Gorham State [now the University of Southern Maine] was a liberal arts normal school mostly educating teachers. Actually, I began as a biology major [but eventually] switched and became a history major.

During my junior year my interest in secondary education really peaked. This was in 1966, and we were imbued with taking up a social field that smacked of giving something to others. There was a real deep sense of the ethical relevance of your job. Careerism wasn't the primary motivation. Teaching was seen as a vocation; it was really about what kind of contribution you could make to public life. I thought teaching sounded like a good profession; working with kids is something I can live with. I was very lucky to grow up in that decade because it had a profound effect upon my politics.

I graduated from Gorham State in 1967 certified as a high school teacher, but I immediately went on to get a master's in history at Appalachian State. The anti-war movement in this country was really quite strong then, and I had gotten caught up with a group known as Democratic Socialist Organizing Committee (DSOC) and had been involved in some SDS work prior to that. Well, I had heard that there were chapters all over the country and that a Gorham professor—a history professor—who was in SDS was going to Appalachian State. I didn't know him personally, but I knew he was involved in the anti-war movement. So I applied there, they gave me a scholarship, and I went.

Being at Appalachian State was a profoundly moving experience for me. I became a Teaching Assistant for a guy who was very political, and that was really my first introduction to a kind of discourse which I had to grapple with. I mean, this guy was raising questions that I simply had no answers to. I had no sense that questions could come from a place like that. I mean, he was raising questions that were extraordinary to me. That year proved to be a political education of the absolute first order.

Giroux's political understanding of curriculum would later flourish against the backdrop of conservatism and nationalism. It was during this era that the "unusual" curriculum work begun earlier by Huebner, Macdonald, Berman, and the like seemed most apparent and relevant to a new generation of curriculum thinkers. In fact, by 1979 the political tradition introduced during the field's early years had become elemental:

> The notion was clear that defensible conceptions of curriculum needed to grow from a complex context . . . [and] a broader base of knowledge derived from several disciplines and from practical settings. To this end three categories of literature emerged that: (1) discussed curriculum implications of the changing and pluralistic culture; (2) continued the trend of foundational studies in education by embracing curricular dimensions of them; and (3) exposed and analyzed influences of political and ideological factors on curriculum thought and practice. (Schubert, 1980, pp. 262–263)

These were the years when the various traditions in curriculum studies were joined by and sometimes combined with new disciplines to produce the numerous discourses and texts that have become part of contemporary curriculum work (see Pinar et al., 1995).

Multidimensional and *eclectic* are apt descriptors for the curriculum books published between 1979 and 1983, evident in the most significant contributions of 1979: Eisner's *The Educational Imagination* (third edition, 1994), Goodlad's *Curriculum Inquiry: The Study of Curriculum Practice,* and Apple's *Ideology and Curriculum.* To nobody's surprise, however, conventional texts on curriculum planning, development, management, and theory continued to be good sellers (e.g., English, 1980; Glatthorn, 1980; Hass, 1983; 1987; Oliva, 1982; 1997) as the press for developing curriculum policy and shaping curriculum change in schools rolled on during an era of convention. Moreover, numerous long-standing, standard synoptic texts enjoyed their second (e.g., Tanner & Tanner, 1980; 1995), third (e.g., Trump & Miller, 1979), fourth (e.g., Saylor, Alexander, & Lewis, 1981), fifth (e.g., R. C. Doll, 1982; 1996), and sixth (e.g., Shepherd & Ragan, 1982) editions. Yet change was in the making: shortly after the popular *Models of Teaching* (Joyce & Weil, 1980; 1996) married expert knowledge with the presentation of curriculum content, for example, *Teacher Thinking: A Study of Practical Knowledge* (Elbaz, 1983) would appear, shifting the nature and focus of that discussion.

Curriculum "readers" remained popular, too, as did curriculum books devoted to notions such as change, models, and systems. Two of the more unusual curriculum texts of this period premiered in 1983: Okazu's *The Encyclopedia of Curriculum,* published in Japan, and William van Til's *My Way of Looking at It: An Autobiography,* published by the author.

Okazu's encyclopedia was one of numerous international curriculum publications pouring into the United States between 1979 and 1983. The nature of this work ranged from broad Canadian overviews of curriculum

(Werner, 1979) to Scottish media resources (Gillespie, 1980) and from British attention to school ideology (Barton, Meighan, & Walker, 1980) to curriculum projects in Northern Ireland's postprimary schools (Sutherland, O'Shea, & McCartney, 1983).

As our understanding of curriculum work expanded internationally, so did our awareness of education and schooling as a global (or perhaps multinational) enterprise (Becker, 1979; Berman & Miel, 1983; Hicks & Townley, 1982). This confluence of demands for a workforce to compete in a global economy and the progressive impulse for global education also prompted other conventional curricularists to ponder and speculate (Haas, 1980; Shane & Tabler, 1981). Here capitalism, consumerism, and computerization were joined.

Following publication of the wildly popular book *Mindstorms: Children, Computers, and Powerful Ideas,* educational computing was *the* topic in schools during the early 1980s (Papert, 1980). As Big Blue and an upstart garage-born company, Apple, competed for school space, the number of texts on the curricular and instructional aspects of cyberspace exploded (e.g., Grady & Gawronski, 1983; Kepner, 1982; O'Neil, 1981; Seidel, Anderson, & Hunter, 1982).

The challenging economic conditions of the late 1970s and early 1980s forced more women into the workforce and more families to produce a second income; younger and younger children found their way into the care of others as public schools slowly expanded to include regular kindergarten and even preschool options. Early childhood education as a new service sector in curriculum was under way in earnest.

Federal legislation played a significant role in commodifying other new space for curriculum work, including special, gifted, and multicultural education. Once public education was defined as the least restrictive environment for students with special needs, the special education field grew at a blistering pace in its attempt to situate but not decontextualize its knowledge and economic base. Curriculum texts published between 1979 and 1983 spoke directly to the issue of special needs students in the United States (e.g., Hinson & Hughes, 1981; Radabaugh & Yukish, 1982; Ruxanoff, 1980; Simonson, 1979).

During the early 1980s, popular culture, economics, and politics blurred. For example, bisexual and androgynous pop music images proliferated during the pre-AIDS 1980s. TV fused with music as major recording labels merged with multinational conglomerates and produced megastars: Prince, with his sexually explicit lyrics; Michael Jackson, who coupled romantic lyrics with libidinous dancing; Madonna, who challenged sexual taboos in *Like a Virgin;* and the outrageous campiness of Boy George. Similar images found popularity in movies and plays such as *Tootsie, Victor/Victoria,* and *La Cage aux Folles.* The boundaries, too, between education, entertainment, and business began to erode. Best-selling business books such as *In Search of Excellence* became educational texts, *USA Today* became the country's first stylistically entertaining newspaper, and Channel One became the first nationwide television station to beam news and ads directly into classrooms.

Fact merged with fiction in the 1980s. Television was no longer bounded by the three major networks, computers were no longer restricted to corporations, and the creation of "life" was no longer the exclusive domain of nature. Reagan's Pax Americana mixed easily with top-grossing movies such as *The Empire Strikes Back* and *Raiders of the Lost Ark* and popular televisions shows such as *Morton Downey* and *Family Ties*. On the rebound, it was morning in America, where the stars and stripes fluttered in the breeze of multinational entrepreneurialism, rugged individualism, and nascent nationalism: the invasion of Grenada and the blockade of Nicaragua, the deployment of cruise missiles in Europe and the development of strategic defense capability in the laboratories. A bullish stock market, the successful maiden flight of the U.S. space shuttle *Columbia,* and the victorious U.S. hockey team all shed light in the dawn of the "city on the hill."

In Reagan's America, space—the new Western Frontier of guns and greed—once again captured public attention. From mythic films such as *Blade Runner* and *Star Trek* to the fact-based fiction of James Michener's *Space* or Ron Howard's astronaut film *The Right Stuff,* to the fiction-turned-fact developments of the Hubble Telescope, the first reusable space shuttle, and the orbiting space station, the efforts of NASA again seemed awesome.

VARIED TALE

NASA: THE FALL

The names are familiar: *Sputnik* and *Explorer I,* Gagarin and Glenn, *Apollo II* and *Apollo 16, Columbia* and *Challenger.* Like these icons of space exploration, the history of America's exploration of space is rooted as much in myth as in reality. Beneath the veneer of a monolithic NASA and our nation's space policy lay competing factions and interests whose goals and motivations varied as much as galactic configurations.

President Kennedy's 1961 decision to announce a human lunar landing by the end of that decade brought together corporate, military, educational, political, and scientific interests. His was an inspiring goal and a calculated strategy. With the successes of the Soviet space program and the well-publicized missile launch failures of the United States, technological backwardness and international humiliation gripped the American psyche. These early aerospace failures

(continued)

were, in part, a reflection of the post-Korean War era. The Eisenhower distrust of the military-industrial complex translated into fewer military expenditures and a three-year loss of 143,000 jobs throughout the military-industrial manufacturing sector. The new Kennedy administration appeared equally lackluster about new military projects.

Kennedy sought to jump-start America's space program not only to elevate its image at home and abroad but also to strengthen civilian control over the military and shore up several constituent groups. Fueled by the 1960s faith in science and technology coupled with a systems management approach, Kennedy's program would wrench military control from space endeavors and subordinate the military's view that "space is a place, not a mission" to NASA's orientation of exploration and experimentation.

Within Kennedy's calculation, too, was the importance of the South for the 1964 presidential election and the critical role of key Dixie senators for prospective domestic legislation. Seeking to corral Texas and Florida, Kennedy understood the political power of massive federal outlays in space facilities. By the end of the decade, $146 billion had been spent for research and development, with another $46 billion in direct expenditures—nearly 20% of which landed in a handful of pivotal southern states. Just as the huge influx of military bases had found root in southern soil a generation or two earlier, so this era brought another wave of federal largesse: Huntsville's Marshall Space Flight Center, New Orleans's Michoud's Assembly Facility, Cape Canaveral's Manned Space Center, and Houston's Land Operations Center.

The economic and political benefits of outsourcing contracts for the new space programs were significant. Billions of corporate-directed dollars found their way to a handful of businesses, including North American Aviation, McDonnel Aircraft, General Electric, Boeing, and Grumman. Though the technology transfer brought about some consumer goods, ranging from freeze-dried food and thermal underwear to cordless razors and nonstick cookware, most applications directly benefited industry and the military. As the number of scholars with expertise in science, engineering, and computer technology exploded exponentially, major institutions of higher education reaped huge windfalls through direct and indirect research grants, new facilities and equipment, and subsidized graduate student and faculty support. Federal support for university scientific and research endeavors increased from $170 million at the midpoint of the Eisenhower era to $1.1 billion at the height of the Great Society in 1965. By 1979, more than 400 institutions, located in every state and two territories, had received NASA funding.

In its early years, NASA was less of a single organization than a series of interlocking corporations, including elements of the old National Advisory Committee on Aeronautics (NACA). These groups represented different constituencies with different philosophies and histories. The three research centers located at Lewis, Ames, and Langley—given their experimental aircraft history—emphasized repeated testing coupled with extensive research. From the Army Ballistic Missile Agency, German rocketeers worked in Huntsville and Michoud, highlighting their own technical capability, which, though allowing for contracting of system hardware and software, focused on in-house building, launching, and controlling satellites. From the Air Force Ballistic Missile Program came a centralized management culture along with a greater emphasis on ground tests and overall system testing.

The space program, then, was the product of a variety of different interests represented by groups that at times had different goals and strategies though they shared a commitment to science, business, and the military—not unlike the newly emerging field of curriculum studies, unified in its opposition to positivism, capitalism, and militarism. It was only due to NASA's high-profile image and performance record that its administrators were able to rise above these more parochial interests. Yet by the time Neil Armstrong fulfilled Kennedy's mandate, this concert of interests was already unraveling. The Vietnam conflict, which escalated under Johnson, resulted in a bloated federal budget (the federal expenditures of one year amounted to more than the entire decade of the lunar project) while the military-industrial-educational infrastructure facilitated the war effort and radicalized a generation of curriculum workers. As the 1970s approached, NASA's budget was already shrinking and its workforce diminishing.

Even before the July 1969 lunar landing, the Nixon administration considered alternative NASA missions in a post-*Apollo* space program. The most ambitious was a human landing on Mars by 1980 (at a projected cost of $100 billion), with lesser projects including an orbiting space station and reusable shuttle craft. NASA itself was divided regarding the priority of these missions, though ultimately, all of these high-profile projects failed to gain support. NASA's post-*Apollo* prospects quickly ran up against a conflation of liberal congressional opponents more concerned with meeting earthly social goals, antiwar activists skeptical about the militarization of space, a public at large increasingly disillusioned by the failure of technology and science to create a new society, and a military–industrial complex already overcommitted to Vietnam resources.

Set adrift in the political arena, the space program unraveled because it lacked a coherent mission, long-term strategic policies, and consistent and adequate funding. The era when NASA largely controlled space operations and influenced space policy while receiving a near carte blanche for expenditures was at an end. It was time for NASA to transform itself.

Freedom and Beyond

During the Nixon years, while NASA transformed itself and presidential politics entered contemporary infamy, Henry Giroux was transformed by the politics of teaching and curriculum. Soon he would join in the transformation of the curriculum field, articulating one of a burgeoning number of competing interests that reflected different priorities and nuanced philosophies.

I left Appalachian State a highly politicized guy in 1968, ready to go into teaching. I went to Baltimore and taught for a year before ending up in Barrington, Rhode Island, where I taught from 1969 to 1975. That was a very political period in my life because I was heavily involved in reading and study groups. My education around pedagogy, cultural studies, and politics all took place during my years as a high school teacher because the period from '68 to '73 was an immensely political time in this country.

I taught in a high school with three or four others who were political as well, including a guy who eventually became a writer for "The Providence Journal," and another guy who eventually became the music reviewer for "The Boston Globe." We all hung out together and talked about our teaching, so questions of pedagogy were constantly creeping into our discussions all the time—less around pedagogical practices than content. We were really focused on what to give these kids. I remember teaching Wilhelm Reich to the high school kids, and renting films from the American Friends Committee. I bought my own books, put them in the library on reserve, and my kids read those books. I got my own films. I was totally independent of the school's curriculum resources. Plus, I often taught my own courses. I taught a course on feminism, a course on alienation. Remember, this was when social studies was emerging in high schools as an effort to balance the typical focus on history alone. And it really provided an academic opportunity for people like myself because in effect, it opened the way for interdisciplinary teaching in the high school.

But those years also produced some real squabbles. I remember coming home one day—I was teaching a course on feminism that year—and turning on the radio and hearing this right-wing guy saying, "Well, you'll be pleased to know that the author of *Sisterhood is Powerful,* Henry Giroux, is teaching at Barrington High School." Of course, Robin Morgan was the author, not me. Well, immediately the right-wing organized and attacked the books in my class, one of which was a feminist critique of Henry Miller. The protesters objected to all of the language being used to identify *Miller's* sexist language, including Miller's language *itself.* Suddenly, all of my books were taken off the library reserve shelf and I had to appear at a public meeting with 300 people to defend the books. But I won the battle. I won the argument. Fortunately, I was lucid enough to convince the liberals in the audience that the real issue to consider was critical thinking. I argued that without being able to enlarge different theoretical discourses, students would be provincial and unprepared for college, or citizenship for that matter. My argument wasn't against censorship, it was for pedagogical practices that promoted critical agency. And from that struggle I learned that the real issue is to make appeals for the possibility for students being the best that they can be, which means that they sometimes have to cross borders that are uncomfortable for them. That was a deep and profoundly political moment for me because it transformed the nature of my own discourse about how to talk about issues. Rather than focus on the issue as inherently wonderful in itself, I learned to focus on the relationship between issues and how they structured or affected people who took them up. And that's a very different kind of argument.

Henry remembers these as "open space" times for teachers, absent today's "heavy-handed curriculum mandates." This was also the period during which he sought a way to talk about the elements of his teaching that he disliked. He recalls reading *Pedagogy of the Oppressed* (Freire, 1970) one night and realizing the following morning that it had changed his life. He describes what happened afterward:

> The following year I left high school teaching and headed to Carnegie-Mellon. What happened was, I attended an inservice seminar on Kohlberg's stages of moral development, given by Edwin Fenton, and ended up asking Fenton a lot of political questions. Ted Fenton was a very open guy, a very wonderful, sweet man who was willing to suspend his own fascination with people who supported his views. He recognized that my oppositional positions articulated something that he could accept as important and so, among those in attendance, he singled me out. He recruited me to Carnegie-Mellon to do a doctorate.

The degree of curricular freedom enjoyed by Giroux and other teachers in the late 1960s and early 1970s evaporated with the press for curriculum evaluation. As we discussed earlier, this widespread interest developed naturally from the heavily funded national curriculum projects of the 1960s. A topic of interest not only in policy and practical situations but also in concept and theory, curriculum evaluation remained popular throughout the late 1970s and early 1980s.

While veterans in the field such as Cronbach (1982; Cronbach et al., 1980) and Stufflebeam and Webster (1980) were joined by others (e.g., Boruch, Wortman, & Cordray, 1981; McCormick & James, 1983) in their efforts to explore this highly sophisticated terrain, efforts were under way to complicate the landscape of perceiving and judging curricular efforts. E. Davis (1980), for example, suggested that teachers could be their own curriculum evaluators, and Guba and Lincoln (1981) began their work in naturalistic forms of evaluation at the same time that Stephen J. Gould published *The Mismeasure of Man* (1981) in an attempt to confound our ways of thinking about what we "know."

The book that caught the widest attention with respect to curriculum evaluation, however, was Eisner's *The Educational Imagination*. The ideas he presented, while obviously new with respect to his aesthetic perspective, were as eclectic in their purpose (i.e., highly sophisticated and critical paths toward making pragmatic decisions related to practice) as were Eisner's teachers at Chicago. Eisner dedicated this book to five of those "teachers who made a difference": Phil Jackson, for a sense of the passionate; Frank Chase, for a sense of the compassionate; Ben Bloom, for a sense of the rational; Joe Schwab, for a sense of the classical; and John Goodlad, for a sense of the practical.

Discontent and Divergence in the Field

Philip Jackson, whose curriculum work continues to influence the field, accepted AERA's (Division B, Curriculum Studies) invitation to present its second state-of-the-field address in 1979. Responding to Pinar's 1978 address and borrowing the sentiment expressed by Eisner in our opening excerpt, Jackson titled his thoughts "Curriculum and Its Discontents" (1980). Briefly, Jackson recognized Michael F. D. Young and David Hamilton of Britain, Ulf Lundgren of Sweden, and William Pinar, Joseph Schwab, Henry Levin, and Elliot Eisner (his former student) of the United States as among the "discontents" who were shifting the nature of curriculum work. Jackson discussed two particular shifts: one "toward a wide assortment of intellectual traditions," which he characterized as "decidedly left of center," and the other a shift in direction between academics and practitioners, with some discontents moving closer to and another group moving further from practitioners (Pinar et al., 1995, p. 233). With calculated humor, Jackson pondered the changing nature and purpose of the curriculum field and expressed caution with regard to the presence and efforts of these discontents. (For a detailed account of Jackson's points and the follow-up reactions to them, see Pinar et al., 1995, pp. 233–236.)

Jackson's 1979 AERA presentation succeeded in fanning the maelstrom prompted by Pinar's 1978 address, pushing lots of people's "hot buttons" with his thoughts—including Henry Giroux's.

> Carnegie-Mellon had a very active social studies curriculum development agenda when I arrived there in 1975. Besides Fenton, I began working with Tony Penna, who really began to introduce me to critical curriculum theory in a very profound way. Tony and I were very interested in the notion of hidden curriculum. I also explored social studies as a critical practice because Ted was doing that kind of work, but I was interested, from a political perspective, in broader issues of curriculum theory and practice.
>
> So my interest in the curriculum field began to emerge right then in 1975, at Carnegie-Mellon. I defined myself as a curriculum theorist then, even though there were a lot of laments about whether or not the field was dead at that time. At the same time, there was a lot of work emerging from Bill Pinar, Michael Apple, and others in which curriculum theory was being highly politicized from at least three or four different perspectives. As for that period being identified as a time for reconceptualizing curriculum, it never occurred to me that Bill Pinar was attempting to define a school of thought by using that term. I mean, I saw that term as a verb more than I did a noun. Yet, a lot of people read that term as an attempt by Bill to in some way establish a kind of incestuous theoretical political community.

I never read it that way. There were too many diverse people who took up the term to have it be one of membership in an exclusive club.

Henry found a "forum for communities of like-minded people" in the annual AERA conferences. Connecting with curriculum people as diverse as Roger Simon, Jean Anyon, David Purpel, and Madeleine Grumet, he sensed the excitement of "fighting real dinosaurs" while shaping a new curriculum discourse. Having completed his doctorate and taken a position at Boston University two years earlier, his 1979 attendance at AERA proved historic. As he tells it:

I went to a session at AERA in 1979 where Phil Jackson and a number of others were supposed to be talking about the reconceptualist movement. Well, Jackson got up and made a joke of it. I was sitting with Bill Pinar and Roger Simon, and I turned to Roger and said, "Somebody has got to respond to this. This is absolutely outrageous that they're doing this." So I got up to respond and they said, "Come up to the microphone." I was terrified. I mean, I was a young assistant professor . . . and I was utterly terrified. But I went up and I bumbled my way through a response. Afterward, Ron Brandt, the Editor of ASCD's *Educational Leadership,* came up to me and said, "Why don't you write a piece on this?" So I did.

"Toward a New Sociology of Curriculum" was a sort of official response to what I thought was a very distorted, highly prejudicial, terribly misrepresenting, and utterly unfair attempt by mainstream "liberal" curricularists to come to grips with some of the discourses that Pinar and others were developing. But that piece cost me a significant number of contacts in my career. A number of unusual things happened and I really became black-balled. I had to live with the legacy of that speech and article for quite some time afterwards; the event got me labeled as a radical Marxist writing about curriculum. Actually, I never really saw it as more than an introductory piece that I hoped people would read. I had no indication that it would have any influence whatsoever, except to maybe open up a few eyes and allow people to realize that there are alternative discourses around that they could appropriate.

VARIED TALE

NASA: WEATHERING THE COMING STORMS

Like the newly emerging divergent curriculum field that Pinar proclaimed in 1978 and Giroux defended in 1979, NASA had also undergone a metamorphosis. At its outset, NASA was considered a high-performance governmental organization, with its leaders overcoming or circumventing bureaucratic impediments toward their mission. By 1975, however, NASA was spending at

(continued)

one-quarter of the level it had eight years earlier and the number of contractors working with NASA had dropped by two-thirds. Reductions in force began in 1972 and extended through 1975, devastating NASA's high-performance culture.

As NASA reduced its overall workforce, however, administrative employees increased in number and were twice as likely as engineers or scientists to receive promotions. With declining budgets and dwindling political payoffs, top administrators grew less able to insulate NASA from outside political and economic forces. The James Webbs and Wernher von Brauns were gone, and a new generation of managers, such as James Fletcher, assumed a more practical approach to space leadership. With the space program's tasks largely reduced to launching weather and communication satellites, public opinion of the program's importance continued to decline.

As the U.S. space program struggled to survive congressional underfunding, public disinterest, and loss of a coherent long-term strategy and organizational ethos, the Soviets successfully launched their Salyut 6 space station in 1977, housing cosmonauts in space for nearly a year at a time. By 1981, an even larger Soviet modular space station, Salyut 7, was operational.

In 1978, NASA celebrated the completion of its second decade in existence, its organizational structure and ethos now transformed. As the force of NASA's original "technical culture" became a memory and shuttle flights became more routine and repetitive, its new, administrative culture developed a reliance on outsourcing more and more technical activities. By 1989, 88% of total NASA moneys went to such contractors. Although NASA still championed its role as an R&D organization in which innovation and change were foremost, many of its employees felt otherwise. In this tense environment of the early 1980s, with its decreased tolerance for failure and sparse support for testing (and, thus, potentially wasting material resources), a greater reliance on computer simulations, ground tests, and self-correcting in-flight devices took hold. As NASA lost its technological expertise, surrendered control to external contractors, and even delegated much of contractor oversight to consulting firms, its employees found dwindling rewards for either quality or control. Nevertheless, NASA had again become an organization with a purpose.

A variety of outsiders aided in the rebirth of NASA and the transformation of the space program. The formation of space interest groups, initiated by the L-5 Society established in 1975 around the ideas of Princeton physicist Gerard O'Neill, was followed the next year by Wernher von Braun's National Space Institute, which boasted 30,000 members favoring general space exploration. By 1980, Carl Sagan's Planetary Society, with 125,000 members, lobbied for scientific (rather than commercial or military) space exploration, supporting funding for the Galileo probe but not for the Reagan administration's Strategic Defense Initiative, popularly known as Star Wars.

Nearly 100 space groups were active by 1983, ranging from the Planetary Society to smaller and more focused membership organizations such as the

Space Cadets, formed by Nichelle Nichols of *Star Trek,* and the Hpatia Cluster, which represented feminist interests in space. Political action groups that promoted conservative, promilitary space policies also emerged, including the American Space Foundation and High Frontier, which by 1985 had 50,000 members.

Finally, two specific trade groups proved potent in the repopularization of space endeavors: the National Coordinating Committee for Space—whose member groups included 21 corporations, 52 universities, and 5 national trade and professional societies—and the Aerospace Industries Association, composed of 58 corporations. In 1981, the former group submitted a consensus document to the Reagan administration entitled "Future Directions for National Space Policy," and the latter group successfully lobbied to prohibit NASA from flying communications satellites on the shuttle and to allow private enterprise to engage in space flight.

Such trade group influence *was also evident in the formation of the bipartisan* congressional Space Caucus, organized in 1982 by Representatives Daniel Inuit of Alaska and Newt Gingrich. The caucus served as a forum for members interested in space exploration and commercialization as well as a coordinating arm for legislation in the three major committees that deal with space policy.

By the mid-1980s, NASA had weathered its worst storm to date. Having gone from a pre-*Apollo* no-holds-barred vision of humans conquering space to a bloated, esoteric gaggle of self-insulated scientists and experts who could not seem to organize themselves to cope successfully with external realities, NASA's leaders literally reinvented the organization's culture and operational structure. And though no American astronauts would visit space between 1975 and the first orbital flight of the space shuttle in 1981, dozens of special interest groups helped bring NASA back into cultural prominence. Shaped by economic constraints, political pressure, managerial culture, and renewed public interest, NASA's high-profile space shuttle program would take the agency and the country itself to the frontiers of the new millennium.

Orbiting Outside the Curriculum Field

The role of diverse special interest groups in the resurgence of NASA's importance was similar to the role of divergent interest groups in the reshaping of contemporary curriculum work; perhaps the only common characteristic of the different interest groups in curriculum was an opposition to the Tylerian status quo. Henry Giroux recognized some of these diverging interests at the time:

> We were reconceptualizing the field. But meanwhile, there was a lot of fallout from the more heavy political types and others who somehow wanted to distance themselves. There was enormous division even then among and

within various groups. For example, one division was around economics and culture. At the time, the work of Michael Apple and others was about political economy and economics. Culture was not much of an issue for them—certainly not as a determining force in its own right. Whereas Bill Pinar and others were attempting to take up culture as a force equally as significant as certain economic determinations. So they talked about language and psychoanalysis and sexuality. In a way that was really quite remarkable in that these were all taboo topics.

At the same time, Henry recognized a growing collection of "divisive networks" represented by different universities—Ohio State, Teachers College, Madison, Wisconsin, and Stanford—and laying claim to differing curriculum legacies. Being "unattached," he could remain interested in the entire field and benefit from its varied representatives. As he notes:

I thought Dwayne Huebner's work was stunning when I read it; and Maxine Greene has always been a source of enormous inspiration for me. I thought Jim Macdonald's work in curriculum theory was the most progressive I had seen during the late 70s and early 80s. Bill Pinar had an enormous influence on me in terms of the early edited books that I read. Michael Apple's *Ideology and Curriculum* was enormously significant for me, as were Tony Penna's, Jean Anyon's, and Tom Popkewitz's early work. I found Ulf Lundgren's work very important in terms of looking at European perspectives. Stanley Aronowitz's work in education was utterly brilliant. And, of course, Paulo Freire more than anyone.

I found myself reading a lot of different people, including Michael Young, Valerie Walkerdine, and Geoff Whitty. I was also reading theoretical work not directly connected to education, including Herbert Marcuse, Walter Benjamin and other members of the Frankfurt School. Like anything else, Marxism has a number of theoretical discourses and I found myself appropriating the more critical work and bringing that to education.

At the time, I was also finding a close intersection with the new sociology of education emerging in England. I began to bring those fields together and talk about the new sociology of curriculum. That was an attempt to in some way rephrase the field by virtue of appropriating a different language—to bring in the Frankfurt School stuff. I was writing about critical theory and cultural politics, infusing that language into curriculum theory while Michael Apple and others were talking about the political economy of curriculum theory. And although their focus created a much needed discourse, my work has always been more expansive, focusing on broader critical traditions, particularly critical considerations of radical democracy, power, and culture in ways that might be helpful for theorists trying to in some way establish wider interdisciplinary spaces and political projects when considering curriculum theory and practice.

The distinctions in contemporary political scholarship noted by Giroux—distinctions among the varied Marxist discourses in this case—would eventually become linked to internecine struggles, often as much about individual and collective identities as they were about individual and collective ideas. Having succeeded in illustrating that their work was *not* about the dominant curriculum paradigm, many new curricularists were busy distinguishing themselves from each other as well.

During the early 1980s the ideas that were shaping contemporary curriculum work grew in both number and sophistication. While much of this development is apparent through professional journal publications and conference presentations (see Pinar et al., 1995), curriculum books provide undeniable evidence that the state of the field had changed. Like a leaky faucet, the post-World War II trickle of nonmainstream curriculum books—which grew persistently during the late 1960s and early 1970s—had become a slow but continuous flow by the early 1980s. Just as historical work had become a valued and respected discourse within contemporary studies (e.g., Berman, 1982; Bullough, 1981; Hug, 1979; Kaestle, 1983; Schubert, 1980), curriculum books representing political (by far the most prolific discourse), phenomenological, and other discourses or texts numbered more than a dozen by 1983.

And like the curriculum field, books about education and schooling from this period suggest a similar diversity. From the 1981 publications of Wigginton's Foxfire experiment and Holt's invitation to homeschooling, to the 1982 appearance of noted efforts to understand school change published by both Fullan and Sarason and the philosopher Mortimer Adler's promotion of the Paideia Proposal, to the remarkable 1983 collection of descriptive studies of schools published separately by Boyer, Goodlad, and Lightfoot, coinciding with the education community's introduction to Schön's *Reflective Practitioner,* education-related books in print by 1983 suggested limitless possibilities for understanding schooling and curriculum differently. As events unfolded, however, this curriculum smorgasbord would be overshadowed in national importance by the publication of *A Nation at Risk* in 1983. Once again, the connections between curriculum work and the results of schooling would be criticized, only this time, the blame would be spread beyond the curriculum field itself into the schools and universities that prepared schoolteachers.

Having authored, coauthored, or coedited five curriculum books by 1983, Henry Giroux had begun to see limitations within the curriculum field and its historic linkages to schools and schooling.

> I left Boston University in 1983, but by that time I was losing my interest in curriculum theorizing—in part, because it was about the schools. To me, the field of curriculum theory is about theories of schooling and really not about broader issues such as popular media or popular culture.

Question

Do you agree that the field of curriculum theory is not about broader issues such as popular media or popular culture?

There was also a limited number of journals you could write for if you were in curriculum, and those journals were almost completely dominated by particular schools of thought. By that time, I was being invited to a lot of places and writing for a lot of journals outside the more narrow curriculum field. The most interesting journals were cropping up elsewhere, outside of education, and the more interesting people in curriculum theory had begun to move out. So by the mid-80s, I felt that the field was much too narrow for me. That's around the time I quit attending AERA. I wanted to widen and broaden my correspondence with teachers, and so I situated myself more broadly within the field of education and addressed the educational force of the wider culture, including but not limited to schools.

VARIED TALE

NASA: RECONCEPTUALIZING SPACE

Giroux's suggestion that the contemporary curriculum field needs a more expansive and well-articulated mission brings us back to the born-again NASA of the early 1980s. Ultimately, the efforts and activities of trade in combination with political and space-related interest groups helped significantly to reinvigorate the U.S. space effort in general and NASA in particular. NASA received its first clear mandate since the Kennedy administration and moved from primarily a political showcase to a commercial zone of opportunity. Handed Reagan's space policy, NASA established an office of commercial programs in 1984 to encourage entrepreneurial activity by providing seed money and reducing bureaucratic impediments. Corporations such as RCA and Hughes Aircraft, for example, began Landsat—an earth observation satellite program that markets its data though private enterprise. In addition to the Department of Commerce, the Department of Energy and the Department of Transportation, among others, funneled substantial financial and bureaucratic resources into NASA's efforts.

As space became more commercialized in the 1980s, it also became more militarized. From the Kennedy administration to the eve of the Reagan era, overall military spending as a percentage of the federal budget had been halved. As part of the Reagan administration's goal of rearming and modernizing the military, the 1981 Department of Defense space budget actually exceeded NASA's expenditures. The enormous funding and political support for the Strategic Defense Initiative (a.k.a. Star Wars) and the space resources needed for the operation of intercontinental ballistic missiles enabled the military to assume a leadership role in U.S. space policy. From the joint chiefs of staff, who help to oversee space activities, to the Air Force, whose deputy undersecretary for space systems supervises the National Reconnaissance Office as well as Space Command, the Department of Defense was now a major factor in NASA's future. The Kennedy administration's position of civilian control over space and the Johnson administration's goal of demilitarizing space had both been vaporized.

Continuing Journey, Different Hurdles

By the summer of 1983, as *Pioneer 10* traveled the 2.7 billion miles beyond earth to leave our solar system, the space program had departed from its trajectory set a generation earlier. A new configuration of interest groups finding voice within a changed sociopolitical landscape had reconceptualized the U.S. space effort.

By that fall, efforts to understand curriculum through political, gendered, autobiographical, aesthetic, and other texts had found their way into the syllabi of curriculum teachers around the United States; even the most conventional courses would have difficulty ignoring the growing accumulation of issues and ideas being produced by the new vanguard of contemporary curriculum studies. At the same time, the curriculum field was about to experience another wholesale pummeling. Like the post-*Sputnik* hullabaloo, the post-*Nation at Risk* period would bolster the field's most conservative, conventional elements. But as "the nation's schools slipped further [during the 1980s] into the hands of the business community, the politicians, bureaucrats, and the social engineers, the scholarly field of curriculum detached itself, and concentrated on understanding curriculum in all its complexity" (Pinar et al., 1995, p. 236).

This "detached," scholarly field of curriculum would face continued internal struggles throughout the decade. As Pinar and his colleagues (1995, p. 238) put it:

> By the early 1980s, the movement to reconceptualize the curriculum field lost the cohesive bonds that maintained the coalition during its first years of struggle and enthusiasm. Opposition to the traditional field was no longer powerful enough a force for coalition, as the movement had succeeded in delegitimating the ahistorical, atheoretical field of the pre-1970 period. With the continued resistance of Marxist scholars to a multiple-perspective conception of reconceptualization

and curriculum, with the emergence of autobiographical studies as a major force in the field, with the concurrent expansion of existential and phenomenological scholarship . . . , with the burgeoning of feminist theory, and the appearance of poststructuralism in curriculum studies, the original reconceptualist movement can be said to have disappeared. Its success was its demise as a movement.

The implications of both the detachment of curriculum scholarship and the demise of the movement to reconceptualize curriculum work are explored in the following chapters.

Visitor Bibliography   Henry Giroux

Giroux, H. (1999). *The mouse that roared: Disney and the end of innocence.* Lanham, MD: Rowman and Littlefield Press.

Giroux, H. (2000). *Impure acts: The practical politics of cultural studies.* New York: Routledge.

Giroux, H. (2001a). *Stealing innocence: Corporate culture's war on children.* New York: St. Martin's Press.

Giroux, H. (2001b). *Theory and resistance in education.* (Revised Edition) Westport, CT: Bergin and Garvey.

Giroux, H. (2001c). *Public spaces/private lives: Beyond the culture of cynicism.* Lanham, MD: Rowman and Littlefield.

Giroux, H. (2002). *Breaking into the movies: Film and the culture of politics.* Malden, MA: Basil Blackwell Publishers.

Giroux, H. (2003). *The abandoned generation: Democracy and the culture of fear.* New York: Macmillan Palgrave.

The Uncertainties of Contemporary Curriculum Work (1984–2002)

8

Implosion and Consolidation: Marginalized Voices

Jean-Francois Lyotard's *The Postmodern Condition: A Report on Knowledge* was translated into English in 1984. Within that book, "Lyotard brought together for the first time diverse threads and previously separate literatures in a prophetic analysis . . . believed to signal an epochal break not only with the so-called 'modern era' but also with various traditionally 'modern' ways of viewing the world" (Peters, 1995, p. 387). With respect to the status and functions of knowledge in highly technological societies, Lyotard asserted that "the traditional [scientific] legitimating 'myths' or 'metanarratives' of the speculative unity of all knowledge and its humanist emancipatory potential have allegedly fallen away. Knowledge and power have been revealed as two sides of the same coin." He explained his assertions through an "analysis of language-games signaling both a return to pragmatics and an elevation of narrative as a mode of thinking in its own right" (Peters, 1989, p. 93).

The timing of this English translation is as significant to our story as Lyotard's prophetic analysis, for this postmodern turn in how we come to understand our world washed over the curriculum field. More than an intellectual phenomenon, however, the postmodern condition forever disrupted much about life, at least as we had come to make sense of it.

▨ Juxtapositions

Disjunctive, contradictory, and *unsettling* are apt descriptors for both postmodernism and the year 1984. On a wind-swept battlefield at Normandy, U.S. President Ronald Reagan and other world leaders commemorated the 40th anniversary of D-Day as Soviet cold warriors Breshnev, Andropov, and Chernenko succeeded one another in quick fashion. Meanwhile, on the Westernized island of Hong Kong, representatives of the United Kingdom and China finalized an agreement to return this capitalist isle to communist rule. On the floor of the Rift Valley of Kenya, a 5-million-year-old jawbone of *Australopithecus afarensis*, our earliest known ancestor, was unearthed. While DNA analysis revealed the genetic difference between chimpanzees and humans to be barely 1%, the Texas Board of Education debated a decade-old ban on the teaching of evolution as scientific fact. In Paris and Atlanta, researchers announced the discovery of HIV as half a million AIDS cases were reported worldwide and *Advocate Men* premiered in gay bookstores. There were also odd cultural juxtapositions: Neil Simon's *Biloxi Blues* and Larry Kramer's *The Normal Heart* played on Broadway; Boy George and George Michael produced platinum-selling albums; Garrison Keillor's *Lake Wobegon Days* and Anne Tyler's *The Accidental Tourist* sold briskly at bookstores; and *The Color of Money*, *The Color Purple*, *Back to the Future*, and *Blue Velvet* ran in cinemas.

As American politics and culture imploded, an ever greater concentration of wealth coupled to technological advances arose. The year 1984 marked the world's largest corporate merger (Standard Oil of California acquired Gulf Oil) and the country's highest rate of bank failures since 1937, resulting in an eventual $300 billion government bailout. Meanwhile, Silicon Valley entrepreneurs amassed huge fortunes by launching mouses, 32-bit chips, and enhanced software packages as genetic engineering and fingerprinting opened up new investment opportunities. Scientists engineered the first frozen embryo birth and the first surrogate conception and cloned their first mammal (a sheep) and their first extinct species (a zebra fish).

Similar to the varied expansion of culture and technology, the curriculum books of 1984 showed an expanding and unsettling diversity as witnessed by their titles: Finn and others fought "against mediocrity" and J. L. Miller made "eccentric propositions" while Raywid and her associates found "pride and promise" within the same teachers and schools that both Brown and Darling-Hammond found near "crisis." Dunkel produced an "epitaph for innovation" in the year that Noddings explored "intuition" and Gilbert offered an "impotent image of ideology." Craft talked of "multicultural opportunities" while Eisner presented evaluation as an art, Rubin saw artistry in teaching, and both Tom and Noddings (in her book *Caring*) discussed morality and teaching.

The 1980s saw a new generation of curriculum workers entering the field. One among this generation, James T. Sears, began his writing career by quoting Ecclesiastes: "One generation passeth away, and another generation cometh." Graduating from Indiana University in 1984 under the tutelage of Norm Overly (an Ohio State graduate who studied with Paul Klohr), Sears presented his vision for the curriculum field at the 1982 Curriculum Theory Conference held in Airlie, Virginia:

> The generation of Michael Apple and Bill Pinar is giving birth to another group of curriculum theorists. As part of that new generation, I acknowledge my intellectual debt to them as well as to their mentors and to their mentors' mentors. As part of that new generation, I recognize that their critiques and theoretical programs now require an intellectual and cultural closeness with our constituency in order to effectively shape schools of the future and to reshape theories of the past.
>
> My colleague, Patti Lather, argues that we must develop a sense of "apocalyptical humility" rooted in a respect for and understanding of the earnest practitioner . . . In the past, these people have been chided for their lack of social vision, intellectual abilities, and educational commitment. In the future, these people must become our collaborators in curriculum research, our allies in political action, and our disciples through pedagogical practice.
>
> Moses shepherded his people for 40 years as they traversed the arid Sinai land. This experience fostered reflection, cleansed the spirit, and renewed commitment. Nearing the journey's end, Moses gazed across the Jordan River from Mount Nebo. He saw Cannan, the future homeland of his children and his children's children. He rested on the mountainside. The prophecy was fulfilled.
>
> My generation must depart the solitude of the desert and thin air of the mountain to journey into the "promised land." Within this land of valleys the common practitioner dwells. The land belongs to neither the theorist nor the practitioner. If it is to belong to any, then it must belong to all. Only through collective struggle will this land blossom and bear fruit. . . .
>
> Theory must be tempered with practice. . . . Without such tempering, the generational dialectic ceases; the prophecy is unfulfilled. (Sears, 1985, pp. 24–25)

This newest generation of individuals, earning their curriculum doctorates during the 1980s, had less in common with each other, not to mention with their predecessors, than had previous generations. The gender mix had shifted considerably, the racial and ethnic composition showed signs of variation, and members' points of origin had multiplied well beyond the curriculum hotbed universities of Ohio State; Madison, Wisconsin; Chicago; and Teachers College. Further, this contemporary group exhibited a far more eclectic range of backgrounds and interests—including their personal and professional ties to teaching and schooling—that allowed them to understand their field in complex and sometimes paradoxical ways.

Reclamations and Reformations

Tom Barone

VISITOR In this chapter, three contemporary curriculum workers illustrate these differences and, as a group, reflect an array of curriculum discourses that distinguishes the field in the postmodern age. The first, Tom Barone, professor of education at Arizona State University, was completing his sixth year as a faculty member at Northern Kentucky University in 1984.

> I grew up in New Orleans. My parents, grandparents, uncle and aunt owned an Italian seafood restaurant there. My family lived in what's called the Gentilly area, very close to Lake Pontchartrain. My family on my father's side is Italian; I'm third generation. They were always restaurateurs and none had gone to college or had ever seen that as a way of making their way in the world. But somehow it was always expected that I would go to college, moreover, that I was going to be something close to a medical doctor or a dentist.
>
> I recall that I was always the person in our family who was much more sympathetic to the position of blacks. In fact, my family was flat out racist and I recall always being uncomfortable with that. And, of course, Vietnam was happening. I had a professor at Loyola University of the South who was quite skeptical about the war. We had to write position papers; that assignment was an act of clarification for me.

Entering Loyola in 1964 as a premed student, Tom's transformative experience occurred in the summer between his sophomore and junior years. "I worked at a small hospital in inner city New Orleans. It was then I decided this was not what I was cut out to do." Switching his major to history and political science without regard for the career implications, he remembers:

> I really didn't decide on going into education until my fifth year. It happened that a friend, who was teaching in a small, private high school, decided to leave and recommended me to the headmaster there. So, in 1968, I took this job teaching history and government. I quickly decided I really liked doing that, so I agreed to work toward my permanent teaching credentials and continued teaching there until 1974. For me, becoming a teacher was extremely accidental.

Teaching and Theorizing

By the mid-1980s, teachers were center stage in the curriculum field as their work (Connell, 1985) and the study of curriculum—at least for some—became inseparable (see, for example, Apple, 1986; Barrow, 1984; Clandinin, 1986; Jackson, 1986; Lieberman & Miller, 1984; Powell, 1985). One result of this blurring was the metamorphosis of a long-standing debate concerning whether and how curriculum ought to relate with classroom teaching and the institutional processes of schooling. Another was a growing disillusionment among some curriculum workers at the annual curriculum theory conferences held at Airlie House in Virginia from 1979 through 1982 and then at the Bergamo Center in Ohio.

The annual conference was unraveling as the "reconceptualists"—a term long abandoned by its creator, Bill Pinar—splintered into a multiplicity of genres. Decade-long theoretical fissures, such as those between Michael Apple and Bill Pinar, had expanded and become exposed in personal conflicts at Bergamo, where divisions erupted between feminist men and women, economic and cultural Marxists, poststructuralists and postmodernists, lesbians and gay men. Sources of these frictions included the proper relationships between theory and practice, the use of language to clarify or obscure curricular insights, and the authority of the curriculum theorist vis-a-vis the classroom teacher. For example, critics eventually shut down the gathering's annual "title contest," which awarded dinner prizes to those contributing the most clever fictional paper titles—a comic reminder, for some, of the distance between the conference and the classroom. Others more directly challenged conference participants. In one paper, Sears (1988) critiqued the language games played by some contemporary curriculum scholars, comparing these theorists with those cavorting in the illusionary safety of Berlin cabarets while events such as Crystal Neicht unfolded. In another, Ellsworth (1989) challenged critical theorists by asking a disarmingly simple but heretical question: Is critical pedagogy really empowering? All the while, contemporary curriculum discourses multiplied, accumulating such forms as mythopoetics, semiotics, ecology, Ricoeurian hermeneutics, aesthetics, psychoanalysis, postformalism, biographic and autobiographic praxis, deconstructionism, race, teacher lore, feminist methodology, and queer theory.

Controversies within contemporary curriculum work that centered on theory and practice resulted in the development of a special issue of *Theory Into Practice* (Vol. 31, No. 3, Summer 1992) entitled "Grounding Contemporary Curriculum Thought" and edited by James Sears. Placed throughout this chapter are excerpts from this special issue penned by authors who represent different perspectives in this theory-practice debate. In the first of these, Bill Schubert describes how the many classroom teachers (also theorizers) with whom he works enhance his curriculum theorizing.

PRIMARY DOCUMENT EXCERPT

Practitioners Influence Curriculum Theory

by William H. Schubert

My commitment to interest-based project learning was influenced by reading Dewey ... [though] my interest in Dewey's work would not have been as receptive had it not been for my work with elementary students in student teaching. Similarly, even that practice cannot be seen as the initiatory point, because I decided to be a candidate for teaching certification for more academic reasons; namely, I wanted to share with others the powers of ideas in making sense of one's life....

My elementary school teaching experience taught me that the question of greatest import was a philosophical curriculum question: What is worthwhile to know and experience? This Spencerian question (Spencer, 1861) must flow in the lifeblood of teachers in their daily activities. Everything they do is contingent upon some image of what is worth knowing and experiencing. Moreover, to address this issue seriously invokes questions about what it means to live a good life and contribute to a society. It probes to basic values about human nature and the nature of reality, the character of knowing and knowledge, the aesthetics of environmental patterns and images that guide educative decision and action, the nature of sound reasoning, and the continuous quest to seek goodness in the lived consequences of educational decisions....

My teaching of graduate students, thus, became an inquiry into their images of curriculum development as teachers. I was bombarded by story after story of teachers who found generic curriculum guides and textbook recipes inadequate, and writing lesson plans to be an exercise without mileage beyond the student teaching experience....

William Pinar (1975) drew together writings by Greene, Phenix, Macdonald, Huebner, and . . . [others] under the label "curriculum theorizing." The term, I felt, enlivened the work of curriculum theorists, taking away the necessity of producing theory, which carries a more brittle and dusty image of something finished and on the shelf . . . Theorizing was a kind of reflection, an image of the need for continuous reconceptualizing of the flow of experience. It seemed implied that this would include theorizing by practicing educators, but the reconceptualist image was too often relegated to academics alone.

The best teachers I have known as graduate students seriously strive to engage in their own version of curriculum theorizing.... If given a chance, teachers who theorize not only test ideas they find in graduate school in their practice setting, they also test the worth of what they read and hear in graduate studies with ideas generated from practice....

[Teachers] who are immersed in practice have again taught me that we need additional information upon which to make sound curricular decisions. We need general knowledge about the implicit curriculum that resides in spheres of student life outside of school, and perhaps more, we need to encourage and enable educators to discover the idiosyncratic patterns of outside curriculum in the lives of students in their schools and classrooms, and what they have learned from these outside curricula.

One of the greatest contributions scholars can make is to acknowledge and facilitate such inquiry by teachers.... Similarly, one of the greatest contributions teachers can make (and have made to my theorizing) is to tell scholars more about the ways they theorize in the concreteness of their educational settings.

Source: Schubert, W. H. (1992). Practitioners influence curriculum theory: Autobiographical reflections. *Theory Into Practice, 31*(3), 236–243. From a theme issue on "Grounding Contemporary Curriculum Thought." Copyright 1992, College of Education, The Ohio State University.

The End of Science in the Postmodern Era

The importance of what students learn from the implicit curricula, noted Schubert, is found beyond classrooms. These idiosyncratic patterns of "external" (to school) learning have a kind of paradoxical relationship to the "concreteness" of teachers' classroom workspaces. Ultimately, Schubert joined with Lyotard in raising questions about legitimate knowledge and the hegemony of the scientific metanarrative.

Lyotard's major working hypothesis was "that the status of knowledge is altered as societies enter what is known as the postindustrial age and cultures enter what is known as the postmodern age" (Lyotard, 1979/1984, p. 3). Articulating antimodernist views of the primacy of scientific knowledge, he argued that "the 'leading' sciences and technologies—cybernetics, telematics, informatics, and the growth of computer languages—are all *significantly language based* and have transformed the two principal functions of knowledge: research and the transmission of acquired learning" (Peters, 1989, p. 98, emphasis in original). Thus, the relationship between language and the creation and transmission of knowledge becomes problematic in terms of justifying and controlling knowledge.

For Lyotard, "science has always justified its claim to truth—and thus power—by having recourse to the dominant 'metanarratives' of metaphysical philosophy" (Lea, 1987, p. 89). Briefly, these metanarratives or stories (which provide legitimacy to all other stories) claim that social emancipation is achieved through the acquisition of ever more refined forms of scientific knowledge. More knowledge allows us to take greater control over our physical world. As cognitive beings, we are ultimately in search of metaphysical myths—transcendent, unified, or totalizing forms of explaining our unity and being. Lyotard and other postmodernists characterized these metaphysical myths as being in crisis, as harmful to smaller, oppositional narratives, and as ultimately losing their authority in the postmodern age. Lyotard analyzed these crises by exploring both scientific knowledge and its sustaining metanarratives as language games.

A language game is played by two or more people in conversation. Each sort of utterance—denotative, prescriptive, performative, and so forth—becomes a separate language game in that it has its own rules concerning what it is, what it means, how it is used, and the like. In a given conversational exchange, therefore, numerous such games will exist, each with a unique set of rules. No two games will necessarily relate because each sentence is a move that may establish a new rule (and so a new game). Thus, what we have are agreements between and among people to play these language games with the utmost communicative flexibility. What we cannot have, using this analysis, is a situation in which any single utterance or collection of utterances has meaning or value *outside* of the game and its players—unless the game is being controlled. Metanarratives represent such institutionalized or controlled discourses.

The metanarratives that serve to legitimize science and scientific knowledge are, for Lyotard, nothing more than grandly constructed language games. Given that no game translates into another, and that each game contains the potential for flexibility of moves, there can be no grand, legitimating metanarrative for science, no unifying principle, no universal metalanguage. In essence, there can be no more "science" as we know it: a search for some ultimate and collective truth.

Question

What are examples of past and present metanarratives in education?

Despite more than two decades of assault against scientific curriculum making, mainstream curriculum texts still identified with scientific interests in curriculum design, development, and implementation. Complementing the 1984 republication of Caswell and Campbell's 1937 *Readings in Curriculum Development* was an array of traditional synoptic texts (e.g., R. C. Doll [sixth edition 1986; 1996]; Hass, 1987; McNeil, 1985; 1996; Ornstein & Hunkins, 1988; 1993; 1998; P. H. Taylor & Richards, 1985;

Unruh & Unruh, 1984; Wiles & Bondi, 1984; 1998; Wulf & Schave, 1984). The field, too, remained obsessed with subject-specific knowledge, ranging from the arts (Abbs, 1987), history (Portal, 1987), and the humanities (Cheney, 1987), to science (Champagne & Horning, 1987), mathematics (McKnight et al., 1987), and technology (Committee on Research in Mathematics, Science, and Technology Education, 1985).

In *Content of the Curriculum* (1988), for example, Ron Brandt presented the 1988 ASCD yearbook as a collection of essays detailing what schools should teach in 10 content areas. Viewed as timely in light of recent attacks on curriculum workers (e.g., A. Bloom, 1987; Cheney, 1987; Hirsch, 1987; Ravitch & Finn, 1987), Brandt decided against "responding in kind" and for "the continuing struggle of deciding what schools should teach" (Brandt, 1988, p. 3). After employing Eisner and Vallance's (1974) conflicting conceptions of curriculum, Brandt noted that "discussions of curriculum necessarily proceed from assumptions about the nature of knowledge and the purposes of education" (p. 5). However, he then shifted this truism to the background to bring focus to questions of subject matter content within largely ahistorical, apolitical, and narrowly defined disciplinary contexts.

In contrast, others challenged educators to think beyond technical designs and traditional organizations of subject matter (e.g., Aronowitz & Giroux, 1985; Bowers, 1984; Schön, 1987; Soltis, 1987). A variety of works (e.g., Anther, 1987; Lloyd, 1987) seemed to intersect with a more complicated picture of the struggles inherent within curriculum work (Popkewitz, 1987), ranging from social issues (Molnar, 1987) and nonsexist curricula (Parker, 1984) to contextualized knowledge (Altbach, 1987) and multiple ways of knowing (Eisner, 1985).

These challenges to the scientific metanarrative were eventually felt in the synoptic textbook market. J. P. Miller and Seller's *Curriculum: Perspectives and Practices* (1985) was unusual at the time because it presented three differing metaorientations or positions to curriculum (transmission, transaction, and transformation) along with philosophical, psychological, economic or social, and historical contexts for each position. Further, their "transformational" position included ideas that connected elements of mysticism, transcendentalism, spirituality, and humanism to curriculum work. The following year, Schubert's synoptic text *Curriculum: Perspective, Paradigm, and Possibility* (1986) fully integrated an historical context within a panoramic representation of curriculum studies and became the first such text to deal seriously with the "reconceptualization" of the curriculum field. Clearly, undermining given frameworks—be they cultural or curricular—was the game in play by the mid-1980s as a host of contradictory images lay strewn across the social and educational landscapes.

Textual Paradoxes in Life and Print

Crack first appeared on urban streets in 1985—the same year that the 99-year-old Coca-Cola morphed into New Coke (then back into Coca-Cola Classic), that Barbie dolls surpassed the entire U.S. population in number, and that the amount of time American youth spent gazing at television screens exceeded their classroom instructional time. The following year, as the country held its first official observance of Martin Luther King Day, the Supreme Court affirmed, in a 5–4 decision, a Georgia statute, and declared that civil rights do not extend to the "fundamental right [of] homosexuals to engage in sodomy."

And while actor-turned-president Ronald Reagan addressed the nation about a secret arms deal, stunned television viewers witnessed a resurrected Bobby Ewing on *Dallas*, learning that the entire 1985 viewing season merely represented a dream.

The curriculum field mirrored these paradoxical phenomena as "the effort to understand curriculum as poststructuralist, deconstructed, postmodern text . . . burst onto the scene" (Pinar et al., 1995, p. 514). In curriculum books, many new voices collided while engaging in analytic explorations and language games. In 1985, Cookson and Persell published *Preparing for Power* in contrast to the third edition of McNeil's *Curriculum: A Comprehensive Introduction*; Ravitch produced *The Schools We Deserve* while Fantini and Sinclair gave us *Education in School and Non-school Settings,* and Oakes presented *Keeping Track: How High Schools Structure Inequality* as Rosales-Dordelly and Short offered us *Curriculum Professors' Specialized Knowledge.*

Mary-Ellen Jacobs

VISITOR These paradoxes were often played out in the daily lives of those preparing to become curriculum workers. Like Tom Barone, our next two contemporary curriculum workers explored medical careers. Mary-Ellen Jacobs spent 14 years working in the medical field while maintaining strong personal interests in writing, literature, and women's studies. Eventually, however, she too would embark on a teaching career. Currently serving as Head of the English Department at Palo Alto College in San Antonio, Mary-Ellen was born in Baltimore.

> My father was a civilian chemical engineer working with chemical and biological warfare for the military. My mother was an elementary teacher before she moved into high school English, eventually teaching English at a community college. My original goal in life was to be a pharmacist.
>
> I was with the nuns in grades 1–9. 1 switched over to a public high school when I was in 10th grade because the Catholic school didn't have

adequate science equipment. I was also able to do music and drama in the public high school. English was always a part of my life, though, and I've always been a reader and a writer. Drama was another powerful element in my life.

After graduating from high school in 1967, Mary-Ellen entered Alverno College, a Catholic women's college in Milwaukee, to study the arts as a double major in English and French. The following summer, she took her first-ever job at a nursing home, where she was "petrified of the patients." Within a few months, though, she had developed a rapport. Meanwhile, Mary-Ellen sensed "that my pursuit of the arts was just self-gratifying in contrast to nursing—which was doing something to help other people." She had also realized that Alverno was "too small for my tastes" and transferred to Marquette University to major in journalism.

The first week I was there I got myself a job as a nurse's aide at a nursing home in Milwaukee. That blew my parents away! After that first semester, I became disenchanted with journalism, so I switched to the nursing program, and my parents again hit the ceiling. As soon as I'd done that, my father told me that if I wanted to be a nurse, I could get some tuition help through the Army Nurse Corps' student nurse program. And I joined up.

As a nursing student, Mary-Ellen was "way off the edge," writing poetry about her psychiatric nursing experiences, "that my instructors said they couldn't understand. I often felt like I shouldn't even be there."

During senior year, Mary-Ellen entered a national writing contest sponsored by the *American Journal of Nursing*. Her poem about open-heart surgery patients won first place, entitling her to attend a weeklong writers' conference at Middlebury College in Vermont. "It was a powerful experience which left me feeling torn about who I was at that point. Nursing was something I did, but I always knew there would be something else that I would do."

After graduating from Marquette in 1971, she spent the next three years as an Army nurse. Returning to school for premed studies, she eventually applied for medical school admission. "But in the mid-'70s, as a nurse and a woman applying for a position in medical school, the question was, 'Why do you want to be a physician? You already have a career.' After two years of medical school rejections, I decided to head for the best graduate program in English."

Mary-Ellen began graduate study at the University of California-Davis in 1977, where she earned her master's degree in English and became intrigued by women's studies. "It struck me that there were no jobs at all for people with Ph.D.s in English," she soon realized. Reentering the Army allowed her to pursue and complete an anesthesiology program, after which she was assigned to Walter Reed Army Medical Center. Unhappy with that particular posting, she "went, anyway—in part knowing that the University of Maryland was close, and that it had a very fine women's and gender studies program."

Susan Edgerton

VISITOR

As Mary-Ellen Jacobs practiced anesthesia in Washington, D.C., Susan Edgerton was busy cloning DNA at the Louisiana State University School of Medicine. With undergraduate and graduate degrees in chemistry, Susan's search for an appropriate life fit eventually drew her into the classroom and, in time, into the curriculum field. Susan is currently an associate professor at Massachusetts College of Liberal Arts, but her roots are southern:

> My parents still live in Ruston, Louisiana, in the same house I grew up in. My father was a professor of special education and my mother was an occupational therapist at the Ruston State School, where children who were not wanted for one reason or another were sent to live. So as a young child, I saw children in situations that were difficult, and a lot different from my own.

For the most part, Susan was very quiet—a "good girl. I did everything I was supposed to do, and I hated it. I also hated school for the most part." Leaving high school in 1973, she headed west to the University of Texas in Austin.

> Going to college was one of the operational assumptions in our family. At least it felt that way to me. I was confused about what made me uncomfortable with high school because I had always been a good student. My parents were very progressive, liberal democrats: my father raged and ranted over the injustices he saw when he was out in schools, and he would talk about that at home about better ways of doing things. So while I saw some things that I really didn't like and couldn't put a finger on about schooling, I also saw schooling, or education, as liberating and valuable and potentially much different from what I had experienced.

After a year in Texas she returned home. Graduating from Louisiana Tech in 1977 with a chemistry degree, she completed a master's degree in organic chemistry in 1983, although she had become interested in philosophy. "I was also interested in teaching. . . . Part of what kept me away from teaching was that I did not want to do something that was a traditional female occupation. So, I ended up in chemistry."

Following her master's coursework, Susan went back to the University of Texas to work on a doctorate in organic chemistry and natural products synthesis:

> I was very uncomfortable. The program was extremely male dominated, which is not untypical of graduate programs in the physical sciences. Also, I was not fully committed to the program because it just didn't encompass everything I was interested in, yet it demanded complete and total commitment to a pretty narrow realm.

With an uncertain confidence, she returned to Louisiana and a job at the Louisiana State University School of Medicine.

Mary-Ellen and Susan sought an equilibrium between what they felt compelled to do socially and how they desired to live personally. This relationship between self and society has long been a dynamic within curriculum work as well, as those who approach curriculum from a primarily political-social vantage point have a tendency to "erase the individual and his or her experience in a fascination with abstractions such as 'cultural reproduction.'" However, in the words of Pinar et al. (1995, p. 565), "the individual is social and society is comprised of individuals." Indeed, it is this antagonistic blend of the political and autobiographical that unites the three distinctive biographies in this chapter—and that underlies Deborah Britzman's contribution to the 1992 special issue of *Theory Into Practice*.

PRIMARY DOCUMENT EXCERPT

Structures of Feeling in Curriculum and Teaching

by Deborah P. Britzman

Feelings are made in social relationships. The structure of feelings, then, alludes to the complex array and disarray of the feelings, desires, and commitments toward social life that students already hold because of the lives they live. While institutional structures strongly affect thought and feelings, rarely is there space for articulation. This dynamic between structures is, for the most part, fundamentally experienced as antagonistic.

I stress these relationships between institutional structures and structures of feeling because part of my commitment as a teacher educator is to encourage future teachers to articulate the relationship between the perspectives and identity struggles of their students and what this means in terms of their own pedagogy and identities. . . . At the same time . . . I am obligated to understand the perspectives of those I encounter in teacher education in order to do more with my own. . . .

June Jordan's (1988) essay, "Nobody Means More to Me Than You and the Future Life of Willie Jordan," offers a powerful example of what issues are at stake when teachers and students make sense of the relationships between curriculum and social life. . . . Jordan re-constructs how she must first persuade her African-American students to look again at the treacherous meanings and antagonistic relations of power summoned by language when dominant forms of

White English are the criteria from which to judge literacy and oral forms of Black English. The academic socialization of these students made it impossible to value their own voices and encounter the texts of their own culture on its own creative terms.

Question

Like Schubert, Britzman tells of stories and histories in relation to their contexts. How does such attention to people's situated lives pertain to curriculum work?

The dilemmas of students dismissing outright the more distressing relations between stories and histories also work through . . . an introductory summer seminar [I teach] in English education. The seminar is composed of graduate students in English studies. It is their first encounter with questions of pedagogy in English education.

Graduate students in the English seminar seem to hold tightly to the construct of the rugged individual; in the power to single-handedly rise above not just the constraints of history and culture—the messiness of everyday life—but the constraints of identity, social location, and power. Insofar as rugged individuals would like to see themselves as the sole authors of their identity, they are resistant to acknowledging the fact that sociality is governed by relations of power, and relations of power regulate the self.

The pedagogical problem was how to link [their] stories to the larger histories of domination and subordination and thus understand individual lives in relation to the social contexts they act within. At the same time, their concerns forced me to rethink my own expectations of how students should respond.

What kinds of subjugations were working within my teaching practices? On one level, I was enacting my own extensive academic socialization by assuming the curriculum as the only authorized experience. Swallowing my astonishment meant that I had to take as credible the kinds of complications these students offered. As I struggled to make sense of which problems students were responding to, I now believe they were responding to the spaces in my own pedagogy, of how we go about the vulnerable work of connecting individual lives to persistent social dilemmas, and of how we learn to tolerate the detours of experience—the times when learning does not mean progress and when curriculum antagonizes the students' hopes and desires.

On another level, the subjugating moments of this seminar eased when we began to address the complications that do spring from the underside of teaching and learning. And yet, the meanings of subjugation are far more slippery than the teacher's power to authorize experience. The dynamics of subjugation are also enacted when students dismiss the stories and lives of others as irrelevant to their own.

There still remains the dilemma of what it might mean to consider the vulnerabilities of experience: the clash between one's theories of how individuals should act and the actual enacted practices that beguile the meanings we make. These are the more interesting dilemmas posed by theory and practice. Exploring the controversies of our time coincidentally means attending to the controversies and deep investments of the self. The social orientation may well begin to open spaces for new relationships between theory and practice; it might create more critical ways for addressing the uneasy relationship between structures of feelings and structures of institutions. The disturbing continuities between the academy and the field, then, may be more significant than what is presently being perceived.

Source: Britzman, D. P. (1992). Structures of feeling in curriculum and teaching. *Theory Into Practice*, 31(3), 252–258. From a theme issue on "Grounding Contemporary Curriculum Thought." Copyright 1992, College of Education, The Ohio State University.

Implosion and the Search for Efficiency

Greatly influenced by the humanities, the arts, and social theory, the postmodern curriculum era witnessed the emerging of a complex collection of curricular forms and understandings. These genres, or to use Pinar's organizational schema, "discourses," will likely shape contemporary curricular efforts well into the next century.

By mid-decade, the "majors" of the curriculum field—including Ohio State, Teachers College, and Stanford—were giving way to diverse, first-rate graduate programs producing a new generation of curriculum workers. Curriculum work, though, still revolved around one of four major philosophical approaches well articulated in *The Struggle for the American Curriculum* (Kliebard, 1986/1995). In the mid-to-late 1980s, interest groups ranging from the most traditional (Kliebard's "humanists") to the more radical (Kliebard's "social meliorists") continued their decades-long quest for the hearts and minds of America's youth.

Within curriculum books we find that as historians such as Kliebard (2004) and Cuban (1986) situated present-day problems and issues of education, others focused on its positive (e.g., Smith, Meine, Prunty, & Dwyer, 1986; van Til, 1986) or seamier pasts (e.g., Franklin, 1986; Hampel, 1986; Shor, 1986). This same traditional range was evident in books about schooling and life in schools as well, with some authors (e.g., Joyce, 1986) wishing to "improve" schools and others (e.g., McLaren, 1986) aiming to bring a meliorist critique to how participants make sense of these institutions.

Perhaps the most vivid display of this range can be seen among the publications about teachers and teaching. On the one hand we find

Handbook of Research on Teaching (Wittrock, 1986), accompanied by the third edition of the popular *Models of Teaching* (Joyce & Weil, 1986/1996) and the government's own *What Works: Research about Teaching and Learning* (U.S. Department of Education, 1986). Meanwhile, Clandinin (1986), Connelly and Clandinin (1988), and Jackson (1986) penned more complex thoughts on what teachers do well, Egan (1986) pushed the conversation of teaching toward "story telling," and van Manen (1986) spoke of teaching's "tone." From the critical tradition, Apple (1986) explored the political economy of class and gendered relations in *Teachers and Texts*, Wexler (1987) conducted a *Social Analysis of Education*, and Giroux examined the role of *Teachers as Intellectuals* (1988b) and *Schooling and the Struggle for Public Life* (1988a). Meanwhile, Shor explained the application of *Freire for the Classroom* (1987), Beyer and Apple (1988) investigated politics, problems, and possibilities in *The Curriculum*, Roman and Christian-Smith (1988) considered *Feminism and the Politics of Popular Culture*, and Lesko (1988) described Catholic high school rites in *Symbolizing Society*.

Most oddly juxtaposed in 1988 were Laurel Tanner's conventionally grounded *Critical Issues in Curriculum* and William Pinar's eclectic *Contemporary Curriculum Discourses*. Tanner, editing Part I of the NSSE's 87th yearbook, identified "school administrators and supervisors and professors of curriculum and supervision" as diverse curriculum workers who "share responsibility for the interactive functions of curriculum development and professional development" (L. Tanner, 1988, p. 1). Meanwhile, Pinar (1988a, p. 8) declared victory for the "reconceptualists," observing "that Tylerian dominance has passed." In lyric praise of his generation's efforts, he continued: "Like a disappearing star in another galaxy, however, it takes some years for everyone, depending upon his or her location, to see this. The fact is that to a remarkable extent reconceptualization has occurred." As a footnote to this statement, itself symbolic, he added:

> While the academic field of curriculum studies has been reconceived, the major ideas which constitute the contemporary field of study have yet to make their way to colleagues in elementary and secondary schools. (p. 13)

In short, curriculum writers offered a good deal of new and intriguing attention to teachers' work during this decade. While Pinar recognized the absence of these fresh understandings among elementary and secondary educators, Laurel Tanner placed the responsibility for addressing the field's "critical issues" in the lap of school administrators and curriculum professors. At the time, the likely success of directly transmitting such new thinking and critical issues to teachers through a hierarchical "trickle down" model of curriculum development or professional development was slim at best.

Question

In what various ways do teachers come to know and understand new and different ways of thinking about curriculum work?

This post-Tylerian transformation of the curriculum field, though, was already undergoing its own transformation. The various groupings articulated by Kliebard (humanists, developmentalists, social meliorists, and social efficiency advocates) and Pinar (political analysis, aesthetic criticism, phenomenological studies, and feminist studies) were giving way to more complex or fractured discourses. Pinar recognized this trend, admitting that his as well as others' work "fits in no one category easily" (1988a, p. 7).

Categorically Denied

Similarly, the music industry would lose its identifiable range of musical genres (rock, country, soul, and classical). In 1984, when RCA released a five-record set, *Elvis: 50th Anniversary Collection*, the coveted Grammys, awarded by the National Academy of Recording Artists and Sciences, were swept by Michael Jackson, who won an unprecedented eight awards. A dozen years later, with the music industry consolidated through megamergers and vertical and horizontal integration, the number of record labels and Grammys had ballooned, with multigenre acts Seal and Annie Lennox dominating the annual event. Lyotard's postmodern condition indeed!

Lyotard's critique of technologized postindustrial Western thought and life, in *The Postmodern Condition* (1979/1984), centers on the growing need to reduce language to its most efficient uses. He refers to this phenomenon as the performativity principle, noting that this principle comes into play in various aspects of life—including the production and transmission of knowledge—that succumb to a logic of performance aimed at maximizing the overall efficiency of some greater system. When this happens, what Lyotard refers to as a "terroristic denial of difference," occurs: all language games are treated as equal in service to some pre-established whole; those that do not serve this common end disappear. Ultimately, this technological understanding or rationale for developing, transmitting, and legitimating knowledge replaces a philosophical understanding.

To prevent this, Lyotard suggests that we "move to a notion of the unrepresentable, to that . . . which resists the logic of performativity and which therefore serves as the basis for an idea of justice based on the acceptance of . . . multiple discourses or differends" (Poster, 1992, p. 574). As we have illustrated, performativity remained a force within the curriculum field, though an unmistakably diminishing one as growing numbers of curriculum writers struggled to represent the unrepresentable. Examples of curriculum's multiple discourses during this period include *Human Interests in the Curriculum* (Bullough, Goldstein, & Holt, 1984), *Interpreting Education: Science, Ideology, and Values* (Edel, 1985), *The Tone of Teaching* (van Manen, 1986), *"The Having of Wonderful Ideas"* and *Other Essays on Teaching and Learning* (Duckworth, 1987), *Changing Our Minds* (Aiken, Anderson, Dinnerstein, Lensink, & MacCorquodale, 1988), and *Reading Curriculum Theory* (Reynolds, 1989). Although one may find evidence of a central or core position (e.g., feminism or political analysis) within these examples, naming or categorizing such texts would be the sort of futile exercise abandoned as nonsensical by contemporary curriculum workers.

Yet while differences grew among cutting-edge curricularists, many educational writers sought unifying themes or denounced the trend toward "disunifying" the culture. Fantini (1986) and Tomlinson and Walberg (1986) spoke, still, of excellence in schools; T. Gordon (1986) addressed the link between democracy and progressivism; and Wigginton (1985) kept spinning folktales of the Foxfire experience. Others continued to extol continuity (e.g., Chittenden & Kiniry, 1986; Gorwood, 1986), the core curriculum (e.g., Gorter, 1986; G. Kirk, 1986), and the field's bedrock practice of curriculum planning (e.g., Kelly, 1986; Lawton, 1986; Leithwood, 1986). Curriculum-specific texts emphasized the bread-and-butter aspects of curriculum work such as leadership (Glatthorn, 1987), management (English, 1987), basic skills (Choate, 1987), and course design (Earl, 1987). This "terroristic denial of differences" within curriculum studies and education generally would continue for decades.

VARIED TALE

POPULAR MUSIC: PERFORMATIVITY AND UNREPRESENTABILITY

We can see the emerging acceptance of multiple discourses at work in the evolution of both the music industry and the contemporary curriculum field. From the postwar to the postmodern era, the largest recording labels, or "majors," have consistently accounted for the majority of volume and revenue. This handful of labels has also generally dominated the recording industry's chart list. During the late 1940s and early 1950s, four majors (Decca, Capitol, RCA/Victor, and Columbia) produced about 70% of the *Billboard* hit records. By the early 1960s, however, these labels accounted for only one-quarter of the Top-Ten hits. The British invasion of rock music, coupled with California surf

(continued)

music and later with the Haight-Ashbury sound, enabled the majors to once again control hit record production; by 1979, 86% of *Billboard* activity was back in their hands.

In 1983, the music business was recovering from the great Crash of '79, which witnessed corporate downsizing and the release of numerous artists from their contracts. Factors ranging from economic hard times, fragmentation of AM radio listeners, and a dwindling teenage market to home taping, the decline of disco and the jukebox, and the rise of punk (not to mention multimillion-dollar recording contracts) resulted in a nearly $1 billion decrease in revenue during the interim four years.

Faced with decreasing sales, increasing costs, organizational overhead, and the bureaucracy of these corporate giants, independent record companies grew in the early 1980s, increasing their single record share from 6 to 15%. Historically, independent record companies (known as "indies" or specialties) have focused on specialized genres of music considered too financially or politically risky for the majors. This "communal music" such as the hillbilly and race records of the 1920s and 1930s, appeared on blues, jazz, and country labels including Blue Note, Vocalion, Commodore, Brunswick, and Okeh. Beginning in the 1950s, the Motown label produced its "Detroit sound" with artists such as the Miracles, Marvin Gaye, Stevie Wonder, and later the Supremes and the Jackson Five all recording on Motown or its subsidiary labels, Tamal and Gordy. Memphis-based Sun Records, which produced rhythm and blues (R&B) and country rock, represented notable artists including Elvis Presley, Johnny Cash, Jerry Lee Lewis, Carl Perkins, and Junior Parker. In the 1960s and 1970s, other indies secured marketing niches by forming around one artist, such as A & M (Tijuana Brass), Apple (the Beatles), and Capricorn (the Allman Brothers Band). By the 1990s, however, many independent labels had been acquired by the majors with the rest marketing primarily in the gospel, folk, classical, children's, and ethnic genres.

Three events in the early 1980s contributed to the rebounding of the music industry: the birth of music video coupled with a $20 million venture between Warner Amex and American Express; the emergence of new blockbuster albums such as *Thriller, Flashdance,* and *Synchronicity;* and the advent of computer disk (CD) technology, which led to consumers replacing their vinyl record libraries and producers increasing their profit-cost ratio. These forces mirrored those of two generations earlier, when the radio and the jukebox rescued the industry during the Great Depression and when, a generation later, Elvis, the baby boom, and the long-playing record ushered in postwar prosperity.

The development of MTV also introduced new, previously underpromoted groups to the 24-year-old and under market—consumers with little interest in aging rock stars or disco. Partly relying on European video clips, extensive exposure was given to "new romantic" groups such as Spandau Ballet, Human League, Depeche Mode, and Duran Duran, which spearheaded the electropop movement of crystalline, electronically synthesized music. Born-again pop stars like David

Bowie, who fused disco and new wave with hits like *Let's Dance*, and the postpunk, Motown-influenced British group Culture Club also benefited from this marriage of music and television. By 1984, as the dollar volume of records surpassed the pre-crash $4 billion mark, MTV was "narrowcasting" a short rotation list of album-oriented and pop rock artists—excluding specialty music such as country, blues, and soul—into 18.2 million homes with a mostly young, white male audience. Soon other cable networks such as the Nashville Network, VH1, and Black Entertainment Television were narrowcasting into other niche markets.

As the record industry consolidated through corporate mergers and the acquisition of independent labels, the mid-1980s marked the beginning of an unparalleled fusion of musical genres and crossover recording artists. By the late 1990s, musician and listener would both splinter into a multiplicity of genres and alter identities. The former architecture graduate and electrical engineer Seal, the son of Nigerian and Brazilian parents, mixed rock, pop, soul, and folk. Similarly, Annie Lennox, a student of flute at the prestigious Royal Academy of Music and later the orange-haired singer of the early 1980s synth-pop band, the Eurythmics, had also hybridized.

Curriculum Sampling

Political analysis of curriculum, the tradition Michael Apple discussed in chapter 5, remained a fundamental discourse within curriculum studies during the early 1980s. However:

> As [political analysis] grew voluminous and more complex, so did the range of interests, incorporating notions of critical pedagogy and literacy as well as issues of race, class, and gender in the 1980s. The next phase, punctuated by heated controversy and criticism from inside as well as outside the sector, was marked by continued incorporation of nearby terrains, including hostile ones, such as feminist, racial, and poststructuralist and postmodern discourses. As the sector expanded, it became divided, and, some would say, self-enclosed. (Pinar et al., 1995, pp. 313–314)

By the closing years of the decade, curriculum workers were borrowing freely from a rapidly growing identity menu. While some were at work developing a "post-liberal" theory of education and curriculum (Bowers, 1987), others clearly had the sense that curriculum had "gone astray" (Hoffman, 1987). As scholars from varied positions and perspectives chose to situate their discussions within the larger context of democracy, citizenship, and public life (e.g., Butts, 1988; Engle & Ochoa, 1988; Giroux, 1988a; Greene, 1988; Jervis & Tobier, 1988), others pushed the epistemological and ideological parameters of curriculum work. Political analysis was well established by the late 1980s (e.g., Beyer,

1988; Dalton, 1988; D. Kirk, 1988), though some of its long-standing proponents had begun to broaden its working parameters (Beyer & Apple, 1988; Giroux, 1988b). Feminist writers (e.g., Aiken et al., 1988) also pushed themselves beyond the political while theorists such as Bowers (1988) and Cherryholmes (1988) had, by this time, staked out ecocultural and poststructural positions. One of the most complex, sophisticated works of 1988 proved to be Madeleine Grumet's *Bitter Milk* (1988a)—a work that brought together numerous intellectual discourses.

Curricularists also focused on teachers (e.g., Beyer, Feinberg, Pagano, & Whitson, 1989; Connelly & Clandinin, 1988; Goodman, 1988; Jackson & Haroutunian, 1989) and the ways in which teachers' and students' lives interact pedagogically (Freire & Faundez, 1989; Oliver & Gershman, 1989). These writers were just as concerned with students "learning to question" the "fractured meaning" of their "lives on the boundary" as they were with exploring "civic education" and the "teacher as text."

Others extended analyses and understandings of pedagogy, curriculum, and the purposes of schools outside of classrooms and schools. Looking to the past to understand present interconnections among economic, cultural, personal, and social forces (I. F. Goodson, 1988; M. B. Katz, 1987; Spring, 1986, 1989), curriculum writers borrowed freely from a variety of academic disciplines while focusing on cultural struggle and everyday life (Giroux & McLaren, 1989; Giroux, Simon, & Contributors, 1989), the competitive ethos (Nicholls, 1989), the moral and spiritual crises in education (Purpel, 1989), and issues of sexual identity (Sears, 1991; 1992c). Much like the music industry, the curriculum field was transforming through its embrace of new and different ideas and interests.

VARIED TALE

POPULAR MUSIC: WHEN THE MUSIC DIED

Of course, American popular music has to some degree always freely borrowed from the musical menu; more critically stated, it "constantly steals from other sources, creating its own encapsulation by transgressing any sense of boundary and identity" (Grossberg, 1990, p. 216). In the 1950s, a subcategory of country music—honky-tonk—blended swing, blues, jazz, and country with lyrics about unrequited loves, barroom brawls, and uncertain jobs sung by the likes of Tammy Wynette and George Jones. Sam Cook, in the early 1960s, merged gospel music with secular themes, helping to found modern soul music, while James Brown stripped gospel blues to minimalist punk and Sly Stone later fused punk with rock. There was also the short-lived band Electric Flag, which combined jazz, country, blues, and rock; Bob Dylan and Donovan's fusion of folk and rock; Linda Ronstadt's and the Eagles' blend of country and rock; and Jackson Browne's country folk. Also during the 1970s the Allman Brothers Band expanded jazz "boogie jams." Bands such as Chicago and Blood, Sweat, and Tears pioneered jazz-rock; Santana added Latin rhythm; and those ranging from progressive rock performers Emerson, Lake, and Palmer to metal guitarist Eddie Van Halen integrated classical music with rock. Other diverse bands such as the Rolling Stones, Canned Heat, Led Zeppelin, and ZZ Top borrowed heavily from early blues, as did guitarists like Bonnie Raitt, Eric Clapton, and Stevie Ray Vaughan.

By the 1980s, musical fusions appeared in unlikely pairings, including Julio Iglesias with Willie Nelson, and the Traveling Wilburys (Bob Dylan, George Harrison, Tom Petty, Jeff Lynne, and Roy Orbison). Meanwhile, the fusion of American and African musical styles abounded in Paul Simon's *Graceland* and the British duo Wham!, while the dance productions of Madonna and Michael Jackson dissolved established notions of pop singing and performing. During this same period, Germany's Das Furlines pioneered the punk-polka genre as England's band the Police blended punkish energy and rock style with reggae and jazz.

We also witnessed the metamorphosis of older stars, sparking new genres or subcategories of music: David Bowie's travels from glitter rock to folk to blues; Neil Young's journey from solo acoustical ballads to sweet country rock to heavy metal distortion; and, most notably, Bob Dylan's transformations all created new musical genres. In the 1970s, Dylan had fused country, folk, and rock music with the advent of *Nashville Skyline*. By the late 1970s and early 1980s, he had christened Christian rock, releasing *Slow Train Coming*, with its single *Gotta Serve Somebody*, garnering Dylan's first Grammy for Best Rock Vocal Performance. By the mid-1980s he had repudiated conservative Christianity with the release of *Infidels* and integrated reggae, dance music, and rap in the album *Down in the Groove*.

The eighties' decade also brought unparalleled success for crossover artists and rap music. MTV's musical specialty show, *Yo! MTV Raps,* hosted by Fab 5 Freddy, popularized this urban folk poetry set to music. Quickly becoming mainstream, the majors bought or forged distributor agreements with independent labels. Hammer, signed by Capitol Records for a multi-album contract, was the first major rap artist to cross over to pop charts with *Please Hammer Don't Hurt' Em*. Another crossover rap group, Arrested Development, blended hip-hop with southern folk blues instrumentation of harmonica and acoustic guitars laced with gospel-tinged lyrics. Run-D.M.C. collaborated with Aerosmith to fuse inner-city rap with heavy metal and attracted a segment of the white, hard-rock audience. And, emerging from the hard-core punk New York underground, the Beastie Boys became the first white group to successfully sell rap, crossing into the mainstream with *License to Kill* in 1986. The American Music Award for Best Black Male Vocal in 1989 was awarded to the British singer George Michael (who is not black), while a year later the white rapper Vanilla Ice hit number one with his album *To the Extreme*.

(continued)

> The disco and punk of the 1970s also set the stage for a number of later genres, including hip-hop, rap, hard-core rock, ballroom, industrial, house, acid jazz, and techno. Hopelessness and despair distinguished the angst and anger of generation X punk, inspired by 1970s artists such as Stiv Bator, The Clash, and Sex Pistols. The early 1980s marked the emergence of urban-based groups such as Black Flag, the Circle Jerks, and Offspring, as independent recording companies tapped into this new genre. One of the best-known bands of the 1980s, the Dead Kennedys, established its label, recording songs such as *Winnebago Warrior, Terminal Preppie,* and *Nazi Punks Fuck Off.* Mostly middle-class, pain-filled youth slam-danced to hard-core music and bought hundreds of thousands of records. Germany's Einstarzencle Neubauten, the world's first industrial band, integrated percussion and guttural vocals with guitar distortions, power tools (ranging from jackhammers to power drills), and other industrial sounds such as amplified air-conditioning ducts and burning oil. A Manchester techno dance band from the late 1980s, 808 State, emphasized groove over technical expertise, contributing to the techno-rave sound with hits like *Pacific State.* House music, originating in Chicago's Warehouse Club (hence its name), technically fused African or Latin rhythms and reverb with deep drum and bass to a sped-up disco beat. A psychedelic version of house music, acid house, emerged later in London. Ultimately, this stylistic fusing and musical boundary devolution made it increasingly difficult for traditional critics and consumers alike to define popular music.

As if "reality" was not hard enough to pin down within the music world, singular readings of reality within politics, culture, and curriculum had vanished as well by the latter part of the decade. Toni Morrison's *Beloved* received the Pulitzer Prize in fiction in the same year that E. D. Hirsch Jr.'s *Cultural Literacy* (1987) and Allan Bloom's *The Closing of the American Mind* (1987) reached best-seller status. Oliver North became a media hero during the televised hearings that implicated him in the Iran-Contra debacle. Meanwhile, President Reagan's response to these congressional testimonies epitomized a postmodern spin: "A few months ago, I told the American people I did not trade arms for hostages. My heart and best intentions still tell me this is true, but the facts and the evidence tell me it's not."

Shifting Ground

As the 1980s ended, the music industry had lost its historically established identity. Struggling to redefine its multiple selves, many of its artists and listeners (old and new) were busy doing the same. While rules changed and foundations shifted or crumbled, identity construction became a part of the decade's shared workload. Members of the music world found themselves both shaping and being shaped by the forces around them as they worked across boundaries and through unknown terrain.

Recall from our introductions to Susan, Mary-Ellen and Tom, that educators, too, had individually and collectively begun these identity reconstruction projects, though in the eyes of some the tensions inherent in choosing direction did not bode well for common hopes. In the following *Theory Into Practice* excerpt, Bill Ayers, a graduate of Teachers College and former SDS leader turned Weatherman, expresses concern about the need to bring together critical theorists and those working in schools.

PRIMARY DOCUMENT EXCERPT

The Shifting Ground of Curriculum Thought and Everyday Practice

by William Ayers

The curriculum is a thing, something bought and sold, packaged and delivered. The teachers are clerks, the line employees doing their jobs. There is virtually no talk among school people of the curriculum as interactive or constructed, of teachers as transformative intellectuals or moral agents.

Question

To what extent does Ayers's opening paragraph ring true about today's school curriculum?

Talk of school improvement generally means buying a different package and inserting it into the existing structures, cultures, and realities. Ideas that are potentially transforming . . . become thus reduced to fit into mindless, airless spaces: "We have a critical thinking unit first thing in the morning." or "We do character ed. just before lunch." The name remains, but the larger reality has overwhelmed whatever might have been hopeful there.

It is a commonplace for academics to be dismissed by school teachers as being impractical, theoretical, philosophical. . . . Equally common (but less discussed at the university) is a practically universal condescension and patronization toward teachers, toward the practical. . . . This is as true for critical theorists as for empirical analytical academics.

The problem is that unlike the "critical theorists" of the 1920s or the 1960s, those who profess critical theory today are most likely to do so in a language that is arid and arcane, and from the relative safety of academe. Critical theorists espouse praxis, a complex integration of political action with intellectual inquiry, but tend to be heavy on the latter and light on the former. Where are the voices of classroom teachers struggling with these questions? Where are the insurgent alternative schools? What role do critical theorists have in making any of this happen?

People involved in changing schools have taken an important first step . . . away from the taken for granted . . . into the unknown. They are searching for new ways of thinking and doing, and they are moving with courage and hope. In this context I have found that no question is too radical, none too provocative. In fact, I have consistently been pushed by parents, students, and teachers to see the workings of politics and power in schools in much greater detail. I often ask school people whose interests are being served here, and I consistently find a complex grasp of the subtleties of control embodied in the lunchroom and the playground as well as the classroom. . . .

Theory is important. Theory helps us to organize the world, to sort out the details, to make some coherent sense out of a kaleidoscope of sensations. Without theory we would collapse exhausted from our encounter with experience. . . . making theory is simply what human beings do. Living in the world is also what we do. . . .

We should be reminded (as the women's movement so powerfully taught) that the personal is political, that we embody a stance and a social statement in our experiences, our choices, our daily lives. We should also know that there is no politics without people, that what we do or do not do matters in its detail. We can, then, stop waiting for the big moment when we can be strong, courageous, and correct, and get on with the business of living as if it made a difference.

We can resist the notion that ideas flow from thinkers to doers. . . . We should resist dogma-theory as a closed, justifying framework that hides reality. We should stay alive to questions, to contradiction, to ambiguity, to the next utterance in the dialogue. And, yes, to spontaneity. We should be for intellect, for a continual desire to see more, to know more. And we should be for a morality linked to action.

[T]here is no proper way to ground curriculum thought in school practice outside of doing it.

Source: Ayers, W. (1992). The shifting ground of curriculum thought and everyday practice. *Theory Into Practice, 31*(3), 259–263. From a theme issue on "Grounding Contemporary Curriculum Thought." Copyright 1992, College of Education, The Ohio State University.

▓ Tom Barone

VISITOR

Tom Barone was drawn to curriculum studies by some of the very ideas Ayers presented—"a continual desire to see more, to know more" and to link morality with action. While seeking his initial teacher certification, Tom enrolled in a curriculum course at the University of New Orleans. In his words:

> That was probably the moment at which I became intrigued with the field of curriculum. I could see how this curriculum course connected with my philosophy background. What appealed to me about education was that it had that balance between thought and practice. I sensed that opportunities were being lost and that the traditional structure of the school was lacking in many ways. I thought maybe what I could do would be to become a teacher educator. Maybe that's the path to power here?

Carefully reading the works of curriculum writers, Tom pondered where to enroll if he was to pursue advanced study. "One night in the Tulane library, I read a couple of articles by Elliot Eisner and knew almost immediately this was the person who made the most sense to me." Tom applied to Stanford in 1974, excited about moving from a more quantitative and technical curricular orientation to one that was more qualitative and holistic:

> Actually, I don't know that I had read any examples of the kind of writing I had in mind at the time. I had read some ethnography and I realized that you could use thick description. I was also interested in the new journalism, reading people like Norman Mailer, Tom Wolfe, and Joan Didion and wondering why the heck can't we write that way and have it be legitimate in terms of educational research. It was considered fairly unusual, radical even, to think about writing the kind of dissertation that I had in mind. But I knew that Elliot would provide a kind of cover for me to do that, which he did.

While at Stanford, Barone also came to understand the curriculum field through courses taught by professors such as Decker Walker, who was working through his naturalistic approach to curriculum development, and Eisner, who "broadened my spectrum of understanding. I remember for the first time really reading Michael Apple's work and being influenced by his ideas, somewhat to the chagrin of Elliot."

After completing his doctorate in 1978 and while teaching at Northern Kentucky University, Tom attended his first reconceptualist conference at Airlie. "It was an eye-opening experience because there seemed to be so much rancor and divisiveness." Among the major curricular camps' representatives "you could actually see the tension in the curriculum field being played out before your eyes. I had previously understood this dissension at an intellectual level with no real sense of the human passion behind it."

Few would deny that, by the late 1980s, curriculum had become an "extraordinarily complicated conversation" (Pinar et al., 1995, p. 848). It had become nearly impossible to categorically place curriculum books. The unusual array of topical curriculum books in 1988, for example—from modular (Moon, 1988) and negotiated (Johnston & Dowdy, 1988) to organic (R. Hunter & Scheirer, 1988) and holistic (J. P. Miller, 1988)—is a clue that the curriculum field, at least with respect to the books one might peruse, had changed.

The publication of the second edition of the popular 1978 reader *Curriculum: An Introduction to the Field* (Gress & Purpel, 1988) was emblematic of the changing times. Consciously organizing previously published curriculum writing to illustrate the field's breadth and complexity, this revision eliminated two former sections: curriculum engineering and the nature and formulation of objectives. In lieu of these traditionally essential curriculum topics, the editors inserted a new section on the hidden curriculum, including work on sex bias, social class, moral education, and cultural politics.

In contrast, William Pinar (1988a) arrayed six perspectives on curriculum theorizing in his carefully titled reader, *Contemporary Curriculum Discourses*. Here, in lieu of talk about subject matter content, curriculum planning, or critical issues, he situated theorizing from varied positions, including political or critical analyses such (Anyon, 1988; Apple, 1988) and phenomenological analyses (Grumet, 1988b; van Manen, 1988). With aesthetic criticism and phenomenology elevated to an equal status with political analysis, for example, readers come away with an overall sense that the curriculum field had indeed, in Pinar's words (1988a, p. 7), become "complicated, with several centers of focus."

No longer contained within conventional discussions of subject matter, organizational schemas, or functional procedures and, for that matter, no longer bound exclusively to schooling, the field's long-standing fascination with institutional discourses had been permanently disturbed—for better or for worse. In place of its "bland eclecticism" and "paradigmatic unity" we see a move "away from curriculum as institutional text" to a situation that, by this time, had become "particularistic and even balkanized" (Pinar et al., 1995, p. 849).

Through biography as curricular text we can see how individuals reconstructed themselves and their work, including the need to reread past decisions and changes. Susan and Mary-Ellen return, below, to share their stories of transformation.

In January 1983, Mary-Ellen Jacobs drove to the University of Maryland campus at College Park to pick up a catalog of spring courses. While visiting the women's and gender studies department, she discovered it offered no evening classes: "Talk about elitism: you could only do women's studies during the day!" Hoping to run the Army's anesthesia school and knowing that the woman then in charge had a Ph.D. in education, Mary-Ellen looked over the graduate course offerings in education. "Wanting to get started immediately," she recalls, "I simply began taking courses. I had no idea what curriculum was, other than the category of space where my courses were located in the catalog."

Toward the end of that first semester, after considering a move from women's and gender studies into education, Mary-Ellen was referred to Louise Berman:

> Louise invited me to an end-of-semester get together at her house the following week—you know, come out and meet students and faculty and talk to them. I did go, but I still had no idea what curriculum was and no idea if I belonged or whether I should get a degree in that area. But I decided to keep taking classes and switch over to the curriculum program.

Taking an introductory curriculum course with Berman, who was using the Saylor, Alexander, and Lewis (fourth edition, 1981) synoptic curriculum text, Mary-Ellen found herself

> totally bored by the whole thing, in part because in [a previous] course we had used Pinar's *Curriculum Theorizing: The Reconceptualists* [1975]. I had to do a paper, and I remember picking up Pinar's book for some reason and really looking at it. I began to see that I could put my knowledge of English and literature together with thinking about nursing education and other aspects of my life. So Pinar's book really changed me.

Although she enjoyed her courses at Maryland, Mary-Ellen began to wonder about her future. "I loved doing clinical anesthesia, but I really loved what I was doing at the University of Maryland, too." In January 1986, she committed to the Ph.D. program full-time, "even though I knew *nothing* about education."

Since she had never taught in public school, she enrolled in a master's program to earn a secondary English teaching certificate.

> I didn't want to be a teacher; I wanted to get my doctorate. But I remained in the program and they arranged a very nontraditional student teaching internship in a whole lot of different schools doing English and language arts with K–12 kids. I was asked to return to teach English at Howard High School the following year while my former cooperating teacher there was out on maternity leave. That year as a teacher really gave me a sense of what schools were about and what I was about as a teacher.

Since 1979, feminism had remained important for Mary-Ellen, so "it wasn't long into my stay at Maryland before I recognized that the curriculum field was contentious." Combining her interests in feminist studies, literature, curriculum, and women as curriculum theorists, her dissertation explored the work of Maxine Greene. Ultimately, Mary-Ellen recognized, "I wasn't just writing about Maxine Greene: in many ways I was writing about myself."

By pursuing her interests in curriculum as a gendered discourse, Mary-Ellen came to appreciate the long history of women who had spent their careers questioning curriculum tradition and waiting to be taken seriously. The most profound aspect of their work is perhaps their persistence in not categorizing or compartmentalizing our understandings of curriculum. Returning again to Pinar et al. (1995, p. 403):

> Perhaps no other single discursive configuration in the field circulates these traditional concepts into a kaleidoscopic theoretical whole as effectively as that sector of scholarship that labors to understand curriculum as gendered text. As the 1990s unfold, feminist curriculum theorists and others committed to gender analysis will no doubt continue to confront the ways all of us . . . are affected . . . by the gender system that forms and deforms us. It is urgent work . . . at the center of the field.

Susan Edgerton, too, works at this central place in curriculum. Like Mary-Ellen, Susan would see the contours and controversies within the curriculum field from her emergent vantage point. While employed as a chemist, she learned of a teaching position in Shreveport at a local private school. Joining the faculty in 1984, she taught one middle school mathematics class along with chemistry, physics, physical science, biology, and advanced-placement chemistry. Yet it was an opportunity to teach anthropology "and do anything with the course I wished" that deeply affected her future:

> I decided to teach cultural anthropology and look at what I was calling at the time contemporary American culture. In other words, we would not focus our gaze on so-called primitive or third-world cultures, but we would focus on ourselves in relation to other cultures. I learned a tremendous amount just preparing for that class, which I taught for three years. And that was a turning point for me, too, because I felt like I had found something that was bringing back earlier interests and combining them with later ones.

While Susan attended graduate classes at Louisiana State University's Shreveport campus, Bill Pinar had become chair of the curriculum department at Louisiana State's main campus in Baton Rouge and created a program that linked graduate study in curriculum at regional campuses with eventual doctoral residency at the main campus. In 1988, Susan left teaching for Baton Rouge and full-time doctoral studies. She remembers:

> Meeting Bill Pinar, eventually, was very important. Bill invited me and Joe Kincheloe to present with him at AERA and Bergamo on something about the South. That exploration ended up becoming a book, *Curriculum as Social Psychoanalysis* [Kincheloe & Pinar, 1991]. To prepare for those presentations, I started reading more literary kinds of things as well as

critical theory, philosophy, etc. But reading Maya Angelou's autobiography sent me in a new direction, because suddenly I discovered literature, which was an important part of my life before. All of a sudden I felt like, why didn't anybody tell me that everything is there; that everything I need, almost, is in literature?

But just being around Bill and the other faculty in Baton Rouge introduced me to a whole new body of literature. The intellectual environment was exciting. He had brought in Leslie Roman and Cameron McCarthy—contemporaries who had worked with Michael Apple at the University of Wisconsin—and Jacques Daignault, Bill Doll, and Tony Whitson. So those were my teachers, primarily, though I also worked with Richard Moreland, a Faulkner scholar in the English Department.

As a doctoral student between 1988 and 1991, Edgerton saw the faculty as respectful of one another and their differences, but she "left that program under no illusions that there was some sort of unified curriculum field."

Metanarratives and Nanonarratives: The Postmodern Curriculum Condition

Throughout the twentieth century, Western philosophers have sought a collective voice to represent unified positions or metanarratives regarding knowledge and truth. Lyotard's *The Postmodern Condition* (1979/1984) represented a clear incredulity toward such metanarratives and universal reason. According to Peters (1995, p. 388):

> the reason why Lyotard's work has given rise to such controversy is that it epitomizes, self-reverentially, the very conditions for discourse in the "postmodern condition." . . . Where multiple parties are involved from a variety of genres of discourse, each with a different perspective or argument.. . . it is perhaps no wonder that there is no one ruling or hegemonic genre, no overarching meta-discourse, language-game or metanarrative, and no rule of judgment applicable to all arguments.

This postmodern medley of nanonarratives promotes cultural heterogeneity and difference while recognizing that such a situation will inevitably contain "differends"—fundamental conflicts between parties that cannot be equitably resolved for lack of a rule applicable to all conflicting parties. For Lyotard, the aim of philosophy is not to resolve differends but rather to detect (a cognitive task) and bear witness to them (an ethical obligation).

Since the mid-1980s, there has been a strong and unmistakable emergence of these nanonarratives within the curriculum literature, all eroding the dominant Enlightenment paradigm and exposing its oppressive metanarratives. Per Lyotard's analysis, the "rule of consensus . . . has been finally rent asunder. The narrative function has been dispersed into many language elements, each with its own pragmatic valencies. We are left with only 'language particles'" (Peters, 1995, pp. 389–390). At decade's end, the relative value of these language particles for the construction and legitimation of curriculum knowledge and identity, as well as the recognition and reading of curriculum texts and discourses, added shape and form to their substance. And, the field evolved into curricular particles.

The positivist metanarrative that had dominated the field since its genesis, and against which oppositional voices had waged unflinching assaults, was now chimeric. These oppositional discourses, including critical theory, feminism, and phenomenology, had enfolded and spawned scores of curriculum genres, including critical postmodernism, feminist poststructuralist methodology, eschatology, and autobiography, and, in the process, created "problems of cross-discourse communication" (Pinar et al., 1995, p. 865).

It was into this fractured curricular world of overlapping and rapidly changing boundaries that the new generation of curriculum workers entered. No longer searching for curricular consensus or consolidation that would merely return us to the state of reductive homogenization of varied multiple interests (which, by design, requires metanarratives), these newest curriculum dissidents were united in their rejection of curriculum "performance" as the power-based legitimizing notion of a technological metanarrative:

> The question (overt or implied) now asked by the professional student, the State, or institution of higher education is no longer "Is it true?" but "What use is it?" In the context of the mercantilization of knowledge, more often than not this question is equivalent to: "Is it salable?" And in the context of power-growth: "Is it efficient?" (Lyotard, 1979/1984, p. 51)

Despite their diversity, all of the *Theory Into Practice* selections excerpted here reject this performativity principle. They differ markedly, however, on the actual and desired relationship between theory and practice. In our final selection from this collection of essays, we turn to William Pinar, who holds fast to the position that pleas for peaceful coexistence between theory and practice relative to curriculum and schooling in particular are misguided and that these "worlds apart" must remain as such.

▼PRIMARY DOCUMENT EXCERPT

"Dreamt into Existence by Others": Curriculum Theory and School Reform

by William F. Pinar

Despite the disguised political motives for the current school reform movement and the "bottom line" character of reform, this is a time of genuine opportunity. I applaud those . . . who embrace this time of opportunity and work with the schools, determined to help realize the educational ideals of teachers, teacher educators, and students. I believe some measure of educationally sound reform can be made at this time.

Perhaps teachers will be granted greater discretion over instructional method, although greater discretion over curriculum strikes me as less likely . . . A change as modest as a return to electives and flexible scheduling would constitute a remarkable advance, even if it represents only an "advance" back to the 1960s.

Many teachers today seem hardened, sullen, brittle, easily indignant. It is as if long ago they lost hope for significant change in the schools. It is as if long ago they lost hope they could teach all children. If that is true, one might say that the times defeated them, not just the massive retreat from the innovations of the 1960s. . . .

Because the organization and culture of the school are linked to the economy, the school is not ideal "ground" for "curriculum thought." For the foreseeable future, teachers will be trained as "social engineers" directed to "manage" learning that is modeled after corporate work stations. Certainly some segment of the curriculum field will devote itself to assist in the design of the corporate school curriculum. However, those of us who labored to reconceptualize the ahistorical, atheoretical field we found in 1970 (Pinar, 1975) have always seen a more complex calling for the curriculum field (Pinar, 1991). The theoretical wing of the reconceived field aspires to ground itself not in the pressured everyday world of the classroom but in worlds not present in schools, in ideas marginal to the maximization of profit, and in lived experience that is not exclusively instrumental and calculative.

These "worlds apart" from the pressure and instrumentality of the daily classroom may seem valueless to the harassed teacher, pressured to raise the test scores of students who may not have eaten that day or slept the night before. As much as we are pulled to help our school colleagues, true help may involve more than the provision of practical answers to everyday problems. Our presence may prove more valuable in the longer term if we continue to point to other worlds, worlds that might enable our school colleagues to achieve sufficient distance from the daily pressure to make a separate peace, while devising creative and self-affirmative strategies for teaching.

If theory does not exist to provide practical solutions to everyday problems, why does it exist?

Theory must create spaces apart from the pressurized sphere of practical activity, spaces in which the demands of the state and of the principal, parents, and students can be viewed, understood, and reframed as questions posed to oneself. By living in worlds apart from the everyday, we might participate in the daily world with more intensity and intelligence.

School reform that moves us from the factory or the assembly-line model of schooling to a corporate model will probably produce welcomed if incremental improvements in test scores and in the quality of life in schools. These would be genuine accomplishments, well worth our labor. However, more profound issues of identity, politics, and experience will tend to be ignored unless theory stays out of bed with practice, continues to wait in other rooms while policy-makers and politicians wrestle with the excitement, pleasure, and frustration of programmatic conceptions. We theorists must continue to create separate rooms of our own in which we try to see past the corporate model, to not necessarily economic forms of human organization, intelligence, and experience. We must not do so with arrogance but with the humility that accompanies the knowledge that we, too, are conceived by others.

What value is theory to the practitioner? To those teachers hardened by 20 years of conservative reaction, it will seem pointless indeed. To the novice teacher eager to earn "merit" salary increases by effective problem solving in the corporate school, it will seem fanciful, perhaps interesting, to be reserved for later, much later. The constituency of theorists may not be in schools at this time. However, if we can teach, if we can make friends with our colleagues struggling in the schools, build bridges between the realms of theory and of practice, create passages—to borrow Daignault's phrase (1992)—to travel from here to there and back again, broadened, deepened, enlivened by the voyage, then we theorists might participate with subtlety and acumen in school reform. Being a theorist does not mean being dissociated or inefficient. Being a theorist does not mean being a celibate in terms of everyday practice. It does not mean one cannot function successfully in the corporate school, providing advice and assistance. Being a theorist does mean that contemporary curriculum organization and the modes of cognition it requires can be bracketed, situated in history, politics, and ourselves. Such theory might allow us to participate in school reform in ways that do not hypostatize the present, but rather, allow our labor and understandings to function as do those in psychoanalysis, to enlarge the perception and deepen the intelligence of the participants.

Theory must stay out of bed with current reform in order to remain free to theorize modes of knowing and knowledge linked with neither the factory nor the corporate model. While harassed practitioners may find such theory not immediately translatable into practical action, they may find that such theory, in underlining the arbitrariness of current practice, provides a lived distance sufficiently apart from the everyday to support self-affirmative, critical, and creative curriculum and teaching.

Source: Pinar, W. F. (1992). "Dreamt into existence by others": Curriculum theory and school reform, *Theory Into Practice, 31*(3), 228–235. From a theme issue on "Grounding Contemporary Curriculum Thought." Copyright 1992 College of Education, The Ohio State University.

▣ Eclectic Connections

Though Jesse Jackson became the first African-American presidential candidate to win several state primaries, George H. W. Bush easily won the general U.S. presidential election in 1988. Bush's call for a "kinder, gentler nation" bathed in "a thousand points of light" promoted volunteerism while Bobby McFerrin's tune *Don't Worry, Be Happy* captured Grammys for both song and record of the year. Two-parent families accounted for only one in four American households, and Tracey Chapman sang of dislocation and unrest.

The following year was marked by other improbable, contradictory images. The Berlin Wall collapsed and a playwright was elected as president of Czechoslovakia. Before leaving our solar system, *Voyager II* (launched in 1977) transmitted data from the planet Neptune, while on this planet, former education secretary William Bennett, now the nation's drug czar, waged a "war" against cocaine (including crack), which was being used regularly by 1 in every 100 sixth graders. And, as Bette Midler and Bonnie Raitt accepted their 1989 music awards, the unconventional-looking pop duo Milli Vanilli, admitting that they never actually sang on their multiplatinum album, raised issues of identity and representation within popular music culture.

Some history, though, changed little. The Chinese army slaughtered demonstrators in Beijing's Tiananmen Square and the United States invaded Central America, arresting one-time ally Manuel Noriega. The year that Francis Fukuyama (in *The National Interest)* announced "the end of history," the aging Rolling Stones grossed some $70 million while on tour. And, as the Rolling Stones extended their quarter century of rock 'n' rolling in 1989, Ronald C. Doll published the seventh edition of his 25-year-old book, *Curriculum Improvement: Decision Making and Process,* the *only* synoptic curriculum text published that year. To be sure, some published works continued to focus on ways for curriculum leaders (Martin, Glatthorn, Winsters, & Saif, 1989) and central office administrators (Pajak, 1989) to develop and document (Armstrong, 1989) or manage (Oliva, 1988/1997; Preedy, 1989) the curriculum. Some, too, wrote on conventional curriculum and instruction topics such as grade-specific efforts (Klein, 1989), computing (Crompton, 1989), and vocational education (Finch & Crunkilton, 1989). A growing number of curriculum writers, though, chose to pursue more complex discussions, sampling from such diverse sources as literary and aesthetic theory, liberation theology and biblical hermeneutics, Vygotskyan social constructivism and Piagetian biological constructivism, chaos theory, postmodern anthropology, Saussurean linguistics, postcolonial theory, semiology, and feminist psychoanalytic analyses. Needless to say, centrists within the field viewed such contributions as intellectual excursions, moving far astray from curriculum and instruction.

V ARIED TALE

POPULAR MUSIC: POSTMODERN POP

From the vantage point of the conventional, popular music, too, had gone astray from its narrow and predictable genres and its historical demarcations by age, gender, and race. So much borrowing, genre bending, and diffusion made it impossible to keep up with the industry's postmodern array of categories and subcategories. Some music does, however, stand out.

Perhaps the subcategory that best characterizes the emergence of the postmodern musical age is hip-hop. Associated with aspects of hip-hop culture such as break dancing, Adidas tennis shoes, crews and posses, oversized pants, graffitied subway cars, and upturned baseball caps, hip-hop used bass lines and looped drum tracks woven with guitar riffs and digitally sampled sound to create counter-hegemonic narratives that reflect urban disillusionment and alienation.

De La Soul was the first of the alternative rap groups, which also included P.M. Dawn and Basehead. Its 1989 album, *3 Feet High and Rising,* went against the hip-hop tradition of machismo rap lyrics. Choosing light rhythms and a quasi-hip attitude, De La Soul sampled from obscure recordings and television shows, clearly signifying the advent of postmodernism: "De La Soul's debut LP was unexpectedly hailed as the Sergeant Pepper of rap, bending the rules of sequencing, referencing and sampling to shape a new form of music. Sonic space was opened up, tracks varied in length, rhyming became more relaxed and informal and a whacky brand of humour was introduced" (Harley, 1993, p. 218). Using instruments of modernist technology such as computers, drum machines, sequencers, and the digital audiotape, sampling and the use of digitally synthesized sounds signaled the arrival of postmodernism to popular music:

> By ripping words away from their socially designated relationships meaning can no longer be assumed and the power to define has been usurped. Avant-garde music frequently employs this strategy of decontextualizing cultural voices. . . . No one final meaning can be constructed from a sound collage. There is no longer an author, just a jumbled concoction of voices vying to be heard above the din. . . . The rearrangement of voices and sound returns musical creation to anyone who chooses to practice the deconstruction . . . . The imagination, as opposed to instrumental reason, is given the chance to direct the flow of sound. Now, all possibilities are available to both the artist and listener . . . [to] the opening of a channel to a subjectivity outside the territory claimed by means-ends rationality. (Coreno, 1994, pp. 210–213)

As the 1980s ended, U.S. music was a $6.5 billion industry domestically, generating sales three times that internationally. Rock music accounted for nearly one-half of record sales, followed far behind by country-western, with about 15%, and classical, with less than 5%. In the curriculum field, "reconceptualist" or contemporary curriculum discourses now accounted for a sizable proportion of presentations at the highly respected AERA annual meetings, as papers and presenters in Division B (Curriculum Studies) reflected the diffuse outgrowth of the once-mischievous Curriculum Theory conferences. Lyotard, it seems, had been correct.

V isitor **Bibliography**   Tom Barone

Barone, T. (2000). *Aesthetics, politics, and educational inquiry: Essays and examples*. New York: Peter Lang Publishing.

Barone, T. (2001a). Pragmatizing the imaginary: On the fictionalization of case studies of teaching. *Harvard Educational Review, 7*(4), 735–742.

Barone, T. (2001b). *Touching eternity: The enduring outcomes of teaching*. New York: Teachers College Press.

Barone, T. (2001c). The end of the terror: Disclosing the complexities of teaching. *Curriculum Inquiry, 31*(1), 89–102.

Barone, T. (2002). From genre blurring to audience blending: Reflections on the field emanating from an ethnodrama. *Anthropology and Education Quarterly, 33*(2), 255–267.

V isitor **Bibliography**   Mary-Ellen Jacobs

Adams, N., Causey, T., Munro, P., Jacobs, M-E., & Quinn, M. (October, 1994). Invisible mending: A reader's theatre performance of teachers' narratives. JCT Conference on Curriculum Theory and Classroom Practice, Banff, Alberta, Canada.

Jacobs, M.E. (1991). *Diary of an ambivalent daughter: A feminist re-visioning of Maxine Greene's discursive landscapes*. Unpublished doctoral dissertation, University of Maryland at College Park.

Jacobs, M.E. (1992). Teacher lore: Learning from our experience. *Teaching Education, 5* (1), 153–157.

Jacobs, M.E. (1993). Teachers' voices for school change: An introduction to educative research. *Teaching Education, 5* (2), 95–97.

Jacobs, M.E. (1998). Living dangerously: Toward a poetics of women's lived experience. In W.C. Ayers & J.L. Miller (Eds.), *A light in dark times: Maxine Greene and the unfinished conversation* (pp. 180–189). New York: Teachers College Press.

Jacobs, M.E., & Munro, P. (1995). (Re) reading women's lives. *Qualitative Inquiry, 1* (3), 327, 19 pp.

Jacobs, M.E., & Roderick, J.A. (1988). Diary of a singular season: Reflecting on dilemmas in teaching writing. *Language Arts, 65* (7), 642–51.

V isitor Bibliography Susan Edgerton

Edgerton, S. H. (1991). "Particularities of 'Otherness': Maya Angelou, Autobiography, and Me." In Joe L. Kincheloe and William F. Pinar (Eds.), *Curriculum as Social Psychoanalysis: The Significance of Place*. Albany, NY: SUNY Press.

Edgerton, S. H. (1993a). "Toni Morrison teaching the interminable." In Warren Chrichlow and Cameron McCarthy (Eds.), *Race, Identity, and Representation in Education*. New York: Routledge.

Edgerton, S. H. (1993b). "Love in the margins: Notes toward a curriculum of marginality in Ralph Ellison's *Invisible Man* and Toni Morrison's *Beloved*." In Louis A. Castenell, Jr. and William F. Pinar, (Eds.), *Understanding Curriculum as a Racial Text*. Albany, NY: SUNY Press.

Edgerton, S. H. (1995). "How to write a lesson plan." In Bill Ayers' edited collection, *Becoming Teachers*. New York: Teachers College Press.

Edgerton, S.H. (1995). "Re-membering the Mother Tongue(s): Toni Morrison, Julie Dash, and Pedagogy." *Cultural Studies* 9(2).

Edgerton, S.H. (1996). *Translating the curriculum: Multiculturalism into cultural studies*. New York: Routledge. Awarded 1997 *Critics' Choice Selection* from the American Educational Studies Association (AESA).

Edgerton, S.H. (1998). "The good fight: Bill Gandall." In W. Ayers, T. Quinn, and J. A. Hunt (Eds.), *Teaching for social justice: A democracy and education reader*. New York: Jointly published by Teachers College Press and The New Press.

Edgerton, S.H. (2000). "Whatever gets you through the night." In M. Morris, M.A. Doll, and W.F. Pinar (Eds.), *How We Work*. New York: Peter Lang.

9

Difference That Breeds Hybridity: Race, Reform, and Curriculum

Responding to the "restoration" of neoconservative political power, Michael Apple, in "The Politics of Official Knowledge in the United States," noted with alarm that questions of curriculum had been reduced to procedural, technical ones. "The right has done a good job of showing that decisions about the curriculum, about whose knowledge is to be made 'official knowledge,' are *inherently* involved in political and cultural conflicts and power" (Apple, 1990, p. 383). In many ways, Apple keenly anticipated the cultural and political tensions that would come to characterize school reform and curriculum in the 1990s. What was unclear, however, was exactly how the curriculum field would respond to the challenges posed by the "free-market ethics" (p. 378) of neoliberalism and the growing governmental interest in school and curriculum reform.

The New World Order

Beyond the threshold of the postmodern age, politics, popular culture, and economics shifted dramatically as the world inched toward the second millennium. From the mid-1980s to the mid-1990s, the top-rated television shows changed from *Dallas* and *Dynasty* to *ER* and *Seinfeld*. In politics, we went from the declaration of emergency law in South Africa to the presidential election of Nelson Mandela, and from "It's morning in America" to the Contract with America. When the cold war officially ended, in 1992, we transitioned from warheads targeted on the "evil empire" to capitalists' invasion of Red Square with hamburgers, soft drinks, and designer jeans. A decade later, as the former head of the KGB reached his Kremlin apogee and glasnost became an apparent aberration in Russian history, the battle between communist and capitalist elites raged internally as former Soviet satellites now orbited NATO and the European Union.

There were also constants during this era. The 1980s had brought the fiscal improprieties of junk bond king Michael Milken and the securities fraud of Drexel Burnham Lambert; the 1990s served up financial misdeeds of trader Nicholas Leeson and the subsequent bankruptcy of Bearings. The American war machine occupied the Persian Gulf and Serbia as a Democratic-controlled Congress held hearings on the Iran-Contra affair; a few years later, a Republican-controlled Congress impeached the President while American forces hunkered down in Bosnia. As the Christian Coalition eclipsed the Moral Majority, scientists went from cloning sheep and extinct species to patenting the first genetically engineered vertebrate and creating antimatter.

Yet the 1990s also made cultural and political differences even more evident in contrary events. O.J. Simpson was found not guilty yet responsible for two murders. Terrorist bombs exploded at the World Trade Center and two teens orchestrated a massacre at Columbine High while federal agents precipitated shootouts at Waco and Ruby Ridge, precursing America's worst case of violent domestic terrorism in Oklahoma City—later eclipsed on an ordinary weekday morning, September 11, 2001. Absent the cold war frame with its ever-present threat of nuclear Armageddon, regional international hostilities escalated along with our own regional and ideological hostilities around environmental, economic, and human rights practices. On 9-11, as Mr. Bush listened to Florida preschoolers reading from a storybook, Americans watched the fiery stories of the Twin Towers—and saw the face of international terrorism in their midst.

This same period produced a consolidation of power and influence for the very rich in America. From 1984 to early 2000, the Dow Jones Industrial Average grew eleven-fold from its average of 1,000 where it had hovered since the mid-1960s. This unparalleled increase of stock valuation was coupled with an equally unparalleled corporate concentration. In the entertainment industry, for example, Viacom acquired Paramount for $9.6 billion, Westinghouse Electric absorbed the last independent network (CBS), Disney bought out Capital Cities/ABC for $16.4 billion, and Time-Warner took over Turner Broadcasting for $19.8 billion. At the precipice of the Millennium, the Dow Jones peaked at 11,723 as 17 dot-com companies eagerly spent over $2 million for 30-second television spots in the January 2000 Super Bowl, AOL merged with Time Warner, the Bill and Melinda Gates

Foundation was formed, and the NASDAQ soon soared past 5,000. A year later—the true beginning of the Millennium—71,921 pilgrims traveled to Tampa's Raymond James Stadium to watch the Baltimore Ravens trounce the New York Giants while just a week earlier George W. Bush, having survived Florida's election balloting debacle, took the oath of office to lead a country where the twin towers of economic and political security were about to collapse. With the bursting of the dot.com bubble, corporate practices also came under greater scrutiny from investors and government watch-dogs alike as a series of high-profile securities and accounting scandals emerged. In late 2001, Enron Corporation filed what was then the largest corporate bankruptcy in American history and, in January 2002, the telecommunications company Global Crossing followed suit. The next June, Enron's auditor, the accounting firm Arthur Andersen, was found guilty of obstructing justice and another telecommunications company, WorldCom, became the largest bankruptcy filing in United States history. Public outcry over these scandals prompted Congress to draft the corporate fraud bill that was reluctantly signed by George W. Bush.

The New Economy, the New World Order, the New Democratic Party—the parlance of the 1990s—seemed to set aside the old categories of social, political, and cultural life. In a rapidly changing and unpredictable world, insistence on ideological and cultural purity was less tenable. Democrats and Republicans swapped ideas and platforms as neoliberals and neoconservatives widened the political spectrum. Like the centaur, the half-man, half-horse figure of Greek mythology, identity was no longer viewed as unitary and stable, but rather as a fluid hybrid of multiple forms and positions.

Hybridity is the term we use in this chapter to denote the character of the new political, cultural, and professional assemblages of this era. For example, hybridity characterizes the fusion of public and private schools we see in areas like charter school legislation, voucher programs, and privatization. And, as we shall see, hybridity helped create the conditions for what we refer to as the "perfect storm," the convergence of events and beliefs that would envelope education. Itself a hybrid of controlled elegance and uncontrollable chaos, the perfect storm, in turn, helped fuel the emergence of multiple political, cultural, and professional hybridities that we will discuss throughout this chapter. It is through the powerful dynamic mix of these hybridities that transgressive acts emerged to challenge the official representations of these events and authoritative beliefs (Bhabha, 2004).

A Perfect Storm

A popular book and subsequent Hollywood movie, *The Perfect Storm* (Junger, 1997), tells the story of the *Andrea Gail* and her crew as they battle three converging weather systems in the Atlantic Ocean in September 1991. Captained by a desperate man determined to bring his overflowing cargo of swordfish to port, the 72-foot ship sailed into a "meteorological hell." With furious seas more deadly than any single storm could produce, the *Andrea Gail* capsized amidst 80 foot waves; all crewmembers were lost.

University of North Carolina law professor, John Charles Boger (2002), contends that three educational developments—student resegregation by race and socioeconomic class, high stakes accountability tied to school reform, and the continuing disparities in school resources and finances—are gathering strength to capsize public education, at least in the American South. Throughout the United States, school districts, captained by determined administrators coping with large numbers of poor and minority children subject to low-stakes curriculum packages and high-stakes testing, are sailing into a "perfect storm."

Our point of embarkation is September 27, 1989, when President George H. W. Bush, the self-described "education president," met with 49 governors during a two-day education summit at the University of Virginia in Charlottesville. Co-chaired by Arkansas Governor Bill Clinton, the group charted national education goals, as politicians turned their attention away from school funding and equal access to educational outcomes and accountability.

Words such as accountability, excellence, standards, and reform, of course, were not coined during this event. From the Committee of Ten to the Woods Hole Conference to *A Nation at Risk*, these concerns have been evident. The summit, however, was a turning point in school reform. Alarmed by the dramatic increase in immigrant populations, a post-industrial economy, and the pressures of globalization, both major political parties began to take great interest in curriculum issues. Certainly, the slow encroachment of the Federal government into education, beginning with the Morill Act of 1862 through the Elementary and Secondary Education Act of 1965, helped create the conditions for this political hybridity: Bill Clinton, a self-anointed "new" Democrat promoting free-market solutions like charter schools and accountability setting the stage for Republican George W. Bush, whose own party had sought to abolish the Department of Education as late as 1996.

Although the ensuing debate among policy-makers and politicians tacked alternatively from local control and school autonomy to centralization and accountability, the elite had set the course for the nation's schools. Meanwhile, curriculum workers—many of whom were far more skeptical about the new educational math (teacher accountability + student testing = quality schools)—were engaged in renegotiating and transgressing the boundaries of curriculum studies.

In part due to this increasing state and federal oversight, but more directly as a result of the theoretical diversification of a field now confronting its own border crossers and fighting a cultural war with religious conservatives, curricularists focused on power, identity, and language. The bread-and-butter of curriculum workers—objectives, curriculum organization, and evaluation methods—was subordinated to concerns about institutional texts and contexts of curriculum work. Although some within the curriculum field refused to shrug off their commitment to schooling, curriculum workers of all theoretical stripes acknowledged the practical impact of these new political challenges.

Nowhere was this acknowledgment more evident than in the intersection of curriculum and cultural studies. What had begun as a school interest among teachers in multicultural education was being "translated" into an academic interest among education professors in cultural studies (Edgerton, 1996). The versatility and complexity of cultural studies widened the meaning of "institutional text" while seemingly increasing the theory-practice gap. Power was no longer simply about domination and resistance; it circulated within all social relations. Identity became "elusive" and multiple. The language of race became a text to be read (Castenell & Pinar, 1993; Yon, 2000). Meanwhile, as issues of power, identity, and language were felt in curriculum workers' everyday lives, the need to connect the seemingly exclusionary binaries of theory and practice *within* the discursive space of schooling became apparent. The new turning point in the curriculum field was its hybridization.

Question

What does it mean to take a hybrid approach to curriculum work? What evidence do you see of the hybridization of the curriculum field today?

Multiculturalism and the Role of the School

In 1913, President Woodrow Wilson applauded the role of public schooling in transitioning immigrant children and youth into their new lives as "Americans" when he said: "The great melting pot of America, the place where we are all made Americans of, is the public school where men of every race and of every origin and of every station of life send their children … [to be] infused with the American spirit and developed into the American man or American woman" (as cited in Swerdlow, 2001 p. 42). Until the mid-twentieth century, the dominant culture of adult, middle-class, Protestant, white European-Americans defined the United States and shaped immigrant students' (in fact, all students') perceptions of the nation's past, present, and future (Taxel, 1997). Most citizens accepted this as a simple social fact—with the exception of a few malcontents. Anthropologist Jules Henry (1963), for example, challenged the role of schooling as an agent of socialization and colonization. Henry thought school (social studies, in particular) taught students to be "stupid" and to accept the culture as given.

Questioning cultural hegemony and breaking the illusion of social consensus were both means and ends of the sixties' social movements. But, as diverse and long-marginalized border voices grew in force, differences between the dominant and minority cultures made it more difficult to control *whose* values, vision, and versions of the American story would or could or should be told in schools. Slowly, notions of accommodation and pluralism replaced melting pot assimilationism, as the dynamic mixing of cultures became more obvious. Through this hybridity, immigrant and other non-mainstream children have come to understand their need to simultaneously become *and define* "American."

Accommodation and pluralism, as advocated in mainstream social studies texts or multicultural curricula, however, are far different from empowerment and resistance resulting from a critical understanding of language, power, and identity. Paradoxically, it is this commingling of cultures (the colonizer and the colonized) that is both enriching and oppressive—differences that breed hybridity and challenge "national" reform.

▰ Peter Hlebowitsh

VISITOR In this chapter, three contemporary curriculum workers represent not only the growing diversity of the nation's population, but also the hybridity of the field. While all three were first classroom teachers, they came to curriculum work for various reasons. The first visitor, Peter Hlebowitsh, a professor at the University of Iowa, found his "American" identity in school. His work as an educator began in a Princeton elementary classroom in 1981. Though certified to teach when he completed college, Peter was no more or less inspirationally or ideologically drawn to this career than were most other classroom teachers or curriculum workers. Growing up in New Jersey as a first-generation American, Peter and his family lived in one side of a duplex; his father was a brick maker, and his mother a seamstress. His parents met in a European refugee camp after Germany's invasion of the Soviet Union. Eventually traveling to Belgium, they immigrated to the United States in 1954:

> We lived in a small part of South River called the Russian Alley. I grew up speaking Russian, though the town, itself, was highly cosmopolitan, with groups of Polish-speaking kids and Hungarian-speaking kids. And, of course, what we called the American kids—second- and third-generation Americans who had lost their strong ethnic identification. I attended elementary school during the Cold War. I spoke Russian when I started school. The school was committed to Americanizing us, so there was no effort whatsoever to be responsive to Russian culture, language, or traditions.

Seemingly, President Wilson's "Americanizing" role for schools contin-ued into the 1950s, as Peter's story indicates, yet by the 1990s the public educational system had become the battleground for politicians and pun-dits engaged in "culture wars," and educators and policy-makers fighting "curriculum wars." Cultural conservatives like former Secretary of Edu-cation William Bennett; former Assistant Secretary of Education, Chester Finn; and another former Assistant Secretary of Education, Diane Ravitch, linked these wars to a crisis in education threatening the nation's social and cultural fabric.

The conservatives' claim of successful assimilation for immigrants in the past was challenged by a diverse group of multiculturalists such as James and Cherry Banks (2005), Sonia Nieto (1999), Christine Sleeter (1999), Carl Grant (2003), Geneva Gay (2000), Catherine Cornbleth (1990), and Cameron McCarthy (1993, 2001). Addressing the failure (or perhaps success) of educational socialization/colonization, these curriculum work-ers advocated various forms of multiculturalism to improve teaching and learning as well as to advance social progress.

Birthed from the civil rights movement of the 1960s, multicultural ed-ucation generally has been viewed as an avenue by which African-Amer-icans and other racial and ethnic groups could reform schools and their curricula to more accurately reflect the experiences, histories, cultures, and perspectives of Americans who were not of European descent. Revis-ing textbooks, hiring more teachers and administrators of color, and ex-panding greater community control of schools, multicultural liberalism seeks simply, but not without difficulty, for all students to "become knowl-edgeable, caring, active citizens" (Banks, 1993, p. 23).

Petra Munro

VISITOR Petra Munro, a professor at Louisiana State University, came to understand multicultur-alism from a unique perspective. Her enculturation experience into American society and schooling was far different from Peter's.

I was born in Germany and came to the United States when I was six years old. I was brought up in the northern suburbs of Chicago, very sheltered, very white, very upper-middle class. When I started first grade I didn't know any English. Probably the pivotal experience that describes my childhood was going up to my teacher one day and curtsying. The kids just burst out laughing because they had never seen anything that hilarious in their lives. So I pretty much became a loner. Because I didn't make a lot of friends and didn't know the language, my escape came through books. I remember spending a lot of my childhood just sitting in my closet reading and writing in my journal.

By the time Petra reached high school, in 1972, she was part of an ex-perimental program, Freshman Studies. All core classes were taught thematically with a project orientation similar to that implemented a generation earlier by progressive educator Carlton Washburne, at nearby Winnetka. While finding this "an incredible experience," she still didn't feel like she "fit in." As Petra remembers:

> I played in the band but I wasn't a real band person. I didn't fit in with the jocks. I just didn't fit into any of the groups. So again, I focused on doing homework and getting straight A's. I got advanced German right away and started reading Hesse, Goethe, and Kafka. I met my best friend from high school in French class. We both read a lot and were curious. You know, you're sort of odd if you were a girl and wanted to be smart.

Of course, being a woman was also being "the other"—a critical concept of post-colonial theory along with hybridity. Culture, though, was unproblematic for the Rudyard Kiplings of education, notably Ravitch, Finn, and Bennett, who initially linked multiculturalism to ethnocentrism, dismissing it as ethnic cheerleading and crossing the line into extremism (Ravitch, 1990b). Rather than viewing culture as hybrid and multivalent, these secular conservatives assumed that culture (itself a cultural construction) was discrete and monolithic. Thus, they viewed multiculturalism as "particularism," "separatist," and "a catch-all term for a panoply of evils, all bent on undermining Western culture" (Cope & Kalantzis, 1993, p. 87). It is this to-the-bunkers defense of Euro-American culture and wielding of colonizing authority against any form of multiculturalism that evidences what radical multiculturalists, employing post-colonial theory, deem as its "totalizing and identity-destroying power" (JanMohamed, 1985).

While supporters and developers of multicultural liberalism describe it as a process of school reform that calls for dialogue and genuine power-sharing among groups (Sleeter, 1999), radical multiculturalists understand the terror in the eyes of the cultural colonialists whose canon they critique and counter-narratives they advance (Gates, 1988; McCarthy, 2001). Cameron McCarthy, a leading curriculum scholar of race and post-colonialism and whose work we will revisit at the end of this chapter, similarly argues that conservative educators and scholars have been so threatened by multiculturalism that we are now experiencing "a virulent reaffirmation of Eurocentrism and Western culture" (1993, p. 290).

The Roots of Difference

During the 1980s, the United States absorbed the greatest wave of immigrants in its history, resulting in the population becoming more ethnically, culturally, and linguistically diverse. The 2000 Census reported that at that time, demographers had projected that by the year 2020, one of every three people in the country would be a minority. That prediction was revised and now the 40-year projection is that one of every two people will be a person of color (2000 Census). The demographics of K–12 students mirror these changes. In 2000, 39% were members of a minority group, with the largest concentrations in the West and the South (2002); the majority of students will be non-white by 2020 (Natriello, McDill, & Pallas, 1990). Hispanic students (those born in, or whose ancestors came from Spanish-speaking countries and those who self-identify as Spanish [Lavin, 1996]) are the fastest-growing student group in the nation's public schools—accounting for 32% of the student body in the West (U.S. Dept. of Education, 2002)—and the lowest student group in educational achievement, with a relatively low probability of attending college (Padron, Waxman, & Rivera, 2002).

Like many Hispanic students, nearly a half-century ago Peter wasn't in the highest ability grouping. Nevertheless, as he worked his way from junior to senior high school, Peter found himself poised for college by his parents, who with no more than a third-grade education, believed "that school was the way to improve your lot." Similarly, Petra knew she was "supposed to go to college" but it was assumed that her road toward self-improvement was to "find a husband." After graduating from high school during the country's bicentennial year, Petra entered DePauw University where she majored in African history and spent the second semester of her sophomore year in Africa. Following this "pivotal experience" she transferred to the University of Illinois, studying with African historians Donald Crummay and Charles Stewart. "That's where I began to connect African history to Marxist theory, to colonial literature, and to theories of oppression, inequality, and exploitation," she recalls, adding: "That's when I first read Freire's *Pedagogy of the Oppressed.*"

Along with the opinion—naïve or not—that higher education is the way to "improve your lot" is the fact that immigrant families often experience economic hardship. This latest and largest wave of immigration contributed to a poverty rate that hit a 20-year high. Taking note, Congress issued its U. S. House Select Committee on Children, Youth, and Families Report in 1989, which highlighted the interplay of the country's ongoing societal and economic changes. The federal government refocused its attention on children and the conditions in their lives that prevented them from being successful in schools.

Historically, newly arrived immigrant children (and children of color, generally) have been viewed as "backward" because they were hard to teach and difficult to manage—that is, they lacked the cultural capital that has traditionally been the currency of exchange in middle-class schools. At the turn of the last century, many were placed in special classes (Franklin, 1994); today, children are labeled "at-risk" if they possess any one of five characteristics: poverty, minority race/ethnicity, limited English proficiency, single-parent family, or mother's lack of a high-school diploma. Children who bring certain medical, economic, cultural, or social "deficits" to learning situations are thus cast into a reformist melting pot because their families are unable or unwilling to assimilate or become pluralized into the dominant culture's middle-class expectations (Swadener, 1990).

Given an increasingly multicultural student body taught by mostly middle-class and middle-aged EuroAmericans (themselves increasingly accountable for their students' high-stakes testing performances) who wield diminishing school resources within a largely mono-cultural curriculum, is it any wonder that these students are labeled "at-risk" and schooled less successfully than all other categories of students (Land & Legters, 2002)? The elements for a "meteorological hell" were converging in schools as they had before wreaking havoc on another institution of American culture: the tobacco industry.

V ARIED TALE

BIG TOBACCO: BIG BROTHER

Many believed that "Big Tobacco" would be brought to its knees by the $246 billion settlement crafted, in late 1998, by the attorneys general of 46 states. Although it may take years to bankrupt the industry, Philip Morris, Brown and Williamson, R.J. Reynolds, and Lorillard—aka Big Tobacco—are looking to greater trade prospects with the most populous country in the world, China, as a profit source. Recent history notwithstanding, Big Tobacco has proven time and again that it can reinvent itself. Having survived its perfect storm, Big Tobacco remains one of the most profitable businesses in the country thanks, in part, to federal assistance.

There may be no other manufactured product as ubiquitous as the cigarette. The modern cigarette—and Big Tobacco—was born in the late 1880s with the invention of the rolling machine. In 1913, R. J. Reynolds revolutionized cigarette advertising by launching one of the most successful campaigns in America, using a Barnum & Bailey circus animal as its model. "Joe Camel" made his the most popular brand in the country.

Cigarette production remained stable until James Buchanan Duke of North Carolina and the National Cigarette Service Committee distributed millions of free cigarettes to the U.S. troops in France during World War I. Cigarette production increased by 633% between 1910 and 1919 while contemporary literature reflected the change—O'Henry's turn-of-the-century short stories never mention smoking, yet by 1926, Hemingway's *The Sun Also Rises* presents cigarette-toting men and women.

Although doctors were beginning to connect smoking with lung cancer as early as 1930, President Franklin Roosevelt declared tobacco an essential wartime crop. Cigarettes were sold at military exchanges and ships' stores tax-free, and distributed free at the front lines as a part of troop "K rations." This federally supported distribution of free cigarettes continued throughout the Korean War and the Vietnam conflict.

As tobacco companies implied that smoking was beneficial—and certainly not deadly—surgery was the only treatment for major internal cancers in the era between the two world wars, with entire lungs removed to stem the disease. In 1927, the American Tobacco Company introduced its Lucky Strike brand and claimed that "physicians endorsed Lucky Strikes." Its advertising slogan, "Reach for a Lucky instead of a sweet," soon pushed this brand into first place, usurping Camel's popularity among male smokers while adding more women to the smoking ranks, although it remained taboo for most.

Edward Bernays, a public relations guru and nephew of Sigmund Freud, taught advertisers how to tap the suffragette masses. Calling cigarettes "torches of liberty," he marched 15 debutantes smoking and waving up Fifth Avenue in New York's Easter Parade of 1929. Newspapers around the world carried that picture, and in just two years, the number of American women who smoked had doubled (Parker-Pope, 2001).

Between 1930 and 1950, cancer-related deaths quadrupled to 20 per 100,000 (Meyer, 1992). As medical studies explored and demonstrated links between smoking and ill health, tobacco companies introduced filter-tipped cigarettes in 1952. In its ad campaign for the new Kent brand, Lorillard called the new smokes "the greatest health protection in cigarette history." Similarly, Liggett's L&M brand became "just what the doctor ordered." Meanwhile, R.J. Reynolds claimed that more doctors smoked Camels than any other brand!

As more medical reports connected health risks with smoking, Big Tobacco executives banded together, forming the Tobacco Industry Research Committee to orchestrate a counter-attack against negative press. Their efforts "focused on recruiting doctors" who did not think that smoking was harmful; "discrediting writers who reported" on the link to cancer; and paying writers to place stories that bolstered the Research Committee's support of smoking as a pleasurable pastime (Parker-Pope, 2001, p. 37). Later disbanded by the 1998 tobacco settlement, this group helped to make the post-World War II cigarette industry one of the most stable in the American economy and among the most profitable of world businesses.

Shifting Political and Curriculum Landscapes

The orchestrated rise of Big Tobacco demonstrates the growing power of the politics of symbolic representation, of controlling the images and social meanings that adhere to a particular product, even one as potentially dangerous as cigarettes. While "spin" has no doubt been around as long as there have been politicians, the aptly named "spin doctor" became an indispensable expert in the selling of a policy or a politician during the last two decades of the twentieth century.

In 1985, following Ronald Reagan's landslide reelection, a group of conservative Democrats founded the Democratic Leadership Council (DLC). Heralding the arrival of the "New Democrat," it sought to craft and advance public policy that "transcend[ed] the stale left-right debate and define[d] a Third Way for governing based on progressive ideas, mainstream values, and innovative solutions that reflect changing times" ("About The New Democrat Movement," n.d, Retrieved December 12, 2002, from http://ndol.org). Critics from within the Democratic Party contended that the DLC was an attempt to shift the party away from the liberal Democratic Party's traditional constituency of organized labor, people of color, and the poor (Nichols, 2000).

Nonetheless, the DLC attracted a new generation of Democratic politicians, mostly Southerners, embracing the organization's philosophy of personal responsibility, mainstream values, and market-based solutions to various public policy issues, including education ("About The New Democrat Movement," n.d, Retrieved December 12, 2002, from http://ndol.org). The DLC's spin that the Democratic Party could only retake the White House by "modernizing" the party's liberal politics appeared valid when, in the 1992 presidential election, former DLC chairman Bill Clinton defeated George Bush by carefully blending DLC themes with populist rhetoric (Nichols, 2000). In some sense, Clinton's election as a "New Democrat" consummated what Michael Apple (1990) has termed the "conservative restoration." Indeed, the term "liberal" had lost most of its conventional meaning throughout the land—much like the word "curriculum."

The demolition of the Berlin Wall and the dissolution of the Soviet Empire, the collapse of the Asian boom and the inflated expectations of technology markets, the presumed linkage between global markets and local democratization, and the breakdown of boundaries resulting in engineered life forms and the North American Free Trade Zone all pushed the world into a state of disequilibrium. Few questioned, however, the underlying relationship between state authority and corporate power.

Not surprisingly, curriculum workers and curriculum reform also experienced disequilibrium during the 1990s. The curriculum field of the past—led by a handful of intellectuals, developed by curriculum workers, dominated by scions of technical or disciplinary mastery, and contested by rival curriculum siblings—no longer existed. Like the music industry, the bending and blending of curricular genres had become the state of the millennial curriculum field—absent institutional consolidation.

During this era in which curriculum scholars worked to be notably different, creating and sustaining a single institutional curriculum identity was impossible. Faculty at those few places with large curriculum studies programs seldom participated in collaborative inquiries once common at Teachers College or Ohio State. Thus, from the beginning to the end of the century, curriculum studies evolved from a handful of renowned sites and programs with collections of noteworthy curriculum luminaries to myriad locations around the country, each housing one or more curriculum people who pursued their individual work of teaching, thinking, and writing about (while occasionally working in schools to develop) curriculum. The result: curriculum hybridity and localized diversity.

Who, then, was the curriculum worker during this last decade of the millennium? Where did one find curriculum literature? Portraying the literature that best exemplifies localized diversity and curriculum hybridity invokes many questions, like: Should curriculum literature be defined as the writings of those who self-identify with the curriculum field through membership in one of several organizations or regular attendance at select national conferences?[1] Should curriculum literature be restricted to books with the term "curriculum" in the title, or to work produced by authors who frequented the pages of prominent, peer-reviewed curriculum journals such as *The Journal of Curriculum Studies, JCT, Curriculum & Pedagogy*, or *Curriculum Inquiry?* Are such journals privileged over practitioner-based magazines like *Educational Leadership* and *Phi Delta Kappan?* Might the curriculum field be more appropriately identified through intellectual genealogy or is the examination of popular culture a more meaningful way of thinking about the curriculum?

Posing these and other questions from multiple positions disrupts the curriculum representations in standard synoptic texts (e.g., R. C. Doll, 1996, ninth edition; Hass & Parkay, 1993, sixth edition [previous editions were edited by Hass]; Henson, 1995; Longstreet & Shane, 1993; Marsh and Willis, 1995; McNeil, 1996, fifth edition; Morrison, 1993; Oliva, 1997, fourth edition; Ornstein & Hunkins, 1998, third edition; Posner, 1995, second edition; Pratt, 1994; Tanner & Tanner, 1995, third edition; Wiles & Bondi, 1993/1998, fourth edition) and reflected the field's postmodern zeitgeist. These synoptic texts canonized the curriculum field, focusing on commonalities and variations that have occurred *within* traditional genres of curriculum discourse. Most of these organizational frames were available under the perennial categories found in Jackson's (1992) *Handbook of Research on Curriculum* and other books that addressed curriculum implementation (e.g., Ben-Peretz, 1990; Fullan, 1991; Hawthorne, 1992; McCutcheon, 1995; Paris, 1993), curriculum evaluation (e.g., Darling-Hammond, Ancess, & Falk, 1995; Wiggins, 1993), and large-scale reform efforts (e.g., Comer, Haynes, Joyner, & Ben-Avie, 1996; Hess, 1991; Hirsch, 1996; M. C. Hunter, 1994; Sears,

---

[1]In the 1990s, these included: Division B (Curriculum Studies) of the American Educational Research Association; the Association of Supervision and Curriculum Development; the Professors of Curriculum group; the Society for the Study of Curriculum History; and the American Association for Curriculum and Teaching.

Marshall, & Otis-Wilborn, 1994; Sizer, 1992). Textual curricular varia-
tions also emerged, including curriculum in small schools (Fliegel &
MacGuire, 1993; Meier, 1995), the hidden curriculum of media and sexu-
ality in classrooms (Ellsworth & Whatley, 1990; Epstein & Sears, 1999;
Trudell, 1993), caring and development of basic beliefs through schooling
(Noddings, 1992, 1993), and students as curriculum theorists (Nicholls &
Hazzard, 1993; Nicholls & Thorkildsen, 1995).

Curriculum workers of the 1990s turned frequently to noncurricu-
larists such as Howard Gardner, Linda Darling-Hammond, Diane
Ravitch, and Carl Glickman. Many within the contemporary curriculum
field also found support from a growing number of full-time consultants
such as Art Costa, Heidi Hayes Jacobs, and William Daggett, who dominated the upscale market of keynote speakers for educational institutes,
conferences, and in-service programs. Even within a more narrow representation of contemporary curriculum literature, one readily found
frequent references to many who did not fall within the traditional education field: Cornel West, Hannah Arendt, Michael Foucault, Richard
Rorty, Amy Gutman, Mary Belenky, bell hooks, Molefi Asante, Clifford
Geertz, and Jean Houston.

The growing authority and power of these new curriculum discourses
or genres (Pinar, 1994, 1998a; Pinar et al., 1995)—born through fusions
and hybrids of personal and professional (con)texts—moved the field's
once-dominant institutional language of curriculum-making into unques-
tionable minority status. For traditionalists like Dan Tanner, this curriculum disequilibrium—which relocated the field well beyond the borders of
curriculum design and development, coupled to the rightward drift of education reform, could not have been worse.

After graduating from Rutgers and earning a degree in social studies
with elementary teaching certification, Peter Hlebowitsh took a long-term
substitute teaching job. The following spring he taught third and fourth
grades in the Princeton Regional Public Schools, where the principal
"allowed me to make mistakes, as long as I didn't repeat them all the time,
so I could grow and develop."

By the time Peter began teaching, in 1981, the curriculum field had already been reconceptualized from its moribund state pronounced by
Schwab a decade earlier. Nevertheless, those loosely called reconceptualists were still plainly in the minority. During his five years in the Princeton schools, there was a renaissance of curriculum thinking as discourses
multiplied to include feminist, racial, neo-Marxist, phenomenological, psy-
choanalytic, and postmodern discourses of various persuasions. Although
a growing number of curriculum workers embraced the field's postmodern
condition (welcoming displacement, irony, and transgression), many—
particularly those from prior generations—were troubled by the emergence of curriculum studies and its distancing from school practice. A few

in the newest generation, like Hlebowitsh, would eventually critique this condition. Unlike senior curriculum traditionalists, Peter prepared to battle the many-headed curricular hydra, known collectively as curriculum studies. Undeterred by the world's postmodern turn, Hlebowitsh and others of this now under-represented group would seek to restore curriculum development as the crown jewel within the field and resurrect its historic leader, Ralph Tyler.

Pursuing a master's degree to elevate his place on the district's pay scale, Peter first encountered his intellectual métier, who was teaching at Rutgers:

> It was complete fortuity that I chose curriculum, which connected me with Dan Tanner. Certified as a school teacher, I had had a lot of education classes. But in Dan's classes, I suddenly discovered a whole new, re-negotiated way of looking at the school, the study of education, and interaction with children. Dan is very much committed to seeing the school as this upbuilder of democracy, this engine of social reform and progress.

Peter was enamored by Tanner's "adventuresome life" of traveling, writing, consulting, and meeting important people. Pursuing his doctorate at Rutgers, Hlebowitsh gained "a better sense of the important contribution that curricularists can make to giving coherence and identity to the school experience." He continues:

> As a doctoral student planning to become a participant in the curriculum field, I think I was made well aware of its varied traditions. Dan, of course, had that big textbook which he believes is representative of the traditions of the field [Tanner & Tanner, 1995]. But he also insisted on us reading primary materials. It was clear that Dan was working out of the tradition of Dewey, and identified himself as a social experimentalist, or a progressive experimentalist. He did spend a lot of time fashioning the other perspectives or traditions, mainly the child-centered, the social efficiency, and the subject-centered traditional humanist traditions.

These traditions did not include those embraced by the reconceptualists. Viewed as outside the curriculum field's boundaries, Tanner simply chose to ignore them; for Peter, reconceptualism soon became his bette noire. After graduating in 1987 from Rutgers, he taught courses from general methods to introduction to research at Long Island University's C. W. Post campus. Two years later he became the general program director for the curriculum theory and development program at the University of Houston. While teaching a doctoral seminar in curriculum theory, Peter says, "I began to get interested in this whole section of the field that Dan Tanner hadn't paid much attention to, [and] I spent a great deal of my time trying to formulate a new, more detailed criticism of this newest paradigm because I felt it was actually threatening the very heart and soul of the field itself."

Driven not only by a desire to revise the reconceptualists' allegedly faulty historical accounts and assaults on the field's forbearers (especially Ralph Tyler), Peter, like William Reid (1992) and William Wraga, hoped to stem the field's hybridization. Arising from the cacophony of post-traditional curriculum voices would come, faintly and slowly at first, an aria of such simple purity of purpose as to silence the curricular confusion of Bergamo.

Cultural Combatants, Curriculum Warriors

Efforts to revise revisionist history and corral cacophonistic identities emerged elsewhere, too. At the Republican National Convention in 1992, for example, conservative politician Pat Buchanan declared, "There is a religious war going on for the soul of America" (Hunter, 1993). This pronouncement represented a political volley in an increasingly acrimonious public debate over which competing cultural and moral values were of most worth. Eventually, the standards movement would be caught up in this national debate.

This clash of values had been brewing in education for some time, represented by the curriculum wars on both coasts. In the mid-1980s, the National Endowment for the Humanities funded an assessment of history and literature knowledge among 17-year-olds conducted by the National Assessment of Educational Progress. The results were published in *What Do Our 17-Year-Olds Know?* (1987), written by Diane Ravitch and Chester Finn, who wondered

> whether the younger generation is culturally illiterate. The spread of remedial reading and writing classes on college campuses has contributed to the sense that our society is breeding a new strain of cultural barbarian, one who cannot read or write except at the most rudimentary level and who possesses virtually no knowledge except that conveyed through the television set. (p. 13)

While the overall results of the assessment were open to interpretation, many specific findings (for example, only one in every three 17-year-olds knew that the Civil War occurred between 1850–1900) were easily sensationalized, lending credence to claims that young people lacked basic cultural knowledge.

In his popular book *Cultural Literacy*, E. D. Hirsch (1987) argued that "a content-neutral conception of educational development," which he identified with the work of Rousseau and Dewey, threatened the country's cultural cohesion (p. xv). A core body of shared knowledge, argued Hirsch, was especially important in an increasingly diverse society, and he included in his book a list of "what literate Americans know" (p. 146). The writings of Hirsch (along with Allan Bloom [1987], Ravitch, and Finn)—

bolstered by the political rhetoric of presidential aspirant Pat Buchanan and Congressman Newt Gingrich, the moral certitude of religious right televangelists, and the social commentaries of radio personalities like Rush Limbaugh—heightened public awareness of the curriculum wars by popularizing school restructuring, standards, and accountability. This national attention helped translate such educational reforms into public policy as an increasingly diverse citizenry grappled with the public educational system's apparent inability to effectively deal with that diversity. Unlike earlier periods of school reform, however, the symbolic value of winning the culture wars would be very much in play as the standards movement unfolded throughout the 1990s.

Petra's experience as a new teacher in public schools highlights the growing diversity of the country's population. It also tells the tale of moving from a classroom teacher into her work in the curriculum field as a direct result of the burgeoning standards movement that has engulfed the nation since 1989.

In the fall of 1980, with diploma in hand, Petra journeyed to Europe. During the next two years she hitchhiked, worked odd jobs, and engaged in political activities.

> I ended up working with a youth group of Turkish women who had emigrated to Germany for work. Raised as devout Muslims, these young women were not allowed by their parents to go out by themselves or to date. Our program provided a place where they could talk about those kinds of issues. That was really my first experience working with adolescents, and I enjoyed it tremendously.
>
> That got me thinking about maybe working with high school kids. Before that time I had never imagined being a teacher. Never. Teaching was women's work. The other thing that propelled me into teaching was . . . realizing that I had never learned anything about Africa in high school. Being in Ghana and Nigeria and getting a much more global perspective of the world, meeting world health organization people, and seeing how U.S. capitalism was impacting the economies and politics in those countries made me realize the need for African history and Third World history at the high school level.

After her travels, Petra returned to the University of Illinois for graduate study in history. On a lark, she enrolled in an education course taught by social studies educator Ben Cox. Inspired, she switched from history to education. In the fall of 1984, she began her high school teaching career in a Chicago suburb that housed many newly arrived immigrants from Nicaragua, who had fled the Sandinista regime, and from India, Pakistan, and Central America.

> I had several students whose parents had sent them over the border and they were living here by themselves, working the three-to-eleven shift and then coming to school. . . . It must have been a nightmare for the Indian and

Pakistani students to go to school because they were taunted so much. They were just the brunt of the cruelest jokes and comments. The school district really did try to segregate these students off into separate classrooms.

Petra's students from Central America were very poor and knew little of their home country's history, let alone American history—the subject she was to teach them. So, she developed a multi-week unit on pre-Colombian history, tracing America's growth through archeology and the Anasazi Indian mounds. Once outcome-based education (OBE) was implemented in the district, she was told that she had to begin the course with the founding of America by Columbus and that she could no longer teach pre-Colombian history. As Petra recalled: "I was a professional and I did not want to be told by the principal or the social studies coordinator how to teach and what to teach." So she resigned.

Finding her place within the contemporary curriculum field was a welcome challenge for Petra, who enjoyed her intellectually eclectic doctoral program in curriculum. "I basically went to graduate school to figure out what teachers do when they know curriculum is imposed on them. How do you stay in the classroom and negotiate that kind of deskilling . . . which is really what I experienced. And of course, grad school gave me the language to talk about the whole process." Although Petra applied to the University of Chicago, Northwestern, and Stanford, her husband at the time would only move to Oregon. She reluctantly enrolled at the University of Oregon, which "ended up being an incredible experience for me. I mean, it ranks right up there with going to Africa for the first time." She worked with an eclectic group of faculty with strong but very diverse theoretical foundations, including David Flinders (a student of Elliot Eisner), Jan Jipson (who had worked with Michael Apple), Harry Wolcott, and Chet Bowers. She also read heavily:

> That's when I was introduced to Michael Apple, the Berlaks [Berlak & Berlak, 1981], Eisner, and also feminists. At the time, Madeleine Grumet's *Bitter Milk* [1988a] was a revolutionary textbook. I already considered myself a feminist, and I definitely considered myself a political activist. So my first readings in curriculum confirmed that there were people out there who were doing things and thinking in these ways.

In Petra's second year of doctoral work, Jan Jipson took her to Bergamo:

> My very first impressions included wondering about the language and some of the discourses and how convoluted they were. You know, high, high theory. It was exciting to see people grappling with issues like: What kind of language should we be speaking? What's the role of theory in the classroom? Where do feminists fit into the field?

In contrast to Peter, Petra embraced the growing hybridity of the field and welcomed the off-key chorus of curricular discourses.

▓ Bi-Coastal Curriculum Wars ▓▓▓▓▓▓▓▓▓▓▓▓▓▓▓▓▓▓

What does it means to be truly "American"? How is the history of America to be taught? Such questions fueled the curriculum wars of the 1990s, which were primarily fought in states with large immigrant populations. On the key battlefronts of California and New York, educational leaders Bill Honig and Tom Sobol each selected women, Diane Ravitch and Catherine Cornbleth, respectively, to wage war or, in the de-politicized language of reform, to improve school curriculum. *Left Back* and *The Great Speckled Bird* represent their contrasting views.

California symbolized how the nation was changing during this time. The state was absorbing nearly half of all new legal and illegal immigrants (New York, Florida, and Texas gained the majority of the rest [Cornbleth & Waugh, 1995]). Faced with huge numbers of English-as-a-second-language (ESL) students and not enough teachers who could speak the students' languages and dialects, Bill Honig, the state's super-intendent of education, orchestrated the reform of each grade's curricu-lum frameworks. He hired Diane Ravitch, a former adjunct professor of education and history at Teachers College, to develop history frameworks. Adopted by the California state board in 1987 (and reaffirmed in 1997), the frameworks reflected an odd blend of nationalism and pluralism, por-traying America as a land created by many groups of immigrants who share common values and ideals (Ravitch, 1990c). While Ravitch pro-moted her work as an "example of an excellent full-length multicultural curriculum" (1990a, p. 18) other academics (Catherine Cornbleth among them) disagreed. The debate over these history-social science frameworks and their accompanying textbooks, however, began in the public arena.

Ravitch (1990c) viewed her critics as special-interest groups and com-plainers who unreasonably demanded a voice over what was written about them. Women, people of color, and other minorities, in her view, wanted to compel teachers to teach "pretty fictions about the past lest offense be given to someone, somewhere" (p. M8). Considered finished, and rejecting any direct criticisms of its grand historical metanarrative of in-tergroup harmony, California's State Board of Education refused to revise Ravitch's work.

Meanwhile, as the first President Bush was meeting with the nation's governors in Charlottesville, the curriculum war on the eastern front got hot.

Contrary to California's assimilationist view, New York adopted a cur-riculum of inclusion. Non-whites, who made up a growing percentage of the workforce, were not doing as well as children of European descent on "almost every quantifiable measure of performance" (McConnell & Breindel, 1990, p. 20). In response, Commissioner of Education, Thomas Sobol, convened a task force charged with reviewing the State Depart-ment of Education's personnel policies and practices, and determining how well the social studies syllabi and instructional materials reflected the pluralistic nature of American society (Cornbleth & Waugh, 1995).

In its report, "A Curriculum of Inclusion," the task force identified a systematic bias toward European culture in state curriculum materials, denouncing them as representing institutionalized racism (Fullinwider, 1996). Blasting the report as "Europhobic," Ravitch (1990b) decried this as using the history curriculum to improve the "self-esteem and self-respect" of children of color while "children from European cultures will have a less arrogant perspective of being part of the group that has done it all" (p. 351).

Supporting the task force's recommendations, Sobol (1988) cited "a pattern of failure" among students from the cities and rural areas that was "clearly associated with race and poverty." (pp. i–ii). While Sobol's plans and pleas were dismissed in almost every quarter, support came from the state's School Boards Association and from the New York City Board of Education (Cornbleth & Waugh, 1995).

Sobol next formed a social studies syllabus review and development committee made up of a panel of education scholars including (among others) SUNY Buffalo professor Catherine Cornbleth. A highly regarded academic, progressive scholar, and educational researcher, she was tapped by Sobol for her expertise in the areas of history, social education, curriculum studies, and social identities. Another member of the panel was CUNY professor Arthur Schlesinger, Jr., a respected historian and former member of the Kennedy administration. Members were charged with examining the 20-year-old state social studies curriculum and recommending changes in its content and use, with the goal of improving students' understanding of one another, American culture, and the world at large (Sobol, 1990).

In the summer of 1991, the committee's advisory report, "One Nation, Many Peoples: A Declaration of Cultural Interdependence," recommended that the New York social studies syllabi be revised to provide more opportunities for students to learn from multiple perspectives and that racist or sexist language be removed (Sobol, 1990). It also went "beyond affirming multicultural and multiple perspectives to explicitly acknowledge racism. . ." (Cornbleth & Waugh, 1995, p. 121) and advocated a shift from the mastery of information to the development of intellectual processes, with an emphasis on depth, not breadth, and "on the power of analytic thought, not memory alone" (Sobol, 1993, p. 260). Unlike the fabled California history framework heralding the nation's common values and ideals, the New York report offered no common ground. Its most vocal dissenter pronounced it impossible to "ingest" other cultures all at once, "certainly not before . . . ingest[ing] its own. After we have mastered our own culture, we can explore the world" (Schlesinger, 1990, p. A14).

▓▓ Bill Watkins

VISITOR While not an immigrant, our third visitor, Bill Watkins, would certainly have met the government's definition of an at-risk student when he attended public school. Currently, Bill is a professor at the University of Illinois at Chicago who spent his formative university teaching years (1986–1995) at the University of Utah in a joint appointment between the Departments of Education and Ethnic Studies. Born in Harlem, his journey to the curriculum field is far different than that taken by Peter or Petra.

> Early on in my life, my family migrated to southern California. Ours was a small family: mother, father, and two children. Neither of my parents was educated beyond high school. My father was a fundamentalist, Pentecostal, bible-thumping, hellfire, preacher. Our family was very conservative to the point of being puritanical. We pretty much rejected worldly acquisitions. We considered this life as preparation for the next, so not much emphasis was placed on education, except for Bible studies. My church was my world and all of my social interactions with my peers were in that world. But that all changed around the time I was finishing elementary school when my father died of leukemia and my mother remarried a "sinner."

Tracked into vocational courses at a "pretty tough" south-central Los Angeles high school, Watkins was advised to prepare for a life of manual labor. Undeterred, he enrolled in junior college but soon "flunked out," turning to a job in the garment industry. At this point, the "Great Sorting Machine" (Spring, 1989) of our "common culture" had functioned predictably for Bill. After a year of "back-breaking labor," he re-entered college, but

> what happens next is the real transformation. In 1968, the war is beginning to heat up in Vietnam and the civil rights movement is pretty intense. Like many other young men, I decided I'd better find out what this war business was all about since I would probably be there very shortly. Then, a metamorphosis happened: I became interested in the antiwar movement. I started paying more attention to my history and political science classes. I declared a major in poli-sci. I met new friends and remarkably, within a year, I was an honors student!

As a senior, Watkins found himself actively recruited by law schools and graduate departments nationwide. However, the more his "politics became radicalized, the less interested I became in law school." Faced with the decision to enter law school, Bill chose to return home to Brooklyn as a "house husband" and community organizer.

Bill Watkins represented the growing differences in American society—and many Americans were fearful of those judged different. It was perhaps this "difficulty with personal difference" that led Peter Hlebowitsh to accept the Americanizing role of schooling as the child of Russian immigrants, and Petra Munro to become a loner in her elementary suburban school as a

German immigrant. Certainly, most Americans prefer cultural stability and social assimilation to the angst of identity reconstruction and the postmodern revision of our narratives "as we begin to wonder," writes Maxine Greene, about "textual realities and communities of interpretation and multiple points of view" while embracing the "cultural pluralism that now has broken through the silences of the long oppressed, long colonized, long subordinated people: these have led to an interest in situated knowing" (Greene, 1993; retrieved from http://www.ed.uiuc.edu/EPS/PES-Yearbook/93_docs/Greene.HTM).

By mid-century, Americans were situated to know, thanks to Big Tobacco's spin on images of popular culture, that smoking was both medically safe and socially innocuous (or "cool"—depending upon one's age). It would take nearly a half-century of scientific studies, along with a Watergate-like public shock, to convince Americans and their government that smoking and cigarettes were deadly and needed to be monitored and regulated.

VARIED TALE

BIG TOBACCO: "YOU'VE COME A LONG WAY, BABY"

Working together as Big Tobacco to safeguard their collective economic interests, competition among individual tobacco companies remained strong during the 1950s following the introduction of filter-tipped cigarettes. Philip Morris, though, was about to steamroll its competition with the cultural creation of the "Marlboro Man." Tapping into the hybridity of American culture—the comingling of paradoxical images and desires such as the desire to fit in and the belief in rugged individualism—company researchers found that a lone cowboy image appealed to younger male smokers looking to assert their independence, and that women found the cowboy sexy. Marlboro eventually became (and remains) the industry's sales leader, bringing millions of smokers to its brand (Hwang, 1995; Parker-Pope, 2001).

Big Tobacco also entered Americans' living rooms through the family television. Product placement insidiously reinforced the commercials: Phillip Morris sponsored *I Love Lucy* (both Lucy and Ricky smoked on camera); John Cameron Swayze, host of the *Camel News Caravan*, who would die of cancer, was required by the sponsor to have a burning cigarette visible whenever he was on camera. Similarly, product placement agreements with filmmakers began as early as the 1930s with Chesterfield and into the film noir era of the 1940s, culminating in *Superman II*, in which trucks with the Marlboro label (which, in reality, do not exist) appeared throughout the films and ace reporter, Lois Lane, was transformed into a Marlboro chain smoker.

> In 1964, the U.S. Surgeon General declared that smoking causes cancer. Two years later the Federal Trade Commission (FTC) began to control cigarettes. By the end of that decade, every cigarette package carried a warning label, no cigarette advertising could be directed at people under 25 years of age, and claims of healthfulness about filters or cigarette products could not be made. The word "cancer," however, was excluded from warning labels after the tobacco industry volunteered to get out of television advertising.
>
> These restrictions, however, had limited impact as Big Tobacco aggressively pursued other marketing strategies. Knowing that children are the most vulnerable (and valuable) segment of its "starter" population, R.J. Reynolds resuscitated "Old Joe Camel" in 1988 as part of a new marketing campaign. Focusing on convenience stores near high schools and colleges, the company's share of sales increased and children recognized Old Joe as easily as they did Mickey Mouse. All of that success and easy profit came to a screeching halt in 1997 when, in an effort to squelch growing tobacco opposition, R.J. Reynolds agreed to retire Old Joe permanently after the FTC filed a complaint against the company. But worse news lay ahead for both Big Tobacco—and the public schools— as the federal government set its sights on regulation.

Just as Big Tobacco began to morph into new versions of itself, our third visitor, Bill Watkins, accepted a life-altering offer to teach school in Chicago. He recalls that Garfield High School hired him in 1975 "on the provision that I seek state teaching certification. I had no concerns about being a teacher: if anyone was ever prepared to interact with tough, inner-city kids, I was. Besides, I was a people-person and already kind of a street intellectual." Like Petra, he entered teaching with a strong political identity.

As required, Bill enrolled at the Chicago campus of the University of Illinois. "In every course there were Benjamin Bloom, John Dewey, and Ralph Tyler. Nevertheless, I slogged through the certification classes." Realizing that with just a few more courses he would earn a master's degree, Watkins pressed on. His persistence caught the eye of one professor, Bill Schubert:

> He said I'd been one of his best students and wondered if I'd thought about going on? And I said, "Well yeah. Kind of. But I don't think I'll go on in education, because I'm sick of Bloom, Tyler, and Dewey." We had come to know one another and Bill had read many of my papers and saw that I was kind of radicalized and political, so he turned me on to other authors who I found absolutely fascinating. . . . When I read Michael Apple's *Ideology and Curriculum* I found it orgasmic. That one book did more than any other to forever tie me to the curriculum field.

Finding doctoral studies exciting and the program more flexible than that of his previous graduate work, Bill "saw a place for my politics within curriculum studies, a place for a politically conscious individual." As an African-American, he found himself entering the curriculum field at a time when curriculum was coming of age as a racial text with an importance of its own. Tied historically to issues of power and control, racial discourse in curriculum emerged from the postmodern crises of identity and representation.

Question

How do the three visitors (Peter, Petra, and Bill) and their life experiences represent the growing multi-hybridity of the curriculum field and of the role of public schools in fueling that hybridity? To what degree do they coincide with your experiences?

▓ Connecting the Dots of National Education Reform ▓

The 1989 education summit marked a shift in the focus of reform. The general feeling in Charlottesville was that despite grave concerns expressed in *A Nation at Risk* six years earlier, achievement had not significantly improved. That report, issued by the National Commission on Excellence in Education, signaled the development of new priorities for the federal government's approach to education reform—an approach that included the "new basics" of a core curriculum for all students comprised of four years of English, three years of mathematics, three years of science, three years of social studies, and one-half year of computer science.

Unlike those fighting the bi-coastal curriculum wars, summit participants found consensus, stressing the need for a "system of accountability" in the reporting of school, district, and state performance, increased parental choice, school-based management, and alternative certification for teachers. The summit ultimately bridged the unmandated reforms of *A Nation at Risk* of 1983 to the eventual passage of a national education policy called the *No Child Left Behind Act* of 2001. The story of this bridge-building effort suggests an unprecedented incursion of national politics into the lives of educators and curricularists alike.

Shortly after the publication of *A Nation at Risk*, the National Governors' Association (NGA) created seven task forces to study and report on "tough questions" concerning education reform. In 1986, the NGA's forward-looking report, *Time for Results: The Governors' 1991 Report on Education,* declared: "We are ready to lead the second wave of reform in American public education" (National Governors' Association Center for Policy Research and Analysis, 1986, p. 7). The task force on leadership and management, chaired by Arkansas Governor Bill Clinton, recommended that state governments "[p]rovide incentives . . . to promote school site management and improvement . . . [c]ollect statewide information on the process and the outcomes of schooling," and "[r]eward principals and schools for performance and effectiveness" (National Governors' Association Center for Policy Research and Analysis, 1986, pp. 59–60).

There, too, was strong corporate interest in schools as business leaders gained unprecedented levels of input into education policy (Weisman, 1991a). Indeed, President George H. W. Bush actively sought the support of corporate organizations like the Business Roundtable (200 corporate leaders representing the nation's biggest companies, including the major tobacco companies), challenging CEOs to get involved in school reform (Walker, 1989). The Roundtable quickly crafted a nine-point education initiative with which to lobby state legislatures and monitor state progress on school reform (Weisman, 1991b).

Thus, by the time that the first President Bush and the nation's governors gathered for their Virginia summit, many of the recommendations that would find their way into the school reform legislation of the 1990s had already been made. Concluding their meeting on September 28, 1989, they decided for the first time to establish *national education goals* that would "guarantee an internationally competitive standard" in six areas by the year 2000. Their call for national goals did not go unnoticed, as the reform initiatives during the 1980s were of interest to many educators, including Peter, Petra, and Bill.

Peter Hlebowitsh, a new teacher when *A Nation at Risk* was published, remembers it as "hugely influential . . . in terms of scholarship, because it ended up being a pretty big feature of my dissertation. One of the things that interested me was how a little thirty-five-page, poorly written document captured the imagination of the nation. How did that happen?" For Bill Watkins, the answer was simple: the conservative restoration indicated "the realignment of power . . . born out of a politics of hysteria." By 1987, outcome-based education (OBE) hit Petra's school district "like a sledge hammer, along with good old accountability." Once her curriculum became uniform, Petra decided: "That's it. I'm out of here."

Goals 2000

The National Education Goals Panel (NEGP), created in 1990 and consisting of governors, members of Congress, members of the president's administration, and state legislators, quickly recommended that Congress establish a National Council on Education Standards and Testing. *Raising Standards for American Education*, the report issued by this council, recommended creating a permanent body to approve national education standards. In November 1993, the NEGP followed up with *Promises to Keep: Creating High Standards for American Students*. This report focused on

Goals 3 and 4 of the National Education Goals and anticipated the creation of a permanent body, called the National Education Standards and Improvement Council (NESIC), as part of President Clinton's Goals 2000 legislation, which was then being considered by Congress.

Promises to Keep recommended charging the NESIC with reviewing and certifying national content standards in eight subject areas: English, mathematics, science, history, geography, foreign language, citizenship/civics, and the arts. Professional organizations would develop the standards and submit them to the NESIC, which would certify only *one* set for each of the eight subject areas. The resulting NESIC-certified national standards would then be available for use and adaptation by state governments as they developed their own content standards. The standards had to be "academic," "world-class," and "useful and adaptable." Paradoxically, they were to be "voluntary" and originate through "bottom-up development" characterized by "a consensus building process that involves educators, parents and community leaders from schools and neighborhoods across the country" (National Education Goals Panel, 1993, pp. 68–69). Congress passed President Clinton's *Goals 2000: Educate America Act* in March 1994, formally creating the National Education Standards and Improvement Council and setting the stage for the creation and certification of national curriculum standards.

From its inception, Goals 2000 proved to be controversial. Despite its origins in the first Bush administration, many conservatives felt that it was an unacceptable intrusion on the part of the federal government into state and local matters. Perhaps, as Daniel Tanner (1998) argued, Goals 2000 resulted from the failure of state governments to actually do what was necessary to achieve the education goals first proposed in 1989. In any event, the promotion of national standards, even without a mandate, symbolically addressed issues of accountability, shifting the public policy debate away from inputs (the distribution of resources both in and out of schools) toward outputs (measurable assessments justifying the distribution of rewards and punishments to schools and educators). The result was a reform hybrid: standards through standardization.

Congressional Curriculum Convulsions: The National History Standards

In 1992, the National Endowment for the Humanities (NEH), along with the U.S. Department of Education, provided funding to the Center for the Study of History in Schools at UCLA for the development of national history standards that would, in time, be ready for review and certification by the NESIC. Controversy ensued, however, when the standards were released in 1994 and Clinton's new Goals 2000 agenda, including the existence and role of the National Education Standards and Improvement Council in overseeing national standards, came under attack.

On January 18, 1995, Republican Senator Slade Gorton of Washington introduced an amendment to the *Unfunded Mandate Reform Act* to *prohibit* the National Education Standards and Improvement Council (NESIC) from certifying the newly developed history standards. Although their use was completely voluntary, Gorton charged that they would form the basis of a de facto national curriculum, a charge echoed by Democrat Joseph Lieberman in his support of the Gorton amendment. Under the leadership of Newt Gingrich, the House of Representatives voted, in the fall of 1995, to eliminate funding for Goals 2000 altogether. The Senate simply agreed to eliminate the National Education Standards and Improvement Council as a compromise to keep some parts of Goals 2000 funded. By late 1995, the push for voluntary national standards was effectively over.

Senator Gorton's remarks before the Senate are an example of how incendiary the juxtaposition of culture and curriculum wars had become. The following excerpt also underscores how important basic curriculum questions (concerning knowledge and worth, for whom, and at what costs) had become to those at the highest levels of the U.S. government. Note, too, that Gorton is concerned not only with the history standards' content, but with their "philosophical foundation" that, in his view, makes them an "ideologically driven, anti-Western monument to politically correct caricature."

PRIMARY DOCUMENT EXCERPT

Proceedings and Debates of the 104th Congress, First Session (January 18, 1995) by the United States Congress

Mr. Gorton: Mr. President [of the Senate], what is a more important part of our Nation's history for our children to study—George Washington or Bart Simpson? Is it more important that they learn about Roseanne Arnold, or how America defeated communism as the leader of the free world?

According to this document—the recently published "National Standards for United States History"—the answers are not what Americans would expect. With this set of standards, our students will not be expected to know George Washington from the man in the Moon. According to this set of standards, America's democracy rests on the same moral footing as the Soviet Union's totalitarian dictatorship.

Mr. President, this set of standards must be stopped, abolished, repudiated, repealed. It must be recalled like a shipload of badly contaminated food. Today, before our children are asked to spend their evenings studying Bart Simpson instead of Benjamin Franklin's discovery of electricity, these standards must be abolished.

My amendment will stop this set of standards from becoming a guide for teaching history in America's classrooms. In order to stop this perverted idea in its tracks, and to ensure that it does not become, de facto, a guide for our Nation's classrooms, it must be publicly and officially repudiated by this Congress. That is precisely what this amendment seeks to do.

These standards are ideology masquerading as history. These standards would have us reinvent America's history. They are terribly damaging, and they constitute a gross distortion of the American story from its conceptual foundations to the present.

America's story is both triumph and tragedy, but mostly triumph, of flawed yet unprecedented accomplishment. But in this teachers' and textbook manual it becomes a sordid tale "drenched in dark skepticism," as a Wall Street Journal editorial put it, emphasizing what is negative in America's past, while celebrating only politically correct culture and causes.

(I) The Standard Project's Initial Charter

The history standards project began as a response to the alarming illiteracy of our Nation's children about their own, national history. Citizens of a pluralistic, democratic society have a deep, historically based understanding of our liberties' origins and institutions, and appreciate the corresponding responsibilities essential for our survival as a nation, as a people.

Such an appreciation is dependent on a mastery of basic American history. The founding truths of this country may have been self-evident to the Founders, but as studies have demonstrated again and again, they are not genetically transmitted. . . .

(II) We Didn't Get What We Paid For

In 1992, when UCLA's National Center for History in the Schools won the bid to produce national guidelines for American and World history curricula, they were given three basic tasks. . . .

After 2 years and more than $2 million of the American taxpayers' money, the history project has failed to reach any of these goals.

Let members examine a sample of some of the outrageous examples, found on almost every page of these documents. As we look at this material, we should keep in mind that President Bush and all the Nation's Governors, at the national educational summit in Charlottesville, VA, in 1989, recommended the development of national standards based upon what was most worth knowing.

(III) These Proposed Standards Do Not Concentrate on What Is Most Worth Knowing

Examples:

First, George Washington makes only a fleeting appearance in the standards. He is never described as our first President.

Second, the Constitution: The Constitution is not mentioned in the 31 core standards, although the standards mention the Depression three times.

Third, central figures and events in American political, cultural, and scientific life are either barely noted—in a 300 page book—or they simply disappear from the story of America's past. Important historical issues, such as the development of the role of Congress in our Federal Government are not discussed. Under these standards, Paul Revere and his midnight ride will never capture the imagination of our children. Ben Franklin's discovery of electricity will not encourage young scientists to seek out their own discoveries that can change the world.

Fourth, significant historical figures pivotal to America's past, such as Daniel Webster and Robert E. Lee, vanish. Titans who exemplify scientific progress in American history are also omitted from the standards. With these standards in place, our children will not learn of Thomas Edison, Alexander Graham Bell, the Wright brothers, or Albert Einstein. Americans who changed the entire World for the better will cease to exist. . . .

(VI) The Proposed National Standards Are Not Balanced and Objective. . . .

The problem is not one of mere detail. The problem is in its philosophical foundations. Those foundations are fundamentally anti-Western, and anti-American in their conceptual framework. The correction of a few of the worst excesses will not remove that anti-American, anti-Western formulation at its base. And it is a most serious problem. Whether or not the standards are certified by the still to be created Goals 2000 NESIC Board, according to Gilbert Sewall and many others, the way in which the textbook establishment works, this manual, having the extraordinary prestige of being the first national curriculum guide, will become, de facto, official if not strongly repudiated. As Dr. Sewall has stated, "It will be the first draft of the next generation of textbooks.". . .

Mr. President, I have been in favor of national standards. Although I had serious reservations, I added my vote to Goals 2000. The development of this ideologically driven, anti-Western monument to politically correct caricature is not what the Congress envisioned, nor is it what the American people paid for. The purpose of this amendment is therefore publicly to repudiate its continued use and stop its further influence. Should such a project ever be taken up again, and I am not at all sure it should be, in light of this experience, it must be undertaken by scholars with at least a passable understanding of and decent respect for this country and for its roots in Western civilization.

Source: United States Congress. (January 18, 1995). Congressional Record: Proceedings and Debates of the 104th Congress, First Session, 141(10), (pp. S1025–S1028). Washington, DC: United States Government Printing Office.

Republican Senator Jim Jeffords of Vermont and Democratic Senator Edward Kennedy of Massachusetts were among those who spoke against Gorton's amendment, declaring that the review and certification of the standards was a matter for the NESIC and not the U.S. Congress. Despite such concerns, Senator Gorton's amendment passed on a vote of 99–1 (Congressional Record, January 18, 1995).

From National Goals to State Assessments: Educators Lose Control

Another aspect of President Clinton's education agenda in 1994 was state accountability. With passage of the Goals 2000 legislation in the spring of 1994, attention turned toward reauthorization of the Elementary and Secondary Education Act, particularly Title I funds for compensatory education programs. On October 20 of that year, the President signed into law the Improving America's Schools Act, a bill reauthorizing ESEA that, for the first time, linked Title I grants to school reform efforts. This new legislation required states to construct school improvement and assessment plans based on state-developed content and performance standards in at least mathematics and reading. Progress toward meeting these standards was to be measured three times over the course of a student's school experience: between grades 3 and 5, grades 6 and 9, and grades 10 and 12 (*Education Week,* November 9, 1994). States were also authorized to use Title I funds for school-wide improvement projects, provided a certain percentage of students met low-income criteria.

Since 1986, when the National Governors Association began to take the lead in promoting school reform efforts, many state governments had also become active in legislating various kinds of school reform initiatives. For example, spurred into action by a Kentucky State Supreme Court decision that found inequitable school funding to be in violation of the state constitution, that state's legislature passed the landmark 1990 Kentucky Education Reform Act. This act represented the most sweeping statewide reform effort at the time by equalizing state funding, creating a mechanism for school-based decision making, setting performance standards, and instituting a state-directed system of accountability that rewarded schools able to reach the standards and "sanctioned" those that did not. In 1998, the Commonwealth Accountability Testing System established a state-wide basic skills test (administered in grades 3, 6, and 9) with state core content area tests administered variously in all other grades (Kentucky Department of Education, 2000).

This refinement of the Kentucky Education Reform Act illustrates how the focus of school accountability systems evolved from an initial concern with *professional* accountability to one that emphasized *bureaucratic* accountability (Darling-Hammond & Ascher, 1991). Bureaucratic accountability rests on procedural, top-down directives, whereas professional accountability requires teachers to make their own decisions concerning students (Darling-Hammond & Ascher, 1991). Included in Kentucky's original reform legislation was an effort to promote school-based decision making throughout the state, a response to the recommendations from the Carnegie Forum on Education and the Economy (1986), which balanced more decision-making autonomy on the part of schools in exchange for increased accountability. Yet, as the 1990s progressed, rigid accountability displaced school autonomy as schools came under fire for not performing— just as did Big Tobacco.

Question

One might argue that educational accountability, today, is both professional and bureaucratic. What evidence do you see that supports such a position?

VARIED TALE

BIG TOBACCO: ACCOUNTABILITY AND GLOBALIZATION

Throughout the 1980s and early 1990s, Representative Henry Waxman of California had doggedly summoned Big Tobacco executives to appear before the House Subcommittee on Health and Environment. In 1994, seven officers of major tobacco companies testified that nicotine was not addictive. Captured in a photograph by *The New York Times,* the seeming indifference of Big Tobacco to its customers drew the attention of many people, two of whom would eventually help to shape the fate of the industry in this country: Merrel Williams, a paralegal for Brown & Williamson (B & W), and Jeffery Wigand, a research scientist for the same company. A son of smokers and a smoker himself, Williams had ferreted away thousands of pages of secret documents showing that the company knew, as early as 1963, that cigarettes were addictive, and outlining its campaigns to attract new smokers or "starters" (Parker-Pope, 2001). These documents were delivered to an anti-tobacco activist and tobacco researcher, Stan Glantz (Gibbs, 1998), and eventually made their way on to the Internet, thus making them available to attorneys and clients.

Williams provided the documents, and Wigand, the famous whistle-blower of a CBS *60 Minutes* episode and the subsequent movie, *The Insider,* became the federal government's interpreter of those pages. Infuriated by Big Tobacco's testimony in 1994, Wigand decided to break his silence in a deposition, claiming that B & W hid research, refused to make cigarettes safer, and even used a compound

(continued)

found in rat poison in certain types of pipe tobacco. The actions of these two men lent tremendous weight to numerous impending lawsuits.

In November 1998, the attorneys general of 46 states and five U.S. territories signed a $246 billion settlement with tobacco companies to be paid out over 25 years in lieu of suing them for the health care costs of smokers. The settlement bans cigarette advertising on billboards and restricts sponsorship and marketing (Fairclough, 2002) in stadiums and at sports events (Hall, 1998). It also funds a $1.5 billion anti-smoking campaign, and restricts lobbying by tobacco companies against state legislation aimed at curbing youth smoking.

As a part of the agreement, the companies posted millions of pages of secret internal documents to the Internet, thus leading to an increase in successful lawsuits against them. Between 1954 and 1998, only three smokers (out of 800 cases) won their cases against Big Tobacco; since 1999, smokers have won one out of every three (Sherrid, 2002).

Despite the government's aggressive tactics, its relationship to Big Tobacco remains problematic. Nearly half the cost of a pack of cigarettes comes from federal, state, and local taxes. Yet the same U.S. Department of Agriculture that imposed quotas to limit the amount of tobacco produced also operated a price support program for tobacco farmers that did not end until late 2004 (University of Tennessee: Agriculture Policy Analysis Center Web site: http://agpolicy. org/tobquota.html).

The 1998 tobacco settlement—a potential death knell—was not even a knockout punch to the industry. As the curriculum field morphs and changes to fit the new political and social landscape of government intervention in schooling, so has Big Tobacco successfully retrofitted itself to a new economic reality after the federal government settlement. Philip Morris became the corporate hybrid Altria Group (one of the world's largest food and beverage companies marketing processed foods [e.g., Kraft] as well as tobacco) and reported huge profit increases in the year after the settlement (Fonda, 2001). Altria also provided the start-up money, in 1995, to form the Center for Consumer Freedom, which fights smoking bans in restaurants. This nonprofit group also aggressively challenges nutritionists and critics of the fast-food industry through lobbying and media ads. Although just a few lawsuits have been filed linking fast food to health problems, "trial lawyers are circling and are starting to turn food into the new tobacco" (Warner, 2005, p. 9).

Although the tobacco industry remains profitable in this country (teen smoking has increased among males and females in all ethnic and racial groups, but especially among young people of color [Beck, 1998]), it has moved vigorously into Eastern Europe, Russia, and Asia. More than 1.1 billion people around the world purchase more than 15 billion cigarettes daily (Parker-Pope, 2001). Given its prospects for economic renewal through worldwide expansion, Big Tobacco is one of the great American success stories of the last century and will probably remain so for the new Millennium, championing the slogan, "You've come a long way, baby."

▓ A Pedagogy of Poverty

In the same year that Big Tobacco reached its settlement, the Center for Education Reform, the Thomas B. Fordham Foundation, Empower America, and the Heritage Foundation sponsored an update to the *Nation at Risk* report. *A Nation "Still" at Risk* claimed that American schools were continuing to fail because the gap in the quality of schools was based on poverty and race. Citing these as moral reasons for change, the update offered two main renewal strategies: standards, assessments, and accountability along with competition and choice (U. S. Department of Education, 1998).

By 2001, 49 states had developed versions of these strategic renewal strategies. Not only did virtually every state create its own educational standards; 28 implemented state-mandated assessments, with 17 states instituting promotion and retention standards based on these assessments (Fuhrman, 2001; Viadero, 2003). In the view of some, though, this "whips and chains" mentality, dependent upon standards-based assessment to determine which schools, teachers, and students are successful, is one of the major obstacles for true school reform.

In Texas, for example, the primary motivation, initially, for education reform was low teacher salaries (McNeil, 2000). However, the appointment of billionaire businessman and presidential candidate H. Ross Perot to lead the state's educational reform brought a corporate sensibility that valued quality control and a clear, measurable return on investment. The result was a reform package that imposed a tightly controlled "top-down structure" of school and curriculum governance while still offering "too few resources" (p. 187). McNeil (2000) convincingly documented the effects of such standardization in Houston, Texas, where the so-called "Texas miracle" began. Building on the insights of Michael Apple regarding teacher "de-skilling," McNeil, in her study of teachers working in Houston magnet schools, found that

> [t]he proficiency system [implemented in the Houston Independent School District] threatened the quality of the curriculum by institutionalizing a consensus curriculum, by divorcing the knowledge of the teacher from the curriculum, by divorcing the knowledge and questions held by students from the required content, and by subjecting all knowledge to a fragmentation filter that artificially altered its substance. (p. 205)

Peter Hlebowitsh and Petra Munro have reflected on similar experiences. When Peter started teaching, before the publication of *A Nation at Risk*, he was fortunate to have a principal who granted a large measure of autonomy to her teachers: "I think one of the key ingredients in being a good school teacher is to have what I used to call discretionary space. . .

You also need room to try new things, to try to be more innovative and creative. My principal allowed me to do that." In contrast, Petra, whose teaching career began a year after the report was released, had a different experience: "We were monitored by the principal and department chairs to make sure we were following correct OBE procedures."

Touting his educational "miracle," the former Texas governor turned U.S. President, George W. Bush, signed into law the No Child Left Behind (NCLB) Act in January of 2002. As the first reauthorization of the Elementary and Secondary Education Act since 1994, NCLB in many ways looked backward. The Act disbanded the National Education Goals Panel (created during his father's administration) and continued much of what was contained in the ESEA reauthorization signed by President Clinton. It required states to use their assessments in measuring reading and mathematics achievement in grades 3–8 but to use National Assessment of Educational Progress (NAEP) tests on a sample of fourth and eighth graders every other year (*Education Week*, January 9, 2002). States were further required to demonstrate academic proficiency for all students within 12 years. Students attending schools unable to make adequate progress for two years were given the option for school choice. NCLB put the public education system on notice: perform or, just as Ravitch (1992) had warned, "they will forfeit their claim to public support" (p. 11).

A decade after Ravitch's prescient words (above) during the debate over multiculturalism, the nation, in 2002, was even more diverse. Yet, instead of admonishing public schools to teach all children a common heritage and an awareness of their shared American identity, NCLB demands, simply, that we teach all children. Period! From the vantage point of curriculum workers like Bill Watkins, this difference is "the blueprint for the end of universal education, and the retreat to education as privilege as opposed to right." This "curriculum of end results" has provided the necessary third ingredient for a "perfect storm" in public education.

NCLB's educational centerpiece is an enhanced "teaching to the test" mentality with its over-reliance on drill and practice, lecture, and rote learning. This "pedagogy of poverty" encourages passivity in students while stifling creativity, curiosity, and the development of critical-thinking and problem-solving skills—all necessary for a democratic citizenry (Irons, 2002; Padron, Waxman, & Rivera, 2002; Rueda & McIntyre, 2002). With the over-reliance on prefabricated curricular programs in many schools with large, at-risk Title I populations, teachers must literally read scripted lessons to students. Neither students nor teachers make pedagogical choices.

The popular reading program *Open Court*, for example, mandates that all students complete every activity at a prescribed pace. The reading lesson lasts two to three hours every day, with most of that time spent in whole group instruction. From the beginning to the end of each lesson, the teacher's every word and action are prescribed.

Hailed as a successful, research-based reading program (especially for poverty-level children), *Open Court* is used in one of every eight elementary schools in California (and in many other states across the country)—though *without* support from the state's reading/language arts experts. And research studies reflect this missing endorsement. Focused on the use of *Open Court* in 153 California schools, Moustafa and Land (2001) found that schools implementing this reading program were more likely to have the *lowest* standardized test scores in their respective school districts. These researchers suggest that its use limits economically disadvantaged children because the reading program does not teach comprehension as a part of instruction.

Haberman (1996), who first labeled such programs of instruction as a "pedagogy of poverty," contends that they appeal to people who believe that students have to be forced to learn and should not be allowed choices (a sign of permissiveness). Those who favor this type of instruction believe that curriculum *transmits* knowledge, skills, and dispositions; that students need to be controlled, especially those who are "at-risk" and lack the requisite learning skills and habits of the dominant culture; and that professional educators must be held to bureaucratic accountability. Inevitably, it is "at-risk" students who are most negatively affected by this type of instruction. Typically in the past, and ever-increasingly so now, many of these students are immigrants (or children of immigrants) who do not yet understand democratic principles (Haberman, 1996).

Adopting a pedagogy of poverty in service to reform-mandated measures of standardization creates a system of "subtractive schooling," separating students from their teachers, their courses, their education, and their identities (Valenzuela, 1999). For children of recent immigrants in particular, such schooling signals them to *not* conform, for to do so "is to risk losing one's cultural identity" (McNeil, 2000, p. 249). Research reports document that the curricular decisions and accountability measures undertaken by school systems in Texas and North Carolina, for example, had been detrimental for African-American students (Ladd, 1999; Smith & Mickelson, 2000). Students are further distanced by a generic curriculum constructed for its ease in testing and computer scoring rather than on the basis of students' needs, learning styles, or cultural backgrounds. Sadly, reform designed to reduce learning disparities, curriculum calibrated to a core body of shared knowledge, and standardization followed to achieve high standards have "widen[ed] the educational inequalities and mask[ed] historical and persistent inequities" (McNeil, 2000, p. 230). Just as the common school was imagined to Americanize or assimilate newly arrived immigrants in the nineteenth and twentieth centuries, current policy language urges not only a common culture but a uniform set of standards reflecting a "tangible commonality" (Cornbleth, 2000, p. 215) shared among the numerous and diverse groups that populate our country. The cultural conservatives' strategy "to contain diversity and difference through a standardized education—with national standards in core subjects, national assessments and a de facto national curriculum" (Cornbleth & Waugh, 1995, p.15), appeared to be successful—but at the price of relinquishing greater control to federal and state governments, widening the academic achievement gap, and placing the nation at greater risk than it had been two decades earlier. Such are the consequences of the hybridity of educational reform.

Resegregation and Student Learning

As school reform and accountability are forcing many teachers into practicing a pedagogy of poverty with their students—more and more of whom are "at-risk" and children of color—the issue of race has once again become central to who goes to school where, and with whom. In a trio of U.S. Supreme Court rulings (*Dowell*, *Freeman*, and *Jenkins* cases) between 1991 and 1995, schools in Oklahoma City; DeKalb County, Georgia; and Missouri reverted to the separate but unequal pattern of the Jim Crow era. Today, *none* of the 25 largest, central U.S. city school systems serves a majority of white students, even though each of these locations contains a white majority population. Nearly two-thirds of the country's black children live in these cities and now attend segregated schools. Since the 1971 *Swann* ruling enforced busing in the Charlotte-Mecklenberg (North Carolina) school system, 10 million white families nationwide have moved out of cities and into suburbs, or have put their children in private schools, leaving inner-city schools with large numbers of children of color. The converse exists in the suburbs, where this influx has created white segregated schools (Irons, 2002).

Schools remain unequal because segregation by race correlates with segregation by poverty. Since a significantly large number of African-American, Hispanic, and Native-American children live in low-income households, the implications for resegregation of public schools should be clear: as schools grow more racially segregated, they will also "re-stratify along economic lines producing more high poverty schools populated disproportionately by non-whites" (Boger, 2002, p. 29). A further implication of resegregation for testing and accountability was demonstrated more than 40 years after the 1960 Coleman report: student achievement is closely linked to the educational background and aspirations of other students in the school. "In fact, . . . the social characteristics of a student body were the single most important factor in predicting minority student achievement" (Boger, 2002, p. 27). Studies done in later decades confirmed this finding (Kennedy, 1986; Mayer & Jencks, 1989; White, 1982; Wolf, 1977).

At the start of the 1990s, the "curriculum wars" in California and New York centered on controlling people and their school-based knowledge—albeit from different ideological positions. It appeared that state educational leaders like California's Bill Honig and New York's Tom Sobol, in collaboration with their selected experts and the business community, would dominate and direct this conversation about ideas and content toward results and measures, rather than a deeper understanding of the consequences of an increasingly diverse school population. By the beginning of the millennium, however, the federal government had effectively taken firm control of both the agenda and the conversation of educational reform.

Cultural Studies: The Ultimate Hybrid

Many working in the curriculum field responded to the new political landscape of school reform by combining and developing interdisciplinary approaches, particularly in the area of cultural studies. In his introduction to *Curriculum: Toward New Identities* (1998), Bill Pinar notes, "[W]e curricularists are no longer the major stakeholders in school curriculum. Instead of wringing our hands over lost influence in the schools and rejection by teachers (and policy-makers and parents and politicians), we might commit ourselves to understanding what curriculum is, has been, and might be" (p. xiii). Pointing toward the creation of new identities, Pinar anticipated a growing interest in the interdisciplinary possibilities of cultural studies: "As the effort to understand curriculum as political text continues to collapse," he wrote, "more scholars can be expected to move to this terrain" (p. xv).

One such scholar is Cameron McCarthy, whose "The Devil Finds Work: Re-reading Race and Identity in Contemporary Life," a chapter in his book *The Uses of Culture* (1998), serves as our final primary source document and illustrates the influence cultural studies has had on the curriculum field.

First developed in Great Britain in the 1950s, cultural studies offered curricularists the kind of theoretical hybridization that combined political critique with the postmodern rejection of "metanarratives." Stuart Hall, a leading and influential cultural theorist, likened some forms of cultural studies to "Marxism without guarantees." Examples of such metanarratives include stable, essentialized notions of race, gender, class, and identity.

Notice in this excerpt how McCarthy characterizes the "new racial times" that have created opportunities for rethinking the relations among identity, popular culture, and education. Also consider how McCarthy makes reference to cultural and political *hybridity* without using that term.

PRIMARY DOCUMENT EXCERPT

The Devil Finds Work: Re-reading Race and Identity in Contemporary Life

by Cameron McCarthy

We are living in new racial times, new racial circumstances. Racial dangers have multiplied, but so have the possibilities for renewal and change. We are living in a historical moment in which the racial order is being reconfigured in the tiniest crevices of everyday life. As I have stressed throughout this book, we need new ways to talk about race and identity to help us better understand the powerful rearticulations that are taking place in popular culture and in the commonsense of the whole body politic. One of these significant new developments is the growing anxiety and restlessness that characterize the white middle class. This tumult and restlessness are most strongly foregrounded at the level of the production of identities and representations. We are living in a time of the production of crass identity politics. By identity politics I mean the strategic deployment of the discourse of group distinctiveness in everyday struggles over political representation and scarce resources (the distribution of goods and services) in education and society. Far too often, identity politics are discussed in ways that suggest that only minority groups—particularly African Americans and Latinos—practice, promote, and benefit from identity politics. The case may further be made that minorities are the only ones who experience the effects of these politics in terms of the fragmentation of identity and symbolic and social disorientation and dislocation. This is manifestly false; white people also practice and benefit from identity politics. Nowhere is this more powerfully registered than in popular culture. As indicated earlier, one has only to look at the respective coverage of whites and minorities on the evening news to see the coordinating role the media play in the elaboration of white identity and the corresponding disorganization and subversion of minority identity formation. . . .

Recoding Racial Identity

. . . It is [the] blend of the educational and the popular that I want to explore briefly here, for one of the current difficulties in the educational literature on race relations is its refusal of the popular. American middle-class white youth and adults know more about inner-city blacks through the media, particularly, television and film, than through personal or classroom interaction or even in textbooks. Nowadays, textbooks are looking intertextually more and more like TV with their HD graphics and illustrations and their glossy, polysemic treatment of subject matter. In addition, anti-institutional educational projects such as Teach For America— with its mission to save the urban poor for god, for capitalism, and for country— are deeply inscribed in a language of the racial other pulled of the television set, as we will see in a moment. We live in a time when "pseudo-events"—as Daniel Boorstin (1975) called media-driven representations in the 70s—have usurped any relic of reality beyond that which is staged. Media simulations have driven incredibly deep and perhaps permanent wedges of difference between the world of the suburban dweller and his inner-city counterpart. Argues Boorstin (1975, p. 3): "we have used our wealth, our literacy, our technology, and our progress, to create a thicket of unreality which stands between us and the facts of life." It is these "facts of life"—notions of what, for example, black people are like or what Latinos are like—that are invented and reinvented in the media, in popular magazines, in the newspaper, and in television and popular film. In this sense, popular culture is always a step ahead of educational institutions in terms of strategies of incorporation and mobilization of racial identities. As authors such as Katherine Frith (1997) point out, by the end of the teenage years, the average student will have spent more time watching television than he or she would have spent in school. It is increasingly television and film, more so than the school curriculum, that educate American youth about race.

The War Over Signs

Even more crucially . . . contemporary conflicts in education and in popular culture are fundamentally battles over signs and the occupation and territorialization of symbolic as well as material resources and urban and suburban space. Central to these developments is the rise of resentment politics. In his *Genealogy of Morals* (1967), Friedrich Nietzsche conceptualized resentment as the specific practice of identity displacement in which the social actor consolidates his own identity by complete disavowal of the merits and existence of his social other. This practice of ethnocentric consolidation and cultural exceptionalism now characterizes much of the tug-of-war over educational reform and multiculturalism. This battle over culture, self, and group has spread throughout society as a whole. Resentment and racial reaction therefore define school life as expressed by the extent to which the culture war over signs and identity in the practices has infiltrated everyday life. Education is indeed a critical site in which struggles over the organization and concentration of emotional and political investment and moral affiliation are taking place. These battles over identity involve the powerful manipulation of group symbols and strategies of articulation and rearticulation of public slogans and popular discourses. These signs and symbols are used in the making of identity and the definition of social and political projects. An important feature of these developments is the radical recoding and re-narration of public life now taking place. As I noted in "Reading the American Popular," traditional distinctions between conservatives and liberals, Democrats and Republicans, the Left versus the Right have collapsed. Radically distorting and conservative energies and drives have taken over the body politic, displacing concerns about inequality and poverty. What we have is the mushrooming of opportunistic discourses activated within the suburban middle class itself.

These discourses center on the protection of the home and the defense of the neighborhood from inner-city predators. They narrate the presentation of the nostalgic ancestral record of the group and its insulation from the contaminating racial other. These opportunistic discourses spawned within the last decade and a half foreground new priorities in the public arena: concerns with identity, history, popular memory, nation, family, crime, and so on, now drive the engines of popular will and the public imagination. This shift away from the issue of social inequality of the 60s and 70s means that America is now willing to spend more on law enforcement and prisons than it is on educating inner-city youth. On the other hand, some minority advocates seem more preoccupied with cultural assertion and cultural distinctiveness than with the bruising socio-economic isolation of minority youth.

Source: McCarthy, C. (1998). *The uses of culture.* New York: Routledge. Reprinted with permission.

McCarthy's argument allows us to consider the politics of the curriculum wars, the Senate debate over the National History Standards, the national fixation on school reform, as evidenced by federal legislation like Goals 2000 and No Child Left Behind, and the story of Big Tobacco, for that matter, as struggles over the "group symbols and strategies" that not only shape and control national, social, and cultural agendas but define "appropriate" individual and collective relationships to those agendas as well.

The forces of race, reform, and a pedagogy of poverty lie in place across the United States, darkening the educational skies for millions of children and linking inextricably to the health and viability of the historic curriculum field. Yet, even within this perfect storm, curriculum stubbornly remains a site for the struggle of *meaning*, not just over what's worth knowing, but also over how people understand themselves and others.

■ And . . . So . . . "Where Are You/We, Anyway?" ■

What unites the three biographies of Bill, Peter, and Petra in their work toward understanding curriculum is the personal meaning this work has for each of them, and its connections to the rest of the world. While these three curriculum workers represent once-stable categories of race, class, and gender, their biographies reflect how they have worked to understand themselves, the work of schools, and the role of curriculum's work within their lives. Yet, together they also evidence the field's hybridity. A Deweyian pragmatist, Peter is passionate about conserving the field and returning it to the democratic mission of public education; Petra, as a feminist with a strong sense of history and post-colonialism, illustrates the continued movement of our field from local public schools to global influences; and Bill, by his racial identity and corresponding emphasis on African-American history as a part of curriculum work, underscores the field's silent ignorance regarding matters of race and racism.

By the end of the 1990s, it was clear that the curriculum field had moved beyond neat categorization. As we noted earlier in the chapter, many who did not identify as curriculum scholars per se nonetheless exerted a great deal of influence on teachers and policy-makers. Diane Ravitch, Howard Gardner, and Linda Darling-Hammond, to name but a few, continue to contribute significantly to debates over what should be taught in schools. Even billionaire publisher Walter H. Annenberg might be said to have influenced the curriculum field of the 1990s, when in December of 1993, he announced in a White House ceremony that he would donate $500 million to public schools. Labels that made sense as the curriculum field experienced growth and expansion in the 1970s and 1980s reached the limits of their descriptive power in the 1990s. More theoretically complex than ever before, the interdisciplinary, even transdisciplinary, nature of contemporary curriculum work has matured and flourished.

One sign of this flourishing is the diversification of curriculum conferences. In 1999, the Bergamo Conference, which we introduced in chapter 6, returned to its namesake location outside of Dayton, Ohio, and continued to attract curriculum scholars like Mary Aswell Doll, Marla Morris, and Greg Dimitriadis working the edges of curriculum theorizing. The personal tensions and theoretical fissures discussed in chapter 8 prompted some participants at that conference to create a new association, the Curriculum and Pedagogy Group. First convened in 2000 in Austin, Texas, this group represented in many ways the aspirations of the "second wave" of curriculum theorizing, the goal of which was to bring to school contexts some of the theoretical insights of the preceding decades. Other curriculum scholars like David Flinders and Marcela Kysilka prefer the American Association of Teaching and Curriculum (AATC), which was founded in 1993 to promote the curriculum field as a national "learned society." As part of the growing interest in the international dimensions of curriculum work, Bill Pinar and Janet Miller founded the American Association for the Advancement of Curriculum Studies (AAACS), the U.S. affiliate of the International Association for the Advancement of Curriculum Studies (IAACS). It is rather difficult to say precisely what distinguishes each of these groups and conferences from the other in terms of their sessions and participants. But perhaps in seeking the hybridity of theory and practice, these newest conferences and organizations are aimed to some degree at the transformative potential of teacher education, curriculum, and life in schools.

However, even with the proliferation of curriculum conferences, some of the old tensions between theory and practice remain. Journal articles stimulating the debate continue to pop up with regularity. William Wraga, a professor of educational administration at the University of Georgia, published an article in the January–February 1999 edition of *Educational Researcher* titled "'Extracting Sunbeams out of Cucumbers': The Retreat from Practice in Reconceptualized Curriculum Studies." Arguing that "[r]econceptualized curriculum studies have continually sought to distance theory from practice" (p. 4), Wraga (1999a) charged Bill Pinar and other so-called reconceptualists with abandoning schools by retreating into theory and refusing to address "real" curriculum problems. Invited to respond, Pinar (1999) drew on the public controversy surrounding the 1998 Southern Baptist Convention's official adoption, into its Message of Faith, of a statement that read, "A wife is to submit herself graciously to the servant leadership of her husband. . ." In titling his response "Gracious Submission," Pinar likened Wraga's argument to a "reassertion of heterosexual male privilege" driven by the desire to see the feminized realm of practice "graciously submitting" to the masculine demands of theory. In contrast to this traditional gendered narrative, Pinar offered, reconceptualists believe that theory and practice engage as equals in the "complicated conversation . . . that is the curriculum" (p. 15). Wraga was unconvinced. "The arrogation of the curriculum field continues," he noted in his rejoinder (1999b, p. 16).

This dissonance between Pinar and Wraga illustrates the centrality of the debate concerning the real or imagined distance between curriculum theory and practice. The decade of the '90s illustrates both the stakes of this debate and the fact that there is no easy divide between each of its terms. Does the curriculum field exist "in a state of perpetual crisis" (Wraga & Hlebowitsh, 2003, p. 425), or is "crisis" more productively read as a sign of growth and vitality? It is difficult to say, precisely. However, the most effective way to address the unforeseen challenges of school reform and curriculum conflict in the twenty-first century may be through the strength that honored diversity can bring to the collective wisdom of the curriculum field.

V isitor Bibliography   Peter Hlebowitsh

Hlebowitsh, P. S. (1992a). Amid behavioral and behavioristic objectives: Reappraising appraisals of the Tyler Rationale. *Journal of Curriculum Studies, 24*(6):533–547.

Hlebowitsh, P. S. (1992b). Critical theory versus curriculum theory: Reconsidering the dialogue on Dewey. *Educational Theory, 72*(1):69–85.

Hlebowitsh, P. S. (1993). *Radical curriculum theory reconsidered: A historical perspective*. New York: Teachers College Press.

Hlebowitsh, P .S. (1995). Interpretations of the Tyler Rationale: A reply to Kliebard. *Journal of Curriculum Studies, 27*(1):89–94.

Hlebowitsh, P. S. (1999a). The common unity and the progressive restoration of the curriculum field. In L. Behar-Horenstein and J. Glantz (Eds.), *Modern and postmodern perspectives in the curriculum field*. New York: Greenwood.

Hlebowitsh, P. S. (1999b). The burdens of the new curricularist. *Curriculum Inquiry, 29*(3):355–364.

Hlebowitsh, P. S. (2005). *Designing the school curriculum*. Boston: Pearson/Allyn & Bacon.

Visitor Bibliography   Petra Munro

Adams, N., Causey, T., Jacobs, M., Munro, P., Quinn, M., & Trousdale, A. (1998). Womentalkin': A reader's theatre performance of teachers' stories. *International Journal of Qualitative Studies in Education, 11*(3):383–395.

Crocco, M., Munro, P., & Weiler, K. (1999). *Pedagogies of resistance: Women educator activists 1880–1960*. New York: Teachers College Press.

Munro, P. (1996). Resisting "resistance": Stories women teachers tell. *Journal of Curriculum Theorizing, 12*(1): 16–29.

Munro, P. (1998a). *Subject to fiction: Women teachers' life history narratives and the cultural politics of resistance*. London: Open University Press.

Munro, P. (1998b). Engendering curriculum history. In W. Pinar (Ed.), *Curriculum: Toward new identities* (pp. 263–294). New York: Garland Press.

Munro, P. (1999). "Widening the Circle": Jane Addams, gender and the redefinition of democracy. In M.S. Crocco & O.L. Davis, Jr. (Eds.), *"Bending the future to their will": Civic women, social education, and democracy* (pp. 73–91). Boulder, CO: Rowman & Littlefield.

Visitor Bibliography   Bill Watkins

Watkins, W. H. (1993). Black curriculum orientations: A preliminary inquiry. *Harvard Educational Review, 63*(3):321–338.

Watkins, W. H. (1994). Pan-Africanism and the politics of education: Towards a new understanding. In S. Lemelle & R. D. G. Kelley (Eds.), *Imagining home: Class, culture and nationalism in the African diaspora* (pp. 351–360). London: Verso.

Watkins, W. H. (Fall/Winter 1995–96). Thomas Jesse Jones, social studies and race. *International Journal of Social Education, 10*(2): 124–133.

Watkins, W. H. (1998). A pedagogy for the dispossessed. *Journal of Interdisciplinary Education, (2)*:8–18.

Watkins, W. H. (2000). Our country is rich, our people are poor: Education, justice and the politics of structural adjustment. In W. Ayers, M. Klonsky, & G. Lyon (Eds.), *A Simple Justice* (pp. 9–12). New York: Teachers College Press.

Watkins, W. H. (2001a) *The white architects of black education: Ideology and power in America, 1865–1954*. New York: Teachers College Press.

Watkins, W. H., Lewis, J., & Chou, V. (Eds.). (2001b). *Race and education: The roles of history and society in educating African American students*. Boston: Allyn & Bacon.

10

Imagining the Postmillennial Curriculum Field

How do we understand the millennium's opening decade in which America's division into blue and red states is nearly as divisive as its split between blue and gray six generations earlier? Where the fracturing of global markets, the movements toward local democratization, and the breakdown of disciplinary boundaries enabling engineered life forms and cyber-biotechnology have pushed the world into a state of uncomfortable reorientation around issues of state power and corporate authority vis-à-vis democracy and democratization, globalization and postcolonialism, technology and ethics? Here we explore the paradox of *consolidated diversity* by returning to several of our cultural icons from previous chapters and introducing others as we situate ourselves within the contemporary curriculum field and peer into its near future.

Democracy, Globalization, and Technology

One of the seeming ironies of this new millennium is the push for democracy within an era of corporate consolidation and globalization. Technology makes each possible. The image of M1A2 Abrams tanks (with a commander's independent thermal viewer, and digital data bus and radio interface unit providing a common picture among all tank commanders of the 4th Infantry Division) rolling into a newly "liberated" Baghdad absent throngs of cheering Iraqis (promised by former Halliburton CEO, Vice-President Richard Cheney, and fellow former CEO Defense Secretary Donald Rumsfeld) captures the apparent paradox of "Operation Iraqi Freedom."

Halliburton International, which retains ties to Cheney in unexercised stock options and deferred salary, garnered contracts worth more than $1.7 billion for its work in Iraq within a year of the "operation." Two years later, in mid-2005, internal Pentagon audits had red-flagged nearly $1.4 billion in Halliburton invoices, including $45 cases of soda and $100-per-bag laundry service; meanwhile Iraqi contracts to the energy services and construction company topped $18 billion. Across its operations in 120 countries, Halliburton has raked in billions of additional dollars—and more red flags. French officials have been probing allegations of millions of dollars in Nigerian oil kickback monies involving Halliburton while officials in Kazakhstan had initiated criminal proceedings for $250 million due to tax evasion.

Although Halliburton purportedly is in alignment with the Bush administration's agenda to evangelize the world for democracy, it has, in a world of postmodern mysteries, simultaneously contributed to genuine grassroots democracy: from Internet sites like Halliburtonwatch.org, the 2-million-plus on-line activists of MoveOn.org, and Ralph Nader's democracyrising.com to mega-networking groups such as the World Movement for Democracy, "responding to the unprecedented global interchange of people, ideas, and goods that has transformed the world" (www.wmd.org). As Halliburton investors readied themselves for their 2005 shareholders meeting at the Four Season's hotel in downtown Houston, Texas, local activists employed a

> "people power" strategy of direct action and popular education to exact social, political and economic costs on Halliburton for their operations in Iraq. In the spirit of the Serbian Otpor student movement, privatization resistors in Bolivia, and Filipino "People Power" which brought down dictator Ferdinand Marcos, as well as the rich tradition of America's own social movements, Houston activists already have been using community dialogue, teach-in's, film screenings, Halliburton counter-recruitment, humor, non-violent direct action and resolve to stop the war profiteers. (Parkin, 2005, paragraph 15)

A similar pattern can be found in the consolidation of the media industry, which includes music, film, newspapers, magazines, sports, television, radio, and publishing, led by media giant AOL/Time-Warner (whose board members are interlocked with 28 other major corporations, including Big Tobacco giant Phillip Morris), and followed quickly by other cartel conglomerates like Walt Disney, General Electric, and Viacom. These media weddings represent

> the grand convergence of the previously disparate US culture industries—many of them vertically monopolized already—into one global

superindustry providing most of our imaginary "content." The movie business had been largely dominated by the major studios in Hollywood; TV, like radio before it, by the triune axis of the networks headquartered in New York; magazines, primarily by Henry Luce (with many independent others on the scene); and music, from the 1960s, mostly by the major record labels. Now all those separate fields are one, the whole terrain divided up among the giants—which, in league with Barnes & Noble, Borders and the big distributors, also control the book business . . . For all the democratic promise of the Internet, moreover, much of cyberspace has now been occupied, its erstwhile wildernesses swiftly paved and lighted over by the same colossi. (Miller, 2002, paragraph 2)

In 2003, the five-member Federal Communications Commission approved rules permitting increased media consolidation and saturation of the American market. The FCC's chairman, Michael K. Powell (son of then Secretary of State Colin Powell) proclaimed that these new regulations were "a careful balance that does not unduly limit transactions that promote the public interest, while ensuring that no company can monopolize the medium." Both Democrat-appointed commissioners opposed the decision that "empowers America's new media elite with unacceptable levels of influence over the media on which our society and our democracy so heavily depend" (Teinowitz, 2003).

Under these new rules, media conglomerates can saturate U.S. cities by owning up to three stations in the largest markets, while newspaper owners may now acquire broadcast stations; broadcasters may now effectively control the airways of stations beaming into 9 out of 10 American homes. In short, within a single large or medium-sized market, a corporation could own the cable system, a newspaper, eight radio stations, and three television stations.

Accompanying this ever-increasing consolidation is the phenomenon we call "consolidated diversity." Taking advantage of technology, media niches are ever more narrowly defined. The rapidly growing Hispanic population, for example, is dissected into consumer groups and then marketed via radio and television giants Clear Channel, Hispanic Broadcasting Corporation (the former being HBC's largest single shareholder), Univision Communications (which, like HBC, is controlled by non-Hispanics and whose proposed $3.1 billion merger was approved by the FCC in 2003), Telemundo (owned by General Electric), and Galavision (the top Spanish-speaking cable system, also owned by Univision) (Gregor, 2002). For example, *Ay Que Noche!* was launched to cater to the late-night 18 to 35 group (representing more than $300 billion in purchasing power—about half of all Hispanic spending) as an alternative to mainstream, late-night talk shows (Narvarro, 2003). Meanwhile, *Despierta America* has successfully delivered an older market for Hispanic households seeking alternatives to the mainstream morning shows, while the long-running *Sábado Gigante* continues its weekly variety and game show with celebrity guests.

From satellite radio to iPods, niche marketing has produced the illusion of diversity where conformity actually prevails. Clear Channel, which operates more than 1,200 radio stations (including 14 in San Diego alone), for instance, selects music

> based on whether artists pay Clear Channel promotional fees or whether Clear Channel agrees with their politics or message. Clear Channel's cost saving measures and "efficiencies" have virtually eliminated local music and local news, relying on national play-lists, centralized news services, and technology that allows central programmers to add local "color" at delivery. Clear Channel also determines which talk show hosts get syndicated on its stations, ensuring carriage of one point of view in every market to the virtual exclusion of all others. (Media Consolidation/Encouraging Diversity in the Electronic Media, 2004, paragraph 2)

This radio behemoth has now set up multiple podcast feeds from select stations. And, the corporation even set up a fake pirate radio station in Akron with messages bleeding into its official stations, such as: "Gone are the days of multiple viewpoints and opinions. Instead we get corporate mandated opinions from talking heads. Corporate controlled music playlists, and so on." The ploy, apparently, was to use "this 'guerilla' marketing to convert one of their stations to a new 'alternative' or liberal talk format . . .," thus further expanding its niche markets (Radio Free Clear Channel, 2005, paragraph 2).

If democracy means choices, then consumers-as-citizens are enjoying greater democracy today than in the era of three national television networks, one or two hometown newspapers, and a handful of locally owned AM radio stations. But, is that the litmus test for democratic communities—be they countries or classrooms? What roles do citizens have within globalized communities controlled by corporations? What are the options for democratic action in this new millennium of *Roller Ball*-like entertainment and politicians often in the pockets of big business?

Incredibly, globalization intensified by technology is also producing genuine democratic action. To cite one case: An alliance of San Juan union members and everyday persons, in early 2005, petitioned the FCC to deny a license to television station WLII, citing "cultural insensitivity." The Alliance of Puerto Rican Artists and Support Groups charged that media giant Univision, which acquired the station three years earlier, had now

> all but dropped local production of telenovelas and game shows in favor of canned programming from Mexico and Venezuela, the source of most of Univision's production. Puerto Rican programming has dropped from about 50 programs a week down to only three. . . . (Puerto Rican Community Groups Attack Univision Broadcasting License, 2005, paragraph 2)

Such unlikely intersections of democracy and globalization via technology are also apparent in education and the field of curriculum.

Globalizing the Curriculum

Curriculum concerns in the United States historically have been shaped in response to globalization. The influx of immigrants at the turn of the last century and the concomitant increase of secondary schools contributed to the NEA's Commission on the Reorganization of Secondary Education's 1918 report, *The Cardinal Principles of Secondary Education*. As in most educational reform that followed over the decades, educational goals preceded school reform. In contrast to later reform efforts, such as *A Nation at Risk*, democracy (civic education) was one of its seven goals:

> The goal of civic education is to develop an awareness and concern for one's own community. A student should gain knowledge of social organizations and a commitment to civic morality. Diversity and cooperation should be paramount. Democratic organizations of the school and classroom as well as group problem solving are the methods that this principle should be taught through. (Available at http://www.nd.edu/~rbarger/www7/cardprin.html)

The 1918 NEA report, like government initiatives later in the century (e.g., the 1958 National Education Defense Act, the 1983 *A Nation at Risk,* and the 1993 *National Excellence: A Case For Developing America's Talent*) assumed that the aim of government-supported schools went well beyond academic preparation envisioned by the *Committee of Ten* report issued in 1892; public school curriculum was foremost about pursuing the nation's agenda. Unlike the 1892 report chaired by Harvard president Charles Elliot, these twentieth-century reports stressed the importance of preparing youth for a world of work in the context of global change—be it the emergence of America as a global power following World War I and facing waves of Eastern European immigrants, or as a response to presumed Soviet hegemony through the technological triumph of Sputnik, or the worsening performance of American children relative to the children of former World War II adversaries Japan and Germany—this country has become obsessed with the measurable academic progress of America's school children compared to those of other industrialized nations. For example, in its FY 2006 budget request, the U.S. Department of Defense requested $10 million for a new National Defense Education Program (NDEP) "for reasons of national, homeland, and economic security" to meet the challenges of the Asian tiger economies by training youth for science and engineering careers as well as foreign languages, particularly in aerospace and energy-related industries, and military and intelligence communities; it was endorsed by the Association of American Universities (Destler Testimony, 2005, paragraph 5).

Strangely enough, however, it is the United States that has exerted—intentionally and unintentionally—the greatest worldwide influence on education. From postwar education reconstruction in Japan to postcolonial assistance in the Philippines, federal agencies like the U.S. Information Agency, often working hand-in-glove with transnational but U.S.–controlled organizations like the World Bank and the International Monetary Fund, have and are Americanizing school systems from Thailand to Turkey. As "developing countries" confront a Pandora's Box of crises like AIDS, poverty, ethnic and religious conflict, and massive ecological degradation, they also must deal with the cultural stripping of their indigenous heritage as well as economic colonialism—all in the name of democracy. As issues of globalization grow in complexity and become more controversial, large-scale protests in cities where the World Bank and the Group of Eight meet are now common occurrences. Confronting such global issues cannot but have an influence on the work of curriculum scholars in this new millennium—particularly since curriculum workers have played such an instrumental role in the past.

Early International Influences

Throughout the nineteenth century, the United States often looked to Europe, particularly to England and Prussia, for guidance in establishing the foundations of its educational system. As common schools became more popular and state-supported systems of education began to take hold, Prussia served as a model for developing the school systems in America—as evident in the Committee of Ten report. European influence was felt on the curriculum as well, as the educational theories of Johan Pestalozzi and Friedrich Froebel, with their emphasis on nurturing the child, took hold. Two of the most influential nineteenth-century Europeans were Johann Herbart and Herbert Spencer. In the late 1880s, Herbart's students popularized his ideas, and they had great influence on U.S. educators studying in Germany. In 1895, Charles DeGarmo became the first president of the National Herbart Society for the Scientific Study of Education.

The Progressive Era marked a reversal in the flow of ideas. By 1920, the United States had become a global power, having picked up colonies in the Philippines and Puerto Rico as the victor in the Spanish American War. It, too, had replaced Great Britain as the world's banker, as the dollar became the world's de facto currency and American capital was exported throughout the world—including cultural and intellectual capital. With the latter, "progressive" educators played an important role. Paul R. Hanna, for example, was identified by *Time* magazine as "Stanford's ambassador to the U.S. Government." Consulting in countries from Yugoslavia to the Philippines, Hanna's

> particular concern was that children involve themselves in community projects to improve certain aspects of life. By doing so, they would learn the practical means of change and gain confidence in their abilities to manipulate those means to advantage. He promoted his concept of the community school through numerous publications, but his most effective promotion was through his work developing community schools in the Philippines. . . . [S]chools should help children understand the changing social, political, and economic worlds in which they live so that they can mold those worlds to their own needs. . . . Hanna understood as well as any educational leader of his time that the accumulation of capital fuels development in market economies, and that human capital is a vital resource. Ignoring that factor in developing curriculum for economic and social modernization was futile, but Hanna's conception of addressing private sector concerns in the curriculum went beyond simplistic ideas of vocational education for industrial and agricultural workers. As he had in the United States during the Great Depression, he perceived the need for schools to help children understand market economics, technological development, international relations, and a myriad of other complex concepts in order to contribute to their nation's, and their region's, development (Stallones, 2002, pp. 278–279)

Hanna's work in the Philippines continued the hegemony of American colonial influence. American education officials insisted on the exclusive use of English in the public schools, for example, well into the 1940s with Filipino students reading Western authors such as Henry Wadsworth Longfellow, William Shakespeare, and Matthew Arnold. *The Song of Hiawatha* was a mandatory part of the elementary curriculum just as *The Merchant of Venice* was at the high school level. In 1929, one American schoolteacher reported the following practice in literature classes in the Philippines:

> The course in literature was a misnomer. It should have been called "The Comparative Anatomy of our Best Works." We skinned participles and hung the pelts on the blackboard to dry. We split infinitives, in much the same manner as a husky midwestern youth splits a stick of wood. We hammered the stuffing out of the compound and complex sentences, leaving the mere shells of their selves. We took our probes and dug into the vitals of literary masterpieces, bringing their very souls to the light of day. . . . We analyzed sentences and defined words— in short, we completed the course, as outlined, including the most important thing: the correct manner of passing the final examinations. (Martin, 2002, p. 78)

Martin (p. 82) concludes, "The combined power of the canon, curriculum, and pedagogy constituted the ideological strategies resulting in rationalizing, naturalizing, and legitimizing myths about colonial relationships and realities"—a conclusion also reached by former Stanford student Douglas Foley (1984), who studied Hanna's community and vocational educational work in the Philippines.

Hanna earned his doctorate in 1929 from Teachers College, where he then joined the faculty, which included George S. Counts, who would later serve as a member of the Educational Survey Commission to the Philippines and Associate Director of Teachers College's International Institute. After World War II, Counts worked with General Douglas Macarthur's team of advisors concerning the reconstruction of education in Japan. Columbia University played a major role with the Carnegie Foundation in globalizing education. Indeed, Carnegie's president, Frederick Keppel (a Columbia alumnus and former undergraduate dean), was assistant secretary of war before becoming Carnegie Corporation's first president in 1923.

> His background in Washington and Columbia along with Carnegie's endowments to the British dominions and colonies, brought together a set of interests that coincided with growing U.S. foreign affairs involvement in the Pacific region. . . . (White, 1996, paragraph 10)

Like other so-called progressive educators, Hanna, who founded the Stanford International Development Education Center, has come under criticism "as an instrument of Western cultural imperialism," notes Stallones (2002, p. 296), whose biography on Hanna was published by the conservative Hoover Institute. Stallones admits that "the criticism is valid to an extent," as Hanna, a diehard Republican and a senior fellow at the Hoover Institution, was

> an unabashed booster of Western models of democratic development. In the early phase of his international career he joined wholeheartedly in the cold war struggle against communism, at least rhetorically. Nevertheless, he was critical of the damage Western imperialism had done to educational, political, and economic systems abroad. His educational proposals for foreign countries were directed at empowering the common people in the same way as his efforts at home had. For Hanna, using the foreign schools as a tool of economic development was a logical extension of using domestic schools for the same purpose during the Depression. He legitimately may be accused of naiveté, but not of collusion with the worst aspects of imperialism. . . . (Stallones, 2002, p. 296)

The complex and seemingly contrary curricularist Paul Hanna also had a long relationship with the United Nations Educational, Scientific, and Cultural Organization (UNESCO).

▉ UNESCO

The curriculum becomes a tool for colonization when it imposes a particular "view" or organizational schemata for understanding and categorizing the world, or privileges certain kinds of knowledge and perspectives over others. Historically, most of the so-called "third world" was colonized economically by Western nations desiring those lands for their resources. Schooling, like other institutions, was used to support these efforts, creating an indigenous middle-class of clerks, bureaucrats, and schoolteachers. As such, there was little "liberal education," nor was there much interest on the part of western colonizers to promote what Brazilian educator Paulo Freire has termed "liberatory education." In 1922, for instance, the Phelps-Stokes Fund of New York published the report of a commission led by Thomas Jesse Jones. The commission had studied schools throughout Africa, ultimately recommending that "the basis of African mass education should be in the adoption and adjustment of western knowledge to the needs and circumstances of individual and community life and Africa," borrowing heavily from the "recently published Cardinal Principles in the United States" (Connell, 1980, pp. 318–319).

Question

How were what Connell calls "the colonial and western patterns of schooling" (p. 424) seen as appropriate to non-Western and developing countries during the early twentieth century? How might we judge such patterns in today's world?

Numerous U.S. curriculum workers participated in these colonizing efforts, including some—like Paul Hanna and George Counts—whose philosophy and, perhaps, intentions were contrary to the aims of Western hegemony. Following World War II, U.S. dominance of the international scene expanded, creating opportunities for American thinking about education to gain an international foothold. Vivian Edmiston Todd, the Curriculum Specialist for the Supreme Command of Allied Powers under General Macarthur, was a student of Ralph Tyler's at the University of Chicago. She wrote of Tyler's influence on the development of curriculum in postwar Japan. In her role as curriculum specialist, Todd was responsible for strengthening the "democratic tendencies of the Japanese people" after the Emperor had been deposed. Another of her duties was to use Tylerian practices and principles to develop a curriculum that would propel Japan's economy to leading nation status by teaching inquiry and practicing "equality of educational opportunity for all" (Todd, 1986, p. 61).

The end of the war also saw the creation of UNESCO. Although there had been earlier international organizations that dealt with education (most notably the International Bureau of Education, directed by Swiss psychologist Jean Piaget), in 1946 UNESCO was established as the United Nations agency concerned with educational and cultural issues. Originally designed to promote international peace through education and cultural understanding, its primary focus soon turned to the developing world, where pre-World War II colonialism was rapidly giving way to post-colonial independence. Taking a broad view of education, UNESCO employed literacy and equal educational opportunities as a vehicle toward improved standards of living, international peace, and global penetration with enormous efforts and monies expended on teacher training for adult and rural education.

UNESCO's first Director General, Julian Huxley (1947), referenced mainstream curriculum thinking of the time by noting:

> Those who can profit by working for a university degree of the present type constitute only a proportion of the population, whether the proportion be 20 or 40 or even 60 per cent: for the remainder to attempt it is a waste of their own money, of the time and talents of university teachers, and of public money. (p.32)

The solution, according to Huxley, was the "accurate study of the distribution of intelligence and other educational aptitudes, in as many populations as possible" (p. 32). As Connell (1980) notes, "UNESCO produced reports, newsletters, pamphlets, statistical analyses, journals, and books that provided information and guidance to educators throughout the developing world in the course of the educational revolution that they were making" (p. 399).

The United States had a complicated relationship with UNESCO— while it dominated UNESCO through the late 1940s and 1950s, seeing it as little more than a propaganda tool with which to fight the Cold War, by the 1960s American influence in UNESCO was waning. In 1963, George Schuster, who had been a member of UNESCO's executive board and the president of Hunter College, wrote: "There can hardly be a professor of education alive who has not participated in some gathering under UNESCO auspices, unless he has deliberately gone into hiding" (p. 24). Twenty years later, the United States formally withdrew from UNESCO and has maintained observer status ever since.

Globalization and Curriculum Workers

As the United States experiences a number of challenging, often conflicting, aspects of the "global village," curriculum workers will increasingly find themselves having to consider the global contexts of their work. Said differently, our longstanding "observer status" with respect to world events has run its course.

Question

Political scientist Joseph Nye (2002a, 2002b) has noted that in the near future, Internet users living in Asia will probably outnumber their U.S. counterparts by more than half a billion. What are the consequences and the challenges of this likelihood to education and to curriculum?

Globalization generally refers to the increasing integration of financial markets and the removal of barriers to free trade, and has consequences in economic, political, and cultural life. Little (2000, p. 299) defines its economic manifestations as "stateless financial markets; the rising proportion of global trade and investment in developing countries accounted for by transnational companies; the domination of international technology flows by transnational corporations; and the growth of international finance capital." Little further identifies the political manifestations of globalization as

> a decline in state sovereignty; the reduced control of national governments over money supply and regulation of exchange rates; an increase in the power of global, sometimes stateless, organizations [e.g., the World Bank and the International Monetary Fund] over national organizations; and an increase in the propensity for national and local political issues to be played out on the world stage. (p. 299)

In the area of culture, Little identifies the manifestations of globalization as "a convergence of life-style and consumer aspirations among the better off, and the widespread distribution of images, information and values" (p. 299).

Too, globalization can result in dire consequences, including violence, social fragmentation, environmental degradation, economic exploitation, poverty, and health crises (Hoffman, 2002)—issues that certainly belong to curriculum workers. Globalization also has implications for employment, career opportunities, and the transfer of high- and low-skilled labor, requiring the curriculum worker to confront economic and political repercussions of the changing nature of job qualifications and skills. In short, that which affects Beirut and Baghdad influences our U.S. backyard school curricula.

Several curriculum organizations have been formed specifically to work within this global arena. One of the earliest is the World Council for Curriculum and Instruction (WCCI), which has brought curriculum scholars from across the globe together for many years. The origins of WCCI lie with the Association for Supervision and Curriculum Development (ASCD), which had devoted some attention to international educational issues throughout the 1950s and early 1960s (Berman, Miel, &

Overly, 1981). In 1966, working at the behest of progressive educator and ASCD associate secretary Louise Berman, the ASCD executive committee appointed a Commission on International Cooperation in Education. Chaired by Berman and her mentor, Alice Miel, the Commission set about organizing a world conference on education. "In the Minds of Men: Educating the Young People of the World," was held in 1970 in Asilomar, California. More than half of the approximately 300 attendees were from countries other than the United States. The success of the Asilomar Conference encouraged a desire to formally establish an international organization, and within a year, an ad hoc committee of Asilomar participants met to formally propose one. Alice Miel led the effort to draft a constitution for the newly formed World Council for Curriculum and Instruction, which became formally independent from ASCD in 1974. The WCCI has gone on to sponsor a number of global projects, exchanges, and conferences, and gained "consultative status" with UNESCO.

In a short publication for Kappa Delta Pi, *Educating for World Cooperation*, Alice Miel and Louise Berman (1983) wrote about the need for cosmopolitans. Using language reminiscent of Carleton Washburne's (1954), they noted that the word *cosmopolitan* "signifies a citizen of the world, a person free from local, provincial, or national prejudices, one with empathy for many kinds of human differences" (p. 4). They called for "reorienting education toward the world" through an examination of curricular and teaching practices (p. 7), and they advocated a composite of three approaches to curriculum, each with a different emphasis: knowing, being, doing.

Question

In what ways are images like "cosmopolitan" and "global village" promising? Problematic?

More recently, Pinar, Reynolds, Slattery, and Taubman (1995, p. 831) have detailed the "growing internationalization of curriculum theory, inquiry, and practice"—although, as noted previously, curriculum workers associated with the major universities like Teachers College and Stanford have long been involved internationally as have a long list of curriculum scholars. In April 2000, the first in what has become a series of international curriculum conferences was held at Louisiana State University with the purpose of promoting internationalization as "both a forum of curriculum and a problem to which curriculum can be addressed." Unlike other attempts to enter into the global educational arena, Pinar and his colleagues were attuned to the real and perceived influences of Westerners and the ethical and political quagmire of U.S. educational hegemony.

They, too, recognized that globalization was a reality that could, perhaps, best be redressed, broadly speaking, through the internationalization of curriculum studies.

As curriculum workers, we are challenged to understand these intersecting forces of democracy, globalization, and technology in ways that can better direct our efforts. Regardless of our particular relationships with curriculum work (policy, theory, research, design and development, etc.) our primary obligation is to join with others to make a difference in the world. Because our work affects people's lives it must be undertaken in a collaborative—not a cloistered—fashion, representing diverse and divergent voices *and* giving space for voices not previously heard.

As we have illustrated in this chapter, we live in a world of growing mystery and paradox shrouded by a thin veil of illusion. And while the public may look to radio or television talking heads, newspaper or magazine opinion and editorial writers, Internet bloggers, or religious leaders for some way to make sense of that which seems senseless, too few engage in democratic actions that can enlarge our public square. Educators, in general, and curriculum workers, in particular, have a different stake in not only making sense of our world, but in bearing the additional responsibility of representing this world—and various views about it—to others. Whether we connect and communicate via the Internet or caucus groups, through policy gatherings or professional meetings, we must get connected, we must communicate, we must be heard—and we must hear the Other.

Where to begin? Perhaps with current issues; or from a shared need to develop definitions and terminologies; or from a personal need to express belief or disbelief. Perhaps by talking within a small group of unlike-minded colleagues or setting up a website; by volunteering to join (or resign from) a curriculum-related committee or running for public office. What's important is that each of us, as educators involved in a public moral enterprise, seizes opportunities for communication. In the following section, we invite you to see if you can't find a space for joining with our collection of *Turning Points* visitors in such an endeavor.

■ At Play with Outtakes

(Introduced by Dan Marshall)

Our decision to include a collection of visitors within this book proved uniquely rewarding for me, since I had the rare privilege of conducting a somewhat lengthy and open interview with each of these guests. Most of our tape-recorded interviews lasted a good hour and were done over the telephone. Working from a skeletal outline of the book's basic themes and time periods, each interview grew out of a small collection of open-ended questions and, in some cases, one or two particular events that I used as prompts for our conversation.

It was many months (in a few cases more than a year) later that we set to work making decisions about locating our visitors within specific chapters of the book and, ultimately, deciding how and where to afford each visitor an appropriately disruptive personal presence within that chapter. This work was especially wrenching because it required me to disembody each transcript into excerpts and bits of talk. Naturally, much of the substance of each interview ended up on the cutting room floor, as they say.

As we neared completion of the original manuscript (in which Sears, Schubert, and I each wrote a brief collection of thoughts about the future of the curriculum field), we came up with the idea of using these interview "outtakes" in some fashion. Ultimately, we chose to artificially construct what we called "A Final Conversation" among the book's guests. In my mind's eye I imagined all of these visitors gathered together in the back room of a bar or restaurant discussing curriculum. In building this imagined exchange, I hoped that the reader might learn a bit more about each visitor's personality as I arranged the excerpts along topical themes— which, like most "conversations," would tend to wander into other themes and topics. All the while I worked toward a fantasy meeting among these principals, realizing that the chance for such a gathering to occur was slim-to-none because of people's different personalities, experiences, and feelings about curriculum and, in some cases, each other. But I stuck with my fantasy nonetheless, and the "conversation" emerged in print.

In patching together these outtakes we did a few things right and a few things wrong. On the up side, bringing our visitors together at the end of the book provides additional information about their thoughts, feelings, and experiences (and thus about them as individuals), and juxtaposing the outtakes helps, we believe, to clarify—and cloud—their similarities and differences. Too, this effort serves to add a unique element to a book that utilizes multiple, overlapping elements (vectors, primary document excerpts, etc.). On the down side, we were at best unclear and at worst misleading in the introduction to our originally "constructed conversation." Specifically, we did not explain to the reader that we had literally created this exchange of viewpoints, and by not including ourselves within that exchange, we further added to the illusion of an actual or real discussion among the visitors. At the same time, we misnamed this collage of outtakes as a conversation when at best it could be read as dialogue (like that written for a play or a novel) and at worst it would be read as mere talk. As Bill Doll notes in his Prolegomena to this second edition, conversation involves listening, understanding, and personalizing each exchange—a "reciprocal engagement" not possible from a spectator's point of view. This is a powerful criticism that we understand and appreciate.

At the same time, our intention in providing a revised version of this "imagined chat" goes well beyond the playfulness of creating an apparent exchange among a collection of curriculum workers. We do not set out to cleverly pretend with this construction, but rather to offer this particular form of narrative as another invitation and encouragement for readers to imagine themselves participating in this—or any other—exchange of ideas, feelings, and experiences about the work of curriculum.

Our efforts in creating and revising *Turning Points* represent our desire to participate in the "complicated conversation" called curriculum work and, equally important, to welcome and encourage others to do the same. Assuming that our field remains firmly rooted in the fundamental questions raised throughout the previous pages, any and all contemplation of the field's past, present, and future becomes, by definition, necessary and important work that transcends mere intellectual exercise or interest. Such contemplation (and its resulting actions), in all its forms, represents a manifestation of our field's most central questions about worthwhile knowledge and experience. What follows is one example of such work.

A Final Exchange

Alex Molnar: I think curriculum is, as Jim Macdonald used to say, merely a study of how to have a world. This narrow thing called the curriculum field just doesn't hold my interest any longer. What I call the curriculum field is simply whatever I want to do.

James T. Sears: I remember when we first met, Alex, and organized one of the first ASCD networks—the Social Issues Network—in the mid '80s. At that time, there was still a residue of political and cultural consciousness within what I would call the mainstream curriculum field, epitomized by that organization's socially progressive post-WWII legacy. In the course of a generation, though, the field of curriculum—like society generally—has moved at least one standard deviation to the right. And for those of us who are social deviates, like the "muted heretics" of the early sixties, we can either find eddies of truly significant educational reform or abandon the field (recognizing that it is the field which has abandoned our bedrock principles). Like you, I have little interest in what currently constitutes the curriculum field, be it mega-educational organizations like ASCD and AERA or old boy curriculum country clubs like the Professors of Curriculum. I no longer see myself as a "curriculum worker," but just someone who works to slow down the Borg-like assimilationism of the latter days of the American Empire.

Mary-Ellen Jacobs: I've never quite felt like I was a member of the curriculum club. I've always believed that teaching is curriculum. I can't separate the two.

William Schubert: In some respects, I agree with you . . . When I think about the origins of the work that I do as a curriculum professor, I reflect on the skills, knowledge and values that enable me to do this work. Like those whom I try to influence with similar reflective questions, I turn to my childhood and youth. I think back to growing up on a farm in Indiana, . . . and my parents, grandparents, and great aunt who conjured up stories and characters to imagine with me. Too, I reflect on books, movies, and television shows that were sites of thinking aloud about the world and social life. I think about the sports we played and watched, the natural world around us, cooperative work, everyday problem solving, the fun and laughter, and planning for and engaging in extensive family travel during summer vacations.

More than any schooling, my past and present informal experiences with family and friends are the seedbed for almost any skill, knowledge, or value that I could identify. Today, and for the past many years, the most profound curriculum of my life is an outgrowth of interaction with my wife (Ann), children, other family members, friends, the arts, sports, and popular culture.

Dan Marshall: Given all that we've presented within this book, I'm wondering whether readers can actually imagine or categorize themselves as curriculum workers. Clearly, some of us still do while others have re-categorized or re-identified themselves. If nothing else, it's become plain to me that everyone from classroom teachers to school administrators, and from nationally-known psychologists to U.S. presidents have had a go at curriculum work, which suggests not only that the days of the "curriculum expert" are long gone in the minds of most, but that the work of curriculum belongs, in important ways, to many who do not hold degrees in Curriculum & Instruction.

Petra Munro: If I had to categorize myself, I'd definitely say feminist, though at this point calling myself that is more of a political thing. Having said that, it's also a category I want to give up. For me, things are a lot more ambiguous and recursive, and I must continually question what makes it possible for me to think that there are such things as feminism or poststructuralism—or a field of curriculum. This doesn't frighten me on a theoretical level, but on a political, day-to-day level it does frighten me, because to give up a category has political consequences.

Bill Watkins: I've always seen myself as a social scientist. That's why people like Michael F. D. Young and Basil Bernstein meant so much to me during my studies and allowed me to feel like I had found a place within the fields of education and curriculum.

Alex Molnar: But who's in the field of curriculum? That's kind of a rhetorical question, because to a certain extent you're in the field if people say you are.

Louis Rubin: Fifty years ago when curriculum theorists decided that they could usefully alter the instructional curriculum in a place like

Pasadena, they simply went out and did it. That's what curriculum people were about. Life was in a slower gear then, and there wasn't nearly the amount of bureaucratic congestion we have now.

Today, it's almost impossible to deal with anything related to curriculum in any sort of orderly fashion. For example, when you talk about multicultural education you are talking about many, many different things depending upon the view of the particular person concerned. To some it's equity, to others it's a matter of introducing kids to different cultures, and to still others it's a means of fighting for feminist rights.

Today's curriculum field is definitely alive—not so much because we have really thought through and become immersed in significant curriculum issues, but rather because all of these other issues have come into play. Yet it's all of these related issues that contaminate genuine curriculum improvements and contribute to our getting nowhere.

James T. Sears: There is no question that the field is in a Schwabian cul-de-sac. As we engage in curriculum development and discourse, we need to focus on *everyday* concerns and issues, speaking as boldly as we do clearly. Here, I use the term curriculum in its broadest sense, including all types of formal and nonformal education from the sexual socialization of children into heteronormality to the desensitization of the television viewer who makes no distinction between the "reality" television of *American Idol* and America's Operation Iraqi Freedom. The challenge is not only the clarity of our language when we talk, for instance, about multicultural education/cultural studies, but articulating sociopolitical concerns and reframing the issues for a citizenry dumbed-down by years of schooling. But, whose curriculum concerns and what issues? Issues such as peace and sustainability, democratic responses in an era of standardization, and malnutrition of the body and the spirit are what the field should be addressing in practical and political arenas. Scholarship and research—with lucidity, thoroughness, and equanimity—should be handmaidens in this venture. The political insularity of contemporary curriculum discourse coupled to the shortcoming of conventional curriculum development is the real contaminant facing this new millennial generation of curriculum workers. The failure to address this, as Schwab noted two generations ago, means that we are moribund—going nowhere. Many of us attending curriculum conferences are already among the walking dead.

Petra Munro: I'm not sure I agree that we're getting nowhere, but that very perception is one important reason why I think people in curriculum theory have to stick together—because I think we are under attack in some ways. I'm very committed to working with teachers and grad students in terms of having ours be a field with a lot of room for them to see themselves in, regardless of their theoretical perspectives. Our field is enriched through its diversity. To be continually rethinking and questioning our assumptions within the political context of education—that's our work. Yet if we alienate teachers, there's no hope that we'll survive.

Susan Edgerton: There's a great deal of pressure on people in our field to connect our work with schools, and that's got both positive and negative aspects. Negatively, schools co-opt us and we can't theorize, independently, as we might be able to. Positively, if we theorize without any sense of what's going on in schools at all we're liable to never be translated. I have enough of a political agenda to think that being translated matters. So we need to connect with schools while also trying to simultaneously disconnect to some extent, to work back and forth between those, and to translate.

Peter Hlebowitsh: The source of that pressure is obvious to me. If you look across the social landscape, schools appear ever more important in the lives of children. Given the perturbations we see in society, the role of school in the life of the learner seems to be taking on more significance rather than less, and if that's the case, then somebody's got to take that on and deal with those kinds of things. It would be my hope that schools of education would have a hand in that. And if they do, only curricularists would be able to do that well because they would have the widest lens.

Patrick Roberts: I agree. As curriculum workers, we need to disrupt the trends that we think are moving schools in the wrong direction. I think we can do that, but it requires us to be proactive, to set the agenda for school reform rather than simply respond to it after the fact. We need to seize the initiative in some way, which I think means embracing the spectrum of our theoretical and practical interests. We need to avoid contributing to the reification of the theory/practice debate. While it can be usefully dialogic, that debate is a red herring when it comes to our work with schools.

Tom Barone: But our lens isn't wide enough for me. I hope that we begin to think about the field of curriculum more broadly than just the property of curriculum theorists. We've become so very narrow that we speak only to ourselves, even as the major decisions about our lives are being made elsewhere. I don't know why there can't be a lot more teachers who are also curriculum theorists, and I'm hoping for this kind of democratization of the curriculum field.

Louise Allen: I agree that we spend far too much time speaking to ourselves. I am perplexed, however, as to how we, as curriculum workers, can help teachers see themselves as part of "the complicated conversation" that Pinar has called our work, especially since so many teachers see curriculum as coming in boxes from publishers and other corporate entities. The larger issue here, of course, is the idea of democracy—not only for the field, but in schools—and in our country. Where/how do we enable teachers to have a democratic classroom and where/how do teachers get to participate in a democratic school? Certainly, if what to teach is limited to materials written by someone else, envisioning democratic curricular choices will be that more difficult for teachers whose eyes have been shuttered. Can curriculum studies open them?

Henry Giroux: To begin, curriculum theorists should be less incestuous. I drifted away from the curriculum field, in part, because I was interested in combining a number of fields, and curriculum theory basically had no discourse to do that at the time. I also felt that it was getting boring. I really didn't see a lot of new work emerging, although it always suggested it was new. People didn't read the history of the field well and consequently, they re-invented parts of that field thinking that they were inventing something different.

Mary-Ellen Jacobs: I have to disagree. What was so radically new to me about reconceptualized curriculum was its attempt to combine a lot of different disciplines—philosophy, psychology, literature, and curriculum— and weave them together to help us see classrooms, teachers, and teaching differently.

On the other hand, maybe the problem with becoming interdisciplinary is that we lose the base, which is to help put schools and teaching and the experience of classrooms in a provocative light. That's really the base of all this interdisciplinarity, isn't it? But we've become so interested in extending the tower that we've maybe lost sight of its base.

Peter Hlebowitsh: That's why we need some reconciliation within the contemporary curriculum field. I think the field has to talk about its base— the burdens that have to be carried by all of us, including the new curricularists: burdens of practice, unity, design, and especially history. We've raised the issue of history: I feel there's been complete mismanagement in our historical interpretation, especially the position that the whole history of the curriculum field is somehow equated with Franklin Bobbitt and social efficiency; that the whole field is somehow captured by this malevolent desire for social control and that Tyler, himself, was a behaviorist with genes from Franklin Bobbitt.

Alex Molnar: The curriculum field has long lacked an historical understanding of itself. For me, curriculum is a manifestation of industrial culture relative to, for example, the collapse of the nation state as an organizing principle and the ascendance of international capital markets as the dominant factor in the construction of social life around this planet. Curriculum is very much a piece of those historical developments. Yet few curriculum writers do much with this in terms of its practical manifestations in the daily lives of children and teachers in the schools, and how what is taught comes to be taught.

Janet Miller: I disagree. Today's curriculum studies range from historical works to issues of development to far-reaching analyses of discourse. I think such a range has really broadened and enlivened and made richer the whole study of the field.

Peter Hlebowitsh: But not without problems. While the curriculum field has developed a tolerance for many views, we now need what Bill Wraga calls a restoration: We've had a reconceptualization and now we need a restoration back toward where the institutional traditions of the field point. Embedded in that is bringing the field back to seeing the public school as its main constituency and working with the highest of ideals toward the widest public mandate.

Henry Giroux: But understand that the notion of "widest public mandate" takes us into other terrains, including culture and politics.

Actually, I found the earlier phases of the contemporary field, between the 1960s and the early 1980s, to be much more political than the later phases.

Bill Watkins: I liked the curriculum field a lot more in the mid-1980s than I did in the mid-1990s. I felt it was a lot more focused, then. I felt real connected to the discourse between 1978 and 1988, especially, but some of the stuff today I just don't feel connected to.

But I feel real comfortable with what I'm doing today. I see myself as standing on the shoulders of DuBois and other black radical educators. I think there's a place within curriculum studies for me, and I feel compelled to take my place.

Michael Apple: When I was a doctoral student there was no doubt in our minds about such generational shifts. As students, we knew that we were standing on people's shoulders, yet Huebner and others insisted we weren't to be clones.

Arthur Foshay: I, too, have been very much aware of a passage of generations. For example, by the time the major curriculum projects of the '60s arrived, the curriculum generation of the '30s had come to an end. As part of a second generation of curriculum people I was very much drawn into the curriculum work of the 1960s—as Caswell was a generation earlier.

Michael Apple: But when I work with doctoral students I want them to stand on the models that I was given and at the same time to reconstruct them. As Huebner and others at Teachers College would eventually say, "Okay, now become yourself." That's my task—that kind of generational shift.

Louise Berman: My advising experiences at TC were different. Alice Miel established a healthy setting for furthering independent and interdependent thinking and feeling by using a non-directive approach. Now there were times when I wish she would have said, "Do this" or "Do that," but such direction was infrequent from her. In my own advising I want to get out of students' way but I also want to energize them and to ignite some kind of intellectual spark. To strike that balance is really, really tough.

Michael Apple: Actually, I'm not comfortable with taking this talk about generational shifts too far. That's one of the reasons why I rejected totally any language that talks about curriculum reconceptualists. Unlike some, I think that's a total misreading of history. We are simply standing on the shoulders of very, very long and valuable traditions that have their roots in the very beginning of the curriculum field.

Dan Marshall: But those roots have spread both deep and wide. From the outset, curriculum work has been about schools and classrooms, teachers and students, teaching and learning—all in play together within changing social, intellectual, cultural and political contexts that exist during particular historical moments. At their most basic, our multiple traditions all represent efforts of different sorts to understand and orchestrate—even steer and control—how the future should look. And those traditions were rooted in public schooling.

However, our traditions (and I think we have some younger ones at this point) are being taxed incredibly by the ever-expanding and complex array of worksites. Our tap root may still remain deeply connected to the nation's public schools, but can't our traditions also spread and take root in today's expanding field of non-school curriculum sites?

Janet Miller: We also need to acknowledge these traditions in their broadest sense. For example, a very strict, standard, narrow definition of curriculum studies prohibits people from exploring. Loosening this previously narrow definition has incredibly enriched the field and provided numerous avenues for curriculum inquiry. The strength of what's happened during the curriculum field's last forty years has permitted this variety of breadth and depth of perspective. I think it's done nothing but enrich our understanding of what we might begin to conceptualize as curriculum.

Arthur Foshay: I'm not so sure. I think the field is in disarray.

Louise Berman: I too am thoroughly pessimistic about today's curriculum field, though I think that our current situation simply has to play itself out.

Bill Watkins: But isn't the same thing true in many different academic disciplines? I think we're at a crossroads in our intellectual life in this country, going through a period of confusion, fragmentation, even reaction before things change. I'm hoping to maintain my own focus during this period of haziness and confusion within a curriculum field that's becoming so complicated, complex, multi-dimensional and chaotically postmodern that it's not really going to be a field much longer—if it still is. And I believe that this period will continue for a while. Where it's going to go after that, I don't know, though I hope it turns in a different kind of direction.

Susan Edgerton: What's to become of the field of curriculum? Who knows? Some of the issues around its identity parallel those that cultural studies faced in England back when they were trying to decide whether or not to departmentalize. I think that curriculum faces some of the same dilemmas. To define ourselves so that we survive institutionally might undermine the very kinds of things that we really want to do.

Patrick Roberts: But we may have no other choice. Schools of education are increasingly caught up in the accountability and assessment movement. I think it is vitally important that those of us who identify with the curriculum field provide a counter-narrative to this trend. That means making the case for our own relevance as a field within the academy.

James T. Sears: Agreed. But we must become foot soldiers in the cultural war against standards and standardization.

Petra Munro: I see different trends beginning. Within the curriculum field, we've gone from a kind of technical to a more political and even personal perspective on understanding things. But I think we're going to have to go beyond those and integrate some very different perspectives, including ecological and spiritual ones.

Tom Barone: For me, the narrative tradition has become very important within the field of curriculum. The practitioner side of me has always resonated with this notion of storytelling, and I believe that curriculum theory as a form of discourse is secondary to narrative.

Michael Apple: What I want is for students to be political, with the understanding that there are many forms of politics. As students of curriculum, I want them to care about a particular tradition that stems from a particular question that I've tried to transform, which is not *what* knowledge is most important, but *whose* knowledge.

Louise Allen: Having our students be political and understand all of curriculum's political variations is critical to schools and curriculum. My great fear, however, founded in my work with school administrators in a large metropolitan center in NC, is that they are told by their supervisors NOT to contact their state and U.S. representatives; they are told to leave "the politics" to the school board and other district representatives who are better able to deal with those issues. In other words, not only has the work of teachers been "dumbed down," but the same process, politically, at least, is also happening to principals. How can we teach this political savvy, model it, and pray that our students—whether teachers or principals—get to practice what they have learned?

Tom Barone: But aren't we saying, in a sense, that the kind of theoretical position anyone adopts in curriculum work or, more broadly, in terms of how they view the world, depends almost entirely upon the individual's life story and the kinds of people and stories you come into contact with during your life?

William Schubert: That's exactly what I'm saying. I'm *not* advocating an ignoring of tradition or the removal of curriculum studies from its original role of service to schools. I *am* advocating that the neglected curricula that daily shape the character and ideals of us all be given due attention along with our focus on schools.

In the long run, I doubt that schools as we know them will prevail. Moreover, the curriculum field itself will need to be radically altered if it is to respond intelligently, compassionately, and imaginatively to the multiplicity of educational journeys on which we have already embarked in today's world, not to mention the yet unknown journeys that the future has in store. How we respond to these journeys, how we infuse them with meaning, purpose, critique, and compassion, depends on what realms of practice and policy our field will embrace. For me, these include the school *and* the host of neglected realms of curriculum from those in families and homes, churches, scouts, clubs, and gangs to television, movies, print media, software, video and video games, music, and a whole array of artistic, scientific, technological, interpersonal, psychological, political, and cultural experiences. We can't be content to be harbingers only of what schools alone might be; rather, we should expand our horizons to see curriculum as whatever brings insight, meaning, and contributory action. We need to study these *whatevers,* learn from them, and promote human growth through collaboration inspired by such study.

James T. Sears: Entering the new millennium, it certainly appears that the nature of curriculum work is again changing as the nature of education changes—in large part due to our entrance into the cyber age and, with it, the slow but irreversible devolution of modernist institutional structures. The emergence of the Internet, coupled with the rapid development of computerized communications, is leading to rapid and radical institutional changes from the workplace to the classroom. The virtual workplace, in which individuals are linked to cyberspace, is already replacing work cubicles and the morning rush hour. As corporations become more information driven and further reduce overhead in global competition, this trend will shift from phenomenon to norm. Thus, once-chided curricularists will find themselves allied with curriculum workers, as those operating from more modernist frameworks—be it progressivism, neo-Marxism, or positivism—find themselves quickly distanced from cyberculture—and the curriculum field. Indeed, the game has changed.

Ultimately, the common school of the modernist era will not simply be linked *into* cyberspace, it will *be* cyberspace. Schools and curriculum will cease to exist as we have known them since the days of Horace Mann. The current movement toward charter schools, homeschooling, and corporate-operated educational academies is ending the hegemony of government-run public schools and the role of the public educator, replacing the corporation as educational arbiter. But soon, new informational technologies—only now on the horizon—will end the industrial age of schooling and its reliance on the print medium, teacher as mediator of knowledge, curriculum scope and sequence, and school buildings.

Modernist theories that presuppose discipline boundaries, hierarchical structures, and enfleshed identities will be irrelevant in this cyber-culture. Virtual communities linking Web sites, databases, and chat rooms with traditional forms of media communication such as television, music, and film will constellate the new "net.culture" currently leveling knowledge boundaries, flattening hierarchical communications, and disembodying racial, gender, and sexual identities. And, it is at this juncture that democracy, globalizations, technology—and the curriculum—will intersect.

Momentary Thoughts

As the preceding exchange suggests, imagining the postmillennial curriculum field is uncomfortable work. Many of us who continue to embrace the label of curriculum worker remain uncertain about the construction (and constructors) of our curriculum identity as it relates to institutional and intellectual life. We remain perplexed about our "property rights," particularly those boundaries having to do with membership, language, and audience. Articulating our base(s) has become as doggedly problematic as representing our traditions and our histories. That our genealogy is still dominated by the presence and work of Eurowhites and males only enhances these problems.

Yet we leave this project feeling edgily optimistic about the future of our field and assuredly addled about future turning points in curriculum. More importantly, in one sense, we cling to the belief that our most pressing challenges may lie, as Janet Miller (1997, p. 2) points out, in how we respond to each other and to those around us:

> Given that myriad and diverse versions of what counts as curriculum studies now circulate at the [AERA] Annual Meeting as well as in our research and practices, I suggest that we pay attention to the ways in which we are *responding* to those various versions that frame our field.

Like all curriculum workers, it remains your responsibility to respond.

Afterword: The Age of Pluralism

Wilma S. Longstreet,
University of New Orleans

The wealth of textures and diversity that have characterized curriculum discourse are captured with great sensitivity in this work. The discouragement of many failed curriculum reforms is equally well represented. The cacophony of points and counterpoints, of interpretations and redefinitions appears to give sustenance to an increasing sense of despair and frustration, a sense of not getting anywhere despite the best efforts of curriculum leaders. It is as though those working in curriculum are caught in an inscrutable maze with all of the exits still hidden.

Ours is a despair born of impatience in a professional field not yet a century old and not yet clear about what its professional work ought to be. With more than 25 years in the field, I find myself hard-pressed to describe the nature of my field. I am still struggling with my own contradictory reactions to the continuing pressure of claims and counterclaims rooted in the inherent diversity of American society. At times, I am disgusted with my field by what appears to be the constant nit-picking of ideas into oblivion regardless of what their worth may be. We have talked about "turning education around" for so long without achieving anything like the reforms envisioned that cynicism has set in and taken its toll on the enthusiasm I once had so much of. I think the field needs to move on in some clear, productive direction—a direction I might not agree with, but one that would allow me to pose my loyal opposition with clarity. Other times, I find the diversity of views— and even the nit-picking—exciting, a part of that greater diversity that contributed to the rise of a new nation with new conceptions of education. The very diversity of our cultural and political origins and our willingness to talk through our diversity gave us the strength as a people to offer educational opportunity to the masses and to create an environment for being together, supportive of both our differences and our socioeconomic well-being.

Most of the public (and this includes curriculum specialists) appears convinced that American education is in a deplorable state and needs radical fixing for the sake of the nation and for the future of our children. According to Berliner and Biddle (1995), the so-called crisis in schooling has been largely manufactured by a government and two American presidents, Reagan and Bush, unprecedentedly involved in massive criticism of the schools. In Berliner and Biddle's words: "Never before had an American government been so critical of the public schools, and never had so many false claims been made about education in the name of 'evidence' " (1995, p. 4). President Clinton, while verbalizing fewer criticisms, has been working to fix what is wrong, which, to judge from his legislative behavior, is primarily low test scores. And, of course, many curricular specialists are convinced there is a great deal wrong because so many schools have become ghettos of poverty. When poverty is not the point, the curricular oppression of each child's creativity and individuality, or the irrelevance of the curriculum to current needs, or the omission of humanities from the course of study, or any number of other concerns convince specialists that school reform needs to happen—indeed, that it is urgent.

But whose demands should become the guiding light of reform? The demands the public makes on the school's curriculum are as disparate as the American public itself. No one institution could succeed in meeting all that has been asked of the schools. If that is true, and most accept it as a truism, then it would appear to follow that a reform bringing some kind of clear focus to the schools is desirable. However, it is not at all clear that the somewhat amorphous quality of the present educational system, characterized by social promotion, standardized testing, and a number of subjects not amenable to standardized testing such as stress management, does not meet and support the cultural and individual diversity of the American public better than a focused program of study, even one focused on higher-level skills such as problem solving and concept building.

Calls for school reform are part of a long-standing American tradition. Every few years a major movement of some kind appears, and I have often sympathized with efforts to redirect schooling. I suppose in my deepest of hearts, like many of my friends and colleagues, I long for the most radical of reforms, a revolution. After all, this nation grew from the revolutionary roots of democracy, and a sense of revolution has persisted throughout our history, permeating all of our cultural lives. We have lived through the agrarian revolution, the industrial revolution, the information revolution, the media revolution—including a revolution in journalism known as muckraking—and even a revolution in education that led to greatly increased accessibility by the masses and a curriculum reconfigured to better serve the economic interests of the nation. We have pursued reforms of every kind, recognizing that the upheavals of these many revolutions require profound revisions of society's infrastructures. In short, the demand for educational reform has persisted throughout our history. Most of us have, in fact, grown up in the midst of demands for reform, and most of us have accepted that ours is a revolutionary period that requires reform.

It may be time, now, to shed the traditional cloak of revolution and reform. We have been culturally imbued with the idea that revolutions and reforms are part of a necessary upheaval if significant improvement is to occur. Yet there is a linearity to this kind of thinking (i.e., X must happen if Y is to occur) that assumes a singular environment. We are, instead, a nation of diverse environments and a multiplicity of cultures sharing a public arena that could be likened to the Tower of Babel. The time for cultural as well as violent revolutions may have already come to an end in the United States. From the grand perspective of several centuries of history, we have been involved in a growing crescendo of change and an ever-accelerating explosion of knowledge with roots ranging from the Crusades and the Great Plague of 1348 through the Enlightenment and the great periods of discovery and mechanization. (This view is taken by many historians, including Braudel, 1987; 1994.) These revolutions and calls for reform have continued to increase in frequency as the time between their appearances has shortened. As this book makes clear, revolutions and reforms have become a constant of our collective lives. If, however, we reflect on the idea either of revolution or of reform as a constantly present phenomenon, we must surely understand that both have become their own antitheses. If revolution and reform are constant in society, then they have clearly become a stable part of that society. To take this further, if change is a constant, then the cessation of change is the revolution.

I realize there is a certain play on words in my discourse, and I most assuredly do not mean to say that change is over. I am quite convinced that change, and the flexibility it requires, will continue to be a fundamental part of our human experience. Made obvious in *Turning Points,* that experience is full of contemporaneous complexities and contradictions that are multidimensional rather than linear. Given that major cultural changes also occur at different rates and are integrated in varying and unpredictable ways, I am further convinced that the many diversities of this nation will increase and that support for diversity in general is a necessary component of a democratic society.

If we are not willing to allow the majority to tyrannize our many culturally disparate groups, then we need to develop a public arena of institutions supportive of profoundly different values and lifestyles and capable of offering to all similar opportunities and benefits. We are in the midst, as we need to be, of building pluralism into a democratic form of governance. This work is an intimidating undertaking to a curriculum specialist and one likely to grow in complexity.

The schools continue to be one of the first public arenas confronting the challenge of pluralism. The long period of exploding knowledge and cultural upheavals has slowly but surely become an age of pluralism, an age in which we have brought into the very fabric of our intellectual and social lives the idea that many kinds and levels of realities and beliefs exist and that they all, taken together, can yield a better quality of existence.

In American education we have already entered the age of pluralism, an age not only of multiculturalism but also of numerous other diversities, ranging from Howard Gardner's conception of multiple intelligences, to the rise of subjects not based on disciplines, to the development of a system of relative valuing intended to respect the diversity of different cultures and their absolute values while rendering the schools beneficial to all. American schools have long been responsive to the public's diversity and to an array of public demands, each of which could be viewed in its own right as revolutionary change. But instead of revolution, each demand has found a niche in the curriculum, praised by some, derided by others. To understand this situation, we must understand the need for relativity in a pluralistic public arena. Public schools must operate in a milieu of relative values in order to protect each group's and each person's right to hold absolute values and to pursue education, which often reaches the very heart of our cultural differences, in the manner that appears most fitting for each of our many cultural groupings.

It may well be that no one institution can effectively do all the things the schools have been charged with doing. In a strictly organizational sense, as today's businesses and sciences operate, the likelihood of schools succeeding in the eyes of all the disparate groups holding claims over them is at best quite low. Pluralism, rather than any systematic analysis of our curricular structures, has driven responses to public demands. Schools have tried to meet the vocational demands of business and industry; they have from time to time tried to respond to the individual needs of children, though hardly at the level of the autobiographical curriculum so valiantly pursued by Pinar and his followers (e.g., Pinar, 1994); they have collaborated in overcoming social problems, from slowing the spread of AIDS and increasing parenting skills among teenage mothers to helping youngsters manage stress and control violent impulses; they have been involved in sustaining the cultural heritage of children from many backgrounds; and they have been charged with developing values in youngsters whose parents represent very different value systems. Before the twentieth century, expectations such as these for any public educational undertaking would have been inconceivable. As we enter the twenty-first century, the disparateness of the public's demands on education—and on the schools—continues to grow.

In this context, postmodernism has been pivotal to the rise of the age of pluralism in American education. Martusewicz (1992), in her effort to describe the postmodern subject, describes as well the underlying conditions of pluralism in American schooling:

> Post-modernism, alternatively called post-modernity, is characterized by a crisis in legitimation, specifically of knowledge, in which an attitude of suspicion or lack of belief with regard to "the master narratives" prevails. That is, our assumptions about what constitutes everyday knowledge as well as academic knowledge, indeed the very possibility of knowing, have been placed deeply into question. (pp. 131–132)

This postmodern view of knowledge and knowing linked, however unintentionally, to the multicultural roots of America's origins, the vastness of land that afforded disparate groups the privacy and potential for each group's unique development, and a government based not only on principles of democracy but also on protection from the tyranny of the majority have created the circumstances supportive of pluralism, especially in the public schools.

Pluralism in the schools is one of the greatest cultural experiments in human history, and while patience is in order, it is extremely difficult to be patient as our expectations for measurable results in the short term continue to reflect the cultural encapsulation of a modern era already past. Indeed, the subject-oriented national tests that have been pursued by the federal government as the singular remedy or reform for education seem a throwback to the early years of twentieth-century modernism. While society is becoming increasingly diverse and pluralistic, the education of children is being configured through testing as being a clearly delimited, singular set of intellectual experiences. So I find both within myself and around the nation a strange conflict between a pluralistic reality, both of student circumstances and of public demands, and the thrust toward singular change often thought of in terms of upheaval, revolution, and reform. We appear to ignore the many revolutionary elements that have infiltrated American education without any one of them becoming the dominant character of a new conception of education or curriculum: revolutions without revolution or, in milder terms, reform without a victorious reform movement.

In the typically eclectic mode of educators, I want the school's curriculum to accomplish it all. Indeed, in times such as these, we may need it all. Nevertheless, as a curriculum specialist, it has been my lifelong professional endeavor to move beyond the tradition of eclecticism that typically undertakes to make logical transitions among often contradictory diversities and their accompanying cacophony of voices. It is not intellectual or social order that I want but rather meaningfulness and worthwhileness in the midst of all this diversity for all the many disparate needs of disparate populations. I cannot quite define what I understand to be meaningful, not because I cannot recognize it, but because I cannot do so a priori.

We are a nation of complexity and diversity. The metastructures of knowledge that we curricularists have fashioned into school subjects, and the processes by which we do the fashioning, need to become pluralistically sensitive. There needs to be relevance for the individual as well as for society and its subcultures, there needs to be room for doubting knowledge and for suspending doubt, and there needs to be an ever-increasing understanding of uncertainty along with the need to act—even when complexity confuses and frightens us. And somehow, if public schooling is to survive, we need to convince ourselves and numerous others that diversity is the essence of what we are. I sense that *Turning Points* is a passionately unusual and deliberate attempt to do just that.

The time has passed for revolutions to hold the answers. Ah, for the simplicity of a stirring revolution with its clarity of direction and reform.

Afterword to the Second Edition

Democratic Education Through Curriculum Work

Jennifer L. Snow-Gerono,
Boise State University

My consideration of this second edition of *Turning Points* is framed through my perspective as a user of the text. I not only study this book with graduate students in curriculum and instruction but also re-consider the text from multiple viewpoints in my quest for emphasizing democratic education and the democratic *participation* of educators in the political sphere of curriculum, schools, and schooling. My work as a teacher educator unnerves me at times in my efforts to engage the nexus of teacher education and curriculum work. During a local school superintendent's recent presentation in one of my graduate level "Issues in Education" courses, she shared that the *what* of curriculum is no longer within the purview of teachers. Teachers, in her perspective, should only have control over the *how* of curriculum. From her vantage point, how should teacher educators and curriculum workers cultivate colleagues who uphold the ideals of democratic education and more particularly democratic participation within policy and curriculum work?

This second edition of *Turning Points* represents an increasingly important dialogue that must take place in order for educators to democratically engage curriculum and education in the new millennium. Democratic education respects and calls for multiple voices in the deliberative process of what curriculum and education are and should be. These voices may be contentious at times—indeed they are layered—but unless teachers and teacher educators enter the "complicated conversation" of curriculum work, hope for democratic education remains dim. All educators need to recognize their right to *voice* in an increasingly standardized framework for education. Democratic participation mandates the need to work through multiple, complex ideas in a fair, equitable, and just fashion. In *Turning Points*, Marshall, et al. provide a historical yet timely perspective, inviting educators into their dialogue and modeling democratic deliberation of curriculum and schooling in a tone of "optimistic uncertainty" rather than silence or despair.

Indeed, these authors have revitalized their passion for curriculum workers and the meshing of curriculum and pedagogy in this second edition in a manner Pinar originally characterized as "stylistic achievement." This edition maintains its significance in a time of higher standards and accountability for American educators because of its potential for helping readers learn from curriculum history as well as move toward a more participatory democratic education based in curriculum work. My own intentions in using this book include encouraging educators to embrace curriculum work as a means for strengthening democratic education (Gutmann, 1999; Henderson & Kesson, 2004). Curriculum workers in our current climate must learn to work within moves toward high-stakes testing and standardization. Reading *Turning Points* aids, I believe, in understanding curriculum history and the continued need for reconceptualizing our curricular understandings in order to remain true to the historically relevant standards of *democratic* education.

Before continuing my personal call for democratic education through curriculum work, I feel it is important to situate myself within—or without, as the case may be—the curriculum field. I am a teacher educator dedicated to working with/in the dialectic theory and practice provided in education study and enactment. My work in teacher education, spanning initial teacher preparation through continued professional development for educators, represents a deep commitment to upholding democratic ideals in teaching, learning, schooling, and education. Likewise, my work as a professor of curriculum, instruction, and foundational studies leads me again and again to the study of *Turning Points* with graduate students—often K–12 teachers, technology educators, administrators, or even philosophers and policy people—working toward a doctorate in school improvement. We struggle together to understand education policy and curriculum, always hopeful for transformation.

In her original Afterword for *Turning Points*, Wilma Longstreet identifies public schooling as "one of the first public arenas confronting the challenge of pluralism" (p. 246). I agree with her that "we are a nation of complexity and diversity." And, I too, struggle between hope and despair in working toward a democratic curriculum, a democratic *education* for an increasingly pluralistic public. Being a relative newcomer to the field of curriculum, I actively choose to lean toward hopefulness, even in an era of high stakes testing and accountability in U.S. public policy. My hopefulness is enhanced in reading this second edition of *Turning Points* for the following reasons: (1) its continued call for democratic deliberation in curriculum work and education; (2) its vivid message that curriculum work, however it may be titled, is an important response to the current trends of many states to act in accordance with current education policy; and (3) its sustained position that the memoir genre provides excellent scaffolding for new curriculum workers as they explore curriculum history and strive to make meaning of curriculum in their own varied discourses and responsibilities. This third point is, in my opinion, a particular strength for those working within current education policy. This edition contains specific updates and connections to public policy that guide new curriculum workers, perhaps more accessibly than other media due to its memoir format, toward collective reflection.

If nothing else, *Turning Points* exemplifies the "complicated conversation" in which curriculum workers have engaged in order to reconceptualize work once bound by scientific prescriptions of curriculum. Of late, it appears as if we are being dragged backward to such prescribed, standardized curriculum work. The dialogue throughout *Turning Points* exemplifies democratic deliberation of curriculum policy and welcomes new curriculum workers' participation. In personal communication with one of my doctoral students about the timeliness of *Turning Points* in her graduate education, she shared the following: "*Turning Points* made me want to engage in long conversations with the authors . . . and engage them in dialogue about curriculum work and its limitless possibilities. *Turning Points* gave me a space—a safe space—in which to think about the human element in curriculum study. It provided me with a reality check of sorts, for it reassured me that my political slant and my position against the scientifically proven methods were rooted in a deep, philosophical traditions shared by others" (Debra Yates, personal communication, 1/8/2005). This safe space was cultivated by the book's structural and personable implicit invitation to engage in democratic deliberation over what curriculum work can and should be. This invitation seems even more explicit in the second edition of *Turning Points*.

Longstreet calls for "meaningfulness and worthwhileness" in her original Afterword. This meaningfulness and worthwhileness should be framed within historical conceptualizations of curriculum and schooling where democratic participation includes curriculum workers of all positions—teachers, teacher educators, philosophers, theoreticians, practitioners, policy-makers and the *public* at large. What makes democratic education a participatory act is the ability and willingness to engage in such conversations and dialogues. Therefore, I issue a call to all educators to enter the dialogue concerning curriculum work in their current contexts. Several visitors in *Turning Points* encourage such dialogue by voicing tensions surrounding the inclusion of teachers' voices or the translation of curriculum work for public school teachers. Movements toward teacher leadership (Lieberman & Miller, 2004) seem particularly hopeful for bringing teachers into a dialogue over curriculum and pedagogy in schools and public policy. Teacher educators must take up this call to educate teacher leaders who are not only capable of, but also willing and able to further engage, this complicated exchange.

Hence, with a focus on this call to democratic education within curriculum work, *Turning Points* provides me with a bolstered space for hope within the current political climate of *No Child Left Behind*. Any educator engaging in curriculum and pedagogy or study or instruction or *work* has a (re)newed climate of accountability as outlined through today's public policy. Certainly, no curriculum worker strives to leave any child behind in public education. Much of contemporary curriculum history examines whose knowledge counts and whose voices are not only shared but also—and more importantly—heard in curriculum and schooling debates. Without examining the historical roots of the curriculum field, however defined, one does not immediately see the recursive style of school reform, nor perhaps the need for a radical revolution of curriculum and education as described in this book. Yet, as evidenced in this edition's new chapter 9, school and curriculum reform in the 1990s "had been reduced to procedural, technical questions." Such procedural, technical emphases in curriculum and pedagogy do align themselves better with today's structures for standardized assessment. Yet, in connection with the hybridity emphasized in neoliberal politics in the 1990s, education's "perfect storm" has in fact arrived. In my work with practicing and prospective teachers, I see much turmoil over the implementation of prescribed curriculum programs intended to increase standardized achievement as measured by test scores. Even educators dedicated to leaving no child behind seem uncertain as to how to assert their voice—their personal, practical knowledge—in a public dialogue on democratic education. A look at the history of the curriculum reconceptualist movement is helpful in this sense. Ideally, readers see that public democratic education focuses on the success of *all* students, no matter their race, gender, socio-economic status, sexual orientation, or ability, while at the same time valuing contextual diversity in learning and curriculum needs.

Today's curriculum workers must become leaders within a political climate that demands followers. Looking back to *A Nation at Risk* and *Goals 2000* one can see how public policy is embracing not only high standards for American education, but standardization as a goal for the American public. How can our age of pluralism breathe within this context of "outputs" over "inputs"? And, more importantly, what is the curriculum worker's responsibility in understanding and shaping "difference that breeds hybridity"? Where will curriculum and pedagogy fall in current contexts of education? The new chapter 9 in *Turning Points'* 2nd edition merits close attention by those who consider themselves to be bridging a theory and practice gap in their curriculum work. What will happen if we act in opposition to federal mandates to standardize public education? What will happen if we do not?

Finally, the genre of this "*Contemporary American Memoir*" provides excellent scaffolding for new curriculum workers as they explore curriculum history and strive to make meaning of curriculum within their own varied discourses and responsibilities. Another doctoral student who engaged *Turning Points* in a culminating curriculum seminar in her program shared: "The idea of having texts 'talk' to one another . . . has the advantage of presenting information in such a way as to cause the individual reading them to have a kind of mental debate within themselves, to have to sort through the perspectives and hopefully come up with a critical version of their own" (Linda Kirby, personal communication, 1/8/2005). For this reason alone, I am most thankful for *Turning Points* in my work as a teacher educator. The book creates the perfect medium for educators to use as a means for defining curriculum work and placing oneself with/in its kaleidoscope of people, policies, perspectives and practices. I continually use *Turning Points* as an entryway for myself and students to reconsider public education and curriculum as a field of study as well as a field in which we all live and participate.

Curriculum work must include deliberation and action in its future in order for public education and democracy to persevere within current realities of policy trends toward standardization and *one* perception of the good life. *Turning Points* provides a valuable space for curriculum workers to recognize, locate, and engage their struggles—their despair perhaps—within their daily curriculum lives, and see also a hopefulness within curriculum stories and their own call toward the future of the curriculum field—where "an era of complex, deliberative action lies ahead." *Turning Points* calls all readers and educators into democratic deliberation over curriculum and education; heeding this call is a promising step in promoting democratic participation in and for education.

Bibliography

Abbs, P. (Ed.). (1987). *Living powers: The arts in education.* London and Philadelphia: Falmer Press.

About the New Democratic Movement. (n.d.). Retrieved December 12, 2002, from http://ndol.org.

Addams, J. (1981). *Twenty years at Hull House, with autobiographical notes.* New York: Penguin. (Previous editions: 1961, 1924, and 1910)

Adler, M. (1982). *The paideia proposal.* New York: Macmillan.

Ahlum, C., & Fraley, J.M. (1973). *Feminist resources for schools and colleges: A guide to curricular materials.* Old Westbury, NY: Feminist Press.

Aiken, S.H., Anderson, K., Dinnerstein, M., Lensink, J.N., MacCorquodale, P. (Eds.). (1988). *Changing our minds: Feminist transformations of knowledge.* Albany, NY: State University of New York Press.

Aikin, W. (1942). *The story of the eight-year study.* New York: Harper & Brothers.

Airasian, P.W. (1994). The impact of the taxonomy on testing and evaluation. In L.W. Anderson, & L.A. Sosniak (Eds.), *Bloom's taxonomy: A forty-year retrospective.* Ninety-Third Yearbook of the National Society for the Study of Education, Pt. 2, (pp. 82–102). Chicago: University of Chicago Press.

Aitken, J. (1993). *Nixon: A life.* Washington, DC: Regnery.

Alberty, H. (1953). *Reorganizing the high school curriculum.* New York: Macmillan. (1st ed. 1947)

Alexander, W.M., Williams, E.L., Compton, M., Hines, V.A., & Prescott, D. (1968). *The emergent middle school.* New York: Holt, Rinehart and Winston.

Allen, L.A. (1999, April–May). Opening doors and broadening horizons: Laura Bragg and The Charleston Museum. Lecture series for the South Carolina Humanities Council, Charleston, SC.

Altbach, P.G. (1987). *The knowledge context: Comparative perspectives on the distribution of knowledge.* Albany, NY: State University of New York Press.

Anderson, K. (1990, May 17). Welcome to the decade of the moment. *Rolling Stone,* 158.

Anderson, L.W., & Sosniak, L.A. (Eds.). (1994). *Bloom's taxonomy: A forty-year retrospective.* Ninety-Third Yearbook of the National Society for the Study of Education, Pt. 2. Chicago: University of Chicago Press.

Anderson, L.W., Macdonald, J.B., & May, F.B. (Eds.) (1965). *Strategies in curriculum development: The works of Virgil E. Herrick.* Columbus, OH: Charles E. Merrill. (Reprinted 1975 edited by L.W. Anderson, & J.B. Macdonald and published by Greenwood, Westport, CT)

Anther, J. (1987). *Lucy Sprague Mitchell: The making of a modern woman.* New Haven, CT: Yale University Press.

Anyon, J. (1988). Schools as agencies of social legitimation. In W.F. Pinar (Ed.), *Contemporary curriculum discourses* (pp. 175–200). Scottsdale, AZ: Gorsuch Scarisbrick.

Anyon, J. (1997). *Ghetto schooling.* New York: Teachers College Press, Columbia University.

Appadurai, A. (1990). Disjuncture and difference in the global cultural economy. In M. Featherstone (Ed.), *Global culture* (pp. 295–310). London: Sage.

Apple, M. (2000a). The hidden curriculum and the nature of conflict. In W. Pinar (Ed.), *Curriculum studies: The reconceptualization* (pp. 95–119). Troy, NY: Educator's International Press.

Apple, M. (2000b). Scientific interests and the nature of educational institutions. In W. Pinar (Ed.), *Curriculum studies: The reconceptualization* (pp. 120–130). Troy, NY: Educator's International Press.

Apple, M.F., & Beane, J.A. (Eds.). (1995). *Democratic schools.* Alexandria, VA: Association for Supervision and Curriculum Development.

Apple, M.W. (1979). *Ideology and curriculum.* London: Routledge.

Apple, M.W. (Ed.). (1982). *Cultural and economic reproduction in education.* London: Routledge & Kegan Paul.

Apple, M.W. (1986). *Teachers and texts: A political economy of class and gender relations in education.* London and New York: Routledge & Kegan Paul.

Apple, M.W. (1988). Social crisis and curriculum accords. *Educational Theory, 38*(2), 191–201.

Apple, M.W. (July/August 1990). The politics of official knowledge in the United States. *Journal of Curriculum Studies, 22*, 377–383.

Apple, M.W. (1993). *Official knowledge: Democratic education in a conservative age.* New York: Routledge.

Apple, M.W. (1996). *Cultural politics and education.* New York: Teachers College Press, Columbia University.

Appleby, R.S. (1997, March 14). Among Catholics, it's crisis all over. *Commonweal, 124*(5), 17–20.

Armstrong, D.G. (1989). *Developing and documenting the curriculum.* Boston, MA: Allyn & Bacon.

Aronowitz, S., & Giroux, H.A. (1985). *Education under siege: The conservative, liberal, and radical debate over schooling.* South Hadley, MA: Bergin and Garvey.

Ashe, A., Jr., & Rampersad, A. (1993). *Days of grace: A memoir.* New York: Alfred A. Knopf.

Association for Supervision and Curriculum Development (1957). *Research for curriculum improvement.* 1957 ASCD Yearbook. Washington, DC: Author.

Association for Supervision and Curriculum Development (1962). *Perceiving, behaving, becoming: A new focus of education.* 1962 ASCD Yearbook. Washington, DC: Author.

Association for Supervision and Curriculum Development (1963). *The unstudied curriculum: Its impact on children.* Washington, DC: Author.

Atkin, R. (1997, September 5). Is tennis a winner in US? Despite some dire assessments, there are signs of an upswing. *Christian Science Monitor,* p. 12.

Ayers, W. (1992, Summer). The shifting ground of curriculum thought and everyday practice. *Theory Into Practice, 31*(3), 259–263.

Bagley, W.C. (1905). *The educative process.* New York: Macmillan.

Bailyn, B. (1960). *Education in the forming of American society.* New York: Vintage.

Baker, E.L., & Popham, W.J. (1973). *Expanding dimensions of instructional objectives.* Englewood Cliffs, NJ: Prentice-Hall.

Banks, J. (1993). Multicultural education: Development, dimensions, and challenges. *Phi Delta Kappan, 75*(1), 22–28.

Banks, J. (2002). *Introduction to multicultural education* (3rd ed.). Boston, MA: Allyn & Bacon.

Banks, J., & Banks, C. (2005). *Multicultural education: Issues and perspectives* (5th ed.). Boston: Allyn & Bacon.

Baroni, D. (1992, December). Fear and trembling in the nineties. *Cosmopolitan, 156–159.*

Barrow, R. (1984). *Giving teaching back to teachers: A critical introduction to curriculum theory.* London, Ontario: Althouse Press.

Bartecchi, C., & MacKenzie, T. (1995). The global tobacco epidemic. *Scientific American, 44*(5), 44–51.

Barton, L., Meighan, R., & Walker, S. (Eds.). (1980). *Schooling, ideology, and the curriculum.* London: Falmer Press.

Beane, J.A. (1993). *A middle school curriculum* (2nd ed.). Columbus, OH: National Middle School Association.

Beauchamp, G. (1973). Basic components of a curriculum theory. *Curriculum Theory Network, 10,* 16–22.

Beck, E.T. (1989). *Nice Jewish girls: A lesbian anthology.* Boston: Beacon Press.

Beck, J. (1998, April 30). How the so-called tobacco settlement is being polluted. *Chicago Tribune, 25.*

Becker, J.M. (1979). *Schooling for a global age.* New York: McGraw-Hill.

Bell, R. (Ed.). (1971). *Thinking about the curriculum.* Bletchley, Bucks, England: Open University Press.

Bellack, A.A., & Kliebard, H.M. (Eds.). (1977). *Curriculum and evaluation.* Berkeley, CA: McCutchan.

Benham, B. (1981). Curriculum theory in the 1970s: The reconceptualist movement. *JCT, 3*(1), 162–170.

Ben-Peretz, M. (1990). *The teacher-curriculum encounter: Freeing teachers from the tyranny of texts.* Albany, NY: State University of New York Press.

Bereiter, C. (1972). Schools without education. *Harvard Educational Review, 42*(3), 390–413.

Berlak, A., & Berlak, H. (1981). *Dilemmas of schooling: Teaching and social change.* London and New York: Methuen.

Berliner, B.C., & Biddle, B.J. (1995). *The manufactured crisis: Myths, fraud, and the attack on America's public schools.* Reading, MA: Addison-Wesley.

Berman, L.M. (Ed.). (1967). *The humanities and the curriculum.* Washington, DC: Association for Supervision and Curriculum Development.

Berman, L.M. (1968). *New priorities in the curriculum.* Columbus, OH: Merrill.

Berman L.M., Hultgren, F., Lee, D., Rivkin, M.S., & Roderick, J.A. (in conversation with Ted Aoki). (1991). *Toward curriculum for being: Voices of educators.* Albany, NY: State University of New York Press.

Berman, L.M., & Miel, A. (1983). *Education for world cooperation.* West Lafayette, IN: Kappa Delta Pi.

Berman, L.M., Miel, A., & Overly, N.V. (1981). *The World Council for Curriculum and Instruction: The story of its early years.* Bloomington, IN: The World Council for Curriculum and Instruction.

Bestor, A.E., Jr. (1952). Life-adjustment education: A critique. *Bulletin of the American Association of University Professors, 38,* 413–441.

Bestor, A.E., Jr. (1953). *Educational wastelands: The retreat from learning in our public schools.* Urbana, IL: University of Illinois Press.

Beyer, L.E. (1988). *Knowing and acting: Inquiry, ideology, and educational studies.* London: Falmer Press.

Beyer, L.E. (1990). Curriculum deliberation: Value choices and political possibilities. In J.T. Sears & J.D. Marshall (Eds.), *Teaching and thinking about curriculum* (pp. 123–137). New York: Teachers College Press, Columbia University.

Beyer, L.E. (Ed.). (1996). *Creating democratic classrooms: The struggle to integrate theory and practice.* New York: Teachers College Press, Columbia University.

Beyer, L.E., & Apple, M.W. (Ed.). (1988). *The curriculum: Problems, politics, and possibilities.* Albany, NY: State University of New York Press.

Beyer, L.E., & Liston, D.P. (1996). *Curriculum in conflict: Social visions, educational agendas, and progressive school reform.* New York: Teachers College Press, Columbia University.

Beyer, L.E., Feinberg, W., Pagano, J.A., & Whitson, J.A. (1989). *Preparing teachers as professionals: The role of educational studies and other liberal disciplines.* New York: Teachers College Press, Columbia University.

Bigge, M.L. (1992). *Learning theories for teachers* (5th edition). New York: Harper Collins. (Previous editions 1982, 1976, 1971, and 1964)

Blanshard, P. (1949). *American freedom and Catholic power.* Boston: Beacon Press.

Bloom, A. (1987). *The closing of the American mind: How higher education has failed democracy and impoverished the souls of today's students.* New York: Simon and Schuster.

Bloom, B.S. (1994). Reflections on the development and use of the taxonomy. In L.W. Anderson & L.A. Sosniak (Eds.), *Bloom's taxonomy: A forty-year retrospective.* Ninety-Third Yearbook of the National Society for the Study of Education, Pt. 2 (pp. 1–8). Chicago: University of Chicago Press.

Bloom, B.S., Engelhart, M.D., Furst, E.J., Hill, W.H., & Krathwohl, D.R.

(1956). *Taxonomy of educational objectives, handbook 1: Cognitive domain.* New York: David McKay.

Blount, J. (2004). *Fit to teach: Same-sex desire, gender, and school work in the twentieth century.* Albany, NY: State University of New York Press.

Bobbitt, F. (1918). *The curriculum.* Boston: Houghton Mifflin. (Reprinted 1972 by Arno Press and Norwood Editions.)

Bobbitt, F. (1924). *How to make a curriculum.* Boston: Houghton Mifflin. (Also Norwood Editions)

Bode, B.H. (1927). *Modern educational theories.* New York: Macmillan.

Bode, B.H. (1938). *Progressive education at the crossroads.* New York: Newson.

Boger, J. C. (2002). Education's 'perfect storm?' Racial resegregation, 'high stakes' testing, & school inequities: The case of North Carolina. Paper presented at the Conference on The Resegregation of Southern Schools: A Crucial Moment in the History (and the Future) of Public Schooling in America. Chapel Hill, NC.

Booker, C. (1981). *The seventies: The decade that changed the future.* New York: Stein and Day.

Boorstin, D. (1975). *The Image: A guide to pseudo-events in America.* New York: Antheum.

Boruch, R.F., Wortman, P.M., & Cordray, D.S. (1981). *Reanalyzing program evaluation.* San Francisco: Jossey-Bass.

Boswell, J. (1980). *Christianity, social tolerance, and homosexuality: Gay people in Western Europe from the beginning of the Christian era to the fourteenth century.* Chicago: University of Chicago Press.

Bowers, C.A. (1984). *The promise of theory: Education and the politics of cultural change.* New York: Longman.

Bowers, C.A. (1987). *Elements of a post-liberal theory of education.* New York:

Teachers College Press, Columbia University.

Bowers, C.A. (1988). *The cultural dimensions of educational computing.* New York: Teachers College Press, Columbia University.

Bowers, C.A. (1992). *Education: Cultural myths and the ecological crisis: Toward deep changes.* Albany, NY: State University of New York Press.

Bowers, C.A., & Flinders, D.J. (1990). *Responsive teaching: An ecological approach to classroom patterns of language, culture, and thought.* New York: Teachers College Press, Columbia University.

Bowles, S., & Gintis, H. (1976). *Schooling in capitalist America: Educational reform and the contradiction of economic life.* New York: Basic Books.

Boyer, P. (1993). The postwar period through the 1950s. In M.K. Cayton, E.J. Gorn, & P.W. Williams (Eds.), *Encyclopedia of American social history,* (Vol. 1, pp. 205–218). New York: Charles Scribner's Sons.

Boykin, K. (1996). *One more river to cross: Black and gay in America.* New York: Anchor Books.

Brameld, T. (1956). *Toward a reconstructed philosophy of education.* New York: Dryden Press.

Brandt, R.S. (Ed.). (1988). *Content of the curriculum.* Alexandria, VA: Association for Supervision and Curriculum Development.

Braudel, F. (1994). *A history of civilizations* (R. Mayne, Trans.). New York: A. Lane. (Original work published 1987)

Brickman, W.W. (1974/1976). *Bibliographical essays on curriculum and instruction.* Folcroft, PA: Folcroft Library Editions (Reprint of 1948 edition)

Britzman, D.P. (1991). *Practice makes practice: A critical study of learning to teach.* Albany, NY: State University of New York Press.

Britzman, D.P. (1992). Structures of feeling in curriculum and teaching. *Theory Into Practice, 31*(3), 252–258.

Brown, B.R. (1984). *Crisis in secondary education: Rebuilding America's high schools.* Englewood Cliffs, NJ: Prentice-Hall.

Bruner, J.S. (1960). *The process of education.* Cambridge, MA: Harvard University Press.

Bruner, J.S. (1966). *Toward a theory of instruction.* Cambridge, MA: Harvard University Press.

Buber, M. (1952). *Eclipse of God: Studies in the relation between religion and philosophy.* New York: Harper.

Bullough, R.V., Jr. (1981). *Democracy in education: Boyd H. Bode.* Bayside, NY: General Hall.

Bullough, R.V., Jr., Goldstein, S., & Holt, L. (1984). *Human interests in the curriculum: Teaching and learning in a technological society.* New York: Teachers College Press, Columbia University.

Bullough, R.V., Jr., Knowles, J.G., and Crow, N.A. (1991). *Emerging as a teacher.* New York: Routledge.

Burke, A., Conard, E.U., Dalgliesh, A., Garrison, C.G., Hughes, E.V., & Thorn A.G. (1924). *A conduct curriculum for the kindergarten and first grade.* New York: Charles Scribner's Sons. (See Hill, 1923)

Burnett, R. (1996). *The global jukebox: The international music industry.* New York: Routledge.

Butler, J. (1990). *Gender trouble: Feminism and the subversion of identity.* New York: Routledge.

Butler, J. (1993). *Bodies that matter: On the discursive limits of "sex."* New York: Routledge.

Butts, R.F. (1988). *The morality of democratic citizenship.* Calabasas, CA: Center for Civic Education.

Callahan, R. (1962). *Education and the cult of efficiency*. Chicago: University of Chicago Press.

Cannon, R.E. (1983). *A synthesis of opposing conceptions of two major curriculum approaches within the field of curriculum*. Unpublished doctoral dissertation, Georgia State University.

Carey, P.W. (1993). *The Roman Catholics*. Westport, CT: Greenwood Press.

Carger, C.L. (1996). *Of borders and dreams: A Mexican-American experience of urban education*. New York: Teachers College Press, Columbia University.

Carlson, D.L. (1992). Ideological conflict and change in the sexuality curriculum. In J.T. Sears (Ed.), *Sexuality and the curriculum* (pp. 34–58). New York: Teachers College Press, Columbia University.

Carnegie Forum on Education and the Economy Task Force on Teaching as a Profession. (1986). *A nation prepared: Teachers for the 21st century*. New York: Carnegie Forum on Education and the Economy.

Carroll, J. (1963, May). A model of school learning. *Teachers College Record, 64,* 723–733.

Carter, D. (1988). *The final frontier: The rise and fall of the American rocket state*. London: Verso.

Casey, K. (1993). *I answer with my life: Life histories of women teachers working for social change*. New York: Routledge.

Castenell, L.A., & Pinar, W.F. (Eds.) (2003). *Understanding curriculum as racial text: Representations of identity and difference in education*. Albany: State University of New York Press.

Caswell, H.L. & Associates. (1950). *Curriculum improvement in public school systems*. New York: Bureau of Publications, Teachers College, Columbia University.

Caswell, H.L., & Campbell, D.S. (1935). *Curriculum development*. New York: American Book Company. (Reprinted 1978 by R. West)

Caswell, H.L., & Campbell, D.S. (Eds.). (1937). *Readings in curriculum development*. New York: American Book Company. (Reprinted 1984 by Darby Books, Darby, PA)

Caswell, H.L., & Foshay, A.W. (1950). *Education in the elementary school* (2nd ed.). New York: American Book Company. (First edition 1942 and third edition 1957)

Cayton, M.K., Gorn, E.J., & Williams, P.W. (Eds.). (1993). *Encyclopedia of American social history, Vol. 3*. New York: Charles Scribner's Sons.

Census: Hispanic dropout numbers soar. (n.d.). Retrieved on October 11, 2002 from CNN.com.

Chaikin, A. (1996, February). Aiming high in hard times. *Popular Science, 248* (2), 50–54.

Chamberlin, D., Chamberlin, E., Drought, N.E., & Scott, W.E. (1942). *Did they succeed in college?* New York: Harper & Brothers.

Champagne, A., & Horning, L. (1987). *The science curriculum: This year in school science 1986*. Washington, DC: American Association for the Advancement of Science.

Charters, W.W. (1923). *Curriculum construction*. New York: Macmillan. (Reprinted 1924, 1925, 1929, and 1938; 1971 by Arno Press, NY)

Cheney, L.V. (1987). *American memory: A report on the humanities in the nation's public schools*. Washington, DC: National Endowment for the Humanities.

Cherryholmes, C.H. (1988). *Power and criticism: Poststructural investigations in education*. New York: Teachers College Press, Columbia University.

Chittenden, P., & Kiniry, M. (Eds.). (1986). *Making connections across the curriculum.* New York: St. Martin's Press.

Choate, J.S. (1987). *Assessing and programming basic curriculum skills.* Boston: Allyn and Bacon.

Chopin, K. (1976). *The awakening: An authoritative text, contexts, criticism.* New York: Norton. (Original work published 1899)

Christian-Smith, L.K. (1991). *Becoming a woman through romance.* New York: Routledge.

Clandinin, D.J. (1986). *Classroom practice: Teacher images in action.* London: Falmer Press.

Clandinin, D.J., & Connelly, F.M. (1992). Teacher as curriculum maker. In P.W. Jackson (Ed.), *Handbook of research on curriculum* (pp. 363–401). New York: Macmillan.

Coates, J. (1997, July 13). Can Microsoft master success? *Chicago Tribune,* Section 1, pp. 1, 10.

Collings, E. (1923). *An experiment with a project curriculum.* New York: Macmillan Company.

Collins, M.J., & Fries, S.D. (Eds.). (1991). *A spacefaring nation: Perspectives on American space history and policy.* Washington, DC: Smithsonian Institution Press.

Comer, J.P., Haynes, N.M., Joyner, E.T., & Ben-Avie, M. (1996). *Rallying the whole village: The Comer process for reforming education.* New York: Teachers College Press, Columbia University.

Commission on the Reorganization of Secondary Education (1918). *Cardinal principles of secondary education: A report of the Commission on the Reorganization of Secondary Education appointed by the National Education Association.* Washington, DC: GPO. (Available at http://www.nd.edu/~rbarger/www7/cardprin.html).

Committee on Research in Mathematics, Science, and Technology Education

(1985). *Mathematics, science, and technology education: A research agenda.* Washington, DC: National Academy Press.

Conant, J.B. (1959). *The American high school today: A first report to interested citizens.* New York: McGraw-Hill.

Connell, R.W. (1985). *Teacher's work.* Sydney and Boston: Allen & Unwin.

Connell, W.F. (1980). *A history of education in the twentieth century world.* New York: Teachers College Press.

Connelly, F.M., & Clandinin, D.J. (1988). *Teachers as curriculum planners.* Toronto: OISE Press; New York: Teachers College Press, Columbia University.

Cookson, P.W., Jr., & Persell, C.H. (1985). *Preparing for power: America's elite boarding schools.* New York: Basic Books.

Cope B. & Kalantzis, M. (1993). Contradictions in the canon: Nationalism and the cultural literacy debate. In A. Luke & P. Gilbert (Eds.), *Literacy in contexts: Australian perspectives and issues* (pp. 83–177). St Leonards, Australia: Allen and Unwin.

Coreno, T. (1994). Guerilla music: Avant-garde voice as oppositional discourse. In J. Epstein (Ed.), *Adolescents and their music* (pp. 189–224). New York: Garland.

Corey, S.M. (1953). *Action research to improve school practices.* New York: Bureau of Publications, Teachers College, Columbia University.

Cornbleth, C. (1990) *Curriculum in context.* London: Falmer

Cornbleth, C. (2000). National standards and curriculum as cultural containment. In C. Cornbleth (Ed.), *Curriculum, politics, policy, practice: Cases in comparative context* (pp. 211–238). Albany: State University of New York Press.

Cornbleth, C., & Waugh, D. (1995). *The great speckled bird: Multicultural politics and education policymaking.* New York: St. Martin's Press.

Counts, G.S. (1932). *Dare the school build a new social order?* New York: John Day. (Also 1969 by Arno Press, New York)

Cremin, L. (2000). Curriculum making in the United States. In W. Pinar (Ed.), *Curriculum studies: The reconceptualization* (pp. 19–35). Troy, NY: Educator's International Press.

Cremin, L.A. (1961/1964). *The transformation of the school: Progressivism in American education, 1876–1957.* New York: Vintage.

Cremin, L.A. (1976). *Public education,* New York: Basic Books.

Crompton, R. (Ed.). (1989). *Computers and the primary curriculum, 3–13.* London: Falmer Press.

Cronbach, L.J. (1982). *Designing evaluation of educational and social programs.* San Francisco: Jossey-Bass.

Cronbach, L.J., Ambron, S.R., Dornbusch, S.M., Hess, R.D., Hornik, R.C., Phillips, D.C., Walker, D.F., & Weiner, S.S. (1980). *Toward reform of program evaluation: Aims, methods and institutional arrangements.* San Francisco, CA: Jossey-Bass.

Cuban, L. (1986). *Teachers and machines: The classroom use of technology since 1920.* New York: Teachers College Press, Columbia University.

Cuban, L. (1989). The 'at-risk' label and the problem of urban school reform. *Phi Delta Kappan, 70*(10), 780–801.

Cummings, P. (1957). *American tennis: The story of a game and its people.* Boston: Little, Brown.

Daignault, J. (1992). Traces. In W.F. Pinar & W.M. Reynolds (Eds.), *Understanding curriculum as phenomenological and deconstructed text* (pp. 195–215). New York: Teachers College Press, Columbia University.

Dalton, T.H. (1988). *The challenge of curriculum and innovation: A study of ideology and practice.* London and New York: Falmer Press.

Darling-Hammond, L. (1984). *Beyond the commission reports: The coming crisis in teaching.* Washington, DC: Rand Corporation.

Darling-Hammond, L., Ancess, J., & Falk, B. (1995). *Authentic assessment in action: Studies of schools and students at work.* New York: Teachers College Press, Columbia University.

Darling-Hammond, L., & Ascher, C. (1991). *Accountability mechanisms in big city school systems.* (Digest No. 71). New York: ERIC Clearinghouse on Urban Education. (ERIC Document Reproduction Service No. ED334311)

Davis, A. (1929, December). The Negro deserts his people. *Plain Talk, 5,* 49–54.

Davis, A., Burleigh, B.B., & Gardner, M.R. (1941). *Deep south: A social anthropological study of caste and class.* Chicago: University of Chicago Press.

Davis, E. (1980). *Teachers as curriculum evaluators.* Sydney, Australia: Allen & Unwin.

Davis, O.L. (Ed.). (1976). *Perspectives on curriculum development, 1776–1976.* 1976 ASCD Yearbook. Washington, DC: Assocation for Supervision and Curriculum Development.

DeCastell, S., & Bryson, M. (Eds.) (1997). *Radical Interventions: Identity, politics and difference / s in educational practice.* Albany: State University of New York Press.

Deford, F. (1997, December 29). Seasons of discontent. *Newsweek,* pp. 74–75.

Delpit, L.D. (1995). *Other people's children: Cultural conflict in the classroom.* New York: New Press.

Destler Testimony. (2005, May 17). Committee on Appropriates Subcommittee on Defense, U.S. Senate. Retrieved August 22, 2005 from http://www.aau.edu/budget/DestlerTestimony51705.pdf.

Dewey, J. (1897). My pedagogic creed. *The School Journal, 54*(3), 77–80.

Dewey, J. (1902). *The child and the curriculum.* Chicago: University of Chicago Press.

Dewey, J. (1913). *The school and society.* Chicago: University of Chicago Press.

Dewey, J. (1916). *Democracy and education.* New York: Macmillan. (Reprinted 1966 by the Free Press)

Dewey, J. (1929). *The sources of a science of education.* New York: H. Liveright.

Dewey, J. (1938). *Experience and education.* New York: Macmillan.

D'Emilio, J. (1983). *Sexual politics, sexual communities: The making of a homosexual minority in the United States, 1940–1970.* Chicago: University of Chicago Press.

Doll, R.C. (1996). *Curriculum improvement: Decision making and process* (9th ed.). Boston: Allyn & Bacon. (Previous editions 1992, 1989, 1986, 1982, 1978, 1974, 1970, and 1964)

Doll, W.E. (1993). *A post-modern perspective on curriculum.* New York: Teachers College Press, Columbia University.

Doll, W.E. (2005). The culture of method. In W.E. Doll, M.J. Fleener, D. Trueit, & J. St. Julien (Eds.), *Chaos, complexity, curriculum and culture* (pp. 21–75). New York: Peter Lang.

Donmoyer, R. (Ed.). (1993). *At risk students: Portraits, policies, programs, and practices.* Albany, NY: State University of New York Press.

Donmoyer, R., Imber,M., & Scheurich, J.J. (Ed.). (1995). *The knowledge base in educational administration: Multiple perspectives.* Albany, NY: State University of New York Press.

Drumheller, S.J. (1972). *Teacher's handbook for a functional behavior-based curriculum.* Englewood Cliffs, NJ: Educational Technology Publications.

Duberman, M. (1993). *Stonewall.* New York: Dutton.

DuBois, W.E.B. (1903). *The souls of black folk.* New York: Signet.

Duckworth, E.R. (1987). *"The having of wonderful ideas" and other essays on teaching and learning.* New York: Teachers College Press, Columbia University. (Reprinted 1996)

Earl, T. (1987). *The art and craft of course design.* New York: Nichols.

Edel, A. (1985). *Interpreting education: Science, ideology, and values* (Vol. 3). New Brunswick, NJ: Transaction/Rutgers.

Edgerton, S. (1996). *Translating the curriculum: Multiculturalism into cultural studies.* New York: Routledge.

Education Week. (1994, November 9). *Summary of the Improving America's Schools Act.* Retrieved December 7, 2003, from http://www.edweek.org/ew/ewstory.cfm?slug=10asacht.h14.

Education Week. (2002, January 9). *An ESEA primer.* Retrieved December 7, 2002, from http://www.edweek.org/ew/ewstory.cfm?slug=16eseabox.h21.

Educational Policies Commission. (1948). *Education for ALL American children.* Washington, DC: National Education Association.

Educational Policies Commission (1952). *Education for ALL American youth: A further look* (Rev.ed.). Washington, DC: National Education Association.

Egan, K. (1978). What is curriculum? *Curriculum Inquiry, 8*(1), 65–72.

Egan, K. (1986). *Teaching as storytelling; An alternative approach to teaching and curriculum.* Chicago: University of Chicago Press. (Reprinted 1989)

Ehrenhalt, A. (1995, Summer). Learning from the fifties. *The Wilson Quarterly, 19*(3), 8–29.

Eisner, E.W. (Ed.). (1971). *Confronting curriculum reform.* Boston: Little, Brown.

Eisner, E.W. (Ed.). (1977). *The arts, human development, and education.* Berkeley, CA: McCutchan.

Eisner, E.W. (Ed.). (1985). *Learning and teaching the ways of knowing.* Eighty-Fourth Yearbook of the National Society for the Study of Education, Pt. 1. Chicago: University of Chicago Press.

Eisner, E.W. (1991). *The enlightened eye: Qualitative inquiry and the enhancement of educational practice.* New York: Macmillan. (Reprinted 1998 by Merrill, Upper Saddle River, NJ)

Eisner, E.W. (1994a). *Cognition and curriculum reconsidered* (2nd ed.). New York: Teachers College Press, Columbia University. (First edition 1982 by Longman, New York)

Eisner, E.W. (1994b). *The educational imagination: On the design and evaluation of school programs* (3rd ed.). New York: Macmillan. (Previous editions 1985 and 1979)

Eisner, E.W., & Vallance E. (Eds.). (1974). *Conflicting conceptions of curriculum.* Berkeley, CA: McCutchan.

Elam, S.M. (Ed.). (1964). *Education and the structure of knowledge.* Chicago: Rand McNally.

Elbaz, F. (1983). *Teacher thinking: A study of practical knowledge.* New York: Nichols; London: Croom Helm.

Elliot, M. (1996). *The day before yesterday.* New York: Simon and Schuster.

Ellsworth, E. (1989). Why doesn't this feel empowering?: Working through the repressive myths of critical pedagogy. *Harvard Educational Review, 59*(3), 297–324.

Ellsworth, E., & Whatley, M.H. (Eds.). (1990). *The ideology of images in educational media: Hidden curriculums in the classroom.* New York: Teachers College Press, Columbia University.

Eng, D. & Hom, A. (1998). *Q & A: Queer in Asian America.* Philadelphia: Temple University Press.

Engle, S.H., & Ochoa, A.S. (1988). *Education for democratic citizenship: Decision-making in the social studies.* New York: Teachers College Press, Columbia University.

English, F.W. (1978). *Quality control in curriculum development.* Arlington VA: American Association of School Administrators.

English, F.W. (1980). *Improving curriculum management in the schools.* Washington, DC: Council for Basic Education.

English, F.W. (1987). *Curriculum management for schools, colleges, business.* Springfield, IL: Charles C. Thomas. (Reprinted 1996)

Epstein, D., & Sears, J.T. (1999). *A dangerous knowing. Sexuality, pedagogy, and popular culture.* London: Cassell.

Estava, G., & Prakash, M.S. (1997). *Grassroots postmodernism: Beyond human rights, the individual self, and the global economy.* New York: Peter Lang.

Fairclough, G. (2002, April 22). "Case on children and tobacco ads commences today." *Wall Street Journal, 239* (78), p. B8.

Fantini, M.D. (1986). *Regaining excellence in education.* Columbus, OH: Merrill.

Fantini, M.D., & Sinclair, R. (Eds.). (1985). *Education in school and nonschool settings.* Eighty-Fourth

Yearbook of the National Society for the Study of Education, Pt. 1. Chicago: University of Chicago Press.

Farber, D.A. (1989, July). From Warren to Rehnquist. *Trial,* pp. 124–126.

Feinberg, P.R. (1982). *A Buberian critique of four curriculum theorists.* Unpublished doctoral dissertation, Loyola University of Chicago.

Finch, C., & Crunkilton, J. (1989). *Curriculum development in vocational and technical education: Planning content and implementation* (3rd ed.). Boston: Allyn & Bacon. (First, second, fourth, and fifth editions 1979, 1984, 1993, and 1999)

Fine, M., Weis, L., Powell, L.C., & Mun Wong, L. (Eds.). (1997). *Off white: Readings on race, power, and society.* New York: Routledge.

Finn, C.E., Jr., Ravitch, D., & Fancher, R.T. (Eds.). (1984). *Against mediocrity: The humanities in America's high schools.* New York: Holmes and Meier.

Flesch, R.F. (1955). *Why Johnny can't read-and what you can do about it.* New York: Harper.

Fliegel, S., & MacGuire, J. (1993). *Miracle in East Harlem: The fight for choice in public education.* New York: Times Books.

Flinders, D.J., & Thornton, S.J. (1997). *The curriculum studies reader.* New York: Routledge.

Foley, D. (1984). Colonialism and schooling in the Philippines, 1898–1970. In P.G. Altbach & G.P. Kelly, (Eds.), *Education and the colonial experience* (2nd rev. ed.) (pp. 33–53). New Brunswick, N.J.: Transaction Books.

Fonda, D. (2001, July 2). Why tobacco won't quit. *Time South Pacific, 26,* pp. 46–48.

Ford, G.W., & Pugno, L. (Eds.). (1964). *The structure of knowledge and the curriculum.* Chicago: Rand McNally.

Ford, N.A. (1973). *Black studies: Threat-or-challenge.* Port Washington, NY: Kennikat Press.

Foshay, A.W. (1975). *Essays on curriculum: Selected papers.* New York: Teachers College, Columbia University.

Foshay, A.W., & Wann, K.D. (1954). *Children's social values: An action research study.* New York: Bureau of Publications, Teachers College, Columbia University.

Foster, M. (1997). *Black teachers on teaching.* New York: New Press.

Foucault, M. (1978). *The history of sexuality.* New York: Pantheon.

Foucault, M. (1980). *Power / knowledge: Selected interviews and other writings, 1972–1977.* New York: Pantheon.

Frankenberg, E., Lee, C. & Orfield, G. (2003) *A multiracial society with segregated schools: Are we losing the dream?* Cambridge, MA: The Civil Rights Project, Harvard University.

Frankfurter, F. (1938). *Mr. Justice Homes and the Supreme Court.* Cambridge, MA: Harvard University Press.

Franklin, B.M. (1986). *Building the American community: The school curriculum and the search for social control.* London and Philadelphia: Falmer Press.

Franklin, B.M. (1994). *From backwardness to "at-risk:" Childhood learning difficulties and the contradictions of school reform.* Albany: State University of New York Press.

Fraser, D.M. (Ed.). (1962). *Current curriculum studies in academic subjects.* Washington, DC: National Education Association.

Freire, P. (1972). *Pedagogy of the oppressed* (2nd ed.). New York: Herder & Herder.

Freire, P. (1994). *Pedagogy of hope: Reliving pedagogy of the oppressed.*

(R.R. Barr Trans.). New York: Continuum.

Freire, P. (1996). *Letters to Christina: Reflections on my life and work.* New York: Routledge.

Freire, P., & Faundez, A. (1989). *Learning to question: A pedagogy of liberation.* New York: Continuum.

Frieling, R. (1997, January). Communion with, not under the Pope. *The Ecumenical Review, 49*(1), 34–45.

Frith, K. (Ed.). (1997). *Undressing the ad: Reading culture in advertising.* New York: Peter Lang.

Frymier, J.R., & Hawn, H.C. (1970). *Curriculum improvement for better schools.* Worthington, OH: Charles A. Jones.

Fuhrman, S.H. (2001). Introduction. In S.H. Fuhrman (Ed.), *From the capitol to the classroom: Standards-based reform in the states* (pp. 1–12). Chicago: University of Chicago.

Fullan, M. (1991). *The new meaning of educational change* (2nd ed.). New York: Teachers College Press, Columbia University. (First edition 1982)

Fullinwider, R.K. (1996). Multicultural education: Concepts, policies and controversies. In R.K. Fullinwider (Ed.), *Public education in a multicultural society: Policy, theory, critique* (pp. 3–22). New York: Cambridge University Press.

Gagne, R.M. (1965). *The conditions of learning.* New York: Holt, Rinehart and Winston. (Reprinted 1970, 1977, and 1985)

Gaskell, J., & Willinsky, J. (Eds.). (1995). *Gender in / forms curriculum: From enrichment to transformation.* New York: Teachers College Press; Toronto: OISE Press.

Gates, H.L., Jr. (1988/1989). *The signifying monkey: A theory of African-American literary criticism.*

New York and Oxford: Oxford University Press.

Gates, H.L., Jr. (1992). *Loose canons: Notes on the culture wars.* New York: Oxford University Press.

Gay Left Collective. (Ed.). (1980). *Homosexuality: Power and politics.* London and New York: Allison & Busby.

Gay, G. (2000). *Culturally responsible teaching.* New York: Teachers College Press.

Gibbs, W. (1998). Big tobacco's worst nightmare. *Scientific American, 279*(1), pp. 30–31.

Giddens, A. (1990). *The consequences of modernity.* Stanford, CA: Stanford University Press.

Gilchrist, R.S. (1963). *Using current curriculum developments: A report.* Washington, D.C.: Association for Supervision and Curriculum Development.

Giles, H.H., McCutchan, S.P., & Zechiel, A.N. (1942). *Exploring the curriculum.* New York: Harper and Brothers.

Gillespie, J. (1980). *Media resources in curriculum development.* Glasgow: Scottish Council for Educational Technology.

Giroux, H. (1988). Liberal arts, teaching and critical literacy: Toward a definition of schooling as a form of cultural politics. In W. Pinar (Ed.), *Contemporary curriculum discourses* (pp. 243–263). Scottsdale, AZ: Gorsuch Scarisbrick.

Giroux, H.A. (1979). Toward a new sociology of curriculum. *Educational Leadership.* Vol. 37. (pp. 248–253).

Giroux, H.A. (1988a). *Schooling and the struggle for public life.* Minneapolis, MN: University of Minnesota Press.

Giroux, H.A. (1988b). *Teachers as intellectuals: Toward a critical pedagogy of learning.* Granby, MA: Bergin and Garvey.

Giroux, H.A. (1992). *Bordercrossings.* New York: Routledge.

Giroux, H.A. (1993). *Living dangerously: Multiculturalism and the politics of difference.* New York: Peter Lang.

Giroux, H.A. (1994). *Disturbing pleasures: Learning from popular culture.* New York: Routledge.

Giroux, H.A. (Ed.). (1997). *The politics of hope: Theory, culture, and schooling.* Boulder, CO: Westview Press.

Giroux, H.A., & McLaren, P. (1989). *Critical pedagogy, the state, and cultural struggle.* Albany, NY: State University of New York Press.

Giroux, H.A., Lankshear, C., McLaren, P., & Peters, M. (1996). *Counter-narratives: Cultural studies and critical pedagogies in postmodern spaces.* New York: Routledge.

Giroux, H.A., & Shannon, P. (1997). *Education and cultural studies: Toward a performative practice.* New York: Routledge.

Giroux, H.A., Simon, R.I., & Contributors. (1989). *Popular culture: Schooling and everyday life.* New York: Bergin and Garvey.

Gitlin, A.D. (Ed.). (1994). *Power and method: Political activism and educational research.* New York: Routledge.

Glaser, R. (1963). Instructional technology and the measurement of learning outcomes. *American Psychologist, 18,* 519–521.

Glatthorn, A.A. (1980). *Curriculum development and reform: A practical resource.* Urbana, IL: National Council of Teachers of English.

Glatthorn, A.A. (1987). *Curriculum leadership.* Glenview, IL: Scott, Foresman and Company.

Gleason, P. (1987). *Keeping the faith: American Catholicism past and present.* Notre Dame, IN: University of Notre Dame Press.

Goldman, N.C. (1992). *Space policy: An introduction.* Ames, IA: Iowa State University Press.

Goldstein, W. (1993). Sports in the twentieth century. In M.K. Cayton, E.J. Gorn, & P.W. Williams (Eds.), *Encyclopedia of American social history,* (Vol. 1, pp. 1643–1655). New York: Charles Scribner's Sons.

Goodlad, J.I. (1966). *School, curriculum, and the individual.* Waltham, MA: Blaisdell.

Goodlad, J.I. (1975). *The dynamics of educational change: Toward responsive schools* (introduction by Samuel G. Sava). New York: McGraw-Hill.

Goodlad, J.I., Ammons, M.P., Buchanan, E.A., Griffin, G.A., Hill, H.W., Iwanska, A., Jordan, J.A., Klein, M.F., McClure, R.M., Richter, M.N., Jr., Tye, K.A., Tyler, L.L., & Wilson, E.C. (1979). *Curriculum inquiry: The study of curriculum practice.* New York: McGraw-Hill.

Goodman, J. (1988). The disenfranchisement of elementary teachers and strategies for resistance. *Journal of Curriculum and Supervision, 3* (3), 201–220.

Goodman, J. (1992). *Elementary schooling for critical democracy.* Albany, NY: State University of New York Press.

Goodman, P. (1966). *Compulsory mis-education, and the community of scholars.* New York: VintageBooks.

Goodson, I.F. (1988). *International perspectives in curriculum history.* London: Routledge.

Gordon, L., & Gordon, A. (1990). *American chronicle: Seven decades in American life.* New York: Crown Publishers.

Gordon, T. (1986). *Democracy in one school?: Progressive education and restructuring.* London and Philadelphia: Falmer Press.

Gorter, R.J. (Ed.). (1986). *Views on core curriculum: Contributions to an international seminar.* Enschade, The Netherlands: National Institute for Curriculum Development.

Gorwood, B.T. (1986). *School transfer and curriculum continuity.* London: Croom Helm.

Gottlieb, A. (1987). *Do you believe in magic?: The second coming of the sixties generation.* New York: Times Books.

Gould, S.J. (1981). *The mismeasure of man.* New York: W.W. Norton.

Grady, M.T., & Gawronski, J.D. (1983). *Computers in curriculum and instruction.* Alexandria, VA: Association for Supervision and Curriculum Development.

Graham, R.J. (1991). *Reading and writing the self: Autobiography in education and the curriculum.* New York: Teachers College Press, Columbia University.

Graham, R.J. (1992). Currere and reconceptualism: The progress of the pilgrimage, 1975–1990. *Journal of Curriculum Studies, 24*(1), 27–42.

Grant, C. (2003). *An education guide to diversity in the classroom.* Boston: Houghton Mifflin.

Greenberg, D.F. (1988). *The construction of homosexuality.* Chicago: University of Chicago Press.

Greene, M. (1978). *Landscapes of learning.* New York: Teachers College Press.

Greene, M. (1978). Pedagogy and praxis: The problem of malefic generosity. In *Landscapes for Learning* (pp. 95–110). New York: Teachers College Press.

Greene, M. (1988). *The dialectic of freedom.* New York: Teachers College Press, Columbia University.

Greene, M. (1993). *The plays and ploys of postmodernism.* Presidential Address at the 49th Annual Meeting of the Philosophy of Education Society.

Greene, M. (1995). *Releasing the imagination: Essays on education, the arts, and social change.* San Francisco: Jossey-Bass.

Greene, N. (1990). *Pier Paolo Pasolini: Cinema as heresy.* Princeton, NJ: Princeton University Press.

Greer, C. (1972). *The great school legend.* New York: Viking.

Gregor, A. (2002, September/October). What's Spanish for big media? *Columbia Journalism Review, 5.* Retrieved August 22, 2005 from http://www.cjr.org/issues/2003/5/voice-gregor.asp.

Gress, J.R., & Purpel, D.E. (Eds.). (1988). *Curriculum: An introduction to the field* (2nd ed.). Berkeley, CA: McCutchan. (First edition 1978)

Grossberg, L. (1990). Is there rock after punk? In S. Frith & S. Goodwin (Eds.), *On record* (pp. 111–123). London: Routledge.

Grumet, M. (1988). Feminism and the phenomenology of the familiar. In *Bitter milk: Women and teaching* (pp. 59–74). Amherst, MA: University of Massachusetts Press.

Grumet, M. (1988a). *Bitter milk: Women and teaching.* Amherst, MA: University of Massachusetts Press.

Grumet, M. (1988b). Bodyreading. In W.F. Pinar (Ed.), *Contemporary curriculum discourses* (pp. 453–473). Scottsdale, AZ: Gorsuch Scarisbrick.

Guba, E.G., & Lincoln, Y.S. (1981). *Effective evaluation: Improving the usefulness of evaluation results through responsive and naturalistic approaches.* San Francisco: Jossey-Bass.

Gutek, G.L. (1993). *American education in a global society: Internationalizing teacher education.* New York: Longman.

Gutmann, A. (1999). *Democratic education.* Princeton, NJ: Princeton University Press.

Haas, J.D. (1980). *Future studies in the K-12 curriculum.* Boulder, CO: Social Science Education Consortium. (Reprinted 1988)

Haberman, M. (1996). The pedagogy of poverty versus good teaching. In W. Ayers & P. Ford (Eds.), *City kids, city teachers: Reports from the front row* (pp. 118–130). New York: W.W. Norton.

Halberstam, D. (1993). *The fifties.* New York: Villard Books.

Hall, J. (1998, November 23). *Tobacco settlement may be a lot less historic and heroic than the participants make it sound.* Media General News Service.

Hamilton, D. (1976). *Curriculum evaluation.* London: Open Books.

Hamilton, D., Macdonald, B., King, C., Jenkins, D., & Parlett, M. (Eds.). (1977). *Beyond the numbers game: A reader in educational evaluation.* Berkeley, CA: McCutchan.

Hampel, R.L. (1986). *The last little citadel: American high schools since 1940.* Boston: Houghton Mifflin.

Hannah, L.S., & Michaelis, J.U. (1977). *A comprehensive framework for instructional objectives: A guide to systematic planning and evaluation.* Reading, MA: Addison-Wesley.

Harley, R. (1993). Beat in the system. In T. Bennett (Ed.), *Rock and popular music: Politics, policies, institutions.* New York: Routledge.

Hass, G. (Ed.). (1987). *Curriculum planning: A new approach* (5th ed.). Boston: Allyn & Bacon. (Previous editions 1983, 1980, 1977, and 1974; also 1993 by G. Hass & F. Parkay)

Hass, G., & Parkay, F. (Eds.). (1993). *Curriculum planning: A new approach* (6th ed.). Boston: Allyn & Bacon.

Hawkeswood, W.G. (1996). *One of the children: Gay Black men in Harlem.* Berkeley, CA: University of California Press.

Hawthorne, R.K. (1992). *Curriculum in the making: Teacher choice and classroom experience.* New York: Teachers College Press, Columbia University.

Hay, D. (1973). Idea of renaissance. In P.P. Wiener (Ed.), *Dictionary of the history of ideas* (Vol. 4, pp. 121–129). New York: Charles Scribner's Sons.

Hayles, N.K. (1999). *How we became posthuman.* Chicago: University of Chicago Press.

Heath, R.W. (Ed.). (1964). *New curricula.* New York: Harper & Row.

Heidegger, M. (1966). *Discourse on thinking.* Harper Torchbook. New York: Harper & Row.

Henderson, J.G. (1992). *Reflective teaching: Becoming an inquiring educator.* New York: Macmillan.

Henderson, J.G. (1996). *Reflective teaching: The study of your constructivist practices* (2nd ed.). Columbus, OH: Merrill and Englewood Cliffs, NJ: Prentice-Hall.

Henderson, J.G., & Hawthorne, R.D. (1995). *Transformative curriculum leadership.* Columbus, OH: Merrill; Englewood Cliffs, NJ: Prentice-Hall.

Henderson, J.G., & Kesson, K.R. (2004). *Curriculum wisdom: Educational decisions in democratic societies.* Upper Saddle River, NJ: Pearson/Merrill Prentice Hall.

Henry, J. (1963). *Culture against man.* New York: Vintage Books.

Henry, N.B. (Ed.). (1945). *American education in the postwar period:*

Curriculum reconstructions. Forty-Fourth Yearbook of the National Society for the Study of Education, Pt. 1. Chicago: University of Chicago Press.

Henson, K.T. (1995). *Curriculum development for educational reform.* New York: Longman.

Heppenheimer, T.A. (1992, November). Lost in space: What went wrong with NASA? *American Heritage, 43*(7), 60–71.

Herrick, V.E., & Tyler, R.W. (1950). Next steps in the development of a more adequate curriculum theory. In V. Herrick & R.W. Tyler (Eds.), *Toward improved curriculum theory* (pp. 118–124). Supplementary Educational Monographs. Chicago: University of Chicago Press.

Hess, G.A., Jr. (1991). *School restructuring, Chicago style.* Newbury Park, CA: Corwin.

Hicks, D., & Townley, C. (Eds.). (1982). *Teaching world studies: An introduction to global perspectives in the curriculum.* London and New York: Longman.

Hill, P.S. (1923). *A conduct curriculum for kindergarten and first grade.* New York: Charles Scribner's Sons. (See Burke et al., 1924)

Hilts, P.J. (1996). *Smokescreen: The truth behind the tobacco industry cover-up.* Reading, MA: Addison-Wesley.

Hinson, M., & Hughes, M. (Eds.). (1981). *Planning effective progress: Planning and implementing the curriculum for children with learning difficulties.* Amersham, Bucks, England: Hulton Educational and the National Association for Remedial Education.

Hirsch, E.D., Jr. (1987). *Cultural literacy: What every American needs to know.* Boston: Houghton Mifflin.

Hirsch, E.D., Jr. (1996). *The schools we need: Why we don't have them.* New York: Doubleday.

Hlebowitsh, P.S. (1993). *Radical curriculum theory reconsidered.* New York: Teachers College Press, Columbia University.

Hoffman, C.M. (1987). *Curriculum gone astray: When push came to shove.* Lancaster, PA: Technomic.

Hoffman, J. (2002). *The solidarity dilemma: Globalisation, europeanisation and the trade unions.* Brussels: European Trade Union Institute.

Hosic, J.F., & Chase, S.E. (1926). *Brief guide to the project method.* Yonkers-on-Hudson, NY: World Book.

Hoyle, E. (1972). *Problems of curriculum innovation II.* Bletchley, Bucks, England: Open University Press.

Hoyle, E., & Bell, R. (1972). *Problems of curriculum innovation I.* Bletchley, Bucks, England: Open University Press.

Huber, M. (1981). The renewal of curriculum theory in the 1970s: An historical study. *JCT, 3*(1), 14–84.

Huebner, D. (1966). Curricular language and classroom meanings. In J. Macdonald, & R. Leeper (Eds.), *Language and meaning* (pp. 8–26). Washington, DC: Association for Supervision and Curriculum Development.

Huebner, D. (1967). Curriculum as concern for man's temporality. *Theory into Practice, 6* (4), 172–179. [Reprinted in W. Pinar (Ed.), *Curriculum studies: The reconceptualization* (pp. 237–249). Troy, NY: Educator's International Press.]

Huebner, D. (2000a). Poetry and power: The politics of curricular development. In W. Pinar (Ed.), *Curriculum studies: The reconceptualization* (pp. 271–280). Troy, NY: Educator's International Press.

Huebner, D. (2000b). The tasks of the curriculum theorist. In W. Pinar

(Ed.), *Curriculum studies: The reconceptualization* (pp. 250–270). Troy, NY: Educator's International Press.

Hug, W.E. (1979). *40 years of research in curriculum and teaching*. New York: Teachers College Press, Columbia University.

Hunter, G.H. (1994, November 14). Did you hear the one about Plato? *Newsweek* p. 20.

Hunter, J. D. (July/August, 1993). Before the shooting starts. *Columbia Journalism Review*. Retrieved December 13, 2003, from http://cjr.org/year/93/4/shooting.asp.

Hunter, M.C. (1994). *Enhancing teaching*. New York: Macmillan.

Hunter, R., & Scheirer, E.A. (1988). *The organic curriculum: Organizing for learning, 7–12*. London and New York: Falmer Press.

Hutchins, R.M. (1936). *The higher learning in America*. New Haven, CT: Yale University Press.

Huxley, J. (1947). *UNESCO: Its purpose and its philosophy*. Washington, DC: Public Affairs Press.

Hwang, S. (1995, October 30). 'Smokers' game: Philip Morris passion to market cigarettes helps it to outsell RJR. *Wall Street Journal*, p. A1.

Illich, I. (1971). *Deschooling society*. New York: Harper and Row.

Irons, P. (1994). *Brennan vs. Rehnquist: The battle for the Constitution*. New York: Alfred A. Knopf.

Irons, P. (2002). *Jim Crow's children: The broken promise of the Brown decision*. New York: Viking Penguin.

Jackson, P.W. (1968). *Life in classrooms*. New York: Holt, Rinehart & Winston.

Jackson, P.W. (1980). Curriculum and its discontents. *Curriculum Inquiry, 10*(1), 28–43.

Jackson, P.W. (1986). *The practice of teaching*. New York: Teachers College Press, Columbia University.

Jackson, P.W. (1992). Conceptions of curriculum and curriculum specialists. In P. Jackson (Ed.), *Handbook of research on curriculum* (pp. 3–40). New York: Macmillan.

Jackson, P.W. (Ed.). (1986). *Contributing to educational change: Perspectives on research and practice*. Berkeley, CA: McCutchan.

Jackson, P.W., & Haroutunian, G.S. (Eds.). (1989). *From Socrates to software: The teachers as text and the text as teacher*. Eighty-Eighth Yearbook of the National Society for the Study of Education, Pt. 1. Chicago: University of Chicago Press.

Jameson, F. (1984). Forward. In J.F. Lyotard, *The postmodern condition* (G. Bennington and B. Massumi, Trans.) (pp. vii–xxi). Minneapolis, MN: University of Minnesota Press.

JanMohamed, A. (1985). The economy of Manicliean allegory: The function of racial difference in colonialist literature. *Critical Inquiry, 12*(1), 59–87.

Jay, K., & Young, A. (Eds.). (1972). *Out of the closets: Voices of gay liberation*. New York: Harcourt Brace Jovanovich.

Jeans, S.J. (1937). *The mysterious universe*. Cambridge, England: Cambridge University Press.

Jervis, K., & Tobier, A. (Eds.). (1988). *Education for democracy*. Proceedings from the Cambridge School Conference on Progressive Education, October 1987. Weston, MA: The Cambridge School.

Johnston, G., & Dowdy, S. (1988). *Teaching and assessing in a negotiated curriculum*. Australia: Martin Educational.

Jones, L.Y. (1980). *Great expectations: America and the baby boom generation.* New York: Ballantine Books.

Jordan, J. (1988, August). Nobody means more to me than you and the future life of Willie Jordan. *Harvard Educational Review, 58*(3), 363–374.

Joyce, B., & Weil, M. (1996). *Models of teaching* (5th ed.). Englewood Cliffs, NJ: Prentice-Hall. (Previous editions 1992, 1986, 1980, and 1972)

Joyce, B.R. (1986). *Improving America's schools.* White Plains, NY: Longman.

Junger, S. (1997). *A perfect storm: A true story of men against the sea.* New York: Norton.

Kaestle, C.F. (1983). *Pillars of the republic: Common schools and American society, 1780–1860.* New York: Hill and Wang.

Karier, C.J., Violas, P.C., & Spring, J. (1973). *Roots of crisis: American education in the twentieth century.* Chicago: Rand McNally.

Katz, J. (1976). *Gay American history: Lesbians and gay men in the USA.* New York: Crowell.

Katz, M.B. (1971). *Class, bureaucracy, and schools: The illusion of educational change in America.* New York: Praeger.

Katz, M.B. (1987). *Reconstructing American education.* Cambridge, MA: Harvard University Press.

Kelly, A.V. (1986). *Knowledge and curriculum planning.* London: Harper & Row.

Kennedy, E., & Davis, M. (1993). *Boots of leather, slippers of gold: The History of a lesbian community.* New York: Routledge.

Kennedy, M. (1986). *Poverty, achievement, and the distribution of compensatory services* (D18–D60). Washington, DC: Office of Educational Research and Improvement, U.S. Department of Education.

Kentucky Department of Education. (2000). *Results that matter: A decade of difference in Kentucky's public schools, 1990–2000.* Frankfurt, KY: Kentucky Department of Education.

Kepner, H.S., Jr. (Ed.). (1982). *Computers in the classroom.* Washington, DC: National Education Association.

Kessler, L. (1990). *After all these years: Sixties ideals in a different world.* New York: Thunder's Mouth Press.

Kessler-Harris, A. (1992, October 21). Multiculturalism can strengthen, not undermine a common culture. *Chronicle of Higher Education,* B3, 7.

Kilpatrick, W.H. (1918). The project method. *Teachers College Record, 19*(4), 319–335.

Kincheloe, J.L. (1993). *Toward a critical politics of teacher thinking.* Westport, CT: Bergin & Garvey.

Kincheloe, J.L., & Pinar, W.F. (Eds.). (1991). *Curriculum as social psychoanalysis: The significance of place.* Albany, NY: State University of New York Press.

King, B.J. (1974). *Billie Jean.* New York: Harper & Row.

Kirk, D. (1988). *Physical education and curriculum study: A critical introduction.* London and New York: Croom Helm.

Kirk, G. (1986). *The core curriculum.* London: Hodder & Stoughton.

Klein, M.F. (1989). *Curriculum reform in the elementary school: Creating your own agenda.* New York: Teachers College Press, Columbia University.

Kliebard, H. (2000a). Persistent curriculum issues in historical perspective. In W. Pinar (Ed.), *Curriculum studies: The reconceptualization* (pp. 39–50). Troy, NY: Educator's International Press.

Kliebard, H. (2000b). Bureaucracy and curriculum theory. In W. Pinar (Ed.), *Curriculum studies: The reconceptualization* (pp. 51–69). Troy, NY: Educator's International Press.

Kliebard, H.M. (1970). The Tyler Rationale. *School Review, 78*(2), 259–272.

Kliebard, H.M. (1986). *The struggle for the American curriculum, 1893–1958*. New York: Routledge. (Second edition 1995)

Kliebard, H.M. (1988). Fads, fashions, and rituals: The instability of curriculum change. In L.N. Tanner (Ed.), *Critical issues in curriculum.* Eighty-Seventh Yearbook of the National Society for the Study of Education, Pt. 1 (pp. 16–34). Chicago: University of Chicago Press.

Kliebard, H.M. (2004). *The struggle for the American Curriculum,* 1893–1958 (3rd ed.) New York: Routledge.

Klohr, P. (Ed.). (1967). *Theory Into Practice, 6*(4).

Kohlberg, L., & Mayer, R. (1972, November). Development as the aim of education. *Harvard Educational Review, 42*(4), 449–496.

Kozol, J. (1967). *Death at an early age: The destruction of the hearts and minds of Negro children in the Boston public schools.* Boston: Houghton Mifflin.

Kozol, J. (1991). *Savage inequalities: Children in America's schools.* New York: Crown Pub.

Krathwohl, D.R., Bloom, B.S., & Masia, B.B. (1964). *Taxonomy of educational objectives, handbook 2: Affective domain.* New York: David McKay.

Krauss, C. (1997, September 7). Those are the players, Buffy, not ants in tennis shoes. *New York Times*, p. 2.

Kridel, C., Bullough, R.V. Jr., & Shaker, P. (Eds.). (1996). *Teachers and mentors.* Hamden, CT: Garland.

Krough, D. (1991). *Smoking: The artificial passion.* Oxford: W.H. Freeman.

Kuhn, T. (1962). *The structure of scientific revolutions.* Chicago: University of Chicago Press. (Also 1970)

Ladd, H. (1999). The Dallas school accountability and incentive program: An evaluation of its impacts on student outcomes. *Economics of Education Review, 18*, 1–16.

Lagerfeld, S. (1995, Summer). The edgy decade. *The Wilson Quarterly, 19*(3), 4–5.

Lamar, H.G. (1985). *An examination of reconceptualist-humanistic curriculum theory and the response of Alabama curriculum practitioners of its value commitments.* Unpublished doctoral dissertation, University of Alabama.

Land, D, & Legters, N. (2002). The extent and consequences of risk in U.S. education. In S. Stringfield & D. Land (Eds.), *Educating at-risk students* (pp. 1–25). Chicago: University of Chicago.

Lather, P. (1991). *Getting smart: Feminist research and pedagogy within the postmodern.* New York: Routledge.

Lather, P. (1992). Critical frames in educational research: Feminist and post-structural perspectives. *Theory into Practice, 31*(2), 87–96.

Lather, P., & Smithies, C. (1997). *Troubling the angels: Women living with HIV/AIDS.* Boulder, CO: Westview. (Earlier edition self-published 1995, Greyden Press, Columbus, OH)

Laughery, J. (1998). *The other side of silence.* New York: Henry Holt and Company.

Launius, R.D. (1994). *NASA: A history of the U.S. civil space program.* Malabar, FL: Krieger.

Lavin, M. (1996). *Understanding the census: A guide for marketers, planners, grant writers and other data users.* Kenmore, NY: Epoch Books.

Lawton, D. (1975). *Class, culture, and the curriculum.* London and Boston: Routledge and Kegan Paul.

Lawton, D. (Ed.). (1986). *School curriculum planning.* London: Hodder & Stoughton.

Lea, K. (1987). "In the most highly developed societies": Lyotard and postmodernism. *Oxford Literary Review, 9*(1–2), 86–104.

Lefevre, P. (1997, October 31). Critics, sponsors size up "Critical Mass." *National Catholic Reporter, 33*(46), 6.

Leithwood, K.A. (Ed.). (1986). *Planned educational change: A manual of curriculum review, development, and implementation: Concepts and procedures.* Buffalo, NY: OISE Press.

Lerner, M. (1994). *Nine scorpions in a bottle: Great judges and cases of the Supreme Court.* New York: Arcade.

Lesko, N. (1988). *Symbolizing society: Stories, rites, and structure in a Catholic high school.* New York: Falmer Press.

Letts, W., & Sears, J.T. (Eds.). (1999). *Queering elementary education.* Lanham, MD: Rowan & Littlefield.

Lewis, M.H. (1928). *An adventure with children.* New York: Macmillan.

Lewy, A. (1977). *Handbook of curriculum evaluation.* New York: Longman.

Lieberman, A., & Miller, L. (1984). *Teachers, their world, and their work.* Washington, DC: Association for Supervision and Curriculum Development.

Lieberman, A., & Miller, L. (2004). *Teacher leadership.* San Francisco: Jossey Bass.

Lincoln, Y. (1992). Curriculum studies and the traditions of inquiry: The humanistic tradition. In P. Jackson (Ed.), *Handbook of research on curriculum* (pp. 41–78). New York: Macmillan.

Liston, D.P., & Zeichner, K.M. (1991). *Teacher education and the social conditions of schooling.* New York: Routledge.

Little, A.W. (2000). Globalisation, qualifications, and livelihoods: Towards a research agenda. *Assessment in Education, 7,* 299–312.

Lloyd, S.M. (1987). *The Putney School: A progressive experiment.* New Haven, CT: Yale University Press.

Longstreet, W.S., & Shane, H.G. (1993). *Curriculum for a new millenium.* Boston: Allyn & Bacon.

Lopez, A.L. (1993). *Exploring possibilities for progressive curriculum and teaching in three urban contexts.* Unpublished doctoral dissertation, University of Illinois at Chicago.

Loughery, J. (1998). *The other side of silence: Men's lives and gay identities: A twentieth-century history.* New York: Henry Holt.

Lynd, A. (1953). *Quackery in the public schools.* Boston: Little, Brown. (Original work published 1950)

Lyotard, J. (1984). *The postmodern condition: A report on knowledge* (G. Bennington and B. Massumi, Trans.). Minneapolis, MN: University of Minnesota Press. (Original work published 1979)

Lyotard, J. (1993). *Libidinal economy.* (I.H. Grant, Trans.). Bloomington, IN: Indiana University Press.

Macdonald, J., Anderson, D., & May, F.B. (Eds.). (1965). *Strategies for curriculum development: The works of Virgil Herrick.* Columbus, OH: Charles E. Merrill.

Macdonald, J.B. (1971). Curriculum theory. *Journal of Educational Research, 64*(5), 196–200.

Macdonald, J.B. (1974). A transcendental developmental ideology of education. In W.F. Pinar (Ed.), *Heightened consciousness, cultural revolution,* and curriculum theory: The proceedings of the Rochester conference (pp. 85–116). Berkeley, CA: McCutchan.

Macdonald, J.B. (Ed.). (1996). *Theory as a prayerful act: The collected essays of James B. Macdonald.* New York: Peter Lang.

Macdonald, J.B., & Leeper, R.R. (Eds.). (1966). *Language and meaning.* Washington, DC: Association for Supervision and Curriculum Development.

Macdonald, J.B., & Zaret, E. (Eds.). (1975). *Schools in search of meaning.* 1975 ASCD Yearbook. Washington, DC: Association for Supervision and Curriculum Development.

Mager, R.F. (1962). *Preparing instructional objectives.* Palo Alto, CA: Fearon. (Also 1975)

Mann J. (2000a). Curriculum criticism. In W. Pinar (Ed.), *Curriculum studies: The reconceptualization* (pp. 133–148). Troy, NY: Educator's International Press.

Mann, J. (2000b). A discipline of curriculum theory. In W. Pinar (Ed.), *Curriculum studies: The reconceptualization* (pp. 149–164). Troy, NY: Educator's International Press.

Mann, J., & Molnar, A. (1975). On student rights. In W. Pinar (Ed.), *Curriculum theorizing: The reconceptualists* (pp. 167–172). Berkeley, CA: McCutchan.

Marcus, E. (1993). *Making history: The struggle for gay and lesbian equal rights 1945–1990: An oral history.* New York: Harper Collins.

Marsh, C., & Willis, G. (1995). *Curriculum: Alternative approaches, ongoing issues.* Columbus, OH: Merrill.

Marshall, J.D., & Kincheloe, J. (1998). It's not about the books: Textbook controversies and the need for uncertain conversations. In J.T. Sears (Eds.). *Public education and religion: Conversations for an enlarging public square* (with J.C. Carper) (pp. 85–91). New York: Teachers College Press.

Marshall, J.D., Schubert, W.H., & Sears, J.T. (1994, April). Turning points in contemporary curriculum history. Poster session at the annual meeting of the American Educational Research Association, New Orleans, LA.

Marshall, J.D., & Sears, J.T. (1985). John Holt: In memory. *Changing Schools, 13,*5.

Marshall, J.D., & Sears, J.T. (1990). An evolutionary and metaphorical journey into teaching and thinking about curriculum. In J.T. Sears & J.D. Marshall (Eds.), *Teaching and thinking about curriculum* (pp. 15–32). New York: Teachers College Press.

Marti, J. (1979). *On education: Articles on educational theory and pedagogy, and writings for children from "The age of gold."* (E. Randall, Trans.). New York: Monthly Review Press. (Essays and stories written by Marti between 1875 and 1900, edited by P.S. Foner).

Martin, D.S., Glatthorn, A., Winsters, M., & Saif, P. (1989). *Curriculum leadership: Case studies for program practitioners.* Alexandria, VA: Association for Supervision and Curriculum Development.

Martin, I.P. (2002, February). Pedagogy: Teaching practices of American colonial educators in the Philippines. *Kritika Kultura, 1,* 74–82. Available at http://www.ateneo.edu/kritikakultura/.

Martusewicz, R.A. (1992). Mapping the terrain of the post-modern subject: Post-structuralism and the educated woman. In W.F., Pinar, & W.M. Reynolds, (Eds.), *Understanding curriculum as phenomenological and deconstructed text* (pp. 131–158). New York: Teachers College Press, Columbia University.

Martusewicz, R.A., & Reynolds, W.M. (Eds.). (1994). *Inside out: Contemporary critical perspectives in education.* New York: St. Martin's Press.

Marzheuser, R. (1995, December 2). Differing images of the church. *America, 173*(18), 17–21.

Mayer, S., & Jencks, C. (1989). Growing up in poor neighborhoods: How much does it matter? *Science, 243*, 1441–1445.

Mazza, K. (1982). Reconceptual inquiry as an alternative of curriculum theory and practice: A critical study. *JCT, 4*(2), 5–89.

McCarthy, C. (1993). Multicultural approaches to racial inequality in the United States. In L.A. Castenell & W.F. Pinar (Eds.), *Understanding curriculum as racial text: Representations of identity and difference in education* (pp. 225–246). Albany: State University of New York Press.

McCarthy, C. (1998). *The uses of culture: Education and the limits of ethnic affiliation.* New York: Routledge.

McCarthy, C. (2001). *Reading and teaching the postcolonial.* New York: Teachers College Press.

McCarthy, C., & Crichlow, W. (Eds.). (1993). *Race, identity, and representation in education.* New York: Routledge.

McClay, W.M. (1988, July). Christian unity: A review of the Catholic movement. *Commentary, 86*(1), 70–72.

McConnell, S., & Breindel, E. (1990). Head to come. *The New Republic, 202,* 18–21.

McCormick, R., & James, M. (1983). *Curriculum evaluation in schools.* London: Croom Helm.

McCurdy, H. (1993). *Inside NASA: High technology and organizational change in the U.S. space program.* Baltimore, MD: Johns Hopkins University Press.

McCutcheon, G. (1995). *Developing the curriculum: Solo and group deliberation.* New York: Longman.

McDougall, W.A. (1985). *The heavens and the earth: A political history of the space age.* New York: Basic Books.

McGraw-Hill. (2000). *This is the company: Annual report 2000.* New York: The McGraw-Hill Companies.

McKnight, C.C., Crosswhite, F.J., Dossey, J.A., Kifer, E., Swafford, J.O., Travers, K.J., & Cooney, T.J. (1987). *The underachieving curriculum: Assessing U.S. mathematics from an international perspective* (5th ed). Champaign, IL: Stipes.

McLaren, P. (1986). *Schooling as a ritual performance: Towards a political economy of educational symbols and gestures.* Boston: Routledge and Kegan Paul.

McLaren, P. (1997). *Revolutionary multiculturalism: Pedagogies of dissent for the new millenium.* Boulder, CO: Westview Press.

McMurry, F.M. (1927). Some recollections of the past forty years of education. *Peabody Journal of Education, 4,* 325–332.

McNally, H.J., Passow, A.H., & Associates. (1960). *Improving the quality of public school programs: Approaches to curriculum development.* New York: Bureau of Publications, Teachers College, Columbia University.

McNeil, J.D. (1996). *Curriculum: A comprehensive introduction* (5th ed.). Boston: Little, Brown and Company. (Previous editions 1990, 1985, 1981, and 1977)

McNeil, L.M. (2000). *Contradictions of school reform: Educational costs of standardized testing.* New York: Routledge.

McQuaid, K. (1989). *The anxious years: America in the Vietnam-Watergate era.* New York: Basic Books.

Media consolidation: Encouraging diversity in the electronic media. (2004). Retrieved August 22, 2005 from http://www.mediaaccess.org/programs/diversity/index.html.

Meier, D. (1995). *The power of their ideas: Lessons for America from a small school in Harlem.* Boston: Beacon Press.

Meyer, J. (1992). Cigarette century: History of cigarette use. *American Heritage, 43*(8), 72.

Miel, A. (1946). *Changing the curriculum: A social process.* New York: Appleton-Century.

Miel, A. (1961). *Creativity in teaching: Invitations and instances.* Belmont, CA: Wadsworth.

Miel, A., & Berman, L. (Eds.). (1970). *In the minds of men: Educating the young people of the world.* Washington, DC: Association for Supervision and Curriculum Development.

Miel, A. & Berman, L.A. (1983). *Educating for world cooperation.* West Lafayette, IN: Kappa Delta Pi.

Miel, A., & Kiester, E. (1967). *The shortchanged children of suburbia: What schools don't teach about human differences and what can be done about it.* New York: Institute of Human Relations Press, American Jewish Committee.

Milburn, G. (1992). Do curriculum studies have a future? *Journal of Curriculum and Supervision, 7*(3), 302–318.

Miller, J.L. (1979). Curriculum theory: A recent history. *JCT, 1*(1), 28–43.

Miller, J.L. (Ed.). (1984). *Eccentric propositions: Literature and the curriculum.* Boston: Routledge & Kegan Paul.

Miller, J.L. (1990). *Creating spaces and finding voices: Teachers collaborating for empowerment.* New York: State University of New York Press.

Miller, J.L. (1997, Fall). Notes from the Vice President. *American Educational Research Association Division B—Curriculum Studies Newsletter,* pp. 1–2.

Miller, J.P. (1988). *The holistic curriculum.* Toronto: OISE Press.

Miller, J.P., & Seller, W. (1985). *Curriculum: Perspectives and practice.* New York: Longman.

Miller, M. (2002). What's wrong with this picture? Retrieved August 22, 2005 from http://www.thenation.com/doc.mhtml?i=20020107&s=miller

Miller, N. (1995). *Out of the past: Gay and lesbian history from 1869 to the present.* New York: Vintage.

Millett, K. (1970). *Sexual politics.* Garden City, NY: Doubleday.

Mills, D.Q., & Friesen, G.B. (1996). *Broken promises: An unconventional view of what went wrong at IBM.* Boston: Harvard Business School Press.

Mills, N. (Ed.). (1990). *Culture in an age of money: The legacy of the 1980s in America.* Chicago: Ivan Dee.

Mitchell, S., & Wile, N. (2002). *2001 literacy program evaluation: A report of the evaluation of literacy programs in elementary and middle schools* (EDRS MF01/PC05). Portland, OR: Portland Public Schools Research and Evaluation Department.

Moffett, J. (1994). *The universal schoolhouse: Spiritual awakening through education.* San Francisco: Jossey-Bass.

Molnar, A. (Ed.). (1987). *Social issues and education: Challenge and responsibility.* Alexandria, VA: Association for Supervision and Curriculum Development.

Molnar, A. (Ed.). (1997). *The construction of children's character.* Yearbook of the National Society for the Study of Education, Pt. 2. Chicago: University of Chicago Press and the National Society for the Study of Education.

Molnar, A., & Zahorik, J.A. (Eds.). (1977). *Curriculum theory.* Washington, DC: Association for

Supervision and Curriculum Development.

Moon, B. (Ed.). (1988). *Modular curriculum*. London: Paul Chapman.

Morgan, R. (1970). *Sisterhood is powerful: An anthology of writings from the women's liberation movement*. New York: Vintage Books.

Morris, B. (1972). *Objectives and perspectives in education: Studies in educational theory, 1955–1970*. London: Routledge & Kegan Paul.

Morrison, G.S. (1993). *The contemporary curriculum: K-8*. Boston: Allyn & Bacon.

Morton, D. (1993). The politics of queer theory in the (post)modern movement. *Genders, 17,* 121–150.

Morton, D. (1995). Birth of the cyberqueer. *Publications of the Modern Language Association, 110*(3), 369–381.

Morton, D. (1996). (Ed.). *The material queer: A LesBiGay cultural studies reader*. Boulder, CO: Westview Press.

Moustafa, M., & Land, R. (2001). *The effectiveness of "Open Court" on improving the reading achievement of economically disadvantaged children*. Paper presented at 91st Annual Meeting of the National Council of Teachers of English, Baltimore, MD.

Mulder, R.L. (1983). *A framework for examining reconceptualism and deriving its possible implications for undergraduate liberal arts teacher education*. Unpublished doctoral dissertation, Michigan State University, East Lansing.

Mumford, L. (1934). *Technics and civilization*. New York: Harcourt, Brace. (Reprinted 1963)

Naisbitt, J., & Aburdene, P. (1990). *Megatrends 2000: Ten new directions for the 1990's*. New York: Morrow.

Napoli, M. (2001). Cigarette companies continue to advertise to kids.

Healthfacts. New York: Center for Medical Consumers.

Narvarro, M. (2003, May 22). Media business advertising. *New York Times*. Retrieved August 22, 2005 from http://www.urbanlatino.com/press/nyt_052203.html.

National Commission on Excellence in Education. (1983). *A nation at risk: The imperative for educational reform*. Washington, DC: U.S. Government Printing Office.

National Education Association (NEA). (1918). *Cardinal principles of secondary education: A report of the commission on the reorganization of secondary education*. Washington, DC: U.S. Government Printing Office.

National Education Goals Panel. (1993). *Promises to keep: Creating high standards for American students*. Washington, DC: GPO.

National Education Goals Panel. (1994). *The national education goals report: Building a nation of learners*. Washington, DC: GPO.

National Governors' Association Center for Policy Research and Analysis. (1986, August). *Time for results: The governors' 1991 report on education*. Washington, DC: The National Governors' Association.

Natriello, G., McDill, E., & Pallas, A. (1990). *Schooling disadvantaged children: Racing against catastrophe*. New York: Teachers College Press.

Naumburg, M. (1928). *The child and the world: Dialogues in modern education*. New York: Harcourt, Brace and Company.

Negus, K. (1992). *Producing pop: Culture and conflict in the popular music industry*. London: Edward Arnold.

Neil, R. (1983, September 12). Curriculum and teacher education: An historical case-study.

Unpublished manuscript, University of Alberta, Edmonton, Canada.

Nicholls, J.G. (1989). *The competitive ethos and democratic education.* Cambridge, MA: Harvard University Press.

Nicholls, J.G., & Hazzard, S.P. (1993). *Education as adventure: Lessons from second graders.* New York: Teachers College Press, Columbia University.

Nicholls, J.G., & Thorkildsen, T.A. (Eds.). (1995). *Reasons for learning: Expanding the conversation on student-teacher collaboration.* New York: Teachers College Press, Columbia University.

Nichols, J. (October, 2000). Behind the DLC takeover. *The Progressive.* Retrieved December 8, 2002, from http://www.progressive.org/nich1000.htm.

Niebuhr, H.R. (1956). *The purpose of the church and its ministry: Reflections on the aims of theological education.* New York: Harper.

Nieto, S. (1999). *The light in their eyes: Creating multicultural learning communities.* New York: Teachers College Press.

Nietzsche, F. (1967). *On the geneology of morals.* W. Kaufman. Trans. New York: Vintage.

Noddings, N. (1984). *Caring: A feminine approach to ethics of moral education.* Berkeley, CA: University of California Press.

Noddings, N. (1992). *The challenge to care in schools: An alternative approach to education.* New York: Teachers College Press, Columbia University.

Noddings, N. (1993). *Education for intelligent belief or unbelief.* New York: Teachers College Press, Columbia University.

Nye, J.S., Jr. (2002a, March/April). The dependent colossus. *Foreign Policy, 129,* 74–77.

Nye, J.S., Jr. (2002b). *The paradox of American power: Why the world's only superpower can't go it alone.* New York: Oxford University Press.

O'Brien, D.M. (1996). *Storm center: The Supreme Court in American politics* (4th ed.). New York: W.W. Norton. (Previous editions 1993, 1990, and 1986)

O'Neil, H.F., Jr. (Ed.). (1981). *Computer-based instruction: A state-of-the-art assessment.* New York: Academic Press.

Oakes, J. (1985). *Keeping track: How high schools structure inequality.* New Haven, CT: Yale University Press.

Okazu, M. (1983). *The encyclopedia of curriculum.* Tokyo: Shogakkan.

Oliva, P.F. (1997). *Developing the curriculum.* (4th ed.). New York: Longman. (Previous Editions 1992, 1988, and 1982)

Oliver, D.W., & Gershman, K.W. (1989). *Education, modernity, and fractured meaning: Toward a process theory of teaching and learning.* Albany, NY: State University of New York Press.

Orfield, G. (2001). *Schools more separate: Consequences of a decade of resegregation.* Cambridge: Harvard Civil Rights Project.

Ornstein, A.C., & Hunkins, F.P. (1998). *Curriculum: Foundations, principles, and issues.* (3rd ed.). Englewood Cliffs, NJ: Prentice Hall. (Previous editions 1993 and 1988)

Overly, N.V. (Ed.). (1970). *The unstudied curriculum: Its impacts on children.* Washington, DC: Association for Supervision and Curriculum Development.

Pacelle, R.L., Jr. (1991). *The transformation of the Supreme Court's agenda: From the New Deal to the Reagan Administration.* Boulder, CO: Westview Press.

Padron, Y, Waxman, H., & Rivera, H. (2002). Issues in educating Hispanic students. In S. Stringfield & D. Land (Eds.), *Educating at-risk students* (pp. 66–88). Chicago: University of Chicago Press.

Pagano, J.A. (1990). *Exiles and communities: Teaching in the patriarchal wilderness.* Albany, NY: State University of New York Press.

Pajak, E. (1989). *The central office supervisor of curriculum and instruction: Setting the stage for success.* Boston: Allyn & Bacon.

Palmer, W. (1993). *Films of the eighties: A social history.* Carbondale, IL: Southern Illinois University Press.

Papert, S. (1980). *Mindstorms: Children, computers, and powerful ideas.* New York: Basic Books. (Reprinted 1993)

Parini, J. (1998, July 10). The memoir versus the novel in a time of transition. *The Chroncle of Higher Education,* p. A40.

Paris, C.L. (1993). *Teacher agency and curriculum-making in classrooms.* New York: Teachers College Press, Columbia University.

Parker, B. (1984). *Nonsexist curriculum development: Theory into practice.* The handbook of the Curriculum Design Project at the University of Colorado, Boulder.

Parker-Pope, T. (2001). *Cigarettes: Anatomy of an industry from seed to smoke.* New York: The New Press.

Parkhurst, H. (1922). *Education on the Dalton Plan.* New York: E.P. Dutton & Company.

Parkin, S. (2005, May 10). Taking direct action against Halliburton: *CounterPunch.* Retrieved August 22, 2005 from http://www.counterpunch. org/parkin05102005.html.

Passow, A.H. (Ed.). (1962). *Curriculum crossroads: A report of a curriculum conference.* New York: Bureau of Publications, Teachers College, Columbia University.

Patton, C. (1996). *Fatal advice: How safe sex education went wrong.* Durham, NC: Duke University Press.

Peters, M. (1989). Techno-science, rationality, and the university: Lyotard on the "postmodern condition." *Educational Theory, 39*(2), 93–105.

Peters, M. (1995). Education and the postmodern condition: Revisiting Jean-Francois Lyotard. *Journal of Philosophy of Education, 29*(3), 387–400.

Phenix, P.H. (1964). *Realms of meaning: A philosophy of the curriculum for general education.* New York: McGraw-Hill.

Pichaske, D. (1989). *A generation in motion: Popular music and culture in the sixties* (2nd ed.). Granite Falls, MN: Ellis Books. (First edition 1979)

Pilder, W.J. (1974). In the stillness is the dancing. In W.F. Pinar, *Heightened consciousness, cultural revolution, and curriculum theory: The proceedings of the Rochester conference* (pp. 117–129). Berkeley, CA: McCutchan.

Pinar, W. (1978). The reconceptualization of curriculum studies. *Journal of Curriculum Studies, 10* (3), 205–214. (Reprinted in H. Hiroux, A. Penna, & W. Pinar (Eds.), *Curriculum and instruction: Alternatives in education* (pp. 87–97). Berkeley, CA: McCutchan.)

Pinar, W. (2001). *The gender of racial politics and violence in America: Lynching, prison rape, and the crisis of masculinity.* New York: Peter Lang.

Pinar, W.F. (1974). *Heightened consciousness, cultural revolution, and curriculum theory: The proceedings of the Rochester conference.* Berkeley, CA: McCutchan.

Pinar, W.F. (Ed.). (1975). *Curriculum theorizing: The reconceptualists.* Berkeley, CA: McCutchan. (Republished as *Curriculum Studies:*

The reconceptualization. Troy, NY: Educator's International Press, 2000.)

Pinar, W.F. (1979). Notes on the curriculum field, 1978. *Educational Researcher, 7* (8), 5–12.

Pinar, W.F. (Ed.). (1988a). *Contemporary curriculum discourses.* Scottsdale, AZ: Gorsuch Scarisbrick.

Pinar, W.F. (1988b). The reconceptualization of curriculum studies, 1987: A personal retrospective. *Journal of Curriculum and Supervision, 3*(2), 157–167.

Pinar, W.F. (1991). The white cockatoo: Images of abstract expressionism in curriculum theory. In G. Willis & W.H. Schubert (Eds.), *Reflections from the heart of educational inquiry* (pp. 244–248). Albany, NY: State University of New York Press.

Pinar, W.F. (1992). "Dreamt into existence by others": Curriculum theory and school reform. *Theory Into Practice, 31*(3), 228–235.

Pinar, W.F. (1993, November). *Curriculum development in the USA: Decentralization and the politics of school reform.* Paper presented to the International Seminar on Curriculum and Decentralization, Santiago, Chile.

Pinar, W.F. (1994). *Autobiography, politics, and sexuality: Essays in curriculum theory, 1972–1992.* New York: Peter Lang.

Pinar, W.F. (1998). Introduction. In W.F. Pinar, Ed., *Curriculum: Toward new identities* (pp. ix–xxxiii). New York: Garland Publishing.

Pinar, W.F. (Ed.). (1998a). *Curriculum: Toward new identities.* New York: Garland.

Pinar, W.F. (Ed.). (1998b). *Queer theory in education.* Mahwah, NJ: Lawrence Erlbaum.

Pinar, W.F. (Ed.). (1998c). *The passionate mind of Maxine Greene.* London: Falmer.

Pinar, W.F. (1999). Response: Gracious submission. *Educational Researcher, 28*(1), 14–15.

Pinar, W.F., & Bowers, C. (1992). Politics of curriculum: Origins, controversies, and significance of critical perspectives. In G. Grant (Ed.), *Review of research in education* (pp. 163–190). Washington, DC: American Educational Research Association.

Pinar, W.F., & Grumet, M. (1981). Theory and practice and the reconceptualization of curriculum studies. In M. Lawn & L. Barton (Eds.), *Rethinking curriculum studies: A radical approach* (pp. 20–42). New York: J. Wiley and London: Croom Helm.

Pinar, W.F., & Reynolds, W.M. (1992). *Understanding curriculum as phenomonological and deconstructed text.* New York: Teachers College Press, Columbia University.

Pinar, W.F., Reynolds, W.M., Slattery, P., & Taubman, P.M. (1995). *Understanding curriculum: An introduction to the study of historical and contemporary curriculum discourses.* New York: Peter Lang.

Pope Pius XII (1990). Humani Generis. In C. Carlen (Ed.), *The papal encyclicals, 1939–1958* (pp. 175–184). Ann Arbor, MI: Pierian Press.

Popham, W.J. (1969). *Instructional objectives.* Chicago: Rand McNally.

Popkewitz, T.S. (Ed.). (1987). *The formation of school subjects: The struggle for creating an American institution.* Philadelphia: Falmer Press.

Portal, C. (Ed.). (1987). *The history curriculum for teachers.* London and New York: Falmer Press.

Posner, G.J. (1995). *Analyzing the curriculum.* New York: McGraw-Hill. (First edition 1992)

Posner, G.J. & Rudnitsky, A.N. (1994). *Course design: A guide to curriculum development for teachers.* (4th ed.).

New York: Longman. (Previous editions 1986, 1982, and 1978)

Poster, M. (1992). Postmodernity and the politics of multiculturalism: The Lyotard-Habermas debate over social theory. *Modern Fiction Studies, 38*(3), 567–580.

Powell, J.L. (1985). *The teacher's craft: A study of teaching in the primary school.* Toronto, NY: OISE Press.

Pratt, C. (Ed.). (1924). *Experimental practice in the city and country school.* New York: E.P. Dutton & Company.

Pratt, C., & Stanton, J. (1926). *Before books.* New York: Adelphi.

Pratt, D. (1994). *Curriculum planning: A handbook for professionals.* Fort Worth: Harcourt Brace College Publishers.

Preedy, M. (Ed.). (1989). *Approaches to curriculum management.* Bristol, PA: Open University Press, Taylor & Francis.

Prescott D.A. (1957). *The child in the educative process.* New York: McGraw-Hill.

Pritzkau, P.T. (1959). *Dynamics of curriculum improvement.* Englewood Cliffs, NJ: Prentice-Hall.

Progressive Education Association Publications, Commission on the Relation of School and College. (1943). Adventure in American education, Vol. 5. *Thirty schools tell their story.* New York and London: Harper & Brothers.

Puerto Rican community groups attack Univision broadcasting license. (2005, January 4). Retrieved August 22, 2005 from http://www. reclaimthemedia.org/print.php?story =05/01/04/6968534.

Purpel, D.E., (1989). *The moral and spiritual crisis in education: A curriculum for justice and compassion in education.* Granby, MA: Bergin & Garvey.

Purpel, D.E., & Belanger, M. (Eds.). (1972). *Curriculum and cultural*

revolution: A book of essays and readings. Berkeley, CA: McCutchan.

Quinn, D.M. (1996). *Same-sex dynamics among nineteenth-century Americans: A Mormon example.* Urbana: University of Illinois Press.

Radabaugh, M.T., & Yukish, J.F. (1982). *Curriculum and methods for the mildly handicapped.* Boston: Allyn & Bacon.

Radio free Clear Channel. (2005, May). Retrieved August 22, 2005 from http://blog.stayfreemagazine.org/ 2005/05/radio_free_clea.html

Raffo, S. (Ed.). (1997). *Queerly classed: Gay men and lesbians write about class.* Boston: South End Press.

Raths, L., Harmin, M., & Simon, S. (1966). *Values and teaching.* Columbus, OH: Merrill.

Ravitch, D. (1985). *The schools we deserve: Reflections on the educational crises of our times.* New York: Basic Books.

Ravitch, D. (1990a). Diversity and democracy. *The American Educator, 14*(1), 16–20; 46–48.

Ravitch, D. (1990b, Summer). Multiculturalism: E Pluribus Plures. *The American Scholar, 337–354.*

Ravitch, D. (1990c, September 2). The troubled road to California's new history textbooks. *Los Angeles Times,* M5, M8.

Ravitch, D. (1992). A culture in common. *Educational Leadership, 49*(4), 8–11.

Ravitch, D. (2000). *Left back: A century of failed school reforms.* New York: Simon & Schuster.

Ravitch, D., & Finn, C.E. (1987). *What do our 17-year olds know?: A report on the first national assessment of history and literature.* New York: Harper & Row.

Raywid, M.A., Tesconi, C.A., Jr., & Warren, D.R. (1984). *Pride and promise: Schools of excellence for all the people*. Westbury, NY: America Educational Studies Association.

Razik, T.A. (1972). *Systems approach to teacher training and curriculum development: The case of developing countries*. Paris, Unesco: International Institute for Educational Planning.

Read, H.E. (1958). *Education through art*. London: Faber and Faber. (Previous Editions 1943, 1947 and 1974)

Reid, W.A. (1978). *Thinking about the curriculum: The nature and treatment of curriculum problems*. London: Routledge & Kegan Paul.

Reid, W.A. (1992). The state of curriculum inquiry. *Journal of Curriculum Studies, 24*(2), 165–178.

Reid, W.A., & Walker, D.F. (Eds.). (1975). *Case studies in curriculum change: Great Britain and the United States*. London: Routledge & Kegan Paul.

Report of the Harvard Committee. (1945). *General education in a free society*. Cambridge, MA: Harvard University Press.

Reynolds, W.M. (1989). *Reading curriculum theory: The development of a new hermeneutic*. New York: Peter Lang.

Rice, J.M. (1913). *Scientific management in education*. New York: Publishers Printing Company. (Reprinted 1969 by Arno Press)

Ritter, H. (1986). *Dictionary of concepts in history*. Westport, CT: Greenwood.

Rocke, M. (1996). *Forbidden friendships: Homosexuality and male culture in Renaissance Florence*. New York: Oxford University Press.

Rofes, E. (1998). Innocence, perversion, and Heather's two mommies. *Journal of Gay, Lesbian and Bisexual Identity, 3*(1), 3–26.

Rogan, J. (1991). Curriculum texts: The portrayal of the field, Pt. 2. *Journal of Curriculum Studies, 23*(1), 55–70.

Rogan, J., & Luckowski, J. (1990). Curriculum texts: The portrayal of the field, Pt. 1. *Journal of Curriculum Studies, 22*(1), 17–39.

Rogers, C.R. (1969). *Freedom to learn: A view of what education might become*. Columbus, OH: Merrill.

Roman, L., & Christian-Smith, L. (Eds.). (1988). *Feminism and the politics of popular culture*. London: Falmer.

Rorty, R. (Ed.). (1967). Introduction. In R. Rorty (Ed.), *The linguistic turn. Recent essays in philosophical method* (pp. 1–39). Chicago: University of Chicago Press.

Rosales-Dordelly, C.L., & Short, E.C. (1985). *Curriculum professors' specialized knowledge*. Lanham, MD: University Press of America.

Rosenbaum, R. (1993, September). The know-it-all nineties. *Harper's Bazaar,* 172–176.

Rubin, G. (1975). The traffic in women. In R. Reiter (Ed.), *Toward an anthropology of women* (157–210). New York: Monthly Review Press.

Rubin, L.J. (Ed.). (1977a). *Curriculum handbook: Administration and theory*. Boston: Allyn & Bacon.

Rubin, L.J. (Ed.). (1977b). *Curriculum handbook: The disciplines, current movements and instructional methodology*. Boston: Allyn & Bacon.

Rubin, L.J. (Ed.). (1977c). *Curriculum handbook: The disciplines, current movements, instructional methodology, administration, and theory* (Abridged ed.). Boston: Allyn & Bacon.

Rueda, R., & McIntyre, E. (2002). Toward universal literacy. In S. Stringfield & D. Land (Eds.), *Educating at-risk students* (pp. 189–209). Chicago: University of Chicago Press.

Rugg, H.O. (Ed.). (1927). *Twenty-sixth Yearbook of the National Society for* the *Study of Education.* Bloomington, IL: Public School Publishing.

Rugg, H.O., & Shumaker, A. (1928). *The child-centered school: An appraisal of the new education.* Yonkers, NY: World Book.

Ruxanoff, L.A. (1980). *A curriculum model for individuals with severe learning and behavior disorders.* Baltimore: University Park Press.

Saylor, J.G., Alexander, W.M., & Lewis, A.J. (1981). *Curriculum planning for better teaching and learning* (4th ed.). New York: Holt, Rinehart & Winston. (Previous editions by Saylor and Alexander, 1974, 1966, and 1954 under similar titles)

Schiro, M. (1978). *Curriculum for better schools: The great ideological debate.* Englewood Cliffs, NJ: Educational Technology Publications.

Schlesinger, A. (1990, April 23). When ethnic studies are un-American. *Wall Street Journal*, A14.

Schön, D.A. (1987). *Educating the reflective practitioner: Toward a new design for teaching and learning in the professions.* San Francisco: Jossey-Bass.

Schubert, W.H. (1985). Scholarly contributions of the SIG. In E.C. Short, G.H. Willis, and W.H. Schubert, *The story of the AERA Special Interest Group on creation and utilization of curriculum knowledge, 1970–1984: Toward excellence in curriculum inquiry* (pp. 45–68). State College, PA: Nittany Press.

Schubert, W.H. (1986). *Curriculum: Perspective, paradigm, and possibility.* New York: Macmillan.

Schubert, W.H. (1992). Practitioners influence curriculum theory: Autobiographical reflections. *Theory Into Practice, 31*(3), 236–244.

Schubert, W.H. (1994). Toward lives worth sharing: A basis for integrating curriculum. *Educational Horizons, 73*(1), 25–30.

Schubert, W.H. (1995). Toward lives worth sharing: Historical perspectives on curriculum coherence. In J.A. Beane (Ed.), *Toward a coherent curriculum* (pp. 146–157). Alexandria, VA: Association for Supervision and Curriculum Development.

Schubert, W.H. (1996, Summer). Perspectives on four curriculum traditions. *Educational Horizons, 74*(4), 169–176.

Schubert, W.H. (1997, Spring). Recent curriculum theory: Proposals for understanding, critical praxis, inquiry, and expansion of conversation. *Educational Theory, 47*(2), 261–285.

Schubert, W.H. & Lopez-Schubert, A.L., (1980). *Curriculum books: The first eighty years.* Landham, MD: University Press of America.

Schubert, W.H., Lopez-Schubert, A.L., Herzog, L., Posner, G., & Kridel, C. (1988). A genealogy of curriculum researchers. *JCT, 8*(1), 137–184.

Schubert, W. H., Lopez-Schubert, A. L., Thomas, T. P. & Carroll, W, M. (Eds.). (2002). *Curriculum books: The first hundred years.* New York: Peter Lang.

Schubert, W.H., & Schubert, A.L. (Eds.). (1982). *Conceptions of curriculum knowledge: Focus on students and teachers.* University Park: College of Education, Pennsylvania State University.

Schubert, W.H., & Zissis, G. (1988). Speculation on curriculum from the perspective of William James. *Educational Theory, 38*(4), 441–455.

Schwab, J.J. (1964). Structure of the disciplines: Meanings and significances. In G. Ford & L. Pugno (Eds.), *The structure of knowledge and the curriculum* (pp. 1–30). Chicago, IL: Rand McNally.

Schwab, J.J. (1969a). *College curriculum and student protest.* Chicago: University of Chicago Press.

Schwab, J.J. (1969b). The practical: A language for curriculum. *School Review, 78,* 1–23.

Schwab, J.J. (1978). *Science, curriculum, and liberal education: Selected essays.* Chicago: University of Chicago Press. (See Westbury and Wilcof, 1978)

Seaman, P., Esland, G., & Gosin, B. (1972). *Innovation and ideology.* Bletchley, Bucks, England: Open University Press.

Sears, J. (2006). *Behind the mask of the Mattachine.* Binghamton, NY: Haworth Press.

Sears, J., & Marshall, D. (2000). Generational influences on contemporary curriculum thought. *Journal of Curriculum Studies, 32*(2), 199–214.

Sears, J.T. (1985). Rethinking teacher education: Dare we work toward a new social order? *JCT, 6*(2), 24–79.

Sears, J.T. (1988). *The glass bead game of curriculum theorizing.* Paper presented at the 10th Annual Conference on Curriculum Theory and Classroom Practice, Dayton, OH.

Sears, J.T. (1991). *Growing up gay in the South: Race, gender and journeys of the spirit.* New York: Haworth Press.

Sears, J.T. (1992a). Dilemmas and possibilities of sexuality education. In J.T. Sears (Ed.), *Sexuality and the curriculum* (pp. 7–33). New York: Teachers College Press, Columbia University.

Sears, J.T. (1992b, Summer). The second wave of curriculum theorizing: Labyrinths, orthodoxies, and other legacies of the glass bead game. *Theory Into Practice, 31*(3), 210–218.

Sears, J.T. (Ed.). (1992c). *Sexuality and the curriculum: The politics and practices of sexuality education.* New York: Teachers College Press, Columbia University.

Sears, J.T. (1997). *Lonely Hunters: An oral history of lesbian and gay southern life, 1948–1968.* Boulder, CO: Westview Press.

Sears, J.T. (Ed.). (1998). *Curriculum, religion, and public education: Conversations for an enlarging public square* (with J.C. Carper). New York: Teachers College Press.

Sears, J.T. (2001). *Rebels, ruby fruit, and rhinestones: Queering space in the Stonewall south.* Brunswick, NJ: Rutgers University Press.

Sears, J.T., & Marshall, J.D. (1984). The twilight of public alternative education: Professional malignancy, an historical perspective. *Journal of the Midwest History of Education Society, 12,* 80–92.

Sears, J.T., Marshall, J.D., & Otis-Wilborn, A. (1994). *When best doesn't equal good: Educational reform and teacher recruitment: A longitudinal study.* New York: Teachers College Press, Columbia University.

Sears, J.T. & Williams, W.L. (Eds.). (1997). *Overcoming heterosexism and homophobia.* New York: Columbia University Press.

Sedgwick, E.K. (1990). *Epistemology of the closet.* Berkeley, CA: University of California Press.

Sedgwick, E.K. (1990). *Tendencies.* London: Routledge.

Seguel, M.L. (1966). *The curriculum field: Its formative years.* New York: Teachers College Press, Columbia University.

Seidel, R.J., Anderson, R.E., and Hunter, B. (Eds.). (1982). *Computer literacy: Issues and directions for 1985.* New York: Academic Press.

Shane, H.G., & Tabler, M.B. (1981). *Educating for a new millennium.* Bloomington, IN: Phi Delta Kappa.

Sharp, R., & Green, A. (1975). *Education and social control: A study in progrssive primary education.* London: Routledge & Kegan Paul.

Shepherd, G.D., & Ragan, W.B. (1982). *Modern elementary curriculum.* New York: Holt, Rinehart & Winston. (Previous editions by Ragan and Shepherd, 1977 and 1971; Ragan and Stendler, 1966 and 1960; and Ragan, 1953)

Sherrid, P. (2002, November 4). Smokers' revenge. *U.S. News & World Report,* 44–47.

Shor, I. (1986). *Culture wars: School and society in the conservative restoration, 1969–1984.* Boston and London: Routledge and Kegan Paul.

Shor, I. (Ed.). (1987). *Freire for the classroom: A sourcebook for liberatory teaching.* Portsmouth, NH: Boynton/Cook.

Short, E.C. (1992). Beginning the conversation: Critical analysis of the 1992 handbook of research on curriculum. *Journal of Curriculum and Supervision, 8*(1), 1.

Short, E.C., & Marconnit, G.D. (1968). *Contemporary thought on public school curriculum: Readings.* Dubuque, IA: Wm.C. Brown.

Short, E.C., Willis, G.H., & Schubert, W.H. (1985). *The story of the AERA Special Interest Group on creation and utilization of curriculum knowledge, 1970–1984: Toward excellence in curriculum inquiry.* State College, PA: Nittany Press.

Shuster, G.N. (1963). *UNESCO: Assessment and promise.* New York: Harper & Row.

Silberman, C. (1970). *Crisis in the classroom: The remaking of American education.* New York: Random House.

Silin, J.G. (1995). *Sex, death, and the education of children: Our passion for ignorance in the age of AIDS.* New York: Teachers College Press, Columbia University.

Simonson, L.R. (1979). *A curriculum model for individuals with severe learning and behavior disorders.* Baltimore: University Park Press.

Sinfield, A. (1994). *Cultural politics-queer reading.* Philadelphia: University of Pennsylvania Press.

Sirotnik, K.A., & Oakes, J. (1981). A contextual appraisal system for schools: Medicine or madness? *Educational Leadership, 39,* 164–173.

Sizer, T.R. (1992). *Horace's school: Redesigning the American high school.* Boston: Houghton Mifflin.

Skinner, B.F. (1953). *Science and human behavior.* New York: Macmillan.

Skinner, B.F. (1958). Teaching machines. *Science, 128,* 969–977.

Slattery, P. (1995). *Curriculum development in the postmodern era.* New York: Garland.

Sleeter, C. (1999). Curriculum controversies in multicultural education. In M. Early & K. Rehage (Eds.), *Issues in curriculum: A selection of chapters from past NSSE yearbooks* (pp 257–280). Chicago: University of Chicago Press.

Smith, B.O., Stanley, W.O., Shores, J.H. (1957). *Fundamentals of curriculum development* (Rev. ed.). New York: Harcourt Brace and World. (1950 edition by World Book, Yonkers-on-the-Hudson, NY)

Smith, E.R., Tyler, R.W., & the Evaluation Staff. (1942). *Appraising and recording student progress.* New York: Harper & Brothers.

Smith, L., Kleine, P., Prunty, J. & Dwyer, D. (1992). School improvement and educator personality. In I. Goodson (Ed.), *Studying teachers lives*

(153–166). New York: Teachers College Press.

Smith, S., & Mickelson, R. (2000). All that glitters is not gold: School reform in Charlotte-Mecklenberg. *Educational Evaluation and Policy Analysis, 22*(2), 101–127.

Snyder, B.R. (1970). *The hidden curriculum.* New York: Alfred A. Knopf.

Sobel, R. (1981). *I.B.M.: Colossus in transition.* New York: Times Books.

Sobol, T. (1988). Commissioner's preface: A house divided. In *New York: The state of learning. A report to the governor and legislature on the educational status of the state's schools* (pp. i–v). Albany: New York State Education Department.

Sobol, T. (1990). Understanding diversity. *Educational Leadership, 48*(3), 27–30.

Sobol, T. (1993). Revising the New York state social studies curriculum. *Teachers College Record, 95*(2), 258–272.

Soltis, J.F. (Ed.). (1987). *Reforming teacher education: The impact of the Holmes Group report.* New York: Teachers College Press, Columbia University.

Sosniak, L.A. (1994). The taxonomy, curriculum, and their relation. In L.W. Anderson & L.A. Sosniak (Eds.), *Bloom's taxonomy: A forty-year retrospective* (pp. 103–125). Chicago: University of Chicago Press.

Spencer, H. (1861). *Education: Intellectual, moral, and physical.* New York: D. Appleton.

Spring, J.H. (1972). *Education and the rise of the corporate state.* Boston: Beacon Press.

Spring, J.H. (1986). *The American school, 1642–1985: Varieties of historical interpretation of the foundations and development of American education.* New York: Longman.

Spring, J.H. (1989). *The sorting machine revisited: National educational policy since 1945.* New York: Longman.

Stallones, J.R. (2002). *Paul Robert Hanna: A life of expanding communities.* Stanford, CA: Hoover Institution Press. Retrieved August 22, 2005 from http://www.hoover. stanford.edu/publications/books/ hanna.html.

Stanford, M. (1994). *A companion to the study of history.* Cambridge, MA: Blackwell.

Stanley, W.B. (1992). *Curriculum for utopia: Social reconstructionism and critical pedagogy in the postmodern era.* Albany, NY: State University of New York Press.

Steamer, R. (1986). *Chief justice: Leadership and the Supreme Court.* Columbia, SC: University of South Carolina Press.

Stearns, P.N. (Ed.). (1994). Events. In P.N. Stearns (Ed.), *Encyclopedia of social history* (pp. 252–253). New York: Garland.

Steinberg, D.L., Epstein, D., & Johnson, R. (Eds.). (1997). *Border patrols: Policing the boundaries of Heterosexuality.* London: Cassell.

Stenhouse, L.A. (1975). *An introduction to curriculum research and development.* London: Heinemann.

Stephenson, D.G., Jr. (1991). Introduction: The Supreme Court in American government. In D.G. Stephenson, Jr. (Ed.), *An essential safeguard: Essays on the United States Supreme Court and its justices* (pp. 1–35). New York: Greenwood Press.

Stinson, T. (1993, August 27). Can the sport save itself from itself? *Atlanta Constitution,* pp. 1, 8.

Stratemeyer, F.B., Forkner, H.L., McKim, M.G., & Passow, A.H. (1957). *Developing a curriculum for modern living.* New

York: Bureau of Publications, Teachers College, Columbia University. (First edition 1947)

Strauss, W. & Howe, N. (1991). *Generations: The history of America's future, 1584–2069.* New York: Morrow.

Stufflebeam, D.L., & Webster, W.J. (1980). An analysis of alternative approaches to evaluation. *Educational Evaluation and Policy Analysis, 2*(3), 5–20.

Sutherland, A., O'Shea, A., & McCartney, R. (1983). *Curriculum projects in post-primary schools.* Belfast: Northern Ireland Council for Educational Research.

Swadener, E. (1990). Children and families "at risk:" Etiology, critique, and alternative paradigms. *Educational Foundations, 4*(4), 16–39.

Swerdlow, J. (2001). Changing America. *National Geographic, 200* (3), 42–62.

Taba, H. (1945). General techniques of curriculum planning. In N.B. Henry (Ed.), *American education in the postwar period: Curriculum reconstruction.* The Forty-Fourth Yearbook of the National Society for the Study of Education, Pt. 1 (pp. 80–115). Chicago: University of Chicago Press.

Taba, H. (1962). *Curriculum development: Theory and practice.* New York: Harcourt, Brace & World.

Tanner, D. (1991). *Crusade for democracy: Progressive education at the crossroads.* Albany, NY: State University of New York Press.

Tanner, D. (January, 1998). The social consequences of bad research. *Phi Delta Kappan,* 79(5), 345–349.

Tanner, D. & Tanner, L. (1979). Emancipation from research: The reconceptualist solution. *Educational Researcher* 8(6), 8–12.

Tanner, D., & Tanner, L.N. (1980). *Curriculum development: Theory into practice* (2nd ed.). Columbus, OH: Merrill. (First and Third editions 1975 and 1995)

Tanner, D., & Tanner, L. (1995). *Curriculum development: Theory into practice* (3rd ed.). Columbus, OH: Merrill/Prentice Hall.

Tanner, D., & Tanner, L.N. (1990). *History of the school curriculum.* New York: Macmillan.

Tanner, L.N. (Ed.). (1988). *Critical issues in curriculum.* Eighty-Seventh Yearbook of the National Society for the Study of Education, Pt. 1. Chicago: University of Chicago Press.

Tanner, L.N. (1997). *Dewey's laboratory school: Lessons for today.* New York: Teachers College Press, Columbia University.

Taxel, J. (1997). Multicultural literature and the politics of reaction. *Teachers College Record, 98*(3), 417–448.

Taylor, F. (1911). *The principles of scientific management.* New York: Harper.

Taylor, P.A., & Cowley, D.M. (Eds.). (1972). *Readings in curriculum evaluation.* Dubuque, IA: Wm. C. Brown.

Taylor, P.H., & Richards, C.M. (1985). *An introduction to curriculum studies* (2nd ed.). Windsor, England: NFER-Nelson. (First edition 1979)

Teal, D. (1971). *The gay militants.* New York: Stein and Day.

Teilhard de Chardin, P. (1959). *The phenomenon of man.* (B. Wall, Trans.). New York: Harper and Row.

Teinowitz, Ira. (2003, July 2). FCC makes media ownership rules official. Retrieved August 22, 2005 from http://www.adage.com/news. cms?newsId=38226).

Teitelbaum, K. (1993). *Schooling for "good rebels": Socialism, American education, and the search for radical curriculum.* New York: Teachers College Press, Columbia University.

Theodoracopulos, T. (1993, June 7). Bad sport. *National Review, 45*(11), 63.

Thomas, T.P. (1991). *Proposals for moral education through the American public school curriculum: 1897–1966.* Unpublished Ph.D. dissertation, University of Illinois Chicago.

Thorndike, E.L. (1924). Mental discipline in high school studies. *Journal of Educational Psychology, 15,* 1–22, 83–98.

Tobacco quota buy-out. (2004, 22 December). Retrieved December 28, 2004, from http://agpolicy.org/ tobquota.html.

Todd, V.E. (1986, Spring). Contributions of Ralph W. Tyler to the curriculum field. *Journal of Thought, (21)*1, 61–69.

Tom, A.R. (1984). *Teaching as a moral craft.* New York: Longman.

Tomlinson, T.M., & Walberg, H.J. (Eds.). (1986). *Academic work and educational excellence: Raising student productivity.* Berkeley, CA: McCutchan.

Trudell, B.N. (1993). *Doing sex education, gender politics, and schooling.* New York: Routledge.

Trump, J.L., & Baynham, D. (1961). *Focus on change: Guide to better schools.* National Association of Secondary-School Principals, Commission on the Experimental Study of the Utilization of the Staff in the Secondary School. Chicago: Rand McNally.

Trump, J.L., & Miller, D. (1979). *Secondary school curriculum improvement: Meeting challenges of the times* (3rd ed.). Boston: Allyn & Bacon. (Previous editions 1972 and 1968)

Tsang, D. (1996). Notes on queer 'n Asian virtual sex. In D. Morton (Ed.), *The material queer: A LesBiGay cultural studies reader* (pp. 310–316). Boulder, CO: Westview.

Tyack, D. (1974). *The one best system: A history of American urban education.* Cambridge, MA: Harvard University Press.

Tyler, L.L. (1970). *A selected guide to curriculum literature: An annotated bibliography.* Washington, DC: National Education Association.

Tyler, R.W. (1949). *Basic principles of curriculum and instruction.* Chicago: University of Chicago Press.

Tyler, R.W. (1993). The Tyler rationale reconsidered. In G. Willis, W.H. Schubert, R.V. Bullough, Jr., C. Kridel, & J.T. Holton (Eds.), *The American curriculum: A documentary history* (pp. 393–400). Westport, CT: Greenwood. (Originally delivered by Tyler at the 1976 Milwaukee curriculum conference and published as "Desirable Content for a Curriculum Development Syllabus Today," in A. Molnar and J. Zahorik (Eds.), *Curriculum theory* (pp. 36–44). Washington, DC: Association for Supervision and Curriculum Development, 1977.)

Tyler, R.W., Gagne, R.M., & Scriven, M. (1967). *Perspectives of curriculum evaluation.* American Educational Research Association. Monograph Series on Curriculum Evaluation, No. 1. Chicago: Rand McNally.

U.S. Department of Education. (1986). *What works: Research about teaching and learning.* Washington, DC: Author.

U.S. National Commission on Excellence in Education. (1983). *A nation at risk, the imperative for educational reform: A report to the nation and the secretary of education, U.S.*

Department of Education. Washington, DC: Author.

Unger, I., & Unger, D. (1988). *Turning point, 1968*. New York: Charles Scribner's Sons.

United States Congress. (1995, January 18). *Congressional Record: Proceedings and Debates of the 104th Congress, First Session,* 141(10), (pp. S1025–S1028). Washington, DC: U.S. Government Printing Office.

United States Department of Education. (1998). *A nation "still" at risk: An education manifesto*. Washington DC: Thomas Fordham Foundation.

United States Department of Education, National Center for Education Statistics. (2002). *The Condition of Education 2002*. Washington, DC: U.S. Government Printing Office.

University of Tennessee Agricultural Policy Analysis Center. (n.d.). *Tobacco quota buyout*. Retrieved December 28, 2004, from http://agpolicy.org/tobquota.html.

Unruh, G.G., & Unruh, A. (1984). *Curriculum development: Problems, processes, and progress*. Berkeley, CA: McCutchan.

Urban, W.J. (1992). *Black scholar: Horace Mann Bond, 1904–1972*. Athens, GA: University of Georgia Press.

Valenzuela A., (1999). *Subtractive schooling: U.S.-Mexican youth and the politics of caring*. Albany: SUNY Press.

van Manen, M. (1986). *The tone of teaching*. Portsmouth, NH: Heineman.

van Manen, M. (1988). The relation between research and pedagogy. In W.F. Pinar (Ed.), *Contemporary curriculum discourses* (pp. 437–452). Scottsdale, AZ: Gorsuch Scarisbrick.

van Manen, M. & Levering, B. (1996). *Childhood's secrets: Intimacy, privacy, and the self reconsidered*.

New York: Teachers College Press, Columbia University.

van Til, W. (1983). *My way of looking at it: An autobiography*. Terre Haute, IN: Lake Lure Press.

van Til, W. (Ed.). (1986). *ASCD in retrospect: Contributions to the history of the ASCD*. Alexandria, VA: Association for Supervision and Curriculum Development.

van Til, W., Vars, G.F., and Lounsbury, J.H. (1961). *Modern education for the junior high school years*. Indianapolis, IN: Bobbs-Merrill.

Viadero, D. (2003, February 5). Researchers debate impact of tests. *Education Week*. Retrieved April 7, 2003 from http://www.edweek. org/ew/ew_printstory.cfm?slug=21carnoy.h22.

Walker, D.F. (1990). *Fundamentals of curriculum*. San Diego, CA: Harcourt Brace Jovanovich.

Walker, D.F., & Soltis, J. (1997). *Curriculum and aims* (3rd ed.). New York: Teachers College Press, Columbia University. (Previous editions 1992 and 1986)

Walker, R. (1989, June 14). Bush to appoint group to proffer education ideas. *Education Week*. Retrieved February 10, 2003, from http://www.edweek.org/ew/ewstory.cfm?slug=08340005.h08.

Wall, J.M. (1995, October 18). Changes in attitude: The lost world of the 1950s [Editorial]. *The Christian Century,* 112(29), 947–948.

Walton, S.F. Jr. (1969). *The black curriculum: Developing a program in Afro-American studies* (NAAAE anniversary ed.). East Palo Alto, CA: Black Liberation Publishers.

Ward, L.F. (1883). *Dynamic sociology, Vols. 1 and 2*. New York: D. Appleton.

Ward, L.F. (1893). *The psychic factors of civilization*. Boston: Ginn.

Warner, M. (2005, June 12). Striking back at the food police. New York Times, section 3, p. 9.

Washburne, C. (1954). *Winnetka: The history and significance of an educational experiment*. Englewood Cliffs, NJ: Prentice-Hall.

Washington, W. (1997, September 14). Accept it, America: There is an 'I' in tennis; A racist system must stop rejecting how Venus Williams does things her way. *The New York Times*, p. 28.

Watkins, W.H. (1991). Black studies. In A. Lewy (Ed.), *The international encyclopedia of curriculum* (pp. 779–782). New York: Pergamon Press.

Watney, S. (1987). *Policing desire: Pornography, AIDS, and the media*. Minneapolis, MN: University of Minnesota Press. (Reprinted 1989 and 1997)

Watts, A. (1972). *In my own way: An autobiography, 1915–1965*. New York: Pantheon Books.

Webster, A.F.C. (1990). The shape of the church in the third millennium. *Modern Age, 33* (2), 206–212.

Weeks, J. (1981). *Sex, politics, and society: The regulation of sexuality since 1800*. London and New York: Longman. (Reprinted 1989)

Weinstein, G., & Fantini, M.D. (1970). *Toward humanistic education: A curriculum of affect*. New York: Praeger.

Weisinger, H. (1973). Renaissance literature and historiography. In P.P. Wiener (Ed.), *Dictionary of the history of ideas: Studies of selected pivotal ideas* (Vol. 4, pp. 147–152). New York: Charles Scribner's Sons.

Weisman, J. (1991a, July 31). Educators watch with a wary eye as business gains policy muscle. *Education Week*. Retrieved February 10, 2003, from http://www.edweek.org/ew/ewstory.cfm?slug=10350004.h10.

Weisman, J. (1991b, November 20). Business Roundtable assessing state progress on reforms. *Education Week*. Retrieved February 10, 2003, from http://www.edweek.org/ew/ewstory.cfm?slug=12table.h11.

Wells, M.E. (1921). *A project curriculum: Dealing with the project as a means of organizing the curriculum of the elementary school*. Philadelphia: J.B. Lippincott.

Werner, W. (Ed.). (1979). *Curriculum Canada: Perspectives, practices, prospects*. British Columbia: Center for the Study of Curriculum and Instruction, University of British Columbia.

Westbury, I., & Wilcoff, N.J. (Eds.). (1978). *Science, curriculum, and liberal education: Selected essays*. Chicago: University of Chicago Press. (See Schwab, 1978)

Wexler, P. (1987). *Social analysis of education: After the new sociology*. Boston: Routledge & Kegan Paul.

White, G.E. (1988). *The American judicial tradition: Profiles of leading American judges* (Expanded ed.). New York: Oxford University Press. (First edition 1976)

White, J.P. (1973). *Towards a compulsory curriculum*. London: Routledge & Kegan Paul.

White, K. (1982). The relation between socioeconomic status and academic achievement. *Psychological Bulletin, 461*, 463–464.

White, M. (1996). *Carnegie Corporation travel grants to Australian educators in the 1930s*. Paper presented at the 1996 Australian Educational Researcher and the Australian Association for Research in Education Joint Conference, Singapore. Retrieved August 22, 2005 from http://www.aare.edu.au/conf96.htm.

Whitson, J.A. (1991). Defining and confining the curriculum theories of curriculum and instruction from the Supreme Court. In J. Erdman & J. Henderson (Ed.), *Critical discourse on current curriculum issues* (pp. 107–121). Chicago: Mid-West Center for Curriculum Studies.

Wiener, P.P. (Ed.). (1973). *Dictionary of the history of ideas: Studies of selected pivotal ideas, Vol. 1–4.* New York: Charles Scribner's Sons.

Wiggins, G.P. (1993). *Assessing student performance: Exploring the purpose and limits of testing.* San Francisco: Jossey-Bass.

Wigginton, E. (1985). *Sometimes a shining moment: The Foxfire experience.* Garden City, NY: Anchor Press/Doubleday.

Wiles, J., & Bondi, J.C. (1998). *Curriculum development: A guide to practice* (5th ed.). Upper Saddle River, NJ: Merrill. (Previous editions 1993, 1989, 1984, and 1979)

Wilhelms, F.T. (Ed.). (1967). *Evaluation as feedback and guide.* 1967 Yearbook of the Association for Supervision and Curriculum Development. Washington, DC: Association for Supervision and Curriculum Development.

Williams, W. (1986). *The spirit and the flesh: Sexual diversity in American Indian culture.* Boston: Beacon Press. (Reprinted 1992)

Willis, G.H. (1985). Professional activities of the SIG. In E.C. Short, G.H. Willis, & W.H. Schubert, *The story of the AERA Special Interest Group on creation and utilization of curriculum knowledge, 1970–1984: Toward excellence in curriculum inquiry* (pp. 25–44). State College, PA: Nittany Press.

Willis, G.H. (Ed.). (1978). *Qualitative evaluation: Concepts and cases in curriculum criticism.* Berkeley, CA: McCutchan.

Willis, G.H., & Schubert, W.H. (1991). *Reflections from the heart of educational inquiry: Understanding curriculum and teaching through the arts.* New York: State University of New York Press.

Willis, G., Schubert, W.H., Bullough, R.V., Kridel, C., & Holton, J.T. (Eds.). (1993). *The American curriculum: A documentary history.* Westport, CT: Greenwood Press/Praeger.

Wills, H. (1928). *Tennis.* New York and London: Charles Scribner's Sons.

Winkler, A.M. (1993). Modern America: The 1960s, 1970s, and 1980s. In M.K. Cayton, E.J. Gorn, & P.W. Williams (Eds.), *Encyclopedia of American social history* (Vol. 1, pp. 219–234). New York: Charles Scribner's Sons.

Wittner, L.S. (1974). *Cold war America: From Hiroshima to Watergate.* New York: Praeger.

Wittrock, M.C. (Ed.). (1986). *Handbook of research on teaching* (3rd ed.). New York: Macmillan. (Previous editions 1973 and 1963)

Wolf, A. (1977). *The relationship between poverty and achievement* (Compensatory Study Group). Washington, DC: National Institute of Education.

Woodson, C.G. (1933). *The miseducation of the Negro.* Washington, DC: Associated Publishers. (Reprinted 1972, 1977, 1990, and 1996)

Woodward, K.L. (1997, August). Hail, Mary. *Newsweek, 130*(8), 48–55.

Woyshner, C. (2003/2004). Women's associations and the origins of the social studies: Volunteers, professionals, and the community civics curriculum, 1890–1920. *International Journal of Social Education, 18*(2), 15–26.

Wraga, W. (1999a). Extracting sunbeams out of cucumbers. *Educational Researcher, 28*(1), 4–13.

Wraga, W. (1999b). The continuing arrogation of the curriculum field: A rejoinder to Pinar. *Educational Researcher, 28*(1), 16.

Wraga, W.G. (1994). *Democracy's high school: The comprehensive high school and educational reform in the United States.* Lanham, MD: University Press of America.

Wraga, W. & Hlebowitsh, P. (2003). Toward a renaissance in curriculum theory and development in the USA. *Journal of Curriculum Studies, 35,* 425–437.

Wright, G. (1963). *The core program: Unpublished research, 1956–1962.* Washington, DC: Office of Education, U.S. Department of Health, Education, and Welfare.

Wulf, K.M., & Schave, B. (1984). *Curriculum design: A handbook for educators.* Glenview, IL: Scott, Foresman & Company.

Yon, D.A. (2000). *Elusive culture: Schooling, race, and identity in global times.* Albany: SUNY Press.

Young, M.F.D. (Ed.). (1971). *Knowledge and control: New directions for the sociology of education.* London: Collier-Macmillan.

Zais, R.S. (1976). *Curriculum: Principles and foundations.* New York: Thomas Y. Crowell.

Zimmerman, J. (2002). *Whose America? Culture wars in the public schools.* Cambridge, MA: Harvard University Press.

Name Index

Subject Index